Martial Rose Library
Tel: 01962 827306

To be returned on or ~~before the~~ day marked above, subject to recall.

THE *Expulsion of the* *T*riumphant Beast

GIORDANO BRUNO

TRANSLATED AND EDITED BY *Arthur D. Imerti,* WITH AN INTRODUCTION AND NOTES.

Foreword by Karen Silvia de León-Jones

University of Nebraska Press
Lincoln and London

© 1964 by Arthur D. Imerti
Foreword © 2004 by the University of Nebraska Press
All rights reserved
Manufactured in the United States of America

First Bison Book printing: 1992

Library of Congress Cataloging-in-Publication Data
Bruno, Giordano, 1548–1600.
[Spaccio de la bestia trionfante. English]
The expulsion of the triumphant beast / Giordano Bruno; translated and
edited by Arthur D. Imerti, with an introduction and notes; foreword by
Karen Silvia de León-Jones.
p. cm.
Includes bibliographical references and index.
ISBN 0-8032-6234-5 (pbk.: alk. paper)
1. Christianity—Controversial literature. 2. Hermetism. I. Imerti,
Arthur D. II. Title.
B783.S73E5 2004
195—dc22 2004015753

Reprinted by arrangement with Arthur D. Imerti

KAREN DE LEÓN-JONES

FOREWORD

Few translations of Giordano Bruno's numerous Latin and Italian works are available in English. Among them is Arthur Imerti's 1964 translation of *Lo spaccio della bestia trionfante*, *The Expulsion of the Triumphant Beast*, a standout for its accuracy; its elegance in preserving the syntax and style of Bruno's writing, which is rich in allegories and metaphors; and its fidelity to the conceptual complexity of Bruno's thought. If it is a commonly held belief that something is always lost in translation, then it is safe to say that Imerti has not only translated but transmitted Bruno's text in a way that is unfortunately lacking in many other attempts to communicate Bruno's writings to the English-speaking world.

By choosing to represent Bruno the Nolan's philosophy in all its multifaceted form, Imerti has not conceded to simplifying unnecessarily sometimes convoluted Italian text in order to make the language and ideas more approachable for the contemporary reader. This is a great strength of the work and an achievement for Imerti. Bruno is often considered a thinker whose ideas are difficult to follow in Italian, and the delicacy of interpreting texts that are sometimes obtuse or mannerist in their original language challenges even the most gifted of translators.

Bruno's literary style is an example of the mannerist movement. Bruno was well versed in contemporary literature and even composed poetry, and his work is an example of the literary experiments of the end of the sixteenth century in Italy, like that of the poetry of Giambattista Marino. As Imerti points out in his introduction, Bruno was also a playwright, recognized as one of the best of his generation for his comedy *Il candelaio*, written in Paris in 1582, just two years before *The Expulsion of the Triumphant Beast.*[1] Indeed, Bruno's philosophical dialogues retain much of the theatrical in their composition, particularly in their numerous interlocutors, use of language, and ability to be broken down structurally into different dialogues, or "acts," and even plot elements. All of his works are rich in references to other texts—those of his contemporaries to the ancient classical texts of Rome, Greece, Chaldea, and Egypt. These references are both stylistic and conceptual.

The contemporary reader must keep in mind that Bruno received training from the Dominicans, a medieval contemplative order. As Imerti points out in his introduction, which is largely biographical, this particular order was by the sixteenth century one of the bastions of classical and Christian knowledge. The Dominicans were famous for their rigorous instruction and well-stocked libraries. They are now perhaps more infamous as the order of the Inquisition, established to assure the perpetuity of Catholic faith against the threat of heretics and infidels.

It was Bruno's own order that defrocked him and then condemned him to death for heresy. Although the Dominicans acted zealously as keepers of the faith, especially during the periods identified by modern scholars as the Reformation and Counter-Reformation, it is interesting to note that in the fifteenth and sixteenth centuries, some of the best-known heretics were of this order, including Savanarola, Bruno, and Thommaso Campanella. Perhaps because the Dominicans were the librarians of the early modern period, most of the ancient texts, all of the principle Christian writings, and even some theologically questionable texts, such as those touching on Neoplatonism and mnemonics, were housed in the great monasteries. Bruno acquired the forbidden writings of Erasmus while only a novice in his monastery in Nola, the order's discovery of which precipitated his first rebuke.

Imerti does a fine job of presenting the historical and biographical context of Bruno's writings in general, and *The Expulsion of the Triumphant Beast* specifically, in his extensive introduction to the translation. Rather than repeat information that has already been included, it seems better to expand on what has been presented. It is essential that the reader keep in mind that *The Expulsion* is part of a trilogy of works. [2] Between 1584 and 1585 Bruno wrote three of his Italian dialogues, which are thematically linked. These three works are, in chronological and thematic order: *The Expulsion of the Triumphant Beast* (*Lo spaccio della bestia trionfante*), *The Cabala of the Pegasean Horse* (*La cabala del cavallo Pegaseo*), and *The Heroic Furors* (*De gli eroici furori*). The trilogy is identified as the moral dialogues because the underlying theme is that of the ethics of mutation. Imerti rightly points out that the dialogues are concerned with each individual's obligation to accept being "governed by the religion of reason."[3]

Reason must be understood within the context of Bruno's thought. A Neoplatonist in his philosophical ideas, Bruno understands reason as the opposite of ignorance. Reason in *The Expulsion of the Triumphant Beast* is associated with synderesis, with the natural laws that govern the universe, and, of course, the Platonic notion of the Archetypal Idea. According to Renaissance forms of Neoplatonic philosophy, derived from Marsilio Ficino, the ideas that govern the laws of the universe are divine, communicated directly *mentis a mentis* (to borrow from the fifteenth-century thinker Giovanni Pico della Mirandola), or from one mind to the other.[4] Which is to say that although Bruno can be superficially interpreted as a rationalist, he is not a man of the eighteenth century or the Age of Reason.

For Bruno, the argument in favor of reason outlined in *The Expulsion* reflects the necessity of engaging the mind in the pursuit of understanding the universe. To do so is to follow two Socratic notions recurrent in his oeuvre. The first notion is that there is nothing new under the sun ("Quid est quod est? Ipsum quod fuit? Ipsum quod est. Nihil sub sole novum."[5]). This statement may be seen as a personal credo since Bruno mentions it in his defense during his trial. The second notion is, "All I know is that I know nothing," or, in Bruno's terms, that we must attain a state of ignorance. In *The Expulsion*, ignorance is the preparatory condition for achieving reason. As demonstrated by the interlocutor

Saulino, disciple of Sofia (Wisdom), ignorance is a basic tenet of the Nolan way that the untrained philosopher must follow on the path to wisdom.

The Expulsion of the Triumphant Beast is an introductory dialogue within the trilogy. It outlines the Nolan philosophy by providing the arguments in favor of reason as a means to attain indirect understanding of the Idea. Reason is the preparatory state of the disciple of philosophy who wishes to attain wisdom, like the training of the novice before receiving his orders. Orthodox theology, blind Aristotelianism, and other pedantic attitudes favor the triumph of the beast of ignorance. The transmuted philosopher who passes through a beastly form may conquer the beast of ignorance and be cleansed by the waters of the Idea and thus attain a godlike state of understanding. Essential to the discipline of the initiate are the ethics of mutation. Mutation, through metamorphosis, is associated with the shadow of the Idea, or natural philosophy—the religion of reason. The Socratic principles of *The Expulsion* are then taken to their logical, ethical, and spiritual extreme in Bruno's subsequent works, *The Cabala* and *The Heroic Furors*.

In these two later works Bruno uses allegorical examples of the interlocutor Onorio's metamorphosis into an ass (Cabala) and Acteon's metamorphosis into a stag (Furors) to describe in physical terms the transformation of the person who attains a state of ignorance, one free from the preconceptions perpetuated by Aristotelian pedants and theocrats. To attain true knowledge— to move toward wisdom and understanding, which are the elements of reason—the only path is mutation, the transformation of the mind to a state of readiness to receive the Archetypal Idea. Physical mutation is the consequence of encountering the shadow of the Idea; it must occur to attain the mystical union with the Idea. True wisdom is the direct consequence of true ignorance, a state in which the student of philosophy is a receptacle for a direct transmission of the Idea. In the final dialogue of *The Heroic Furors*, the Idea is eventually communicated as revelation (*mentis a mentis*). Ultimately, once the Idea is revealed, mutation becomes an infinite cycle so that metamorphosis changes into metempsychosis, the Nolan concept of immortality. The Idea itself is the wisdom of the universe, the immortal soul in the realm of divinity claimed by theology.

In the Italian dialogues Bruno systematically undermines institutional religion in favor of synderesis. He does so by dedicating each dialogue to one of the major religions believed to have influenced early modern Christianity. The religions containing elements of divine truth were identified by the Platonic School led by Ficino in the fifteenth century. These include ancient Egyptian worship, considered to be the primordial religion, often confused with Hermeticism. *The Expulsion of the Triumphant Beast* is often hailed as a Hermetic dialogue because of the Lament of Hermes, derived from a Hermetic text well known in the sixteenth century, contained therein. The Lament of *The Expulsion* is actually a representation of the mutation of the institution of religion over time. This is made clear by Jove, who calls the council of gods to warn them of their impending and inevitable mutation. Jove's argument is that the Idea, the basic truth reflected in the laws of the universe, is unchanging, but the form in which the Idea is embodied alters with time. The point of the Lament in *The Expulsion* is not to defend Hermeticism per se; it is to demonstrate that the gods through which the Egyptians and Greeks once worshiped nature were, centuries later, replaced by a new deity—the God of the Jewish and early Christian eras described in *The Cabala*. In *The Cabala* Bruno describes the advent of theology, and its supersedure of natural religion, in elegiac but nostalgic tones similar to those used in the Lament. However, this deity, like the others that preceded Him, must also be replaced. In *The Heroic Furors*, institutional religion is replaced by mysticism—by direct communication with the fount, with the Idea. Bruno's notion of direct communion with God is not the same as what many Protestant movements preached. Essentially, Bruno replaces religion with reason, or theology with natural philosophy (including science).

The trilogy of the Italian moral dialogues is the epitome of the Nolan philosophy. In these works Bruno presents the basic principles that will be recurrent in his later writings, which are, for the most part, Latin scientific treatises dedicated to mathematics and mnemonics.[6] To defend his arguments in his last significant Italian works, Bruno uses all the methods of persuasion at his disposal: philosophy, ethics, magic, the art of memory, allegory.

The richness of Bruno's thought can make the dialogues a difficult read the first time through. Although Bruno wrote in a literary style, today's reader will most appreciate his depth of thought, the complexity of his ideas, and the breadth of his knowledge. And the patient and dedicated reader will find Bruno's basic message—the importance of reason and open mindedness against institutional obscurantism—remains valid today.

Allusions to other works—literary, philosophical, mathematical, and scientific—abound throughout *The Expulsion of the Triumphant Beast*. Bruno also makes constant references to his own earlier works. Thus it is important to keep in mind that many obscure passages in the text either refer to a previous work in which Bruno developed a theme or idea in a more explicit fashion or anticipate arguments and themes to be developed in the two successive dialogues. Two works that most influenced the themes in *The Expulsion* are *The Ash Wednesday Supper* (*La cena de le ceneri*) and *Cause, Principle, and Unity* (*De la causa, principio e uno*). Written in 1584, these two Italian dialogues are essentially metaphysical works that defend Bruno's Neoplatonic principles. Of particular interest to the contemporary reader is the autobiographical element of *The Supper*. Bruno describes events, people, and places of the London of his time in mannerist detail. Bruno includes similar autobiographical elements in *The Expulsion*, although not with the same vividness as descriptions such as crossing London by night provide in *The Supper*. References to himself and his time will undoubtedly pique the curiosity of the reader, allowing the imagination to reconstruct physically, not just metaphysically, the early modern period. Bruno also provides fascinating glimpses of his irascible personality, which shed light on not only his eventual behavior with the Inquisition—his refusal to retract his unorthodox ideas—but also his dedication to and belief in the Nolan way.

Many contemporary critics have researched Bruno's life, so the curious reader will find numerous biographical works available. Scholarly works on Bruno abound, especially because interest in Bruno peaked for the fourth centenary of his death in the year 2000. For the sake of brevity, only those works available in English will be mentioned. There are distinct schools of research on Bruno in the United States, Great Britain, Italy, France, and

Germany; unfortunately, many of the European studies are not available in English, so the following discussion focuses on the American and British schools. Indeed, much British scholarship is dedicated to Bruno's "English experience," his London sojourn between 1583 and 1585. Hilary Gatti is a scholar who has published numerous articles on Bruno in England that are rich in literary and biographical elements.[7]

Among Bruno scholars, the most controversial study is by the British historian John Bossy, who attempted to demonstrate that Bruno was a spy at the court of Elizabeth I.[8] Although many specialists discount Bossy's theory, it remains an intriguing account of Bruno and his time that would undoubtedly assist the general reader to get a feel for the period. For a psychological exploration of the man, the theologian Eugen Drewermann presents a fictionalized account of Bruno's last night (*Giordano Bruno, oder, Der Spiegel des Unendlichen* [Kosel, 1992]). Drewermann bases his account on the trial documents edited by the historian Luigi Firpo, distinguished as the only scholar to date to have had such complete access to the Bruno files in the Vatican library. Unfortunately, the trial documents have not been translated into English.

The best introduction to Bruno's philosophy remains the fundamental text by the Warburg Institute historian Frances Yates. Her *Giordano Bruno and the Hermetic Tradition* (University of Chicago Press, 1964) was the first interpretation of Bruno that dared to go beyond the usual debate of anti-Aristotelianism and Neoplatonism to argue in favor of the art of memory, magic, and Hermeticism—themes that had hitherto been largely ignored or relegated to the esoteric, not serious research. Although Yates overstated Bruno's understanding and use of Hermeticism, her many writings on Bruno provide a clear and readable overview of his thinking, bringing Bruno into the mainstream of philosophical research.[9] Yates influenced every future generation of philosophy scholars, not to mention general readers interested in esoteric thinking. Her gift is in making Bruno's complex mind reachable. Yates started a trend in British Bruno studies that became an international phenomenon; her works are translated into every major European language.

Throughout the 1980s Bruno studies essentially were still concerned with magic, the art of memory, and Hermeticism. Historians of ideas such as Edward Gosselin, also a translator of *The Ash Wednesday Supper*, see Bruno within the context of Hermeticism and occultism in the early modern period. [10] Yates certainly influenced the historian of religion Ioan Culianu, who used Yates's works as secondary sources in his courses at the University of Chicago. In *Eros and Magic in the Renaissance* (University of Chicago Press, 1987), Culianu's interpretation of Bruno lay in the detailed analysis of Bruno's Neoplatonic magic, especially the theme of metamorphosis and metempsychosis in the Italian moral dialogues. It is a good introduction to the trilogy. For a more literary analysis of the theme of metamorphosis, Nuccio Ordine's *La cabala dell'asino* (*Giordano Bruno and the Philosophy of the Ass* [Yale University Press, 1996]) deals primarily with the second dialogue of the trilogy, but Ordine's numerous references to *The Expulsion* provide the context for his argument on the recurrent satirical theme of the ass.

As a tribute to a great Bruno scholar who published extensively on the Nolan within a philological context, it is important to mention Giovanni Aquilecchia, the University of London professor emeritus. Aquilecchia edited the critical editions of many of Bruno's works, including the Italian dialogues. Imerti's translation of *The Expulsion of the Triumphant Beast* is based on Aquilecchia's text. Because Aquilecchia's scholarship on Bruno spanned a lifetime, it is impossible to cite all of his publications, which cover many aspects of Bruno's life and thought. One specific contribution worth mentioning is the interest Aquilecchia generated in the literary aspect of Bruno's writings, which were an aspect of Bruno studies in English literature from his era to the present day.

Another trend in scholarship focuses on Bruno's mathematical and scientific ideas, many contained in his Latin treatises. Wayne Schumaker develops the connection between natural magic, derived from Yates's work, and the origins of modern science. [11] Giovanni Aquilecchia also wrote on the philological aspect of Bruno's mathematical works. [12] Allison Coudert has gone further in reevaluating Bruno's mathematical ideas by citing him as the source of Liebniz's *Monadology*. [13] Stephan Clucas has published on Bruno's *ars memorandi* as a scientific method linked to the mathematical circles active in England at the end of the sixteenth century. [14]

In the twentieth century Bruno is best remembered as a martyr for his scientific ideas. Bruno sparked the imagination of the fiction writer, including authors such as James Joyce and Samuel Beckett, as well as the scholar. He was even mentioned in the science-fiction novel *He She and It* (1991) by Marge Piercy. In Europe Bruno has been the subject of various theatrical works, in Italian and English, that began to appear in the 1990s and usually reenact the trial and Bruno's last hours. Bruno's appearance in popular literature and theater reflects a trend toward the general public's growing interest in the philosopher. It is a fascination that sparked events all over the world in the year 2000.

NOTES

1. For a Hermetic reading of the comedy, see Jo Ann Cavallo's article, "The Candelaio: A Hermetic Puzzle," *Canadian Journal of Italian Studies* 15 (1992): 47–55.

2. Karen de León-Jones, *Giordano Bruno and the Kabbalah: Magicians, Prophet and Rabbis* (New Haven: Yale University Press, 1997; reprint, Lincoln: University of Nebraska Press, 2004).

3. In *The Expulsion of the Triumphant Beast*, translated by Arthur D. Imerti (reprint, 2004; Lincoln: University of Nebraska Press, 1964), 26.

4. See the online translation (with commentary) of Giovanni Pico della Mirandola, *Conclusiones nongentae*, into English and Italian: www.brown.edu/Departments/Italian_Studies/pico/ [June 10, 2004].

5. Giordano Bruno, *De la causa* (Padua: CEDAM, 1941), 246.

6. The only full treatise on mnemonics by Bruno translated recently into English is *On the Composition of Images, Signs and Ideas* [*De imaginum, signorum, et idearum compositione*], translated by Charles Doria, edited by Dick Higgins (New York: Willis, Lock and Owens, 1991).

7. Hilary Gatti, *The Renaissance Drama of Knowledge: Giordano Bruno in England* (London, 1989).

8. John Bossy, *Giordano Bruno and the Embassy Affair* (New Haven: Yale University Press, 1991).

9. See Frances Yates, *The Art of Memory* (Chicago: University of Chicago Press, 1966) and *Collected Essays: Lull and Bruno* (London: Routledge, 1982).

10. Edward A. Gosselin, "Bruno's 'French Connection': A Historiographical Debate," in *Hermeticism and the Renaissance: Intellectual History and the Occult in Early Modern Europe*, edited by Ingrid Merkel and Allen G. Debus (Washington DC: Folger Shakespeare Library, 1988), 166–81. See also *The Ash Wednesday Supper*, edited and translated by Edward A. Gosselin and Lawrence S. Lerner (Hamden CT: Archon Books, 1977).

11. Wayne Shumaker, *Natural Magic and Modern Science: Four Treatises, 1590–1657* (Binghamton NY: Medieval and Renaissance Texts and Studies, 1989).

12. Giovanni Aquilecchia, "Bruno's Mathematical Dilemma in His Poem 'De minimo,'" *Renaissance Studies* 87 (Jan. 1992): 1–17.

13. Allison Coudert, *Leibniz and the Kabbalah* (Dordrecht: Kluwer Academic Publishers, 1995).

14. See Stephan Clucas, "In campo fantastico: Alexander Dicson, Walter Warner and Brunian Mnemonics," in *Giordano Bruno, 1583–1585: The English Experience* (London: Warburg Institute, 1995).

Dedicated to my beloved wife, Frances

Editor's Preface

In my translation, I have endeavored to convey to the reader not only the literal meaning of *Spaccio de la bestia trionfante* but also its style. With this aim in mind, I have made every effort to preserve the flavor of Bruno's poetical prose, without violating the spirit of the English language. When necessary, however, I changed the word order, modified the punctuation, paragraphed passages that ran on for several pages, and broke up involved sentences especially after clauses ending with a colon or semicolon, where a change of subject was indicated. Wherever I felt that the antecedents in Bruno's involved sentence structure were ambiguous, I inserted them either in the text itself or in bracketed interpolations, so as to be helpful to the reader. As for the capitals to indicate abstractions and personifications, I followed, with some exceptions, the text collated and annotated by Giovanni Gentile.[1]

From the incomplete and anonymous English translation of *Lo spaccio* I have borrowed the title, *The Expulsion of the Triumphant Beast,* and on rare occasions, a single word.

I take this opportunity of thanking my colleague Dr. Eugen Kullmann of The New School for Social Research for his thorough reading of my introduction and translation and for his sagacious recommendations.

For their patient reading of my introduction and their most helpful criticism, I wish to thank Dr. Maristella Bové Lorch, chairman of the Department of Italian, Barnard College, Dr. Peter M. Riccio of the Department of Italian, Columbia University, and Dr. John C. Nelson of the Department of Romance Languages and Literature, Harvard University.

I am also indebted to Dr. Paul O. Kristeller of the Department of Philosophy, Columbia University, for having read the "Explanatory Epistle," and given me the benefit of his authoritative advice.

I wish to express my appreciation to Dr. Hans Jonas of the Graduate Faculty, New School for Social Research, and Dr. Edgar R. Lorch of the Department of Mathematics, Columbia University, for their valuable suggestions concerning my translation of the passages dealing with mathematics; to the late Dr. Arthur Jeffery, executive officer of the Department of Near and Middle East Languages, Columbia University, for his scholarly assistance in the interpretation of the passages concerning "Pixide" and "Semammeforasso"; to Dr. Sol Tax, chairman of the Department of Anthropology, University of Chicago, for his expert opinion concerning the passage on the Aztec Calendar; to Dr. Marjorie Milne of the Metropolitan Museum of Art for her aid in the identification and interpretation of various obscure passages dealing with mythology; and to Mr. Ernst Pomeranz of The New School for having checked several of my translations from the Latin.

I am grateful, indeed, for the kindness shown to me by the

staff of the various departments of the Butler Library at Columbia, especially by Mr. Kenneth Lough and Miss Alice Bonnell. I deeply appreciate the generosity of the Yale University Library for having lent me a rare copy of the anonymous and incomplete translation of *Lo spaccio*.

My warmest thanks go to my friends Mrs. M. F. Loewenstein, Mrs. Harold Maslow and Mrs. Arthur Douglass, Jr., for helping to lighten the burden of my research; to my dear friend Mr. Joseph Bercovici, writer, editor, and lover of philosophy, for his intelligent reading of, and sagacious comments upon, various parts of my manuscript.

I can only inadequately express my indebtedness to the indefatigable volunteer workers of the American Red Cross, the Jewish Guild for the Blind, and the New York Ethical Culture Society for having transcribed *Lo spaccio* and other works into Braille.

I extend my most cordial thanks to my editor, Miss Katherine Morgan, for her pertinent suggestions on stylistic matters, and to the director of the Rutgers University Press, Mr. William Sloane, without whose ardent championship of my manuscript this book could not have been possible.

I am profoundly indebted to an autodidact, my dear father, Mr. Vincent A. Imerti, who first called to my attention the existence of Bruno when I was a youth of seventeen.

The work on Bruno's challenging text, which with some periods of intermission has absorbed my energies for nine years, could never have been pursued and completed without my devoted wife's unselfish help, encouragement, understanding, and sympathy. In every phase of my work—research, translation, editing, revision, and endless typing—she has been my constant and cherished companion.

Arthur D. Imerti

New York City
February, 1963

Contents

EDITOR'S
INTRODUCTION

I

THE MAKING OF A HERETIC

The last sixty years of the sixteenth century represent a period of great upheaval for all of Europe, and especially for Italy. Renaissance Italy, the focal point of Western culture, was most sensitive in her reactions to the religious, political, and military events that shook Europe during this era. Consequently, the Reformation, the Counter-Reformation, the Inquisition, and the struggle between Spain and France for supremacy over the Italian peninsula, culminating in the triumph of Spanish autocratic rule, profoundly disturbed the intellectual climate of that unhappy country. It is an irony of history that at the very time the intellectual and religious freedoms of the Italians were at their lowest ebb, Italy should produce some of her most daring thinkers: Cardano, Telesio, Galileo, Campanella, and Bruno.[1] Certainly, the most heretical of these was Giordano Bruno, philosopher, poet, dramatist, and martyr in the cause of intellectual freedom.

Giordano Bruno was born in 1548 in Nola, a town near Naples situated on the lower slopes of Mount Cicala.[2] For centuries Nola had been a large and flourishing community; however, by Bruno's time it had been reduced to one tenth of its former size as a result of invasions, volcanic eruptions, and plagues.

In 1562 Bruno was sent to study in Naples, a city which had

been thrown into confusion by the forceful imposition, in 1547, of the Inquisition by the Spaniards. In that city Bruno studied literature and philosophy. The inquisitive and highly sensitive young man found himself in an intellectual environment colored by the polemics between the humanists favoring the Christian commentaries upon Aristotle and those favoring the Averroistic exegesis of the Greek philosopher, and between the Neo-Platonists and the Aristotelians. We do not know to what extent the young scholar engaged in these controversies; but there is little doubt that his intense antipathy to Aristotelian philosophy, then regaining its former ascendancy, and to the humanists, whose emphasis upon philology he deplored, stems from this early period. We know, however, that by the time he entered the Monastery of San Domenico Maggiore in 1565, the controversies had profoundly weakened the young man's belief in the doctrine of the Christian Trinity.[3]

Bruno's decision to enter the monastery, despite his religious doubts was "the gravest mistake of a career that was uniformly unfortunate."[4] Perhaps his reason for doing so was his great admiration for Thomas Aquinas; or perhaps, as J. Louis McIntyre suggests, he joined the Dominicans because their powerful order offered a rare educational opportunity to boys of poor families.[5]

While in San Domenico, Bruno read omnivorously in philosophy, theology, and literature, and was attracted to the mnemonic works of Ramón Lull.[6] At this time his rebellious nature began to assert itself. On one occasion he disposed of his images of the saints, and on another he encouraged a fellow novice to forego the reading of the *Istoria delle sette allegrezze,* in favor of *Vita de* [sic] *Santi Padri*.[7] For these manifestations of rebelliousness he received a warning from the authorities of the monastery.

When, in 1576, charges of heresy were drawn up against Bruno by the Neapolitan Inquisition, which accused him of insubordination to the monastic authorities during his novitiate, he fled to Rome. There he was informed by the Roman Holy Office that one hundred thirty accusations of heresy had been drawn up against him, among them the charge that he had read several books by Erasmus.[8] Faced with another trial, the Nolan shed his ecclesiastical garments and took flight from the Eternal City.

During the same year Bruno spent brief periods of time in Genoa, Turin, Savona, and Noli. In 1577, he moved on to Venice, where he published his first book, *Dé segni dé tempi,* a work now lost.[9] Unable to find employment in that city, he left after a few weeks for Padua. There he met some fellow Dominicans who convinced him that it would be prudent for him to wear the garb of his order. After living for some time in Brescia and Bergamo, the Nolan went to Milan, where he first heard of Sir Philip Sidney, a man who was to play an important role in his life during his stay in England.

Bruno left Milan in 1578, with Lyons as his destination. Interrupting his journey upon reaching Chambéry, he spent several months in a Dominican monastery. Here he was warned by an Italian priest that he would not be welcome in Lyons. Heeding this warning, he decided to proceed to Calvinist Geneva.

Bruno's unfortunate decision to go to Geneva, a city where the authority of Aristotle was as unchallenged as it was in Rome and where Michael Servetus and other thinkers had been martyred, cannot help but lead us to reflect upon the perplexing alternatives with which he was so often faced.

In Geneva, Bruno became acquainted with the Marchese di Vico, one of the illustrious Italian Protestant exiles who lived in that city. He sought to make it clear to the Marchese that he was not interested in accepting Calvinism, but merely wished to live and work undisturbed. However, many pressures were brought to bear upon him, accompanied by warnings that unless he accepted the religion of the city he would not be permitted to reside there.[10]

Bruno's devotion to truth and his intolerance of pedants led him to write a leaflet against the arrogant and influential Antoine de La Faye, an Aristotelian professor of philosophy and biographer of Theodorus Beza, pointing out no less than twenty errors in one of his lectures.[11] Incensed by Bruno's act of defiance, the Geneva authorities ordered his arrest, demanded that he destroy the copies of his leaflet, and apologize to the irate M. de La Faye.[12] Although at first reluctant, Bruno finally yielded to these demands. However, deeply humiliated by this episode and embittered for the rest of his life against Calvinists, pedants, and

Aristotle, he left the city of Geneva to resume his wanderings until he reached Lyons, where he resided for a period of four weeks.

Bruno lived in Toulouse from 1579 to 1581, in which period he took his doctorate in theology at the university. After he was appointed to a chair in philosophy, he delivered a series of lectures on Aristotle's *De anima.* His nonconformist views on the Greek philosopher, however, brought upon him the wrath of his students.[13] When the storm and fury of the religious civil wars broke upon Toulouse, a stronghold of Protestantism, Bruno sought refuge in Paris.

Bruno's genius was recognized soon after his arrival in Paris in 1581, when he delivered a series of thirty lectures on the thirty divine attributes as expounded by Thomas Aquinas. The deep impression that these and subsequent lectures must have made upon his hearers is revealed to us in the testimony of the Bohemian John â Nostitz, a disciple of Bruno's in the French capital. He declared his admiration for Bruno's enormous erudition, prodigious memory, and eloquence.[14]

When enthusiastic reports of Bruno's intellectual abilities reached Henry III, he summoned the Italian to an audience for the specific purpose of ascertaining whether his gifts of memory were the result of natural endowments or of magic. Bruno assured the French monarch that his memory was solely the result of study and application. Deeply impressed by the philosopher's explanation, the king conferred upon him the privilege of delivering extraordinary lectures in Paris.[15] In the final pages of *Spaccio de la bestia trionfante,* published in 1584, a grateful Bruno refers to Henry as "Questo Re Cristianissimo, santo, religioso e puro. . . . Ama la pace, conserva quanto si può in tranquillitade e devozione il suo popolo diletto. . . ."[16] ("This most Christian, holy, religious, and pure king. . . . He loves peace and, as much as it is possible, maintains in tranquillity and devotion his beloved people. . . .")

The period of relative tranquillity and security enjoyed by Bruno in Paris was one of the most prolific in his career. He dedicated his *Ars memoriae* and *De umbris idearum* [17] to His Majesty. Both works are inspired by Ramón Lull's theories on the mnemonic art. In *Ars memoriae* this art, according to Spampanato, becomes "a mnemonic device endeavoring to choose and determine some images around which the rest can be grouped." [18] On the other hand, *De umbris idearum* "gives the metaphysical basis of the art of memory." [19]

His *Cantus circaeus* [20] is dedicated to Henry's natural brother, Prince Henry of Angoulême. This work "offers first a practical application, and secondly a more elementary account of the theory and practice" of his mnemonic system. [21] Still another mnemonic work inspired by Lull was published in Paris in 1582, under the title of *De compendiosa architectura et complemento artis Lullii.* [22]

This happy period of Bruno's life was unfortunately terminated by the renewal of the bloody religious war. Bruno, whose unorthodox views were irreconcilable with those of both Catholics and Protestants, realized that his life was now in danger and determined to leave France forthwith. He succeeded in obtaining letters of recommendation from Henry III to the French ambassador in London, Michel de Castelnau, Sieur de la Mauvissière.

Such was the reputation of Bruno's iconoclastic attitudes, however, that Sir Henry Cobham, the British ambassador in France, declared in a letter to Sir Francis Walsingham, Queen Elizabeth's Secretary of State, that Bruno's religious views could not be trusted. [23]

Before taking up residence in the home of Castelnau, Bruno sojourned at Oxford from April to June, 1583, where he lectured on philosophy. His decision to teach at that university, then an uncompromising seat of Aristotelianism, [24] seems to have been motivated by his deep-seated need for economic and professional security. For, as Mrs. Singer observes, "It is hard to imagine a less congruous figure in the Oxford of that day. . . ." [25]

The harassed philosopher's mind and character are revealed in the "Epistle" to the Vice-Chancellor, the Masters and Doctors of Oxford, accompanying his *Triginta sigillorum explicatio.* [26] Bruno begins the "Epistle" with an exhortation that the Oxford authorities be "discreet," and then indicates his strong preference for Pythagoras, Parmenides, Anaxagoras, and for the "best philosophers," to whose teachings he states he will add his "new propositions." Bruno declares that he is impelled by the awareness of his own knowledge, and more so by the desire "to manifest the falsity of vulgar philosophy," to prove the truth of his views in spite of the opposition of the garrulous "philosophasters." He expresses the hope that it may not be permitted "to any ass to bray here and there" against his doctrines, and asserts that if he is accepted by Oxford, they will find in him "a man most capable of putting into practice the valor of his powers." [27]

The intellectual climate at Oxford was such that Bachelors and Masters of Art were fined five shillings for each disagreement with the premises of Aristotle's *Organon;* and those whose views were irreconcilable with the opinions of the Stagirite were peremptorily expelled. Bruno tells us in *De la causa* that every student was obligated by oath to heed the following admonishment, which appeared in the university statutes: "nullus ad philosophiae et theologiae magisterium et doctoratum promoveatur, nisi epotaverit e fonte Aristotelis." [28] ("let no one be advanced to the degrees of Master and Doctor of Philosophy and Theology, unless he has drunk from the fountain of Aristotle.")

The philosopher was manifestly unwilling to drink from the "fountain of Aristotle," inasmuch as he disagreed most vehemently with the Greek philosopher's concept of God and the universe. At first Bruno's radical views on metaphysics and cosmology merely encountered a cool reception at Oxford; but soon his fiery temper, bluntness, and lack of tact were to provoke the inevitable break with the university. The incident that brought about the rupture occurred on June 11, 1583, at the Church of the Holy Virgin in the presence of a visiting Protestant nobleman and scholar, Albert Laski, palatine of Sieradia.[29] Bruno became involved in a violent dispute with several Oxford theologians and scholars when he violently attacked some Aristotelian views held by them. Because of this incident the Nolan became *persona non grata* and was compelled to leave the university.

In alluding later to his Oxford controversy in *La cena,* he acidly remarks:

andate in Oxonia, e fatevi raccontar le cose intravenute al Nolano, quando publicamente disputò con que' dottori in teologia in presenza del prencipe Alasco polacco ed altri della nobiltà inglesa. Fatevi dire

*come si sapea rispondere a gli argomenti; come restò per quindeci sillo-
gismi quindeci volte qual pulcino entro la stoppa quel povero dottor,
che, come il corifeo dell' Academia, ne pousero avanti in questa grave
occasione.*

(go to Oxford, and have them tell you about things that befell the
Nolan, when he publicly disputed with those Doctors of Theology in
the presence of Prince Albert Laski, the Polish nobleman, and other
gentlemen of the English nobility. Have them tell you how we were
able to answer their arguments, how that poor doctor on fifteen occasions, during the argumentation of fifteen syllogisms, remained confused like a chick caught in hemp fiber, that doctor whom they placed
before us on that grave occasion as the coryphaeus of the Academy.)

Bruno then contrasts the "incivility and discourtesy" of "that pig,"
as he calls his opponent, with the "patience and humanity" dis-
played by "that other one who indeed indicated that he was a
Neapolitan, born and raised under a more benign sky." [30]

The religious and philosophical doubts engendered by Bruno's
reading of heretical authors during his early years in Naples, his
unhappy experiences with the Neapolitan and Roman Inquisitions, his humiliation at the hands of the Aristotelian Calvinists
in Geneva, his witnessing of the horrors wrought by the religious
civil wars in France, his bitter controversy with the advocates of
Aristotle at Oxford—all contributed to the making of the heretical
author of *Lo spaccio*.[31] Henceforth, the iconoclast resolved to carry
on a merciless war against pedants and pedantry, against the Reformed sects (particularly the Calvinists), and finally against
Christianity itself.

After his unfortunate experience at Oxford, Bruno returned
to London, to live for approximately twenty-seven months at the
home of Castelnau, who employed him as a tutor and gentleman
companion. His stay in the British capital was perhaps the hap-
piest period in the tormented life of a restless wanderer.

In the devoutly Catholic Sieur de la Mauvissière, a scholarly
man endowed with a rare spirit of tolerance and humanity, the
heretic was to find a friend of profound understanding.[32] Bruno
referred to the French ambassador's "longanimity, perseverance

and solicitude," traits which had "won over, obligated, and linked" him to the Frenchman.[33]

Castlenau's kind offices in behalf of his controversial protégé led to Bruno's acquaintance with Robert Dudley, Earl of Leicester, Sir Philip Sidney, John Florio,[34] Sir Fulke Greville, the Italian jurist Alberigo Gentile, and many other intellectuals living in London.

Sir Philip Sidney had studied jurisprudence at the University of Padua, and like most writers and intellectuals of Elizabethan England, was imbued with a love of Italian culture. It is believed that the English poet may have financed the publication of Bruno's Italian works. Bruno dedicated *Spaccio de la bestia trionfante* and *De gli eroici furori* to him. Addressing Sidney in his "Epistola esplicatoria" to *Lo spaccio,* Bruno manifests his indebtedness to him:

Or non so qual mi sarei, eccelente Signore, se io non stimasse il vostro ingegno, non onorasse gli vostri costumi, non celebrasse gli vostri meriti; con gli quali vi siete scuoperto a me nel primo principio ch'io giunsi a l'isola Britannica, per quanto v'ha conceduto il tempo; vi manifestate a molti, per quanto l'occasione vi presenta; e remirate a tutti, per quanto vi mostra la vostra natural inclinazione veramente eroica.[35]

(Now I do not know how I should esteem myself, excellent sir, if I did not esteem your intellect, did not respect your customs, did not proclaim your merits, through which you revealed yourself to me at the very moment I arrived on the island of Britain, insofar as time permitted you. You manifest yourself to many, whenever you have the occasion; and you look upon all with favor to that extent to which your natural and truly heroic inclination indicates you should.)

A misunderstanding that terminated the friendship between Bruno and Sidney's close friend, Sir Fulke Greville,[36] brought about strained relations between Bruno and Sidney. Alluding to his rift with Greville, in the same "Epistola," Bruno exclaims in a tone of repentance:

non permetta il fato, che io . . . come tal volta mi son mostrato sensitivo verso le moleste ed importune discortesie d'alcuni; cossí avanti gli occhi de l'eternità vegna a lasciar nota d'ingratitudine, voltando le spalli a la vostra bella, fortunata e cortesissima patria, prima ch'al meno con segno di riconoscenza non vi salutasse, gionto al generosissimo e gentilissimo spirito del signor Folco Grivello. Il quale, come con lacci di stretta e lunga amicizia, con cui siete allevati, nodriti e cresciuti insieme, vi sta congionto: cossí nelle molte e degne, esterne ed interne perfezioni v'assomiglia; ed al mio riguardo fu egli quel secondo, che, appresso gli vostri primi, gli secondi offici mi propose ed offerse: quali io arrei accettati, e lui certo arrebe affettuati, se tra noi non avesse sparso il suo arsenito de vili, maligni ed ignobili interessati l' invidiosa Erinni.[37]

(may Fate not allow that I . . . since I have sometimes shown myself sensitive to the vexatious and inopportune discourtesies of some people, thus come to leave before the eyes of eternity a note of ingratitude by turning my back upon your beautiful, fortunate, and most courteous fatherland without, at least, a sign of gratefulness, by paying my respects to you, as well as to that most generous and most kind spirit, Sir Fulke Greville. Just as he is close to you in the bonds of intimate and long friendship, in which you were reared, nourished, and raised together, so he resembles you in the many and worthy, external and internal perfections; and, with regard to me, he was that second man who, after your first good offices, extended and offered me the second. These I would have accepted, and he certainly would have effectuated them if the envious Erinys of cowardly, malicious, ignoble, and interested parties had not spread her arsenate.)

Bruno met Queen Elizabeth through Castelnau, and frequently accompanied the French ambassador in his visits to her. The queen was strongly attracted to Italian culture and frequently conversed in Italian with the ladies and gentlemen of her court. Referring to her in glowing terms, the philosopher observes that "in title and royal dignity" she is not inferior to any king, and because of her "judgment, wisdom, council, and rule" she is not easily eclipsed by any other monarch of the world.[38]

In 1585 ill fortune again struck the philosopher. His friend and patron, Castelnau, was recalled to Paris, and Bruno, who had been totally dependent upon the French ambassador, was obliged to return with him to the turbulent French capital.

Bruno reveals nothing concerning his second sojourn in Paris except what we know from the following declaration made at his Venetian trial in 1592:

*E tornando il detto Ambasciator in Francia alla Corte, l'accompagnai a
Paris; dove stetti un altro anno,*[39] *trattenendomi con quelli signori ch'io
conoscevo, a spese però mie la maggior parte del tempo.*[40]

(And since the said Ambassador was returning to the Court in France,
I accompanied him to Paris, where I remained another year, entertain-
ing myself among those gentlemen whom I knew, at my own expense,
however, most of the time.)

In December of 1585 Bruno met Guillaume Cotin, the librarian
of the Monastery of Saint-Victor de Paris. Thanks to the diary
kept by this erudite monk, some invaluable knowledge has come
down to us concerning the philosopher's personality and patterns
of thought, which Cotin gleaned from his conversations with
him.[41]

An entry in the diary, dated December 6, 1585, relates, among
other things, that Bruno was living near the Collège de Cambrai,
that his father was still alive in Nola, and that he was about to
publish a work entitled *Arbor philosophorum.*[42] Pointedly, Cotin
reports that the philosopher was reading Lucretius.

From the December 7 entry we learn that Bruno gave two
reasons for his being compelled to flee Italy. The first was a reference to his having been falsely accused of the murder of a fellow
monk; the second, his need to avoid the inquisitors. During the
same conversation the philosopher boasted that he could teach
anyone the art of "artificial memory" in one hour. Bruno also revealed to Cotin that he detested the "heretics of England and
France," because of their attitude toward good works and their
reliance on faith and justification alone.[43]

We are told that Bruno was quite critical of preachers in general, except Hebrew preachers, whose eloquence and learning he
praised.[44]

Cotin also notes Bruno's strong interest in mathematics. The
philosopher spoke to him of the Italian mathematician, Fabrizio
Mordente, at that time living in Paris, whom Bruno called "the
god of geometricians," whose work, he said, he would undertake
to publish in Latin, since Mordente was not sufficiently conversant
with that language.[45]

The most dramatic entry in Cotin's absorbing diary, however, is the report of still another controversy in Bruno's tempestuous career, arising from a dispute between him and other scholars at the Collège de Cambrai.

On May 28, 1586, the philosopher invited a group of royal lecturers to the Collège to hear him argue against errors in Aristotle. Having completed his lecture, Bruno challenged his audience to come to the defense of the Greek philosopher. His challenge was ignored until a young lawyer, named Rudolphus Calerius, stood up to remark sarcastically that no one had deigned to answer Bruno, because his arguments were deemed unworthy of a response. He then proceeded to argue in favor of the Stagirite. When he had concluded his remarks, he in turn challenged Bruno to refute his arguments. The audience became increasingly hostile, and fearing that he might meet with bodily harm, Bruno decided to leave the building. Thereupon he was seized by several students who insisted that they would not allow him to do so unless he either answered Calerius' challenge or retracted his declarations. They released him after having exacted a promise that he would return the next day to continue the debate. The next day he declined to re-enter the dispute, but instead appointed his disciple, Jean Hennequin, to be his advocate.[46] Hennequin was not successful in sustaining his arguments against Calerius, upon which the audience demanded that Bruno resume his own defense. Sensing the futility of any defense he might make, brilliant and logical though it might be, Bruno declared himself beaten. After this dramatic episode we find no more references to Bruno in Cotin's diary.

In the summer of 1586, the dangers of the religious civil war became more ominous in the French capital, and Bruno was compelled to leave Paris for the second time. He decided to seek a haven in Germany, a country in which he was to encounter Catholics, Calvinists, and Lutherans. His relations with the latter were most cordial, and the philosopher's heretofore critical attitude toward the Germans and Germany, maintained in *Lo Spaccio*, underwent a profound change.[47] Yet his stay in that country was not to be free from controversy.

From a memorandum in the registry of the University of Marburg, dated July 25, 1586, we learn that Bruno was matriculated at that seat of learning for a very brief period. We are told by the rector, Petrus Nigidius, that following his matriculation Bruno requested permission to give public lectures in philosophy. His request was not honored because of what Nigidius considered "grave reasons." Upon learning that his request had been denied, Bruno betook himself to the house of Nigidius.

adeo excanduit [Nigidius informs us], ut mihi in meis aedibus procaciter insultaret, quasi vero in hac re contra ius gentium et consuetudinem omnium universitatum Germaniae et contra omnia studia humanitatis agerem; ac propterea pro membro Academiae amplius haberi noluerit.[48]

(he flew into such a rage that he boldly insulted me in my own house, as if indeed I had acted, in this matter, against the law of all the people and the custom of all the universities of Germany, and against all humanistic studies. And he declared that he therefore no longer wished to be retained as a member of the Academy.)

And thus Bruno's first association with a German university came to an abrupt end.

On August 20 of the same year, Bruno was matriculated at the University of Wittenberg, where he gave public lectures. Here at last he was able to enjoy that intellectual freedom so necessary to a teacher and scholar; and this happy period in the philosopher's life evokes these reflections from Spampanato, the greatest of Bruno's biographers:

He, who since earliest youth had had a natural propensity for philosophy, and had then become so enamored of her and revealed himself so faithful to her as "to hold in contempt, to abandon and to lose his fatherland, home, wealth, honor, and all the things that are ordinarily asked for, desired, and longed for," could finally manifest his own sentiments at Wittenberg.[49]

Bruno's students and colleagues at Wittenberg, although often in profound disagreement with the philosopher's original views, nevertheless gave him their polite and scholarly attention, a marked contrast to the open hostility Bruno had encountered in the universities at Toulouse, Paris, and Oxford.

In 1588, however, the Lutherans at the University of Wittenberg were superseded by the Calvinists, who had declared Copernicus' theories on the universe to be heretical; and Bruno, an ardent champion of Copernicus, finding Wittenberg no longer safe, resolved to leave.

In his *Oratio valedictoria* to the faculty and students at Wittenberg on March 8, 1588, Bruno had words of praise for Martin Luther; and of the Germans the grateful philosopher could now say: "The day the Germans fully evaluated the power of their genius and applied it in higher studies, they would no longer be men but gods." [50]

Later in the same year Bruno found himself in Prague, where he resided until the fall, after which time he moved on to Helmstedt. The Lutheran University of Helmstedt, at which Bruno matriculated on January 13, 1589, was to be a comparatively peaceful refuge for the philosopher until the spring of 1590, when a controversy broke out between Calvinist and Lutheran factions at that institution. Wishing to avoid an evolvement similar to that at Oxford, Bruno left Helmstedt for Frankfurt-am-Main. His reason for choosing the famous book center seems to have been to publish his three great Latin works: *De immenso, De monade,* and *De minimo.*

Since Bruno had published an incredible array of philosophical works whose heretical content had attracted the attention of a small, but influential, group of intellectuals, his reputation as a controversial figure was already well established in Frankfurt-am-Main. He encountered immediate and vigorous opposition from the city authorities. The philosopher's petition to the Senate for permission to remain at the home of Johann Wechel, a friend of Sir Philip Sidney's and one of the partners of the famous publishing house of Wechel and Fischer, did not meet with success. Through Wechel's efforts, however, he found himself quartered in a Carmelite monastery; and it was in this paradoxical environment that he prepared his manuscripts for his Frankfurt publishers.

It is not known why Bruno interrupted his stay in Frankfurt

to go to Zurich. In a letter to Henry Julius, Duke of Brunswick-Wolfenbüttel, on February 13, 1591, Wechel states that the philosopher had been "taken away" from him by a "sudden occurrence while he was preparing to correct the last page of *De minimo*." [51] During Bruno's absence he wrote the dedication to Henry Julius, dated February 15, 1591, and published the work. Bruno returned the following spring to prepare *De monade* and *De immenso* for publication, the second and third of his three monumental Latin works, which with *De minimo* constitute the most mature fruits of his thought and are considered by Spampanato to be his "philosophical testament." [52]

In April of 1591, a certain Giovanni Mocenigo, a wealthy, young Venetian nobleman, chanced upon a copy of Bruno's *De minimo* at a Venetian bookshop owned by Ciotti, a well-known bookseller. As fate would have it, Mocenigo was so impressed by the contents of the work, and especially by its references to the art of memory, that he determined forthwith to ask Bruno to come to Italy to teach him that art. He appealed to Ciotti to supply him with information concerning the philosopher, and Ciotti, who had met Bruno in Frankfurt in 1590, offered to act as an intermediary. Encouraged by Ciotti, Mocenigo addressed two urgent letters to the philosopher in Frankfurt, offering him employment in his home as a tutor. Bruno accepted the offer.

It is difficult to understand why the philosopher decided to return to Italy, whence he was a fugitive from both the Neapolitan and Roman Inquisitions. Perhaps the author of *Lo spaccio* believed that his heretical philosophical and religious ideas might meet, if not with acceptance, at least with toleration in the Republic of Venice; and possibly his yearning for his beloved homeland after an absence of some fourteen years caused him to underestimate the risk involved.

In the early weeks of 1592, Bruno established residence in the home of Mocenigo and began to teach him the arts of memory and of invention. Mocenigo bestowed upon his teacher numerous acts of kindness; and Bruno, disarmed by his apparent friendliness, divulged many of his heretical ontological and epistemological views. It was not long before the Venetian had sufficient grounds for suspecting that he was harboring a man of heretical beliefs;

and when he became dissatisfied with the progress of his studies, he accused Bruno of not teaching him all he knew about the arts of memory, invention, and geometry, threatening repeatedly to denounce him to the Holy Office if he did not teach him what he had promised. Finally the angry and suspicious Mocenigo, fearful of consequences to himself if he continued to extend hospitality to a man of Bruno's unorthodox views, disclosed the nature of the philosopher's remarks to his father confessor and was advised to denounce Bruno.

Meanwhile, Bruno, unaware of Mocenigo's intentions, informed him that he was planning to leave for Frankfurt-am-Main in order to publish some works. Mocenigo accused him of wishing to impart the secrets of his knowledge to others. The following day, aided by several men, the irate Venetian locked the philosopher in an attic, and in the early morning hours of May 22, 1592, betrayed him to the civil authorities who delivered him into the hands of the Inquisition. After being tried by both the Venetian and Roman Inquisitions, he was burned at the stake in Rome on February 16, 1600. The specific charges made by Mocenigo against Bruno will be dealt with in a later discussion of the philosopher's Venetian trial.

Before proceeding with an analysis of *Spaccio de la bestia trionfante* we shall make a cursory examination of Bruno's *Il candelaio* and of his Italian philosophical works, all of which confirm, to a greater or a lesser extent, the controversial tone of *Lo spaccio.*[53]

Bruno published his only comedy, *Il candelaio,* in Paris in 1582.[54] It is considered one of the most brilliant and original Renaissance comedies. In this sometimes autobiographical work, a savage indictment of the pedantry, immorality, and superstition of his day, we find numerous veiled allusions to theologians, scholars, and professors whom Bruno had known as a student in Naples and Nola.

The themes, characters, and situations of *Il candelaio* are most diversified, and, according to Spampanato, the work had a significant influence upon such writers as Molière and Shakespeare. Spampanato points out that no less than ten plots of Molière's were influenced by Bruno's comedy. Bruno's biographer also argues that such Shakespearian plays as *Love's Labour's Lost, As You Like It, Cymbeline, King Lear, Macbeth, The Life and Death of King Richard II,* and *Hamlet* "seem to remind us in some way of characters, scenes, speeches, and ideas of *Il candelaio* and of the *Dialoghi metafisici e morali.*" [55]

Bruno published all of his Italian philosophical works during his London period: *La cena de le ceneri; De la causa, principio et uno; De l'infinito universo et mondi; Cabala del cavallo Pegaseo* con l'aggiunta dell' *Asino cillenico; De gli eroici furori;* and *Spaccio de la bestia trionfante.*[56] These works are written in the dialogue form, a form preferred by the Italian philosophers and moralists of the sixteenth century.

In *La cena de le ceneri,* a dialogue dealing with Bruno's advanced cosmological ideas, wherein the philosopher expounds the Copernican theory, he inveighs against contemporary English scholars in general and Oxford scholars in particular, characterizing the latter as "una costellazione di pedantesca obstinatissima ignoranza, e presunzione mista con una rustica incivilità, che farebbe prevaricar la pazienza di Giobbe" [57] ("a constellation of the most pedantic, obstinate ignorance and presumption, mixed with a kind of rustic incivility, which would try the patience of Job").

The setting of this controversial work evolves from discussions which took place at the home of Sir Fulke Greville on Ash Wednesday in 1584; [58] and McIntyre suspects that it was the sarcastic tone in which Bruno refers to English scholars, and to all classes in the English social structure, that caused the rift between Bruno and Greville.[59]

De la causa, principio et uno, although somewhat less controversial than *La cena,* was none the less equally heretical in its outlook. In this work Bruno establishes the fundamental ideas of his philosophy of nature, inspired by the thinking of pre-Socratic and Neo-Platonic philosophers. He here defends his indictment of the Oxford scholars in *La cena;* and in the following passage we detect his suspicion that their attitude toward him might have been motivated by their xenophobia:

E io dico due cose: prima, che non si deve uccidere un medico straniero,
perché tenta di far quelle cure che non fanno i paesani; secondo dico,
che al vero filosofo ogni terreno è patria.[60]

(And I declare two things: first, that one must not kill a foreign doctor,
because he attempts those cures that the native doctors do not attempt,
second, I say, that for the true philosopher every land is his country.)

De gli eroici furori is an epistemological prose work interspersed with allegorical poems, whose allegory is explained by
the poet-philosopher. Here he establishes the premise that intellectual love is superior to physical love, and declares that the soul
by relentlessly seeking the truth, which is revealed to us in many
seemingly contradictory forms, will, when it shall have acquired
an intellectual understanding of the Deity, ultimately attain peace.
The work also expresses Bruno's contempt for the slavish imitators of Petrarch.

Cabala del cavallo Pagaseo con l'aggiunta dell' *Asino cillenico,*
which is dedicated to an imaginary bishop of Casamarciano and
is strongly suggestive of Erasmus, satirizes mysticism and some
of the fundamental concepts of Christian dogma. The opening
lines of the "Sonetto in lode de l'asino" containing Bruno's
apostrophe to "holy asininity" establish the mood of the work:

O sant'asinità, sant'ignoranza,
Santa stolticia e pia divozione,
Qual sola puoi far l'anime si buone,
Ch'uman ingegno e studio non l'avanza. . . .[61]

(Oh holy asininity! holy ignorance!
Holy foolishness and pious devotion!
You who alone do more to advance and make souls good
Than human ingenuity and study. . . .)

De l'infinito universo et mondi is a daring cosmological work.
Using the theories of Copernicus as a point of departure, the philosopher goes far beyond that thinker in his own speculations
upon the nature of the universe. Attacking the very foundations
of Aristotle's cosmology, he states unequivocally that the universe
is infinite and that there is an infinite number of worlds.

Perhaps nowhere in Bruno's writings is there a more poignant analysis of the philosopher's sense of loneliness and his feeling of persecution than in the following words directed to Castelnau in the dedicatory epistle of this dialogue:

Se io, illustrissimo Cavalliero contrattasse l'aratro, pascesse un gregge, coltivasse un orto, rassettasse un vestimento, nessuno mi guardarebbe, pochi m'osservarebono, da rari sarei ripreso e facilmente potrei piacere a tutti. Ma per essere delineatore del campo de la natura, sollecito circa la pastura de l'alma, vago de la coltura de l'ingegno e dedalo circa gli abiti de l'intelletto, ecco che chi adocchiato me minaccia, chi osservato m'assale, chi giunto mi morde, chi compreso mi vora; non è uno, non son pochi, son molti, son quasi tutti.[62]

(If, most illustrious gentleman, I worked a plough, pastured a flock, cultivated an orchard, and tailored a garment, no one would look at me, few would observe me, by very few would I be reprehended and I could easily be pleasing to everybody. But since I am a delineator of the field of nature, solicitous concerning the pasture of the soul, enamored of the cultivation of the mind, and a Daedalus as regards the habits of the intellect, behold one who, having cast his glance upon me, threatens me, one who, having observed me, assails me, another who, having attained me, bites me, and another who, having apprehended me, devours me. It is not one person, it is not a few, it is many, it is almost all.)

II

Lo Spaccio, ITS FORTUNES,
LITERARY ASPECTS, ALLEGORY,
AND SUMMARY

That *Spaccio de la bestia trionfante* should have been the only work of Bruno's to be singled out by the Roman Inquisition at the summation of his trial is not surprising; for owing to its daring ethical and epistemological speculations, its philosophy of nature, of religion, and of history, the work becomes the embodiment of all that is most heretical in the philosopher's thinking. Bruno, himself, keenly aware of its heretical nature, had the book published in 1584 in an atmosphere of secrecy.[1] Furthermore, in order to make the work appear less suspect, he chose to give Catholic Paris rather than Protestant London as its city of publication.[2] The title page reads as follows:

Spaccio de la Bestia Trionfante, Proposto da Giove, Effettuato dal Conseglio, Revelato da Mercurio, Recitato da Sofia, Udito da Saulino, Registrato dal Nolano.

Diviso in Tre Dialogi, Subdivisi in Tre Parti.

Consecrato al Molto Illustre et Eccellente Cavalliero Sig. Philippo Sidneo.

Stampato in Parigi.

M. D. LXXXIIII.

It is reasonable to assume that Sir Philip Sidney, to whom the philosopher dedicated *Lo spaccio,* with his deeply moving and most revealing "Epistola esplicatoria," circulated it among his friends. But in the years subsequent to the philosopher's burning, few scholars dared to refer to *Lo spaccio* and its author, except to allude to the work as something blasphemous, and to its author as an impious atheist.

By 1712 *Lo spaccio* was almost completely forgotten. However, on May 27 of that year an announcement in *The Spectator* of the sale at public auction of a copy of the work, for the immense sum of thirty pounds, caused a flurry of excitement among English scholars and bibliophiles.[3] The following year there appeared an anonymous English translation of the work.[4]

Spaccio de la bestia trionfante reveals the exuberance of Bruno's personality, his vivid imagination, vast erudition, and daring originality of thought. This great allegorical ethical work contains profound observations and judgments upon history, philosophy, astronomy, the contemporary social and political scene.

Although first and foremost a philosophical dialogue, *Lo spaccio* is also a cleverly contrived work of literature. It consists of ten parts: the introductory "Epistola esplicatoria," and three dialogues, each subdivided into three sections.[5] The subject matter of the third part of the first dialogue is correlated with that of the corresponding part of the second, and with that of parts two and three of the third. Employing as its framework a bizarre astronomical plot, the use of which frequently interrupts the development of his thoughts, the poetically imaginative Bruno proceeds to dazzle his readers with an amazing array of similes, metaphors and allusions to persons, places, and things. Sometimes by means of subtle irony, sometimes by biting sarcasm, and sometimes by the use of paradox, *Lo spaccio* lashes out against the pedants in religion, in science, philosophy, and letters.

Driven by an inner compulsion to express the wealth of ideas suggested by his encyclopedic mind,[6] Bruno wrote with incredible rapidity. Thus, even a cursory examination of the style and language of *Lo spaccio,* with its tropology, its grammatical and factual inconsistencies, its circumlocutions, its prolixity, its diffuseness, its digressiveness, its excessive use of Latinisms and dialecticisms, furnishes us with sufficient evidence to assume that Bruno made only the most superficial revision of his writing, once his thoughts were penned. *Lo spaccio* also abounds in cryptic and paradoxical utterances, which render the interpretation of its passages extremely difficult. At its best, however, the work contains a freshness of invention and a lucidity of expression that are a source of delight and edification.

Bruno admired the satirist Lucian and elected to employ a dialogue form modeled after that Greek writer,[7] rather than after that of Plato, as was the custom among Renaissance writers. Like Lucian's dialogues, Bruno's do not strictly adhere to a central theme. The author of *Lo spaccio* frequently digresses from the thought at hand, now to attack the theories of the Calvinists, now to protest against the Protestant confiscation of Catholic properties, now to insert a brief but pointed remark regarding his astronomical views, at other times to introduce humorous passages, couched so that they may both inform and entertain the reader.

Bruno believed that the poet is intuitive of many philosophical and religious truths. Thus Saulino, one of the principal characters of *Lo spaccio* declares: "Poeti sí, filosofi non mai hanno sí fattamente descritti e introdotti gli dei." [8] ("Poets, indeed, never philosophers, have so described and introduced the gods.") The work contains numerous direct and indirect references to Virgil, Ovid,[9] Lucretius, Seneca, Dante, Petrarch, Ariosto, Tasso, and other poets.

My analysis of the plot of *Lo spaccio* will be predicated upon an examination of its literal, allegorical, and philosophical premises.

That Bruno meant *Lo spaccio* to be, in its literal meaning, an outspoken document is made clear by him in the following passage:

Qua Giordano parla per volgare, nomina liberamente, dona il proprio nome a chi la natura dona il proprio essere; non dice vergognoso quel che fa degno la natura; non cuopre quel ch'ella mostra aperto; chiama il pane, pane; il vino, vino; il capo, capo; il piede, piede; ed altre parti di proprio nome; dice il mangiare, mangiare; il dormire, dormire; il bere, bere; e cossí gli altri atti naturali significa con proprio titolo . . . le imposture per imposture . . . gli filosofi per filosofi, gli pedanti per pedanti . . . le sanguisughe per sanguisughe, gli disutili, montainbanco, ciarlatani, bagattellieri, barrattoni, istrioni, papagalli per quel che si dicono, mostrano e sono. . . .[10]

(Here Giordano speaks in a vulgar manner, freely designates, gives the appropriate name to him to whom Nature gives an appropriate being. He does not call shameful that which Nature makes worthy, does not cover that which she reveals openly. He calls bread, bread; wine, wine; the head, the head; the foot, foot; and all other parts by their own names. He calls food, food; sleep, sleep; drink, drink; and likewise signifies the other natural acts with their proper titles . . . impostures as impostures . . . philosophers as philosophers; pedants as pedants . . . leeches as leeches; useless mountebanks, charlatans, triflers, swindlers, actors, and parrots as they are called, show themselves, and are. . . .)

Because of the heretical character of *Lo spaccio,* Bruno prudently limits himself to giving the reader only a few clues to the allegorical nature of the work. What the author does hint at, however, should be sufficient to enable us to detect and interpret the deeper meanings contained in the fable.

According to the philosopher, the reader's appreciation of this work will depend on his understanding, experience, and open-mindedness. To him he offers this advice and warning:

in questo mezzo ognuno prenda gli frutti che può, secondo la capacità del proprio vase; perché non è cosa sì ria che non si converta in profitto ed utile de buoni; e non è cosa tanto buona e degna che non possa esser caggione e materia di scandalo a' ribaldi.[11]

(let each one gather from this medium the fruits that he can, according to the capacity of his own bowl; because there is nothing so wicked that it may not be converted to the profit and usefulness of good people; and there is nothing so good and worthy that it cannot be the cause and material of scandal for ribalds.)

The three principal characters through whom Bruno unfolds the fable of *Lo spaccio* are Mercury, Sophia, and Saulino. Mercury, who represents "the sense," reveals to Sophia, the symbol of earthly wisdom, the results of the deliberations made by Jove, Momus, and the other gods of the Council. Sophia, in turn, imparts to Saulino, who represents man in search of wisdom, what she has learned from Mercury.[12]

The central figure about whom the fable revolves is Jove, whose metamorphosis into many forms symbolizes the change that "Jove, the soul, and man incur finding themselves" in the fluctuating matter of the universe.[13] He is, according to Bruno, not "too legitimate and good a vicar or lieutenant of the first principle and universal cause," but is, rather, "variable, subject to the Fate of Mutation."

As is each being, guided by intelligence, Bruno's Jove, who "represents each one of us," is a microcosm.

Quel medesimo [declares Bruno] e messo governatore e motor del cielo per donar ad intendere, come in ogni uomo, in ciascuno individuo si contempla un mondo, un universo; dove per Giove governatore è significato il lume intellettuale che dispensa e governa in esso e distribuisce in quel mirabile architetto gli ordini e sedie de virtudi e vizii.[14]

(That same Jove is made the governor and mover of heaven in order that he give us to understand how in every man, in each individual, are contemplated a world and a universe where, for governing Jove, is signified intellectual Light, which dispenses and governs in it [the world], and distributes, in that admirable structure, the orders and seats of the virtues and vices.)

The crisis facing the aging father of the gods is symbolic of the crisis in the life of Renaissance man, profoundly disturbed by new religious, philosophical, and scientific ideas. The schisms, Inquisition, religious civil wars, and invasions produce an insecure individual, convinced that only wealth and power can give him a sense of security. The acquisition of these, however, tends to produce in him a moral and physical decrepitude. Jove's decrepitude, of which his brittle body, his softening brain, the loss of his teeth, his graying hair, his failing vision, his irregular breathing, his slow movements, and his trembling hands are the evidence, symbolizes the decline of majesty, strength, and beauty in man. And the inference we may draw is that not until man's love of wealth and power is converted into a desire for temperance and reason can he truly progress toward goals that will benefit both him and society.

The principal theme of *Lo spaccio* is a satire of the universe as conceived by what Bruno calls the "imagination of foolish mathematicians, and," according to him, "accepted by no less wise physicists, among whom the Peripatetics are the most vain." It deals with the ignorance, superstition, and prejudice, embodied in the "triumphant beast," which Bruno implies have distorted man's reason in all ages and cultures. A "repented Jove" is to clear the firmament of "about forty-eight images," forming the constellations contained in the boreal, zodiac, and austral zones of the heaven.[15] The images represent an equal number of vices to be replaced by the virtues, long banished from their places of glory and esteem. The moral of the work is that not until man is governed by the religion of reason, based on an understanding of the universal laws of nature, will he completely purge himself of the "triumphant beast" within him.

Jove, who has for a long time led a life of dissoluteness, devoting himself almost exclusively to amours and to warlike enterprises, decides to submit himself to a self-examination of his past actions and attitudes. Driven by "synderesis," which Bruno describes as "a certain light which resides in the crow's nest, topsail, or stern of our soul," Jove "wants to effectuate and define that which, for some space of time before, he had proposed and determined."[16] He orders the release of censoring Momus, who because of his frankness had been bound to the star in Callisto's tail. From now on Jove is resolved to accept into his council only those individuals who have attained complete detachment from the pleasures of the flesh, and who are disposed to contemplation and study.

"Like the old lion in Aesop,"[17] declares Bruno, the father of the gods has been reduced to a state of impotence. The altars and temples, once dedicated to him, are now consecrated to satyrs, fawns, and semi-beasts; and only occasionally does he behold ceremonial rites reminiscent of the former religion of the Greeks.

He who has been the victor over the rebellious Typhoeus (Typhon) and Briareus now humbly confesses his present weakness to his fellow gods:

or non ho polso di contrastar a certi mezi uomini, e mi bisogna al grande mio dispetto, a voto di caso e di fortuna lasciar correre il mondo; e chi meglio la séguita, l'arrive, e chi la vence, la goda.[18]

(I . . . now do not have the courage to oppose certain half men, and am compelled, in spite of myself, to let the world run according to the wish of Chance and of Fortune; and may he who best pursues Fortune attain her, and may he who conquers her enjoy her.)

Jove also alludes to Vulcan's waning vigor and weakening will, and to Venus' evanescent beauty.

The father of the gods convokes his council to an extraordinary meeting on the day of the Feast of the Gigantomachy in order to bring about the much-needed reforms in heaven.[19]

In his opening words to the council Jove makes it clear to all that on this occasion, compelled by the seriousness of the situation, he will dispense with the usual oratorical niceties. His words reflect Bruno's impatience with the pedantic grammarians and rhetoricians of his time

Non aspettate, o dei, che, secondo la mia consuetudine, v'abbia ad intonar ne l'orecchio con uno articioso proemio, con un terso filo di narrazione e con un delettevole agglomeramento epilogale. Non sperate ornata tessitura di paroli ripolita infilacciata di sentenze, ricco apparato di eleganti propositi, suntuosa pompa di elaborati discorsi e, secondo l'instituto di oratori, concetti posti tre volte e la lima prima ch'una volta a la lingua. . . .[20]

(Do not expect, oh gods, that I shall, as is my custom, intone into your ears an artful introduction, a polished thread of narration, and a delightful epilogical agglomeration. Do not expect an ornate contexture of words, a polished weaving of my sentences, a rich apparatus of elegant arguments, a sumptuous pomp of elaborate discourses, and, according to the institute of orators, conceits sooner placed three times to the file than once on the tongue. . . .)

Jove reveals to the gods that he has meditated for an entire year upon the agenda he is about to recommend. He indicates that because of the rapes, thefts, murders, and adulteries perpetrated by him and the other gods, deeds recorded forever by history, literature, art, and the heaven [21] itself, it would have been preferable for the gods to have been ignominiously routed by the giants.

The gods must first, according to Jove, cleanse their hearts and consciences through repentance, then dedicate themselves to the love of justice. He argues that they must not only show remorse for misdeeds committed but must also destroy the physical vestiges of a life formerly motivated by inordinate desires.[22]

These grave warnings have a profound effect upon the celestial Senate; and the gods unanimously agree to meet four days hence to effectuate the proposals made by Jove and predestined by Fate.

On the fourth day the gods reassemble; and Mercury, presenting himself before Jove, makes known to him that they are "ready and disposed, without simulation and guile, but with free and spontaneous will, to accept and put into execution that which would be concluded, established, and ordained by the present synod." The father of the gods then expresses the hope that henceforth the day designating the victory of the gods over the giants shall be remembered also as the day on which the gods won the greatest of all victories, the victory over themselves, when "disease, plague, and leprosy are exiled from heaven into the deserts," when "broken is that chain of crimes and smashed is the trunk of errors, which were binding" them "to eternal punishment." He and the heavenly Senate then proceed to purge the heaven of all the vices, which Bruno refers to collectively as "the triumphant beast." This act in the context of Bruno's thought is symbolic of the reformation of human society.

III

THE HERETICAL PREMISES OF
Lo Spaccio, THEIR RELIGIOUS, SOCIAL,
AND POLITICAL IMPLICATIONS

Bruno's opening words to Sidney in the "Epistola explicatoria" of *Lo spaccio* exhort his readers to be guided by the "intellectual sun," symbolic of reason, "the teacher of the senses, the father of substances, the author of life." The philosopher admonishes: "Cieco chi non vede il sole, stolto chi nol conosce, ingrato chi nol ringrazia. . . ." [1] ("He is blind who does not see the sun, foolish who does not recognize it, ungrateful who is not thankful unto it. . . .")

He who had encountered the opposition of the inquisitorial authorities in Italy, the jeers of his students at Toulouse, and the scepticism of his colleagues at Oxford had no illusions as to the reception his ideas would be given by what he calls the multitude of "foolish, perverse, and wicked" pedants who, "under their severe brows and subdued countenances, their profuse beards and magisterial and grave togas, studiously, to universal harm, contain ignorance no less despicable than haughty, and no less pernicious than the most celebrated ribaldry." The philosopher is deeply confident, however, that *Lo spaccio* will be received with favor by men of the caliber of the erudite, open-minded, and generous Sir Philip Sidney, among whom "works and heroic effects will not be believed to be fruits of no value and vain."

Bruno, dedicating to his friend and benefactor "the numbered and arranged seeds of his moral philosophy," indicates that *Lo spaccio* is not his definitive ethical work,[2] although there are certain truths therein expressed, which he insists must be defended against the assaults of "the wrinkles and the brows of the hypocrites." He affirms that his reason for writing these dialogues is not to disapprove of "that which commonly is esteemed worthy of being approved by all wise and good men," but, rather, to reprove the contrary. He expresses the hope "that there be not anyone of so gross a mind, and so malicious a spirit," that he may conclude that what is written in *Lo spaccio* is said by him in a definitive manner. Determined that no one should say that he is taking "aim at the truth," and hurling stones "against the honest, the useful, the natural, and, consequently, the divine," the philosopher voices the hope that his readers will examine and weigh all the evidence objectively before pronouncing judgment.[3]

Bruno's concept of truth is the source of the most heretical premises contained in *Lo spaccio*. Indeed, the eternal search for truth is the very foundation of the ethical system implicit in the work. Few thinkers have possessed Bruno's fanatical devotion to her; few have been willing to die in her cause. The following passage in *Lo spaccio*, uttered by Saulino, with its ardent allusions to truth, is strongly autobiographical:

anzi, con essere più e più impugnata, più e più risuscita e cresce. Senza difensore e protettore si defende; a però ama la compagnia di pochi e sapienti, odia la moltitudine, non si dimostra a quelli che per se stessa non la cercano, e non vuol essere dechiarata a color che umilmente, non se gli esponeno, né a tutti quei che con frode la inquireno; e però dimora altissima, dove tutti remirano e pochi veggono.[4]

(Rather, the more and more she is impugned, the more and more she is resuscitated and grows. Without a defender and protector, she defends herself; and yet she loves the company of a few wise men. She hates the multitude, does not show herself before those who do not seek her for her own sake, and does not wish to be declared to those who do not humbly expose themselves to her, or to all those who fraudulently seek her; and therefore she dwells most high, whither all gaze, and few see.)

Bruno equates truth with Divinity itself, declaring that she is "the divinity and the sincerity, goodness and beauty, of things," the unity and goodness which preside over all things. As cause and principle, she is before all things; as substance, she is in all things. Truth, declares the philosopher, is "ideal, natural, and notional"; or, in other terms, "metaphysics, physics, and logic."

The philosopher maintains that truth cannot be crushed by violence, nor can she be corrupted by time; for she is relative to time, and reveals herself as the substance of things in myriad and ever-changing forms. She is manifest in all living things, operating through the eternal laws of an immanent God identified with a timeless universe, and although she may appear different in each succeeding generation, she is immutable and immortal. That which in the physical world is revealed to us through our senses, says Bruno, and that which we can comprehend, thanks to our intellect, "is not the highest and first truth, but a certain figure, a certain image, a certain splendor of her."

It is Bruno's belief that if man wishes to ascertain truth, he must approach theology, philosophy, and science without any preconceived attitudes. He, as Brunnhofer points out, is "perhaps the only philosopher who does not claim to have an infallible method of arriving at the truth." [5] His impatience with those who lay claim to such "infallible methods" is clearly revealed in the following passage from *De la causa:*

Perché è cosa da ambizioso e cervello presuntuoso, vano e invidioso, voler persuadere ad altri, che non sia che una sola via d'investigare e venire alla cognizione della natura; ed è cosa da pazzo e uomo senza discorso donarlo ad intendere a se medesimo. [6]

(Because it is a thing fit for an ambitious person, and for a presumptuous, vain, and envious mind, to want to persuade others that there is only one way to investigate and to come to the cognition of nature; and for one to convince himself that that is so, is a thing worthy of a mad man and a man without reason.)

The philosopher clung to the belief that there is an element of truth in all doctrines. Thus, in *De umbris idearum* he declares:

Non abolemus Pythagoricorum mysteria. Non parvifacimus Platonicorum fides et quatenus reale sunt nacta fundamentum, Peripateticorum ratiocinia non despicimus.[7]

(We do not abolish the mysteries of the Pythagoreans. We do not belittle the faith of the Platonists and do not despise the ratiocinations of the Peripatetics insofar as these ratiocinations find a real foundation.)

An examination of Bruno's sources, and the conclusions the philosopher draws from them, will aid us in identifying and understanding the "certain truths" he wishes to defend; and we shall observe that although as expressed in *Lo spaccio,* they may indeed at times seem fragmentary and indefinitive, the tone in which they are stated leaves little doubt as to their heretical meaning. Thus, the Roman inquisitors could not help but grasp the significance of the heretical religious philosophy that lends the work its controversial nature. Berti observes that although *Lo spaccio* seems to be, on the surface, an indictment of paganism, it is in effect "the proclamation of natural religion and the negation of all positive religions." [8]

Probably no man did more to focus the attention of Western thinkers upon pre-Socratic philosophers than did Aristotle himself, their greatest Greek opponent; for in order to refute their doctrines, he was compelled to name many of these thinkers in his *Physics* and *Metaphysics.* It was Bruno's close familiarity with Aristotle's works and his dissatisfaction with the Stagirite [9] that, according to McIntyre, "led him into greater sympathy with the nature-philosophers whom Aristotle decried." [10] *Lo spaccio* contains reminiscences of pre-Socratic and Neo-Platonic philosophers whose thinking was considered suspect by the Church. Toward these Bruno maintained the attitude of an eclectic. He does not attempt, as McIntyre points out, "to appreciate their relative value, nor to discover any evolution of thought through the successive systems. From each," continues McIntyre, "he takes that which agrees or appears to agree with his own philosophy, and treats it as an anticipation of, or an authority for, the latter." [11]

Thus, in developing the concept of the Absolute One, Bruno draws upon both Xenophanes, who represents "the static aspect of pantheism," [12] and Heraclitus, who represents the more dynamic

concept of pantheism, that is to say, that of a divinity which manifests itself through the finite. To Pythagoras, Bruno owes his concept of the transmigration of souls.

From Anaxagoras, who was the first to introduce the teleo-
logical principle in the explanation of the universe, Bruno learned
of the relationship existing between Absolute Being and Finite
Being. For his doctrine of "motion and change" he is indebted to
both Heraclitus and Empedocles.

In the imagery of his language, in his dialectic, in his love of
mathematics, in his rational view of life, Bruno shows a close
affinity with Plato. His mysticism and his concepts of "substance"
and "immanence," on the other hand, seem to stem from Plotinus
and other Neo-Platonists.

In *Lo spaccio* Bruno reveals his strong attraction to the mysteries of the Egyptian religion, his curiosity in that cult having
been aroused by his reading of the Hermetic writings of Iamblichus
and of Lucius Apuleius.[13]

It was not the substance of Ramón Lull's teaching but, rather,
his method that attracted Bruno to him; for through this method
the Nolan and many other Renaissance thinkers believed that they
could acquire universal knowledge.[14]

With his theory of the "coincidence of contraries" and his use
of mathematical symbols to explain the Deity, the German cardinal, Nicholas Cusanus, exerted a profound influence upon Bruno.
But, as we shall observe, Bruno's conclusions differ fundamentally
from those of Cusanus.

Bruno's concept of "substance" [15] is, perhaps, the most heretical
premise of *Lo spaccio,* since from it he derives his concept of
"immanence," the source of his religion of nature. His religion of
nature, in turn, becomes the source of his philosophy of knowledge
and of his heretical sociopolitical ideas.

Bruno speaks of an "eternal incorporeal substance" and of an
"eternal corporeal substance." [16] Although, according to him, "eternal incorporeal substance" does indeed have "familiarity with
bodies," it does not become a "subject of composition," since no
part of it can be "changed, formed, or deformed." It is, according
to the philosopher, "the divinity, the hero, the demon, the particular god, the intelligence," the "efficient and formative prin-

ciple," about which the composition of all beings is formed. It is the intrinsic principle and cause of "harmony, complexion and symmetry," and is not an accident derived from these, as taught by Aristotle and Galen, whom Bruno places among "fools under the name of philosophers." In short, it is, according to the philosopher, the "substance which is truly man." Since "eternal incorporeal substance" is rational principle, it is the governor and ruler of the body, and, therefore, superior to and independent of it.

On the other hand, "eternal corporeal substance" emanates from "eternal incorporeal substance." It is not "producible ex-nihilo, nor reducible ad nihilum, but rarefiable, condensible, formable." But whereas "eternal corporeal substance" remains unchanged, "the complexion is changed, the figure is modified, the being is altered, the fortune is varied."

We shall now turn to Bruno's conception of the doctrine of "motion and change." The opening pronouncement of *Lo spaccio*, uttered by Sophia, is a formulation of this doctrine, evolved by Heraclitus and Empedocles. But whereas the doctrine developed by the pre-Socratic Greek philosophers is, more specifically, of a cosmic nature, in *Lo spaccio* Bruno emphasizes the doctrine's ethical implications. Thus, asserting that there would be no pleasure if "bodies, matter, and entity" did not experience "mutation, variety, and vicissitude," [17] Bruno's Sophia declares:

Il stato del venereo ardore ne tormenta, il stato dell'isfogata libidine ne contrista; ma quel che ne appaga, è il transito da l'uno stato a l'altro. In nullo esser presente si trova piacere, se il passato non n'e venuto in fastidio. La fatica non piace, se non in principio, dopo il riposo; e se non in principio, dopo la fatica, nel riposo non è delettazione. [18]

(The state of venereal ardor torments us, the state of requited lust saddens us; but that which satisfies us is the transit from one state to the other. In no present being do we find pleasure, if the past has not become wearisome to us. Labor does not please except in the beginning, after rest; and unless in the beginning, after labor, there is no pleasure in rest.)

In his development of the doctrine of "motion and change" Bruno leans heavily upon the Pythagorean belief in "metempsychosis," a teaching considered heretical by the Catholic Church. For whereas the Church in its Credo unequivocally states its belief in an ultimate return of the soul to its resurrected body, Bruno declares that, guided by the "Fate of Mutation," the soul of man will incur infinite changes of "life and of fortune." He believes that the "High Justice, which presides over all things," will see to it that man is rewarded with a body befitting his conduct in his present state of "metempsychosis." Thus, according to Bruno, a man who has led an "equine or porcine" existence in this life will inherit "equine or porcine" forms in another.

From the consideration of the concept of "motion and change" Bruno is logically led to his interpretation of the doctrine of the "coincidence of contraries," developed by Nicholas Cusanus.[19]

Cusanus maintains that since finite nature is the result of the creative act of an infinite God, those effects which in her seem contradictory to finite minds, do coincide in the mind of God, their creator, who is both the "maximum absolute" and the "minimum absolute." [20]

Bruno believes that "the beginning, the middle, and the end, the birth, the growth, and the perfection of all that we see, come from contraries, through contraries, into contraries, to contraries." He declares that where there is "contrariety, there is action and reaction, there is motion, there is diversity, there is number, there is order, there are degrees, there is succession, there is vicissitude." Every being, then, finds himself "with such a composition, with such accidents and circumstances . . . because of differences which arise from contraries." All contraries are resolved or coincide in one original and prime contrary, "which is the first principle of all the others, which are the proximate efficients of every change and vicissitude." According to the Nolan, that which gives us pleasure and satisfaction is the "mutation from one extreme to the other through its participants and motion from one contrary to the other through its intermediate points." Consequently, there is a greater attraction between two contraries than between like and like.[21]

Bruno, indicating his indebtedness to Cusanus for his "coincidence of contraries," manifests that he considers it not only an epistemological [22] but also an ethical doctrine.[23] The attraction of contraries becomes for him the very basis of social and political relationships. Therefore, he maintains that there is no appreciation of justice where there is no injustice, no appreciation of harmony where one has not experienced its contrary.

Bruno placed Providence next to Truth in his descending ethical scale. Because she is a companion of Truth, she must be of the essence of Truth; and like the latter, she is both liberty and necessity. She is that attribute which links rational beings with Prudence, inherent in "temporal discourse." She is known as Providence when she "influences and is found in superior principles"; as Prudence when she is "effectuated in us." Prudence is, for Bruno, a reflection of Providence, whom he compares with the sun, "as that body which warms the earth and diffuses light." She abides in universals and particulars, having Dialectic as her "handmaiden" and Acquired Wisdom as her "guide." She instills in human beings the faculty of reason, through which they learn to adapt themselves "to things, to times, and to occasions."

As are Truth and Providence, Sophia, or Wisdom, is of two species. The first is "the superior, supracelestial, and ultramundane," which is "invisible, infigurable, and incomprehensible" and is "above all things, in all things, and between all things"; the second species is "the consecutive, mundane, and inferior," which is "figured in the heaven, illustrated in minds, communicated through words, digested through art, refined through conversation, delineated through writings." Bruno identifies Superior Wisdom with Providence and Truth, which are attributes of the Deity. Earthly, mundane Sophia is not of the essence of Wisdom, but merely partakes of her. Bruno compares earthly Sophia with "an eye which receives light and is illuminated by an external wandering light." She is that indispensable faculty through which man contemplates, comprehends, and explains Truth, "toward which, through various steps and diverse ladders, all aspire, strive, study, and, by rising, force themselves to reach."

Bruno is severe with those who knowingly distort wisdom, calling those who claim to know what they do not know, rash sophists; those who deny knowing what they do know, ungrateful to the "active intellect," "injurious toward truth," and "outrageous" toward wisdom. He condemns all those who do not seek wisdom for her own sake, but would rather sell her "for money or honors or for other kinds of gain." Bruno is scornful of those who desire wisdom in order to win acclaim, or "to detract, and to be able to oppose and stand against the happiness" of those whom they may call "troublesome censors and rigid observers."

For Bruno, Law, the daughter of Sophia, who consists of Divine Law [24] and her derivative, the Law of Nations, is the divine instrument through which "princes reign and kingdoms and republics are maintained." She is the "art of arts and discipline of disciplines," through which men of diverse complexions, customs, inclinations, and wills "must be governed and repressed." Because she is conceived differently by different peoples, she adapts herself to "the complexion and customs of peoples and nations, suppresses audacity through fear, and sees to it that goodness is secure among the wicked."

In his peregrinations through war-torn Europe, Bruno had ample opportunity to observe that the lust for power, which characterized his times, had produced a widespread disregard for law and agreements between and within nations, governed by unprincipled absolute rulers, of which Machiavelli's prince was the prototype.[25] Bruno's condemnation of the faithlessness and hypocrisy of princes is a devastating indictment of his times and a refutation of Machiavelli's political philosophy, as it is expounded in *The Prince*. He declares:

Vedete a che è ridutto il mondo, per esser messo in consuetudine e proverbio, che per regnare non si osserva fede. . . . A che verrà il mondo, se tutte le republiche, regni, dominii, fameglie e particolari diranno, che si deve esser santo col santo, perverso, col perverso? e [sic] si faranno iscusati d'esser scelerati perché hanno il scelerato per compagno o vicino? [26]

(See to what point the world is reduced, because it has become custom and proverb that in governing faith is not observed. . . . What will the world come to if all republics, kingdoms, dominions, families, and individuals say that one must be a saint with the saint, perverse with the perverse? And will they excuse themselves for being wicked because they have a wicked man as a companion or neighbor?)

The immoral environment engendered by these absolute princes, influenced by sycophants of every description, helped to create a faithless, dissolute, irresponsible, and indolent upper class. With penetrating insight and subtle irony, Bruno realistically depicts the dissipation of the sons of the rich, surrounded by a host of servants, as they while away the hours "in the house of Idleness." [27]

Bruno was highly critical of the libidinous conduct of both the married and unmarried women of the upper classes. He deplored the consequences of premarital relations of young women, although he did not consider Virginity something worthy in herself, "because," declares Bruno's Jove, "of herself, she is neither a virtue nor a vice, and does not contain either goodness, dignity, or merit." He did evince great concern, however, for women who unwisely submitted themselves to abortions; and he deemed that it would have been better, had they prevented the waste of that seed which could "give rise to heroes." [28]

The lack of interest shown by wealthy women in their children, whom they often entrusted to dirty and incompetent nursemaids, and their preference, instead, for domestic animals, provoked Bruno's indignation. With cutting irony he satirizes the distorted sense of values characteristic of one of these mothers, who addresses her child thus:

O figlio mio, fatto a mia imagine: se come ti mostri uomo, cossì ti mostrassi coniglio, cagnolino, martora, gatto, gibellino; certo, si come ti ho commesso a le braccia de la serva, de la fante, de questa ignobile nutriccia, di questa sugliarda, sporca, imbreaca, che facilmente, infettandoti di lezzo, ti farà morire; perché conviene anco che dormi con ella; io, io sarei quella che medesima ti portarei in braccio, ti sostenerei, lattarei, pettinarei; ti cantarei, ti farei di vezzi, ti baciarei, come fo a quest'altro gentile animale. . . . [29]

(Oh my son, made in my image, as you show yourself to be a man, would that you also showed yourself to be a rabbit, a she-puppy, a marten, a cat, and a sable. Just as surely as I have committed you into the arms of this servant, of this domestic, of this ignoble nursemaid, of this filthy, dirty, drunken woman, so infecting you with her fetidness (because it is also necessary that you sleep with her), she will easily cause you to die. I, I myself should be she who should carry you in her arms, should nourish you, suckle you, comb you, sing to you, caress you, kiss you, as I do with this gentle animal. . . .)

Bruno did not limit himself to satirizing the corruption, despotism, and violence of his times. He proposed as a positive solution the reinstatement of the goddess Law as the moral guide and teacher of nations, who should be especially concerned with "whatever appertains to the communion of men, to civilized behavior." Viewing with alarm the mutual distrust between the governors and the governed, he maintained that the "potent," that is to say those who ruled, should be "sustained by the impotent," or the governed. He insists, however, that "the weak be not oppressed by the stronger."

The state advocated by Bruno must foster "virtues and studies, useful and necessary to the commonwealth"; and its citizens, who most profit from them, should be "exalted and remunerated." Demonstrating a philanthropic concern for the poor, Bruno recommends that they be aided by their wealthy fellow citizens; and in words which might be construed as socialistic, he urges that "the indolent, the avaricious, and the owners of property be scorned and held in contempt." [30]

The citizens of Bruno's state, which should be ruled by laws based on "justice" and "possibility," must not only respect and honor their temporal rulers but also preserve "the fear and the cult of invisible powers." [31]

Despite the fact that out of a sense of gratitude he had extravagant words of praise for such absolute rulers as Henry III of France, Bruno condemns absolutism both in religion and in the state. Advocating the deposition of tyrants and favoring republics, he urges that "just rulers and realms be constituted and strengthened."

Bruno's concept of justice is predicated upon his belief that the state must exert a moral influence upon the lives of its citizens. Therefore, it rests upon the state to see that justice be meted out to all "without rigor," and that it sponsor "Equity, Righteousness," "Gratitude," and "Good Conscience." The state should see to it that individuals be conscious of their own worth, that elders be respected, that equals view one another with equanimity, and that superiors be benign "toward inferiors."

The Roman Republic was for Bruno the symbol of justice, law, and order, that justice, law, and order which he observed in operation in the world of nature. He concurred with Machiavelli in the opinion that Rome attained her leading position among nations, not because she was favored by Fortune, as believed by the ancients, but rather because she practiced virtue. Republican Rome, where the cordial rapport between the state and religion promoted peace and happiness for all its citizens, was for Bruno the ideal state, to be emulated by other peoples. He extolls the Roman people for their "magnanimity, justice, and mercy," qualities which, according to Bruno, made them akin to the gods. Jove's words eloquently express the philosopher's admiration for the Romans:

con gli suoi magnifici gesti, piú che l'altre nazioni, si seppero conformare ed assomigliare ad essi, perdonando a'summessi, debellando gli superbi, rimettendo l'ingiurie, non obliando gli beneficii, soccorrendo a'bisognosi, defendendo gli afflitti, relevando gli oppressi, affrenando gli violenti, promovendo gli meritevoli, abbassando gli delinquenti, mettendo questi in terrore ed ultimo esterminio con gli flagelli e secure, e quelli in onore e gloria con statue e colossi. Onde consequentemente apparve quel popolo piú affrenato e ritenuto da vizii d'incivilitade e barbaria, e piú esquisito e pronto a generose imprese, ch'altro che si sia veduto giamai. E mentre fu tale la lor legge e religione, tali furono gli lor costumi e gesti, tal è stato lor onore e lor felicitade.[32]

(because with their magnificent deeds they, more than the other nations, knew how to conform with and resemble them, by pardoning the subdued, overthrowing the proud, righting wrongs, not forgetting benefits, helping the needy, defending the afflicted, relieving the oppressed, restraining the violent, promoting the meritorious, abasing criminals; and by spreading terror and utmost destruction among the other nations by means of scourges and axes, and honoring the gods with statues and colossi. Whence, consequently, that people appeared more bridled and restrained from vices of an uncivilized and barbarous nature, more excellent and ready to perform generous enterprises than any other people that has ever been seen. And as long as such were their law and religion, their customs and deeds, such were their honor and their happiness.)

Bruno's concept of the Deity as pure rational principle, and as both cause and effect, made all positive religions, with their emphasis on the anthropomorphic attributes of God, repugnant to him.[33] Catholicism was no exception, although the universal structure of the Catholic Church, which united peoples of diverse customs and races, so reminiscent of Rome, strongly appealed to the philosopher. Nevertheless, his sly references to monks, monasteries, and relics hint at his disapproval of some of the basic tenets of Catholicism. His ironic allusions to the New Testament,[34] and particularly his satire of Christ, whose life on earth he allegorizes in Orion, and whose "trinitarian" nature, in Chiron the Centaur, are an implied refutation not only of Catholicism but of Christianity itself.

He assailed the Protestants for their confiscation of Catholic schools, universities, hospitals, and other properties, accusing them of being disseminators of that discord and injustice which wreaked so much suffering and destruction upon Europe, at much inconvenience to himself. Referring to Protestant theologians, constantly bickering among themselves, he caustically remarks:

tra diece mila di simil pedanti non si trova uno che non abbia un suo catecismo formato; se non publicato, al meno per publicare quello che non approva nessuna altra instituzione che la propria, trovando in tutte l'altre che dannare, riprovare e dubitare; oltre che si trova la maggior parte di essi che son discordi in se medesimi, cassando oggi quello che scrissero l'altro giorno.[35]

(among ten thousand such pedants there is not one who has not compiled his own catechism, and who, if he has not published it, at least is about to publish that one which approves of no other institution but his own, finding in all the others something to condemn, reprove, and doubt; besides, the majority of them are found in disagreement among themselves, rescinding today what they wrote the day before.)

He who had suffered humiliation at the hands of the Calvinists at Geneva acrimoniously impugns their doctrine of predestination and their emphasis on faith, reproaching them for wanting "to reform the deformed laws and religions." The Calvinistic belief in predestination, according to Bruno, induced its adherents "to the contempt of, or at least to little concern for, legislators and laws, by giving them to understand that they propose impossible things, and rule as if in jest." The biting sarcasm with which Bruno refers to the Calvinists and their doctrines, typical of his satirical style, is vividly illustrated in the following passage:

E cossí escano da quelle profanate stanze e non mangino de quel pane iscomunicato; ma vadano ad abitare in quelle pure ed incontaminate case, e si pascano di que'cibi, che mediante la loro riformata legge li sono stati destinati, e novamente prodotti da questi personaggi pii che fanno tanto poco stima de l'opere operate, e solamente per una importuna, vile e stolta fantasia si stimano regi del cielo e figli de li dei, e piú credeno ed attribuiscono a una vana, bovina ed asinina fiducia, ch'ad un utile, reale e magnanimo effetto.[36]

(And so let them depart from those profaned dwellings and not eat of that accursed bread; but let them go and inhabit those pure and uncontaminated houses and feed upon those victuals that have been destined to them by means of their reformed law, and recently brought forth by these pious individuals—they who hold completed works in such low esteem, and only because of an importune, vile, and foolish imagination consider themslves rulers of heaven and children of the gods, and believe more in, and attribute more to, a vain, bovine, and asinine faith than to a useful, real, and magnanimous effect.)

Bruno is harsh in his criticism of the Jews, whom he calls the "excrement of Egypt." He maintains that Moses, "who left the court of Pharaoh, learned in all the sciences of the Egyptians," imparted their knowledge to the Jews; and he implies that the evolution of Jewish monotheism, with its emphasis on a personal God, destroyed the concept of the Deity as immanent principle, embodied in the natural religion of the Egyptians.[37]

In his interpretation of the Old Testament Bruno's views clash with both Christian and Jewish teachings. He regards its stories as fables, or metaphorical representations of history, passed on from the Egyptians to the Babylonians and then to the Hebrews. He adduces as evidence of his premise the "metaphor of the raven," which, he declares, was "first found and developed in Egypt and then taken by the Hebrews, through whom this knowledge was transmitted from Babylonia, in the form of a story. . . ."

Bruno is struck by the variations of the Osiris myth in the ancient Mediterranean civilizations, to which he makes a brief allusion.[38] However, he specifically points out analogies between such Greek myths as that of Apollo and the Raven and the biblical Noah and the Raven, between that of Deucalion and Noah, and between that of Cetus and Jonah and the Whale.

The source of the myths shared by the Greeks with the Hebrews, he insists, is not Hebrew but Egyptian. Egypt, indeed, is for Bruno the source of all the myths and fables of the Mediterranean world, all being poetical representations of events dating back to the dawn of Western civilization.[39]

Historically, Egypt represents for Bruno the cradle of Western religion. The Egyptian cult, with its worship of the living effects of nature, seems to come closest to his concept of natural religion. The following quotation from Iamblichus,[40] which in the form of a prophecy laments the disappearance of the natural religion of the Egyptians and the dire effect this loss will have upon humanity, prognosticates a return to the religion of nature; and Bruno's employment of this passage in *Lo spaccio* is most significant:

Non sai, O Asclepio, come l'Egitto sia la imagine del cielo, e per dir meglio, la colonia de tutte cose che si governano ed esercitano nel cielo? A dir il vero, la nostra terra è tempio del mondo. Ma, oimè, tempo verrà che apparirà l'Egitto in vano essere stato religioso cultore della divinitade; perché la divinità, remigrando al cielo, lasciarà l'Egitto deserto; e questa sedia de divinità rimarrà vedova da ogni religione, per essere abandonata dalla presenza de gli dei. . . . O Egitto, Egitto, delle religioni tue solamente rimarranno le favole, anco incredibili alle generazioni future, alle quali non sarà altro, che narri gli pii tuoi gesti, che le lettere sculpite nelle pietre. . . . Le tenebre si preponeranno alla luce, la morte sarà giudicata più utile che la vita, nessuno alzarà gli occhi al cielo, il religioso sarà stimato insano, l'empio sarà giudicato prudente, il furioso forte, il pessimo buono. E credetemi che ancora sarà definita, pena capitale a colui che s'applicarà alla religion delle mente. . . . Soli angeli perniciosi remarranno, li quali meschiati con gli uomini forzaranno gli miseri all'audacia di ogni male, come fusse giustizia; donando materia a guerre, rapine, frodi e tutte altre cose contrarie alla anima, e guistizia naturale: e questa sarà la vecchiaia ed il disordine e la irreligione del mondo. Ma non dubitare, Asclepio, perché dopo che saranno accadute queste cose, allora il signore e padre Dio, governator del mondo, l'omnipotente proveditore, per diluvio, d'acqua o di fuoco, di morbi o di pestilenze, o altri ministri della sua giustizia misericordiosa, senze dubbio donarà fine a cotal macchia, richiamando il mondo all'antico volto.[41]

(Do you not know, oh Asclepius, that Egypt is the image of heaven or, better said, the colony of all things that are governed and practiced in heaven? To speak the truth, our land is the temple of the world. But woe is me! The time will come when Egypt will appear to have been in vain the religious cultivator of divinity, because divinity, remigrating to heaven, will leave Egypt deserted. And this seat of divinity will remain widowed of every religion, having been deprived of the presence of the gods. . . . Oh Egypt, oh Egypt! Of your religions there will remain only the fables, still incredible to future generations, to whom there will be nothing else that may narrate your pious deeds save the letters sculptured on stones. . . . Shadows will be placed before light, death will be judged to be more useful than life, no one will raise his eyes toward heaven. The religious man will be considered insane, the impious man will be considered prudent, the furious man, strong, the most wicked man, good. And believe me, capital punishment will still be prescribed for him who will apply himself to the religion of the mind. . . . Only pernicious angels will remain, who, mingling with men, will force upon the wretched ones every audacious evil as if it were justice, giving material for wars, rapines, frauds, and all other things contrary to the soul and to natural justice. And this will be the old age and the disorder and irreligion of the world. But do not doubt, Asclepius, for after these things have occurred, the lord and father God, governor of the world, the omnipotent provider, by a deluge of water or of fire, of diseases or of pestilences or of other ministers of his compassionate justice, will doubtlessly then put an end to such a blot, recalling the world to its ancient countenance.)

In the words of Isis conveyed by Sophia, Bruno contends that despite the fact that it is true that the Egyptians resorted to some abusive practices in their natural religion, they nevertheless worshiped "the Deity, one and simple and absolute in itself, multiform and omniform in all things"; and therefore, he arrives at the conclusion that their cult was far superior to the anthropomorphic polytheism of the Greeks.

A careful study of *Lo spaccio,* of *De la causa* and of *De l'infinito* would seem to confirm the opinion, held by some scholars, that Bruno was not only a true pantheist but also the direct ancestor of Spinoza.[42] The universe as viewed by both Bruno and Spinoza is governed by an immanent Deity, who is absolute principle; but whereas Spinoza conceives of a static, determined universe, which is merely "the statue of God," [43] Bruno conceives of one containing both necessity and freedom.[44]

Certainly the most heretical aspect of Bruno's philosophy in *Lo spaccio* is his concept of a religion of nature, derived from his doctrine of "immanence."

In developing his concept of "immanence," Bruno establishes the premise that "animals and plants are living effects of Nature," which, he declares, is "nothing else but God in things," or, expressed in other terms, "natura est deus in rebus." [45] Thus, according to Bruno, the universe is an emanation of the Deity within it.[46] Referring to Bruno's universe, Spaventa declares that it is not "the tomb of dead divinity," but rather "the seat of living divinity . . . the true and only life of God." [47] Bruno's Deity, since he is the substance of all things, cannot limit or divorce himself from his infinite universe; for, according to Cassirer, in Bruno's universe, "the one and infinite substance cannot help but reveal itself to itself, in an infinity of effects." [48] Consequently, potency and act coincide in the Deity; and he is one and the same with the reality that emanates from him.

Bruno believes that Divinity, which is latent in nature, "working and glowing differently in different subjects . . . through diverse physical forms in certain arrangements . . . succeeds in making them participants . . . in her being, in her life and intellect." He alludes to the "ladder of Nature . . . by which Divinity descends even to the lowest things," just as all rational beings "by means of a life, resplendent in natural things," rise "to the life which presides over them."

From Bruno's philosophy of nature is derived his philosophy of knowledge. Since multiform nature in which all opposites coincide is, according to him, the infinite emanation of a Deity who is absolute reason, she (nature) is the teacher of all rational beings.[49] The inference that we may draw from *Lo spaccio* is that the more deeply man penetrates into the laws of nature, by virtue of his intellect, the closer will he come to an understanding of the unity that exists between him and the immanent principle. For in Bruno's doctrine, as Cassirer maintains, the "intellect and all its determinations are a representation and so to speak a symbolic imitation of the same original principle from whose foundation nature has its origin." [50] It is, then, through purely intellectual processes, rather than through a mystical experience, that rational beings can become one with God. Upon this point Gentile observes:

The knowledge of divinity as championed by Bruno is not ecstasy, or immediate union, although it is indeed union that it has as its end, whereupon the spirit, as he says, "becomes a god upon intellectual contact with that object, deity." It is a rational process, a discourse of the intellect, a true and appropriate philosophy.[51]

Bruno scoffs at the classical myth of the Golden Age, so often used as a theme by the writers of the Renaissance; for he, like Hegel, concluded that man living in that legendary period of "peace and plenty" was little more than beast.[52] He firmly believes that man, the "artisan and efficient of God, sacred by his very humanity," [53] could reproduce in society the unity and harmony established in the universe by its immanent, rational principle.

Lo spaccio envisages a society in which the natural religion of the Egyptians, in its purest sense, and the speculative intellect of the Greeks would coincide in a sociopolitical structure patterned after that of the Roman Republic. The source of the state, which Bruno conceives of as "an ethical substance," is God, "the absolute reality, or reality which is the principle of all realities." The state envisaged by the philosopher would be one containing a unity of law and religion, rather than a separation of "the divine from law and civil life." [54] In this state, which in some aspects foreshadows Vico's idealization, natural religion, philosophy, the arts and sciences, would combine to form a religion of reason. Of this ideal state, contemplated by Bruno, Giusso declares:

In Bruno, as later in Vico, is designed and prophesied, as the perfect state of civilization, that state in which the arts and the sciences, "since they derive their being from religions and laws, may serve laws and religions." . . .[55]

IV

THE HERETIC AND HIS TRIAL

Although Bruno in his writings often sought to protect himself against suspicion by resorting to allegorical language, in conversation with those whom he considered his friends he was frequently unguarded. Thus, the philosopher's confidential remarks to Guillaume Cotin, and later to Giovanni Mocenigo, give us additional insight into his heretical thinking.[1]

We learn from Cotin's diary that Bruno was compelled to leave Italy "pour éviter," as he asserts, "les calumnies des inquisiteurs, qui sont ignorans, et, ne concevans sa philosophie, le diroyent hérétique." Although generous in his praise of Thomas Aquinas, Bruno refers contemptuously to what he terms the "subtleties of the scholastics." We are told that he inveighed against the Sacraments, and especially the Eucharist, which were all, according to him, unknown to Peter and Paul. He furthermore maintained that when mankind became aware of these matters, the "troubles" that beset religion would be removed, and he hoped that the end of these "troubles" was at hand. He assailed the philosophy of the Jesuits, which, he asserted, dealt only with questions derived "from the text and intelligence of Aristotle."[2]

Giovanni Mocenigo's denunciations of Giordano Bruno were contained in letters addressed by him to the Venetian Holy Office on May 23, 25, and 29, 1592, and were to become the basis of the tribunal's case against the philosopher. Although in the letters the nobleman may have colored his statements, nevertheless, their content reflects the basic thoughts contained in *Lo spaccio.*

Mocenigo made the following accusations: Bruno maintained that the Catholic faith is "full of blasphemy against the majesty of God"; "that there is no distinction of persons in God," and that making such a distinction would imply that God is imperfect; "that the world is eternal"; "that there are infinite worlds"; [3] "that all the operations of the world are guided by fate"; [4] and that "souls created through the operation of nature pass from one animal to another." In other accusations Mocenigo charged that Bruno affirmed that "Christ was a rogue"; and "that if He performed wicked deeds in order to seduce peoples, He could very well have predicted that He would have to be hanged"; that "the miracles" of Christ and His disciples were "apparent"; and that He and His disciples were "magicians." [5]

The letters further reveal that Bruno severely criticized monastic institutions, branding all monks as "asses," and Catholic doctrines as "asinine"; that he considered a blasphemy the Catholic teaching that bread is transmuted into flesh; that he disapproved of the sacrifice of the Mass, stating that "there is no punishment of sins"; that he denied the possibility of the Virgin Birth, and alleged that the actions of the Church of his day were not in harmony with the spirit of the Apostles, who, according to him, converted others to their way of thinking by their preaching and their own good examples; and that Catholics have no proof that their faith has any merit in the eyes of God. According to Mocenigo, Bruno demonstrated "that he wanted to make himself the author of a new sect under the name of a new philosophy." [6] Mocenigo alleged that on another occasion Bruno criticized all religions; but although he insisted that the Catholic faith was in need of great change, he nevertheless admitted that it was the religion that pleased him most. [7] The Venetian stated that Bruno criticized the Church's use of violence against those who did not want to follow Catholic doctrines, asserting that the concept of "not doing unto others that which we would not have done unto us," would be sufficient for society. [8] Bruno is said to have contended that he harmed no one by living and thinking as he saw fit,[9] and to have warned that the world would soon witness a general reform, since, as he claimed, the widespread ignorance and corruption it contained could not continue.[10]

Ever since his student days in Naples, Bruno had been aware of his conflict with society; and although he fervently desired that his views might someday be allowed to coexist with the prevailing attitudes of his time, he nevertheless feared that he would ultimately be overwhelmed. Yet, he lived and thought dangerously; and it is therefore not surprising that, prophetic of his own unhappy fate, he should exclaim:

questo, come cittadino e domestico del mondo, figlio del padre Sole and de la Terra madre, perché ama troppo il mondo, veggiamo come debba essere odiato, biasimato, perseguitato e spinto da quello.[11]

(we see how this man, as a citizen and servant of the world, a child of Father Sun and Mother Earth, because he loves the world too much, must be hated, censured, persecuted, and extinguished by it.)

At the Venetian trial of Bruno, which began on May 26, 1592, we witness a defendant stunned by the swift sequence of events leading to his arrest.[12] If the philosopher showed signs of vacillation during this ordeal, it was because he gradually became convinced of the hopelessness of his position. Hence, motivated by the somber realization that the heretical premises of his *Weltanschauung* made him vulnerable to the relentless assaults of his prosecutors, he alternately denied or justified or offered apologies for many audacious and original ideas developed in *Lo spaccio* and in his more than three score works, dealing with the most diversified religious, philosophical, and scientific themes.[13] In a desperate attempt to save himself, he was humbly to admit that he was in error, plaintively ask forgiveness for his "misdeeds," plead for a *modus vivendi* with the Church, and throw himself upon the mercy of the tribunal.

The inquisitors who tried the philosopher in Venice, and later in Rome, derived their power from the formulation of premises based on an absolute reliance upon the authority of Revelations and scholastic philosophy. Armed with their concept of absolute truth, they believed that all religious, philosophical, and scientific ideas that did not conform with revealed Holy Script were to be opposed by every possible means. Moreover, they were convinced that to confine or destroy the body of one heretic meant the saving of the souls of countless believers, who might otherwise, consciously or unconsciously, fall prey to his heretical beliefs.

Previously the Church had countenanced the tradition among scholars of holding a religious-philosophical dichotomy, a practice which had protected Pomponazzi.[14] Bruno's implied intention, at his Venetian trial, was to resort to that procedure. Referring to his works, he argued that he had always defined his terms philosophically, "according to natural principles and natural understanding, being in no way concerned with that which principally must be maintained according to faith." The defendant maintained that if he, speaking according to his "natural reason," had pronounced impious judgments, it was not "to impugn religion," but rather "to extol philosophy."[15]

Asked whether he had at any time "taught, held, or disputed" in favor of any premise prejudicial to the Catholic Church, he replied that he had not done so directly; and he affirmed that in his *Centum et viginti articuli de natura et mundo, adversus peripateticos,* published in Paris with the consent of the authorities, he had argued "according to natural principles," without prejudice to the truth Catholics were taught to believe "in the light of faith." He maintained that the works of Aristotle and Plato can be read and taught in like spirit, and alleged that these books were likewise "indirectly" contrary to faith in the same manner, or, in his own words, "rather much more contrary than the articles philosophically proposed by me." He asserted that the philosophical arguments he held against Aristotle and his followers would be more fully understood in the light of the premises he established in *De monade, De minimo, De immenso,* and, to a lesser degree, *De compositione imaginum.*[16]

The Nolan, called by Kepler "the defender of infinity,"[17] admitted that in his works he had spoken of the existence of an infinite universe, containing other worlds similar to ours, "an effect of divine infinite potency."

perché [declared the philosopher] io stimavo cosa indegna della divina bontà e potenzia che, possendo produr oltra questo mondo un altro ed altri infiniti, producesse un mondo finito.[18]

(because I considered it a thing unworthy of divine goodness, divine potency, that being able to produce besides this world another and infinite worlds, it should produce a finite world.)

He stated that he agreed with Pythagoras that the earth was another heavenly body, "similar to which are the Moon, other planets and other stars, which are infinite."

Indeed, the philosopher had been deeply concerned with the problem of infinity; for in *De l'infinito* he remarks:

Uno dunque è il cielo, il spacio immenso, il seno, il continente universale, l'eterea regione, per la quale il tutto discorre e si muove. Ivi innumerabili stelle, astri, globi, soli e terre sensibilmente si veggono ed infiniti raggionevolmente si argumentano. L'universo immenso ed infinito è il composto che resulta da tal spacio e tanti compresi corpi.[19]

(One, then, is the heaven, the immense space, the bosom, the universal continent, the ethereal region, through which everything flows and moves. There, innumerable stars, heavens, globes, suns, and earths are seen through the senses, and the existence of infinite numbers is argumented through reason. The immense and infinite universe is the composition that results from such a space and so many bodies comprised within that space.)

And in another passage in the same work, he again develops this thought:

Però per la raggione de innumerabili gradi di perfezione, che denno esplicare la eccellenza divina incorporea per modo corporeo, denno essere innumerabili individui, che son questi grandi animali (de quali uno è questa terra . . . per la continenza di questi innumerabili si richiede un spacio infinito.[20]

(because of the innumerable grades of perfection, however, that must explain incorporeal divine excellence by corporeal means, there must be innumerable individuals, such as these great beings (of which one is this earth. . . . For the containment of these innumerable beings infinite space is required.)

Now, apprehensive that his candid remarks on the nature of the universe might have prejudiced his defense, Bruno, resorting to a new strategy, resolved to explain his views on the nature of God in more ambivalent terms. Thus he affirmed his belief in a "Universal Providence," "by virtue of which everything lives, vegetates, moves, and abides in its own perfection." This "Universal Providence" he interpreted in two manners: the first, "in the manner in which the soul is present in the body," that is to say, everywhere, which Bruno defined as "nature, shadow, and vestige of divinity"; the second, "in the ineffable manner with which God by means of his essence, presence, and potency is in all and above all, not as part, not as soul, but in an inexplicable manner." [21]

Bruno explained that he conceived of Divinity as having three attributes: "potency, wisdom, and goodness," or "mind, intellect, and love, through which things first have their being, the reason of the mind; then, an ordered being, distinguished by reason of the intellect; third, harmony and symmetry, by reason of love." But he declared that these distinctions existed "by way of reason," and not "by way of substantial truth." [22]

The philosopher admitted that because of his "inconstant faith," [23] he had not understood the literal meaning of the Trinity; [24] but he had instead conceived of that doctrine in philosophical terms. He then sought to prove that his philosophical explanation of God did not conflict with either Aristotle's or Thomas Aquinas' conception of the Deity.

In truth, however, the Brunian concept of God was diametrically opposed to that of Aristotle and Thomas Aquinas; for whereas the Deity as defined by them lay outside of the universe, which He as a prime mover willed into existence, Bruno's God, as revealed in *Lo spaccio,* himself determined, is the immanent principle that pervades all nature; and the Nolan's concept of a pantheistic Deity is closely linked with the Pythagorean "soul of the universe," [25] which for him is the formative principle of all things. Bruno refers to this principle in *De la causa:*

Se dunque il spirto, la anima, la vita si ritrova in tutte le cose, a secondo certi gradi empie tutta la materia; viene certamente ad essere il vero atto e la vera forma de tutte le cose. L'anima, dunque, del mondo è il principio formale constitutivo de l'universo e di ciò che in quello si contiene. Dico che, se la vita si trova in tutte le cose, l'anima viene ad esser forma di tutte le cose: quella per tutto è presidente alla materia e signoreggia nelli composti, effettua la composizione e consistenzia de le parti.[26]

(If then the spirit, the soul, the life, is found in all things, and it, according to certain gradations, fills all matter, it certainly becomes the true act and the true form of all things. The soul of the world, then, is the formal and constitutive principle of the universe and of that which is contained in it. I say that if life is found in all things, the soul becomes the form of all things. She presides throughout matter and is dominant in mixtures, effectuates the composition and consistency of the parts.)

Yet the Nolan at his Venetian trial identified the same "soul of the universe" with the third person of the Trinity, asserting that that concept, as he understood it, is the source of the life and soul "of each thing which has soul and life." He attempted to justify this premise by quoting Solomon's "Spiritus Domini replevit orbem terrarum, et hoc quod continet omnia." ("The spirit of the Lord filled the earth and all that it contains.") As further corroboration of his argument, he also quoted lines 724 to 727 from Pythagorean Virgil's sixth book of the *Aeneid:*

> Principio coelum et terras camposque liquentes
> lucentemque globum Lunae Titaniaque astra,
> spiritus intus alit totamque infusa per artus
> mens agitat molem. . . .[27]

(In the beginning the spirit sustains from within the heaven and earth and the waters, the shining orb of the Moon and the Titanic stars; and a soul infused through the members sways the massive structure. . . .)

He referred to the second person of the Trinity as "that wisdom and that son of mind," who, he said, was called "intellect" by the philosophers, and the "Word" [28] by the theologians.

The philosopher was asked whether his views concerning the

"miracles, actions, and death of Christ" contradicted the teachings of the Catholic Church. He replied that he had interpreted Christ's life in the light of the teachings of the Church; and although he admitted that he had stated that "the miracles were testimony of divinity," [29] as he interpreted divinity, he emphasized that he relied more upon the authority of the Gospel.

Bruno's affirmations of his belief in Christ's divinity, prompted by the relentless probing of his judges, stand in direct contrast with his characterization of Christ in *Lo spaccio*, therein allegorically represented by Orion:

Questo [says Bruno in the words of Momus], perché sa far de maraviglie, e . . . può caminar sopra l'onde del mare senza infossarsi, senza bagnarsi gli piedi; e con questo consequentemente potrà far molte altre belle gentilezze; mandiamolo tra gli uomini; e facciamo che gli done ad intendere tutto quello che ne pare e piace, facendogli credere che il bianco è nero, che l'intelletto umano, dove li par meglio vedere, è una cecità; e ciò che secondo la raggione pare eccellente, buono ed ottimo, è vile, scelerato ed estremamente malo; che la natura è una puttana bagassa, che la legge naturale è una ribaldaria; che la natura e divinità non possono concorrere in uno medesimo buono fine, e che la giustizia de l'una non è subordinata alla giustizia de l'altra, ma son cose contrarie. . . .[30]

(This is because he [Orion] knows how to perform miracles, and . . . can walk over the waves of the sea without sinking, without wetting his feet, and with this, consequently, will be able to perform many other fine acts of kindness. Let us send him among men, and let us see to it that he give them to understand all that I want and like them to understand: that white is black, that the human intellect, through which they seem to see best, is blindness, and that that which according to reason seems excellent, good, and very good, is vile, criminal, and extremely bad. I want them to understand that Nature is a whorish prostitute, that natural law is ribaldry, that Nature and Divinity cannot concur in one and the same good end, and that the justice of the one is not subordinate to the justice of the other, but that they [Nature and Divinity] are contraries. . . .)

Bruno's judges, however, not satisfied with his previous statements concerning the nature of the first person, questioned him

again on the subject. Yielding to the persistent pressure of his ex-
aminers, he who had in *Lo spaccio* advocated the existence of an
immanent Deity, now completely reversed himself, declaring: "Ho
creduto e tenuto indubitatemente tutto quello che ogni fedel
cristiano deve creder e tener della prima persona."[31] ("I have believed and maintained without doubt all that which every faithful
Christian must believe and maintain concerning the first person.")

Furthermore, he maintained that he had always held that the
second and third persons were of the same essence as the first,
explaining:

*perché essendo indistinte in essenzia, non possono patire inequalità,
perché tutti li attributi che convengono al Padre, convengono anco al
Figliuol e Spirito santo.*[32]

(because having no distinction in essence, they cannot suffer inequality,
inasmuch as all the attributes that apply to the Father, apply also to
the Son and to the Holy Ghost.)

He admitted, however, having had doubts concerning the incarnation of the second person. Moreover, he asserted that if there were
anti-Trinitarian passages in his writings, they merely served to convey the viewpoints held by Arius and his followers; and he declared that he had believed that the opinions of Arius, which he
deemed "less pernicious"[33] than they were popularly esteemed
to be, had been misinterpreted.

Bruno was questioned whether he had ever in his writings or
conversation, either directly or indirectly, stated anything contrary
to the Holy See. He declared emphatically that although he had
written and said many things that could be construed as deroga-
tory to the Catholic faith, he had not spoken "ex professo,"[34] but
philosophically, and had often reiterated thoughts held by heretics.

Having drawn this damaging admission from the philosopher,
the tribunal insisted upon a more definite statement of his views
on the Trinity. Bruno stated that he had maintained that there is
"a God distinguished into the Father, the Word, and Love, which
is Divine Spirit, and that all three of these are one God in essence."
He emphasized, however, that he had not believed it was fitting to

refer to Him in terms of persons, stating that he had been strengthened in his belief by a reading of the following passage in Augustine: "Cum formidine proferimus hoc nomen personae, quando loquimur de divinis, et necessitate coacti utimur." ("With fear we mention this name of person, when we speak of divine matters, and use it only when compelled by necessity.") He argued that although, because of his lack of understanding, he was beset with doubts concerning the doctrine of the Incarnation, he had not openly denied it, and therefore had not contravened the authority of Scriptures. He terminated his argument by affirming his belief in the "Verbum caro factum est." [35]

The tribunal, referring to Mocenigo's accusation concerning Bruno's opinions on the life of Christ, sought to ascertain whether it was true that he believed Christ to be "not God, but a rogue" who "was able to predict his own death, although he afterward well demonstrated that he was very unwilling to die." [36] The defendant expressed amazement that this question should be put to him.

Bruno defended himself against Mocenigo's accusation that he did not believe in the sacrifice of the Mass, asserting that he accepted the Church's teaching that the bread and wine of the sacrifice truly become the Body and Blood of Christ.

Attempting to defend the orthodoxy of his views concerning the Sacrament of Penance,[37] Bruno declared that he knew that that Sacrament was ordained "to purge our sins," stating that he had "never, never, never" spoken "on this subject," and that he had always maintained that "he who dies in mortal sin is damned." [38]

Bruno admitted that in approximately sixteen years he had visited a confessor only twice. The first of these visits was to a Jesuit in Toulouse; the second, to a Jesuit in Paris, while he was consulting with the Bishop of Bergamo, the nuncio at Paris, and with Don Bernardín de Mendoza on the possibility of being readmitted into the Church. He declared that having been denied absolution, because of his apostasy, he never again went to Mass, stating, however, that he had intended someday to live within his own order as a good Christian.

The tribunal again interrogated him concerning his views on the soul, demanding to know specifically whether he believed that souls pass "from one body to another." He asserted that he had always held, "ex professo" that souls are "subsistent substances" and immortal; that they are "intellective"; and that "they do not pass from one body to another, but that they go to paradise or to purgatory or to hell." Then, endeavoring to justify the Pythagorean concept of the soul, which he held philosophically, he offered the argument that since souls were both "subsistent without the body and inexistent within the body," it was possible for them to pass from one body to another. Previously, Bruno had not only testified that souls were immortal, but, seeking to obviate any possible doubt concerning his belief in the Catholic doctrine of the Resurrection, had hastened to add that he believed even bodies to be immortal; and in an effort to prove the sincerity of his remarks, the author of *Lo spaccio* had quoted from Ecclesiastes: "Nihil sub sole novum: quid est quod est? ipsum quod fuit." [39]

Bruno admitted to his Venetian judges that his assertion to Mocenigo that the Apostles "did more with their preaching, good life, examples, and miracles than could be done today by force" was an implied criticism of the Catholic Church. Seeking, however, to convince them of his preference for the Catholic faith, he referred to a passage in one of his works (the title is indecipherable in the document) in which he had advocated "the extirpation of those who, under the pretext of religion and reform, do away with works." [40]

Asked to give his opinion concerning the "sin of the flesh outside of the Sacrament of Matrimony," the defendant conceded that he had sometimes spoken of this matter, and had stated that it was the least of all sins. Adultery, on the other hand, he considered the worst sin of the flesh, with the exception of the sin against nature. He now admitted that he had been in error when he had condoned fornication, and quoted Paul's admonition against carnal indulgence: "quod fornicarii non possidebunt regnum Dei." [41]

On June 2, 1592, after having completed its day-long examination of Bruno's doctrines, the tribunal summarized its evidence against the author of *Lo spaccio*. It declared that the defendant should not be amazed at having been subjected to the foregoing rigid interrogation, inasmuch as the Holy Office had learned of his sojourn "in so many countries, cities, and places" inhabited by heretics, whom he had befriended. It concluded that since, by his own confessions, he had attended their sermons, he may have maintained "that Christ was not the son of God"; that He "was not incarnated, and born of the Virgin Mary"; and that "humanity and divinity" were not in the same hypostatic union. It then reiterated Mocenigo's specific accusations.[42]

Nevertheless, the tribunal declared that it wished to "beg and supplicate" that since the defendant had on several occasions indicated his willingness to recognize his errors, he continue to "unburden" his conscience by telling the truth. It assured him that he would be extended every consideration necessary for the salvation of his soul, urging him above all to confess "precisely and distinctly the errors and heresies spoken, held, and believed regarding the Catholic faith." [43]

Although the tribunal hinted that it might show leniency toward the philosopher, it nevertheless was determined to subject him to further questioning. Insisting on knowing whether the defendant had been tried and sentenced elsewhere by the Holy Office, and for what specific charges, it demanded "an extended confession" of his entire life which would be "clear, honest, and open." It pointed out that such a confession was necessary so that the defendant might prepare himself to be received "in the bosom of the Holy Mother Church" and be restored as a follower of Jesus Christ. It admonished him, however, that if he obstinately persevered in denying any article pertinent to the Catholic faith, he should not be surprised if the Holy Office proceeded against him "with those terms of justice" [44] which the Catholic Church is wont to use against impenitent heretics.

Confronted with such admonitions, the philosopher proclaimed:

Così Iddio mi perdoni li mei peccati, come ho detto la verità in tutte le cose che mi sono state dimandate e che mi sono riccordato; ma per maggior mia contentezza e sodisfazione andarò anco pensando maggiormente a fatti miei; e se mi occorrerà alla memoria cosa alcuna che abbi detto o fatto contra la fede cristiana e catolica, la dirò liberamente; e così protesto de aver detto il giusto e vero, e de dirlo per l'avenir, e confido di non esser mai convinto in altro.[45]

(So may God forgive my sins, since I have said the truth about all the matters that were asked of me and that I remembered; but for my greater happiness and satisfaction I shall reflect more extensively upon my experiences; and if anything should come to my memory that I have said or done against the Christian and Catholic faith, I shall declare it freely. And likewise I maintain that I have said what is just and true, and that I shall say it in the future; and I confess that I shall never be convinced by another belief.)

The next day the tribunal asked Bruno whether he had reflected upon the previous day's questioning, and then read to him a transcript of the June 2 proceedings. Bruno admitted that having lived with "heretics," he had followed their customs of "eating and drinking foods of all kinds" and that he had eaten meat on Fridays during Lent and on other days of abstinence. He stated, however, that he considered as "pious and holy"[46] the Church's commandment requiring Catholics to abstain from meat on prescribed days. Referring to rites practiced by "heretics," he disclaimed ever having received communion in a Protestant church.

He emphasized that he had given his previous statements concerning Christ, not as defense of his views, but merely as an explanation of them, and that his declarations had given him an opportunity to confess his errors.

The tribunal wished to ascertain whether Bruno believed that "men are created out of corruption like other animals." He asserted that he had never believed this doctrine held by "Lucretius, Epicurus, and other similar men,"[47] although he had discussed it in his works.

In his reply to the tribunal's question as to whether he had ever relied on magic, Bruno stated that he had always held in contempt books on necromancy; but he admitted that since he had shown interest in every aspect of philosophy and had been "curious about all the sciences,"[48] he had confessed to many people that if he had leisure time, he planned to study astrology in order to ascertain whether there was any truth in this art.

The tribunal asked the defendant whether he had "held or said that the operations of the world are guided by Fate, denying God's providence."[49] To this question Bruno replied that he had never spoken of a determined universe, reaffirming his belief in "God's providence." He pointed out that in his writings he had demonstrated how man can oppose Fate, thanks to his free will. Indeed, as we have seen, Bruno did believe in the existence of a limited free will within the framework of determinism.

Bruno could ambivalently state that he believed in "Providence," having in his works occasionally employed this term to designate "Fate." This tendency is evident in the following lines from *Lo spaccio,* wherein Mercury explains to Sophia the workings of Providence:

Ma te inganni, Sofia, se pensi, che non ne sieno a cura cossí le cose minime, come le principali, talmente sicome le cose grandissime e principalissime non costano senze le minime ed abiettissime. Tutto dunque, quantunque minimo, è sotto infinitamente grande providenza. . . .[50]

(But you deceive yourself, Sophia, if you believe that minimum matters are not of so much concern to us as important ones, inasmuch as very great and important things do not have worth without insignificant and most abject things. Everything, then, no matter how minimal, is under infinitely great Providence. . . .)

In a dialogue between Saulino and Sophia in the same work, however, the poet-philosopher expresses his determinism in terms of Fate:

SAULINO. *Volete voi che non conosca Giove la condizion del fato, che per propio e pur troppo divolgato epiteto è intitolato inesorabile? È pur verisimile, che nel tempo de le sue vacanze (se pur il fato gli ne concede), talvolta si volga a leggere qualche poeta; e non è difficile che gli sia pervenuto alle mani il tragico Seneca, che li done questa lezione:*

> *Fato ne guida, e noi cedemo al fato;*
> *E i rati stami del contorto fuso*
> *Solleciti pensier mutar non ponno.*
> *Ciò che facciamo e comportiamo, d'altro*
> *E prefisso decreto il tutto pende;*
> *E la dura sorella*
> *Il torto filo non ritorce a dietro.*
> *Discorron con cert'ordine le Parche,*
> *Mentre ciascun di noi*
> *Va incerto ad incontrar gli fati suoi.*

SOFIA. *Ancora il fato vuol questo, che, benché sappia il medesimo Giove che quello è immutabile, et che non possa essere altro che quel che deve essere e sarà, non manchi d'incorrere per cotai mezzi il suo destino.*[51]

(SAUL. Do you expect Jove not to know the condition of Fate, which according to his own and all too commonly divulged epithet, is called inexorable? It is indeed likely that during the time of his vacations (if indeed Fate grants him any), sometimes he may turn to the reading of some poets; and it is not improbable that the tragedian Seneca will fall into his hands, and will impart to him this lesson:

> Fate guides us, and we surrender unto it;
> And our worrysome thoughts cannot change
> The fixed threads of the warped spindle.
> All things which we do and bear,
> On Fate's lofty decree depend;
> And the harsh sister does not rewind the twisted thread.
> The Fates proceed in a definite order,
> While each of us goes with uncertainty
> Toward his own destiny.

SOPHIA. In addition Fate wills this: that although Jove himself knows that it is immutable and that there can be nothing else except that which must be and will be, he cannot by means of this knowledge avoid meeting his own destiny.)

Bruno was asked by the tribunal: "Are the errors and heresies committed and confessed by you still embraced by you, or do you detest them?" Realizing the defenselessness of his position, the philosopher was now ready to humble himself before his judges:

Tutti li errori che io ho commessi fino al presente giorno [exclaimed Bruno], pertinenti alla vita catolica e professione regulare . . . e tutte le eresie che io ho tenute, e li dubii che ho avuti intorno alla fede catolica ed alle cose determinate dalla Santa Chiesa, ora io le detesto ed aborisco, e ne sono pentito d'aver fatto, tenuto, detto, creduto o dubitato di cosa che non fosse catolica; e prego questo Sacro Tribunale che conoscendo le mie infirmità vogli abbracciarmi nel gremio di Santa Chiesa, provedendomi di remedii opportuni alla mia salute, usandomi misericordia.[52]

(All the errors that I have committed up to the present day, pertinent to Catholic life and to its regular practice . . . and all the heresies that

I have entertained, and the doubts that I have had regarding the Catholic faith and matters determined by the Holy Church, I now detest and abhor; and I am repentant for having done, held, declared, believed, or having meditated upon any matter that was not Catholic; and I beseech this Holy Tribunal that knowing my infirmities it will want to take me into the bosom of the Holy Church, by providing me with remedies suitable for my salvation, and by showing me mercy.)

On July 30, 1592, the last day of the Venetian trial, the tribunal insisted that now the defendant could and should purge his conscience. Bruno asserted that the articles he had confessed sufficiently demonstrated the extent of his excesses, and that he had given the court sufficient ground for suspecting him of heresy; but he protested that he had already shown remorse for his conduct, and had indicated his desire to reform.

The tribunal made a final effort to persuade him to confess whether he was guilty of any other heresies. The philosopher admitted that it was possible that during his long wanderings he might in other ways have deviated from the teachings of the Church, but that he did not remember specifically how and when. Then, kneeling before his judges, he pleaded for forgiveness, declaring that he was ready to accede to every demand submitted to him by the tribunal. But he supplicated the court to mete out any punishment, excessively severe though it might be, except that of a public confession, which would bring dishonor upon the sacred habit he had worn.[53]

During his trial Bruno had entertained strong hopes of avoiding capital punishment; for, indeed, in the sixteenth century only five persons, out of one thousand five hundred and sixty-five tried before the Venetian Inquisition, had been sentenced to death.[54] However, his hopes of obtaining mercy from the Venetian Holy Office were dashed by the intervention of Pope Clement VIII, a pontiff who had, upon ascending the throne of St. Peter, promised to use the severest measures against heretics.

On September 12, 1592, Cardinal Santaseverina, writing in behalf of the Holy See to Fra Giovan Gabriele da Saluzzo, the Father Inquisitor of Venice, demanded that Bruno be surrendered to the papal governor of Ancona for extradition to Rome. On September

17 the Venetian Holy Office agreed to comply, promising to do all in its power to obtain the cooperation of the secular authorities of Venice. But the Venetian Republic, beset by many problems of state, delayed action on this matter for several months; and not until January 7, 1593, after much pressure had been brought to bear by the Vatican authorities, did it agree to the extradition of the philosopher of Nola. On February 27 Bruno was incarcerated in the dungeons of the Roman Inquisition.

Sufficient evidence to enable the Roman Holy Office to pronounce judgment upon Bruno had been supplied by the Venetian tribunal. Yet, for six years (1593 to 1599), the prisoner was ignored, save for a few occasions on which the inquisitors visited or summoned him before them; and except for their censure of the propositions in his defense (September, 1596), and their decision to question him on passages in his writings (December, 1596), no definitive action was taken in his case.[55]

Finally, on January 14, 1599, eight heretical propositions,[56] which Vatican theologians had extracted from his works, were read to the defendant. The crisis in the embattled life of Giordano Bruno of Nola had reached its climax. On January 18 he was allowed a period of six days in which to recant; but in his reply on January 25 he stubbornly insisted upon the right to defend his views. He declared on December 21, 1599, that "he did not want to, nor did he wish to retract"; nor was there "anything to retract." [57]

Despite Bruno's having stated in a letter to the pontiff that he would submit only to the Holy See for a final judgment upon his writings, it was reported to the Holy Office on January 20, 1600, that Pope Clement VIII had decided that extreme measures should be taken against him and that he be committed to secular authorities.

The Roman Holy Office issued a document on February 8, 1600, reviewing the highlights of the Roman proceedings against Bruno. Among other things it alluded to the tone of Bruno's statements found in his letter to Pope Clement VIII, from which it "manifestly" appeared to that body that he was "pertinaciously" persevering in his "errors." Furthermore, the document stated that it had been said of him that while sojourning in England he was considered an "atheist," [58] and that he had composed a book entitled *Trionfante bestia.*[59] The document concludes with an official pronouncement of excommunication against Bruno, declaring that his books should be publicly burned, and their titles placed upon the *Index.*

According to the German, Gaspar Schopp, a witness to Bruno's burning, the condemned philosopher, upon hearing this sentence, is said to have risen and to have exclaimed: "You perhaps pronounce sentence against me with a fear greater than that with which I receive it." [60]

Bruno was consigned to the civil authorities of Rome; and on the morning of February 16, 1600, after a period of eight days during which he had refused to recant, he was brought to the Campo di Fiori to be burned. Before being given to the flames, he was shown the image of Christ, from which he disdainfully averted his gaze.

In an allegorical passage in *De monade,* Bruno seems to have written his own epitaph:

> *Pugnavi, multum est; me vincere posse putavi . . .*
> *Et studium et nixus sors et natura repressit.*
> *Est aliquid prodisse tenus: quia vincere fati*
> *In manibus video esse situm. Fuit hoc tamen in me*
> *Quod potuit, quod et esse meum non ulla negabunt*
> *Secla futura, suum potuit quod victor habere,*
> *Non timuisse mori, simili cessisse nec ulli*
> *Constanti forma, praelatam mortem animosam*
> *Imbelli vitae.*[61]

(Much have I struggled. I thought I would be able to conquer . . .
And both fate and nature repressed my zeal and my strength.
Even to have come forth is something, since I see that being able to
  conquer
Is placed in the hands of fate. However, there was in me
Whatever I was able to do, which no future century
Will deny to be mine, that which a victor could have for his own:
Not to have feared to die, not to have yielded to any equal
In firmness of nature, and to have preferred a courageous death to a
Noncombatant life.)

Although Bruno, like Spinoza and Einstein, was a deeply religious man in a "cosmic sense," he was branded a heretic by an age more religious than scientific. He who had maintained with scientific objectivity that truth is relative, and not absolute, as taught by positive religions, died a willing martyr in its cause.

Speaking of heretics, Albert Einstein, one of the great heretics of our age, said:

it is precisely among the heretics of every age that we find men, who were filled with the highest kind of religious feeling and were in many cases regarded by their contemporaries as Atheists, sometimes also as saints. Looked at in this light, men like Democritus, Francis of Assisi and Spinoza are closely akin to one another.[62]

THE
EXPULSION OF
THE TRIUMPHANT
BEAST

PROPOSED BY JOVE,

ACHIEVED BY THE COUNCIL,

REVEALED BY MERCURY,

NARRATED BY SOPHIA,

HEARD BY SAULINO,

RECORDED BY THE NOLAN

Explanatory Epistle

WRITTEN TO THE MOST ILLUSTRIOUS
AND EXCELLENT KNIGHT,
SIR PHILIP SIDNEY, BY THE NOLAN

He is blind who does not see the sun, foolish who does not recognize it, ungrateful who is not thankful unto it, since so great is the light, so great the good, so great the benefit, through which it glows, through which it excels, through which it serves, the teacher of the senses, the father of substances, the author of life.

Now I do not know how I should esteem myself, excellent sir, if I did not esteem your intellect, did not respect your customs, did not proclaim your merits, through which you revealed yourself to me at the very moment I arrived on the island of Britain, insofar as time permitted you. You manifest yourself to many, whenever you have the occasion; and you look upon all with favor to that extent to which your natural and truly heroic inclination indicates you should.

Then leaving the concern of all to all, and the duty of the many to the many, may Fate not allow that I, since I have sometimes shown myself sensitive to the vexatious and inopportune discourtesies of some people, insofar as my private affairs are concerned, thus come to leave before the eyes of eternity a note of ingratitude by turning my back upon your beautiful, fortunate, and most courteous fatherland without, at least, a sign of gratefulness, by paying my respects to you, as well as to that most generous and most kind spirit, Sir Fulke Greville. Just as he is close to you in the bonds of intimate and long friendship, in which you were reared, nourished, and raised together, so he resembles you in the many and worthy, external and internal perfections; and, with regard to me, he was that second man who, after your first good offices, extended and offered me the second. These I would have accepted, and he certainly would have effectuated them if the envious Erinys of cowardly, malicious, ignoble, and interested parties had not spread her arsenate.

So therefore, reserving for him some other subject matter, here I present to you this collection of dialogues, which certainly will be as good or as bad, as worthy or unworthy, excellent or worthless, learned or ignorant, lofty or base, profitable or useless, fertile or sterile, grave or dissolute, religious or profane, as those into whose hands they may come; some are of one kind, others of another, contrary kind. And since the number of the fools and the perverse is incomparably larger than that of the wise and the just, it follows that if I want to consider glory or other fruits, to which the multitude of voices gives birth, so far removed am I from the expectation of a happy outcome from my study and work that rather I must expect a source of discontent and must esteem silence to be much better than speech. But if I take into account the eye of Eternal Truth, to which things are the more precious and renowned, the more they are, sometimes, not only known, sought after, and possessed by the fewest but also, besides, considered worthless, blamed, and attacked, it happens that the more I strive to cut the course of the impetuous torrent, the more vigor I see added to it by the turbid, deep, and steep channel.

So then we shall let the multitude laugh at, jest at, mock at, and entertain itself, by the masks of the mimical and comical and histrionic Sileni, under which is covered, hidden, and secure the treasure of goodness and truth, as, on the other hand, there are more than many persons who, under their severe brows and subdued countenances, their profuse beards and magisterial and grave togas, studiously, to universal harm, contain ignorance no less vile than haughty and no less pernicious than the most celebrated ribaldry.[1]

Here, many men who cannot sell themselves as learned and good men, because of their goodness and doctrine, may easily come forward, showing how ignorant and vicious we are. But God knows and is acquainted with the infallible truth that just as that type of men is foolish, perverse, and wicked, so I, in my thoughts, words, and deeds, do not know, do not have, do not pretend anything else but sincerity, simplicity, and truth. It will, in such manner, be judged [of me] where works and heroic effects are not believed to be fruits of no value and vain; where to believe without discretion is not considered the highest wisdom; where the impostures of men are distinguished from divine counsels; where perversion of natural law is not looked upon as an act of religion and superhuman piety; where studious contemplation is not madness; where honor does not consist in avaricious possession, splendor in acts of gluttony, reputation in the multitude of servants, whatever they may be, dignity in the best attire, greatness in possessing the most, truth in miracles, prudence in malice, astuteness in betrayal, prudence in deception, knowing how to live in dissembling, strength in fury, law in force, justice in tyranny, judgment in violence—and so it goes with everything else.

Here Giordano speaks in a vulgar manner, freely designates, gives the appropriate name to him to whom Nature gives an appropriate being. He does not call shameful that which Nature makes worthy, does not cover that which she reveals openly. He calls bread, bread; wine, wine; the head, the head; the foot, foot; and all other parts by their own names. He calls food, food; sleep, sleep; drink, drink; and likewise signifies the other natural acts with their proper titles.[2] He regards miracles as miracles; acts of prowess and marvels as acts of prowess and marvels; truth as truth; doctrine as doctrine; goodness and virtue as goodness and virtue; impostures as impostures; deceptions as deceptions; the knife and fire as the knife and fire; words and dreams as words and dreams; peace as peace; and love as love. He regards philosophers as philosophers; pedants as pedants; monks as monks; ministers as ministers; preachers as preachers; leeches as leeches; useless mountebanks, charlatans, triflers, swindlers, actors, and parrots as they are called, show themselves, and are. He regards workers, benefits, wise men, and heroes as the same. Come! Come! We see how this man, as a citizen and servant of the world, a child of Father Sun and Mother Earth, because he loves the world too much, must be hated, censured, persecuted, and extinguished by it. But, in the meantime, may he not be idle or badly employed while awaiting his death, his transmigration, his change.

Let him today present to Sidney the numbered and arranged seeds of his moral philosophy, not in order that he know and understand them as something new, but in order that he examine, consider, and judge them, accepting all that which must be accepted, excusing all that which must be excused, and defending all that which must be defended against the wrinkles and the brows of hypocrites, the teeth and the nose of the presumptuous, the file and the hiss of pedants. Let him admonish the first that they should esteem him firm in that religion which begins, grows, and maintains itself by resuscitating the dead, healing the infirm, and giving of its own goods, and that there cannot be any affection where that of another is ravished, where the healthy are crippled and the living slain. Let him counsel the second that they turn to the Efficient Intellect and Intellectual Sun, imploring it that it give light to him who does not possess it. Let him make the third understand that it is not suitable for us to be as they are—slaves of definite and determined sounds and words.

But, by the grace of the gods, it is permitted us and we are at liberty to make them serve us, to take and accommodate them at our convenience and pleasure. Thus, let not the first be troublesome to us with their perverse conscience, the second with their blind seeing, the third with their ill-employed solicitude; if the first do not want to be accused of foolishness, envy, and malice, the second do not want to be reprehended for their ignorance, presumption, and temerity, the third do not want to be branded with cowardice, frivolity, and vanity; the first for not having abstained from the rigid censure of our judgment, the second for not having abstained from the stubborn calumny of our sentiments, the third for not having abstained from the foolish riddling of our words.

Now, in order to cause anyone who wants, and is able to, to understand my intention in the present discourse, I protest and certify that insofar as it pertains to me, I approve that which commonly is esteemed worthy of being approved by all wise and good men, and reprove the contrary along with the same. And therefore, I pray and beseech all that there be not anyone of so gross a mind and so malicious a spirit that he may want to determine, giving himself and others to understand, that that which is written in this volume is said by me in an assertive manner.[8] Nor (if he wishes to believe the truth) let him believe that I, either through it or through an accident, may at any point want to take aim at the truth, and hurl stones against the honest, the useful, the natural, and consequently the divine. But let him consider as certain that I, for all my striving, expect the contrary. And if, perhaps, it happens that he is not capable of this, let him not determine, but let him remain in doubt until that time when it will have been resolved, after his having penetrated into the pith of the meaning.

Afterward, let him consider that these are dialogues, wherein are interlocutors, who make their own speeches, and by whom are reported the discourses of many, many others, who equally abound in their own meanings, reasoning with that fervor and zeal which, especially, can be and are appropriate to them. In the meantime, let there be no one who will think otherwise than that these three dialogues have been set down and developed only as the material and subject of a future work; because it seems expeditious to me, being of the intention of treating moral philosophy according to the internal light that the divine Intellectual Sun has radiated and still radiates within me, first to set forth certain preludes, in the manner of musicians; to sketch certain occult and confused outlines and shadows, like the painters; to weave and straighten out certain threads, like the weavers; and to lay certain deep, profound, and dark foundations, like the great builders. This only seemed to me to be effectuated more conveniently by placing in a certain number and order all of the first forms of morality, which are the capital virtues and vices, in such a manner that you will see introduced into the present work a repented Jove, whose heaven was full to overflowing with as many beasts as vices, according to the forms of forty-eight famous images, a Jove now consulting about banishing them from heaven, from glory and a place of exaltation, destining for them, for the most part, certain regions on earth and allowing to succeed into those same seats the virtues, already for so long banished and undeservedly dispersed.

Now, while that is put into execution, even if you see things vituperated, which seem to you unworthy of vituperation, things scorned, worthy of esteem, things exalted, worthy of censure, consider all of this instead as being said indeterminately (considered so even by those who, by their authority, can say it) as being put down with difficulty, placed in the arena, set in the theater, all of this waiting to be examined, discussed, and compared when the music has been arranged, the image represented, the cloth woven, and the roof built. In the meanwhile Sophia represents Sophia, Saulino acts as Saulino, Jove as Jove, Momus, Juno, Venus, and other Greeks or Egyptians, dissolute or grave, as what and whichever they are; and [all] can be adapted to the condition and nature that they are able to represent. If you see serious and jocose subjects, consider that they are all equally worthy of being gazed upon with not ordinary lenses.

In conclusion, consider as definite only the order and number of the subjects of moral consideration, together with the foundations of such a philosophy, which you will see therein entirely represented. Moreover, let each one gather from this medium the fruits that he can, according to the capacity of his own bowl; because there is nothing so wicked that it may not be converted to the profit and usefulness of good people; and there is nothing so good and worthy that it cannot be the cause and material of scandal for ribalds. Here, then, considering everything else (whence we cannot gather any worthy fruit of doctrine) as something doubtful, suspect, and impendent, let our final intention be considered to be the order, the initiation, the disposition, the index of the method, the tree, the theater and arena of the virtues and the vices

—where afterward one must discuss, inquire, inform oneself, correct oneself, distend oneself, betake oneself, and pitch one's tent on other considerations, when, determining upon everything according to our own light and intention, we shall explain ourselves in numerous other particular dialogues, in which the universal architecture of such a philosophy will be fully completed and in which we shall reason in a more definite manner.

We here, then, have a Jove, not taken as too legitimate and good a vicar or lieutenant of the first principle and universal cause, but well taken as something variable, subject to the Fate of Mutation; he, however, knowing that together in one infinite entity and substance there are infinite and innumerable particular natures (of which he is one individual), which, since they in substance, essence, and nature are one, likewise, by reason of the number through which they pass, incur innumerable vicissitudes and a kind of motion and mutation. Each one of these natures then, and particularly Jove's, finds itself as such an individual, with such a composition, with such accidents and circumstances, having been placed in number, because of differences which arise from contraries, all of which are reduced to one original and first contrary, which is the first principle of all the others, the proximate efficients of every change and vicissitude. Because of this, just as he, from one who at first was not Jove, afterward was made Jove, so he, from one who at present is Jove, finally will be other than Jove.

He knows that of the eternal corporeal substance (which is not producible *ex nihilo,* nor reducible *ad nihilum,* but rarefiable, condensable, formable, arrangeable, and "fashionable") the composition is dissolved, the complexion is changed, the figure is modified, the being is altered, the fortune is varied, only the elements remaining what they are in substance, that same principle persevering which was always the one material principle, which is the true substance of things, eternal, ingenerable, and incorruptible.

He knows well that of the eternal incorporeal substance nothing is changed, is formed or deformed, but there always remains only that thing which cannot be a subject of dissolution, since it is not possible that it be a subject of composition; and therefore, either of itself or by any accident, it cannot be said to die; because death is nothing but the divorcing of parts joined in a composite, in which state all of the substantial being of each part remaining (which cannot be lost), that accident of friendship, of accord, of complexion, union, and order ceases.

He knows that spiritual substance, although it has familiarity with bodies, must not be considered as really coming into a composition or mixture with them; because this [composition] is brought about, body with body, a part of matter fashioned in one way, with a part of matter fashioned in another. But there is one thing, an efficient and formative principle from within, from which, through which, and around which the composition is formed; and it is exactly like the helmsman on the ship, the father of the family at home, and an artisan who is not external but fabricates from within, tempers and preserves the edifice; and in it is the power to keep united the contrary elements, to arrange together, as if in a certain harmony, the discordant qualities, to keep and maintain the composition of an animal. It winds the beam, weaves the cloth, interweaves the threads, restrains tempers, gives order to and arranges and distributes the spirits, gives fibers to the flesh, extends the cartilage, strengthens the bones, ramifies the nerves, hollows out arteries, fecundates the veins, foments the heart, gives breath to the lungs, succors all, within, with vital heat and radical humidity, in order that the said hypostasis may be composed and the said countenance, figure, and face may appear on the outside.

Thus, the dwelling place in all things said to be animate is formed from the center of the heart, or from something proportionate to it, by its enfolding and shaping the members and conserving those which have been enfolded and shaped. Thus, necessitated by the principles of dissolution, abandoning its architecture, it [the efficient and formative principle] causes the ruin of the edifice by dissolving the contrary elements, breaking the union, removing the hypostatic composition; because it cannot eternally nestle among the same temperaments, perpetuating the same threads, and preserving those same arrangements, in one and the same composite. However, making its retreat from the external parts and members to the heart, and, as if re-gathering the insensible instruments and tools, it indicates clearly that it leaves through the same door through which it once was fitting for it to enter.

Jove knows that it is neither likely nor possible if corporeal matter, which is composable, divisible, manageable, contractable, formable, mobile, and consistent, under the dominion, power, and virtue of the soul, is not annihilable, is not, in any point or atom, annulable, that, on the other hand, the most excellent nature, which commands, governs, presides over, moves, vivifies, vegetates, makes sentient, maintains and contains, should be of a worse condition. Jove knows, I say (not what some fools, under the name of philosophers, want to believe) it is neither likely nor possible that an act that results from the harmony, symmetry, complexion, and, finally, from an accident, because of the dissolution of the composite, should become nothing, together with the composition, any more than the principle and intrinsic cause of harmony, complexion, and symmetry that derive from it, which can no less subsist without the body, than the body, which is moved and governed by it, and united by its presence and dispersed by its absence, can be without it.

Jove considers this principle, then, to be that substance which is truly man, and not an accident which is derived from the composition. This [principle] is the divinity, the hero, the demon, the particular god, the intelligence, in which, by which, and through which, just as diverse complexions and bodies are formed and form themselves, there likewise succeeds being, diverse in species, of diverse names, of diverse forms. This, because it is that [principle] which, as regards the rational acts and appetites, moves and governs the body according to reason, is superior to it and cannot be necessitated and compelled by it.

It follows that by virtue of the High Justice that presides over all things, because of inordinate affects in the same or in another body, it [being] will be tormented and made ignoble, and that it must not expect the government and administration of a better dwelling when it has badly guided itself in the rule of another. Because, then, of its having there led a life, for example, equine or porcine, it will be (as many more excellent philosophers have understood; and I esteem that, if it is not to be believed, it is much to be considered) ordained by Fatal Justice that there be woven about it a prison appropriate to such a crime or offense, and that there be organs and instruments suitable to such a laborer or craftsman.

And so, on and on, always encountering the Fate of Mutation, it will eternally continue to incur many other worse and better species of life and of fortune, according to whether it has conducted itself better or worse in the immediately preceding condition and lot. So we see that man, changing nature and modifying his affects, from a good man becomes wicked, from a temperate man, intemperate; and, on the other hand, that from one who seemed to be a beast, he ends up by seeming to be another better or worse, by virtue of certain delineations and configurations which, deriving from the internal spirit, appear in the body, so that they will never deceive a prudent physiognomist. However, since we see in the faces of many in the human species, expression, voices, gestures, affects, and inclinations, some equine, others porcine, asinine, aquiline, and bovine, so we are to believe that in them there is a vital principle through which, by virtue of the proximate past or proximate future mutations of bodies, they have been or are about to be pigs, horses, asses, eagles, or whatever else they indicate, unless by habit of continence, of study, of contemplation, and of other virtues or vices they change and dispose themselves otherwise.

Upon this sentence (elaborated by us more than the plan of the present passage requires, not extended without great reason) depends the act of repentance of Jove, who is introduced, as is vulgarly described, as a god who possessed virtues and kindness, and possessed human and sometimes brutal and bestial dissoluteness, frivolity, and frailty, as it is imagined that he possessed when it is reputed that he changed himself into those various subjects or forms in order to indicate the mutation of the various affects that Jove, the soul, and man incur, finding themselves in this fluctuating matter. That same Jove is made the governor and mover of heaven in order that he give us to understand how in every man, in each individual, are contemplated a world and a universe where, for governing Jove, is signified Intellectual Light, which dispenses and governs in it [the world], and distributes, in that admirable structure, the orders and seats of the virtues and vices.

This world, taken according to the imagination of foolish mathematicians and accepted by no less wise physicists (among whom the Peripatetics are the most vain, and these are not without present fruit), as first divided into so many spheres, and then separated into about forty-eight images (in which they primarily conceive an octave, stelliferous heaven, partitioned, and called by the vulgar the firmament), becomes the starting point and subject of our work.

Because, just as here, Jove (who represents each one of us), from one who was conceived, was born, and from a child became a young man, and robust, and from such has become and is ever becoming older and older and more infirm, so from an innocent and inept individual, he becomes noxious and able; becomes wicked and sometimes becomes good; from an ignorant becomes a wise individual; from a crapulent, a sober man; from an incontinent, a chaste man; from a dissolute, a grave man; from an iniquitous, a just man. In addition to this, he is sometimes bent because of the strength that is failing him, both driven and spurred on by the fear of Fatal Justice, superior to the gods, which threatens us.

The day, then, on which is celebrated in heaven the Feast of the Gigantomachy (a symbol of the continuous war, without any truce whatsoever, which the soul wages against vices and inordinate affects), this father wants to effectuate and define that which, for some space of time before, he had proposed and determined; just as a man, in order to change his way of life and customs, is first invited by a certain light that resides in the crow's nest, topsail, or stern of our soul, which light is called synderesis by some, and here, perhaps, is almost always signified by Momus.

He, then, proposes to the gods, that is, he exercises the act of ratiocination of the internal council, and goes into consultation regarding what is to be done. Now he calls for prayers, arms his faculties, and adapts his purposes—not after supper and during the Night of Inconsideration, and without the Sun of Intelligence and Light of Reason, not on an empty stomach in the morning, that is to say, without fervor of spirit, and without being well-warmed by the supernal ardor, but after dinner, that is, after having tasted of the ambrosia of Virtuous Zeal and imbibed of the nectar of Divine Love; around noon, or at the point of noon, that is, when Hostile Error least outrages us and Friendly Truth most favors us, during the period of a more lucid interval. Then is expelled the triumphant beast, that is, the vices which predominate and are wont to tread upon the divine side; the mind is repurged of errors and becomes adorned with virtues, because of love of beauty, which is seen in goodness and natural justice, and because of desire for pleasure, consequent from her fruits, and because of hatred and fear of the contrary deformity and displeasure.

This will be considered, accepted, and agreed upon by all, and among all the gods, when the virtues and powers of the soul rally to favor the work and the act of whatever that efficient light defines as just, good, and true, which directs the sense, the intellect, the discourse, the memory, love, the covetous and irascible faculties, synderesis, and will, faculties signified by Mercury, Pallas, Diana, Cupid, Venus, Mars, Momus, Jove, and other divinities.

There, then, where the Bear was, by virtue of the place's being the most eminent part of the heaven, Truth is placed, who is the highest and most worthy of all things, rather, the first, last, and middle; because she fills the area of Entity, Necessity, Goodness, Beginning, Middle, End, and Perfection. She is conceived of in the contemplative, metaphysical, physical, ethical, and logical fields; and with the Bear descend Deformity, Falsity, Defect, Impossibility, Contingency, Hypocrisy, Imposture, and Felony. The seat of the Great Bear, for a reason not to be stated in this place, remains vacant.

Where the Dragon curves and forms an oblique line, in order to be in proximity to Truth, Prudence is placed, with her maidens, Dialectic and Metaphysics; she has standing around on her right, Craftiness, Cunning, and Malice; on her left, Stupidity, Inertia, and Imprudence.[4] She moves about in the area of Consultation. From that place fall Casualness, Unexpectedness, Chance, and Carelessness, with the left and right side bystanders.

Thence, where Cepheus fences alone, fall Sophism, Ignorance of depraved disposition, and Foolish Faith, with their servants, ministers, and bystanders; Sophia,[5] in order to be the companion of Prudence, there presents herself and will be seen moving in the divine, natural, moral, and rational fields.

There where Boötes observes the chariot, Law ascends in order to get close to her mother Sophia; and she will be seen moving about the divine, natural, tribal, civil, political, economic, and personal-ethical areas, through which she ascends to superior things, descends to inferior things, distends and widens herself toward equal things, and turns toward herself. Thence, fall Prevarication, Crime, Excess, and Exorbitance, with their children, ministers, and companions.

Where the Northern Crown shines, the Sword accompanying it, one understands Judgment as the proximate effect of the law and act of justice. The latter will be seen moving in the five areas of Apprehension, Discussion, Determination, Imposition, and Execution; and hence, as a consequence, falls Iniquity, with all its family. By the Crown, which occupies the quiet left side, are represented Reward and Recompense; by the Sword, which the busy right arm rattles, are represented Punishment and Vengeance. Where, with his cudgel, it seems that Alcides is making space for himself after the debate of Wealth, Poverty, Avarice, and Fortune with their gathered courts, Courage, whom you will see moving in the areas of Attack, Resistance, Assault, Preservation, Offense, and Defense, goes to make her residence, from whose right side fall Ferity, Fury, and Pride, and from whose left side, Weariness, Debility, and Pusillanimity; and around whom are seen Temerity, Audacity, Presumption, Insolence, and Familiarity, and opposite her, Cowardice, Trepidation, Doubt, and Desperation, with their companions and servants. She [Courage] moves about in almost all of the areas.

There, where one sees the nine-stringed Lyre, ascends the Mother Muse with her nine daughters, Arithmetic, Geometry, Music, Logic, Poetry, Astrology, Physics, Metaphysics, and Ethics; whence, as a consequence, fall Ignorance, Inertia, and Bestiality. The mothers have the universe as their area; and each of the daughters has her particular subject.[6]

Whither the Swan spreads its wings, ascend Repentance, Purification, Palinode, Reform, and Cleansing; and hence, as a consequence, fall Selfish Regard for Oneself, Impurity, Sordidness, Impudence, and Obstinacy, with their entire families. They move about and through the area of Error and Fault.

Whence is dismissed enthroned Cassiopea, with Haughtiness, Pride, Arrogance, Boastfulness, and other companions, who are seen in the area of Ambition and Falsehood, ascend Moderated Majesty, Glory, Decorum, Dignity, Honor, and other companions, with their courts. These by first choice ordinarily move about the areas of Simplicity, Truth, and similar others, and sometimes, by force of necessity, move in the area of Dissimulation and similar others, which, by accident, can be the refuge of virtues.

Where fierce Perseus shows us the Gorgonian trophy, ascend Labor, Solicitude, Study, Fervor, Vigilance, Commerce, Exercise, and Occupation, with the spurs of Zeal and Fear. Perseus possesses the talaria of Useful Concern and Contempt for Vulgar Wealth, with their ministers, Perseverance, Intelligence, Industry, Skill, Investigation, and Diligence; and he recognizes as his daughters, Invention and Acquisition, each of whom has three vases full of Material Well-Being, Bodily Well-Being, and Spiritual Well-Being. He roams in the areas of Robustness, Might, and Freedom from Harm; Torpor, Sloth, Idleness, Inertia, Indolence, and Laziness, on one flank, flee before him, with all of their families; and on the other, flee Restlessness, Foolish Occupation, Vacuity, Meddlesomeness, Curiosity, Travail, and Perturbation, which issue forth from the area of Irritation, Instigation, Compulsion, Provocation, and other ministers, which build the Palace of Repentance.

To Triptolemus' seat ascends Humanity, with her family, Counsel, Aid, Clemency, Favor, Suffrage, Succor, Delivery, and Relief, with other companions and brothers of these, and their ministers and children, which move about the area characteristic of Philanthropy, whither Misanthropy does not approach, with its court, Envy, Malice, Disdain, Disfavor, and other brothers of these, which roam through the area of Discourtesy and other vices.

To the house of Ophiuchus ascend Sagacity, Keenness, Subtlety, and similar virtues, which inhabit the area of Consultation and Prudence; whence flee Awkwardness, Stupidity, Foolishness, with their throngs, all of which grow in tufts in the area of Imprudence and Inconsideration.

In the seat of the Arrow are seen Judicious Choice, Observance, and Intent, which are exercised in the area of Orderly Study, Attention, and Aspiration; and from there depart Calumny, Detraction, Flattery, and other children of Hate and Envy, who delight themselves in the gardens of Insidiousness, Espionage, and similar ignoble and most base gardeners.

In the space in which the Dolphin forms an arc are seen Love, Affability, and Courtesy, which, together with their companions, are found in the area of Philanthropy and Friendship; whence the hostile and outrageous throng flees, and withdraws to the areas of Contention, Dueling, and Revenge.

Whence the Eagle departs, with Ambition, Presumption, Temerity, Tyranny, Oppression, and other busy companions, for the area of Usurpation and Violence, there go to sojourn Magnanimity, Magnificence, Generosity, and Dominion, which move about in the areas of Dignity, Power, and Authority.

Where formerly was the horse Pegasus, behold Divine Fervor, Enthusiasm, Rapture, Prophecy, and Contemplation, which move about in the area of Inspiration; whence escape afar Ferine Fury, Mania, Irrational Impetuosity, Dissolution of the Spirit, and Dispersion of the Inner Sense, found in the area of Intemperate Melancholy, which is the Cavern of Perverse Genius.

Where Andromeda yields, with Obstinacy, Perversity, and Foolish Persuasion, which are apprehended in the area of Double Ignorance, succeed Facility, Hope, and Expectation, which show themselves in the area of Good Discipline.

Where the Triangle is conspicuous, there Faith, otherwise known as Fidelity, becomes consistent, which is expected in the area of Constancy, Love, Sincerity, Simplicity, Truth, and other virtues, from which are far removed the areas of Fraud, Deception, and Instability.

At the former palace of the Ram, you have placed Episcopacy, Duchy, Exemplariness, Demonstration, Counsel, and Indication, which are happy in the area of Respect, Obedience, Consentience, Virtuous Emulation, and Imitation; and thence depart Bad Example, Scandal, and Alienation, which are tormented in the area of Dispersion, Bewilderment, Apostasy, Schism, and Heresy.

Taurus demonstrates that he has been the embodiment of Patience, Tolerance, Longanimity, Controlled and Just Rage, which are employed in the area of Government, Ministry, Service, Labor, Work, Respect, and others. With him depart Unrestrained Ire,

Anger, Spite, Disdain, Reluctance, Impatience, Lament, Complaint, and Wrath, which are found almost in the same areas.

Where the Pleiades used to dwell, mount Union, Civilization, Congregation, Populace, Republic, and Church, which take their positions in the area of Social Intercourse, Concord, Communion; there, Regulated Love presides; and with them [the Pleiades] are removed from heaven, Monopoly, Throng, Sect, Triumvirate, Faction, Division, and Addition, which incur danger in the areas of Inordinate Affection, Iniquitous Design, Sedition, and Conspiracy, where Perverse Counsel, with all of its family, presides.

Whence depart the Gemini, ascend Figurative Love, Friendship, and Peace, which delight themselves in their own areas; and those banished ones drag along with themselves Unworthy Partiality, which obstinately fixes its foot on the area of Iniquitous and Perverse Desire.

Cancer drags along with himself Wicked Repression, Unworthy Retrogression, Lowly Deformity, and Unpraiseworthy Restraint, the Lowering of the Claws and the Retraction of the Feet from good thinking and doing, Penelope's Reweaving, and similar consorts and companions, which withdraw into and keep themselves in the area of Inconstancy, Pusillanimity, Poverty of Spirit, Ignorance, and many others; and to the stars ascend Righteous Conversion, Repression of Evil, Retraction from the false and iniquitous, with their ministers, which rule themselves in the area of Honest Fear, Regulated Love, Righteous Intention, Laudable Repentance, and other associates, opposed to Bad Progress, to Wicked Advancement, and to Profitable Pertinacity.

Leo drags with himself Tyrannical Terror, Fear, Formidability, Perilous and Hateful Authority, the Glory of the Presumption, and Pleasure of being feared rather than loved. They move in the area of Rigor, Cruelty, Violence, and Suppression, which are there, tormented by the shadows of Fear and Suspicion. And to the celestial space ascend Magnanimity, Generosity, Splendor, Nobility, Pre-eminence, which administer within the area of Justice, Mercy, Just Conquest, and Worthy Condoning, which reach forth toward the study of being loved rather than feared; and there, they are consoled by Security, Tranquillity of Spirit, and their families.

To join Virgo, go Continence, Pudency, Chastity, Modesty,

Shyness, and Honesty, which triumph in the area of Purity and Honor, despised by Impudence, Incontinence, and other mothers of hostile families.

The Scales have always been the archetype of Expected Equity, Justice, Grace, Gratitude, Respect, and other companions, administrators, and followers, which move about in the threefold area of Distribution, Commutation, and Retribution, where Injustice, Disgrace, Ingratitude, Arrogance, and others of their companions, daughters, and administrators do not set foot.

Where Scorpio used to curve his hooked tail and spread his claws, there no longer appear Fraud, Iniquitous Applause, Feigned Love, Deception, and Betrayal, but the contrary virtues, daughters of Simplicity, Sincerity, and Truth, which move about in the area of the mothers.

We see that Sagittarius was the emblem of Contemplation, Study, and Good Applause, with their followers and servants, which have as object and subject the area of the True and the Good in order to form the Intellect and Will, whence are far removed Affected Ignorance and Lowly Unconcern.

There, where Capricorn still resides, you see Hermitage, Solitude, Contemplation, and other mothers, companions, and handmaidens, which withdraw into the area of Absolution and Liberty, in which are not secure Conversation, Contract, Curia, Feasting, and others appertaining to these children, companions, and administrators.

In the place of humid and distempered Aquarius, you see Temperance, the mother of many and innumerable virtues, who particularly shows herself there with her daughters, Civility and Urbanity, from whose areas escape Intemperance of Affects, with Wildness, Harshness, and Barbarity.

Whence, with Unworthy Silence, Envy of Knowledge, and Defraudation of Doctrine, which move in the area of Misanthropy and Baseness of Mind, the Pisces are removed, there are placed Worthy Silence and Taciturnity, which move in the area of Prudence, Continence, Patience, Moderation, and others, from which flee to contrary shelters Loquacity, Multiloquence, Garrulity, Scurrility, Buffoonery, Histrionics, Levity of Intentions, Vain Talk, Whispering, Complaint, and Murmuring.

Where Cetus was grounded, is found Tranquillity of Spirit, which is secure in the area of Peace and Quiet, whence are excluded Storm, Turbulence, Travail, Inquietude, and other associates and brothers.

There, whence Divine and Miraculous Orion disconcerts the Divinities with Imposture, Adroitness, Profitless Courtesy, Vain Prodigy, Prestidigitation, Sleight of Hand, and Knavery, which, as guides, conductors, and doorkeepers, serve Boastfulness, Vainglory, Usurpation, Rapine, Falsity, and many other vices, in whose areas they are active, is exalted Militia, zealous against iniquitous, visible, and invisible powers; it labors in the area of Magnanimity, Courage, Love for People, Truth, and other innumerable virtues.

Where there still remains the representation of the river Eridanus, we must find something noble of which we shall speak at other times; because its venerable theme does not fit in among these others.

Whence the fleeing Hare is driven away, with Vain Fear, Cowardice, Trembling, Diffidence, Desperation, False Suspicion, and other sons and daughters of Father Indolence and Mother Ignorance, is contemplated Fear, the son of Prudence and Consideration, minister of Glory and True Honor, which are able to sally forth from all virtuous areas.

Where, in the act of running after the Hare, Canis Major had distended his back, ascend Vigilance, Custody, Love of the Republic, Guardianship of Domestic Matters, Tyrannicide, Zeal, and Salutiferous Preaching, which are found in the area of Prudence and Natural Justice; and with him, come down Venation and other ferine and bestial virtues, which Jove wishes to be esteemed as heroic, although they move about in the area of Rascality, Bestiality, and Butchery.

Canis Minor drags down with her, Assentation, Adulation, and Servile Flattery, with their companions; and there, on high, ascend Placability, Friendliness, Companionship, and Kindness, which move about in the area of Gratitude and Fidelity.

Whence Navis returns to the sea, together with Lowly Avarice, Deceitful Commerce, Sordid Gain, Fluctuating Piracy, and other infamous companions, and most often vituperous, there go to make their residence Liberality, Courteous Communication,

Timely Provision, Useful Contract, Worthy Pilgrimage, and Munificent Transportation, with their brothers, companions, helmsmen, oarsmen, soldiers, sentinels, and other ministers, which move about in the area of Fortune.

Where the Southern Serpent, called the Hydra, lengthened and spread her coils, Provident Caution, Judicious Sagacity, and Revirescent Virility make their appearance; whence fall Senile Torpor, Stupid Reversion to childishness, with Insidiousness, Envy, Discord, Slander, and other table companions.

Whence the Raven is expelled, with Gloomy Blackness, Croaking Loquacity, Indecent and Gypsy-like Imposture, with Odious Affrontery, Blind Contempt, Negligent Service, Sluggish Sense of Duty, and Impatient Gluttony, succeed Divine Magic with her daughters,[7] Divination and her ministers and families, among which Augury is first and foremost, which are wont to exert themselves for a good end in the area of Military Art, Law, Religion, and Sacerdotal Office.

Where the Bowl is presented with Gluttony and Ebriety, with that multitude of ministers, companions, and bystanders, there is seen Abstinence; there, are Sobriety and Temperance in Living, with their ranks and positions.

Where the demigod Centaur perseveres and is firmly fixed in his sacristy, are together arrayed Divine Parable, Sacred Mystery, Moral Fable, Divine and Holy Priesthood, with their instituters, preservers, and ministers, thence falls and is banished, Anil and Stupid Fable, with its Foolish Metaphor, Vain Analogy, Ineffectual Anagogy, Silly Tropology, and Obscure Representation, with their false courts, porcine convents, seditious sects, confused ranks, disordered orders, deformed reforms, impure purities, filthy purifications, and most pernicious knaveries, which move about in the area of Avarice, Arrogance, and Ambition; over these presides Grim Malice; and blind and crass Ignorance carries on its business.

With the Altar are Religion, Piety, and Faith. And from its eastern corner fall Credulity, with so many follies, and Superstition, with so many concerns, small concerns and very small concerns; from its western side Wicked Impiety and Insane Atheism precipitate.

Where the Southern Crown is in waiting, there are Reward,

Honor, and Glory, which are the fruits of wearisome virtues and virtuous studies, which depend on the favor of the said celestial influences.

Whence is taken the Southern Fish, there is Enjoyment of the said honored and glorious fruits; there, Rejoicing, the River of Delights, the Torrent of Pleasure; there, the Supper; there, the soul

> Feeds the mind, so noble
> That it no longer envies Jove his ambrosia and nectar.[8]

There is the termination of tempestuous travails; there, the Bed; there, Tranquil Repose; there, Secure Quiet.
Vale.

First Dialogue

Interlocutors: SOPHIA, SAULINO, MERCURY

FIRST PART
OF THE *First Dialogue*

SOPHIA. So that if in bodies, matter, and entity there were not mutation, variety, and vicissitude, there would be nothing agreeable,
nothing good, nothing pleasurable.

SAUL. You have demonstrated it very well, Sophia.

SOPHIA. We see that every pleasure consists only in a definite
transit, journey, and motion. Just as troublesome and sad is the
state of hunger; so, displeasing and grave is the state of satiety;
but that which does delight us is the motion from the one [state]
to the other. The state of venereal ardor torments us, the state of
requited lust saddens us; but that which satisfies us is the transit
from one state to the other. In no present being do we find pleas-

ure, if the past has not become wearisome to us. Labor does not please except in the beginning, after rest; and unless in the beginning, after labor, there is no pleasure in rest.

SAUL. If it be so, there is no pleasure without an admixture of sadness, since in motion there is the participation of that which satisfies and of that which wearies.

SOPHIA. You are right. So to what has been said, let me add that Jove sometimes, as if he were bored with being Jove, takes certain vacations, now as a farmer, now as a hunter, now as a soldier; now he is with the gods, now with men, now with beasts. Those who are in villas take their holidays and recreation in cities; those who are in the cities take their relaxation, holidays, and vacations in the country.[1] Walking pleases and benefits him who has been sitting or lying down; and he who has run about on his feet finds relief in sitting. He finds pleasure in the country who has for too long dwelt under his roof; he yearns for his room who is satiated with the country. Association with one food, however pleasing, is finally the cause of nausea. So mutation from one extreme to the other through its participants,[2] and motion from one contrary to the other through its intermediate points, come to satisfy [us]; and, finally, we see such familiarity between one contrary and the other that the one agrees more with the other than like with like.

SAUL. So it seems to me; because justice has no act except where there is error, harmony is not effectuated except where there is contrariety. The spherical does not repose on the spherical, because they touch each other at a point; but the concave rests on the convex. And morally, the proud man cannot get together with the proud man, the poor man with the poor man, the greedy man with the greedy man; but the one is pleased with the humble man, the other with the rich man, the latter with the splendid man. However, if the matter is considered physically, mathematically, and morally, one sees that that philosopher who has arrived at the theory of the "coincidence of contraries" has not found out little, and that that magician who knows how to look for it where it exists is not an imbecile practitioner.[3] All, then, that you have uttered is most true. But I should like to know, oh Sophia, for what purpose, toward what end, you say it.

SOPHIA. What I wish to infer from that is that the beginning, the middle, and the end, the birth, the growth, and the perfection of all that we see, come from contraries, through contraries, into contraries, to contraries. And where there is contrariety, there is action and reaction, there is motion, there is diversity, there is number, there is order, there are degrees, there is succession, there is vicissitude. Therefore, no one who considers well, will ever, because of his being or possession, be abased or exalted in spirit, although in comparison with other conditions and fortunes it may seem to him good or bad, worse or better. Likewise, I with my divine object, which is Truth, as a fugitive for so long a time, occult, depressed, and submerged, have judged that period that is decreed by the ordinance of Fate to be the beginning of my return, appearance, exaltation, and magnificence, to be so much the greater, the greater having been the obstacles.

SAUL. So it happens that for him who wants to raise himself from the earth by jumping more vigorously, it will be necessary that he first bend himself sufficiently; he who endeavors to conquer more efficiently the passing over of a ditch sometimes reduces the difficulty of doing so by stepping back eight or ten paces.

SOPHIA. So much the more then, by the grace of Fate, do I hope in the future for better success, the worse I have found myself up to the present.

SAUL. The more depressed is man
  And the lower he is on the wheel,
  The closer he is to ascending,
  As with it round he turns.
  A man who but yesterday
  To the world gave laws,
  Now upon the block
  Has placed his head.[4]

But be so good, Sophia, as to be more specific in regard to what you plan to say.

SOPHIA. Thundering Jove, after having enjoyed youth for so long a time, has led a reckless existence and has occupied much of his time in war and love. Now, as if subdued by time, he is beginning to break away from lasciviousness, vices, and those tastes which are inherent in virility and youth.

SAUL. Poets indeed, never philosophers, have so described and introduced the gods. So Jove and the other gods grow old? Is it within the realm of possibility that even they will someday have to go beyond the shores of Acheron? [5]

SOPHIA. Do listen, Saulino; and do not cause me to digress from what I propose to discuss. Listen to me until I have spoken.

SAUL. Please do continue speaking. I shall listen most attentively; because I am sure that you will utter only great and serious words. I doubt, however, that my brain is capable of understanding and retaining what you say.

SOPHIA. Entertain no doubt. Jove, I say, is becoming mature. He admits to his council only those persons whose hair is snowy white, whose brows are wrinkled, whose noses are bespectacled, whose beards are white, who have lead in their feet, and who are supported by canes. I say, indeed, that their heads should contain a bridled imagination, cautious thinking, and a retentive memory. Their foreheads should show a quick apprehension, their eyes, prudence, their noses, sagacity, and their ears, attention. There should be truth on their tongues, sincerity in their breasts, and well-directed affections in their hearts. In their shoulders they should show patience, in their backs, forgiveness of wrongs received, in their stomachs, discretion, in their bellies, temperance, in their breasts, continence, in their legs, constancy, and in the soles of their feet, rectitude. In their left hands, they should hold the Pentateuch of Decrees; in their rights hands, discursive Reason, informative Knowledge, regulating Justice, governing Authority, and executive Power.

SAUL. Indeed, Jove is well provided. However, he must first be thoroughly cleansed and purged.

SOPHIA. No longer are there beasts into which he transforms himself; no Europas, who cause him to acquire the horns of a bull; no Danaës, who cause him to acquire the color of gold; no Ledas, who cause him to grow the features of a swan; no Asterian nymphs and Phrygian boys,[6] who cause him to grow the beak of an eagle; no Deoidas [Proserpines], who cause him to become a serpent; no Mnemosynes, who degrade him into a shepherd; no Antiopes, who "semi-bestialize" him into a satyr; no Alcmenes, who transform him into Amphitryon.

For that helm which turned and directed this ship of metamorphosis has become so weakened that it can barely resist the violence of the waves, and, perhaps now, is being driven toward shallow water. The sail is so torn and riddled with holes that the wind tries in vain to swell it.[7] To the oars which, despite contrary winds and violent storms, used to propel the vessel, the boatswain will now hiss in vain, "Steer windward, starboard, in the ship's wake, full speed ahead," because the oarsmen have become like paralytics, no matter how calm and tranquil in its place be Neptune's field.

SAUL. Oh, great misfortune!

SOPHIA. Hence there will be no one who will still speak of and fable Jove as one who is carnal and voluptuary; because the good father's spirit has been subdued.

SAUL. Just as he who had so many wives, so many wives' maids, and so many concubines, who finally, having become most satiated, bored, and weary, said "Vanity, vanity, all is vanity." [8]

SOPHIA. He is thinking of his Day of Judgment, because the period of the more or less, or exactly, thirty-six thousand years is near, as has been made public; at which time the revolution of the year of the world threatens that another Caelus may come to take back his dominion, judging by the change that the motion caused by the vibration of the planets brings about, and by their inconstant and hitherto unseen and unheard-of relationship and behavior.[9] He fears that Fate will ordain that the hereditary succession should not be like that of the preceding great mundane Revolution, but should be most varying and different, however the prognosticating astrologers and other diviners may gabble.

SAUL. So it is feared that some more cautious Caelus may come, who, following the example of Prester John, in order to obviate possible future inconvenience, will banish his sons to the seraglios of [Ethiopian] Mount Amhara; and besides, for fear that some Saturn might castrate him, he must never make the error of not tightening his iron drawers, and must not withdraw to sleep without diamond breeches. Whereupon the afore-mentioned effect having failed, the door will be shut to all other consequences, and in vain shall we await the birthday of the goddess of Cyprus, the depression of lame Saturn,[10] the exaltation of Jove, the multiplication of sons and sons of sons, grandchildren and grandchildren of grandchildren, up to the very generation, the very one which is in our times, and can up to the prescribed term be in future ones.

Nec iterum ad Troiam magnus mittetur Achilles.[11]

(Nor will great Achilles be sent back to Troy.)

SOPHIA. The condition of things, then, being in such a state, and Jove viewing the troublesome memorial of his jaded strength and enervated manliness as the approach of his death, he daily makes warm vows and effuses fervent prayers to Fate, in order that things in future centuries may be disposed in his favor.

SAUL. You, oh Sophia, tell me wondrous things. Do you expect Jove not to know the condition of Fate, which, according to his own and all too commonly divulged epithet, is called inexorable? It is indeed likely that during the time of his vacations (if indeed Fate grants him any), sometimes he may turn to the reading of some poets; and it is not improbable that the tragedian Seneca will fall into his hands, and will impart to him this lesson:

> Fate guides us, and we surrender unto it;
> And our worrysome thoughts cannot change
> The fixed threads of the warped spindle.
> All things which we do and bear,
> On Fate's lofty decree depend;
> And the harsh sister does not rewind the twisted thread.
> The Fates proceed in a definite order,
> While each of us goes with uncertainty
> Toward his own destiny.[12]

SOPHIA. In addition Fate wills this: that although Jove himself knows that it is immutable and that there can be nothing else except that which must be and will be, he cannot by means of this knowledge avoid meeting his own destiny. Fate has ordained prayers, as much for obtaining as for not obtaining; and in order not to burden too much the transmigrating souls it interposes the drinking from the Lethean river in the midst of the mutations, so that through oblivion everyone may be especially affected and eager to preserve himself in his present state.

Therefore, youths do not recall their state of infancy; infants do not long for the state in their mothers' wombs; and none of these longs for the state in that life which he lived before he found himself in such a nature. The pig does not want to die for fear of not being a pig; the horse fears most to lose his equine nature. Jove, because of compelling necessities, greatly fears not being Jove. But Fate's mercy and grace will not change his state without having saturated him in the waters of that river.

SAUL. So that, oh Sophia (an unheard-of thing!), this divinity also has someone to whom he may effuse his prayers? Is he also given to fear of Justice? I used to wonder why the gods greatly feared to forswear the Stygian Swamp; [13] now I understand that this proceeds from the penalty that they too must pay.

SOPHIA. So it is. He has commanded his blacksmith, Vulcan, not to work on holidays; he has commanded Bacchus not to convene his court and not to allow his Euhantes [14] to commit acts of debauchery except during carnival time and the principal feasts of the year, and then only after suppertime, after the setting of the sun, and not without his special and express permission.

Momus, who had spoken against the gods, and had argued, as it seemed to them, too severely against their errors, therefore had been banished from their consistory and from conversation with them, and relegated to the star which is at the tip of Callisto's tail, without the privilege of passing the limit of that parallel under which Mount Caucus lies. There the poor god was weakened by the rigors of cold and of hunger, but now is recalled, vindicated, restored to his pristine state, and made ordinary and extraordinary herald, with the most ample privilege of being able to reprehend vices without any regard to the title or dignity of any person.

He has enjoined Cupid to cease wandering in the presence of men, heroes, and gods so unclad as is his custom; and having enjoined him that he no longer offend the sight of the denizens of heaven by demonstrating his buttocks in the Milky Way and Olympian Senate, but that he go around in the future dressed at least from the waist down, Momus gave him the most strict mandate that he should no longer dare to carry darts except in behalf of natural love; and that he make the love of men similar to that of other animals, making them fall in love during certain and determined seasons. And thus just as for cats March is customary, for donkeys, May, for men let those days be accommodated in which Petrarch fell in love with Laura, and Dante with Beatrice.[15] And this statute is in an interim form, until the forthcoming council meeting, to be held when the sun is at the tenth degree of Libra, situated at the source of the river Eridanus, there where the bend of Orion's knee is.

Then will be restored that natural law, by which it is permissible for each male to have as many wives as he can feed and impregnate; because it is a superfluous and unjust thing and entirely contrary to natural law that upon an already impregnated and gravid woman, or upon other worse subjects, such as others illegitimately procured, who for fear of disgrace induce abortions, there should be spilt that man-producing semen, which could give rise to heroes and fill the empty seats of the empyrean.

SAUL. Well discerned, in my judgment. What more?

SOPHIA. I believe that that Ganymede, who in spite of jealous Juno, was so much in his [Jove's] favor, and who alone was permitted to approach him and extend to him the three-forked lightning, while other divinities reverently kept themselves at a distance of many paces, if at present he has no other virtue except that which is almost lost, it is to be feared that rather than being Jove's page he may favor acting as shield-bearer to Mars.

SAUL. Whence this mutation?

SOPHIA. Concerning Jove's change and why envious Saturn, in past days, with the pretext of fondling him [Ganymede], continued moving his rough hand in such a manner over his chin and vermilion cheeks, it is said that from that touch his face is becoming hairy, that little by little that grace is diminishing which had the power to seduce Jove from heaven, and cause him to be snatched by Jove into heaven, wherefore the son of a human being was deified, and the father of the gods became a bird.

SAUL. Matters too stupendous!

SOPHIA. He has enjoined all the gods not to have pages or gentlemen of the bedchamber of a lesser age than twenty-five.

SAUL. Ah! Ah! Now what is Apollo doing, what is he saying about his dear Hyacinth?

SOPHIA. Of, if you only knew how unhappy he is!

SAUL. I certainly believe that his dejection causes this darkness in the sky, which has lasted more than seven days; his breath produces so many clouds, his sighs such stormy winds, and his tears such copious rains.

SOPHIA. You have guessed it.

SAUL. Now, what will become of that poor child?

SOPHIA. Apollo has made up his mind to send him to study humane letters at some reformed university or school, and to submit him to the rod of some pedant.

SAUL. Oh fortune, oh treacherous destiny! Does this boy seem to you a morsel for pedants? Would it not have been better to place him in the care of a poet, to mold him in the hands of an orator, or to accustom him to the staff of the cross? Would it not have been more expedient to commit him to the discipline of. . . .

SOPHIA. No more, no more! That which must be, shall be; that which had to be, is. Now to complete the story of Ganymede, the day before yesterday, expecting the usual welcome, he, with his customary childish grin, handed Jove his cup of nectar; and Jove, having somewhat fixed his disturbed eyes upon his face, said, "Are you not ashamed, oh son of Tros? Do you think that you are still a child? Perhaps, with the passing of the years your discretion will increase, and you will add to judgment? Do you not realize that the time is past when you used to come to deafen my ears, when as we were leaving through the outer atrium Silenus, Faunus, he of Lampsacus,[16] and others used to deem themselves fortunate if they could have the opportunity of stealing a pinch from you, or at least of touching your garment, and to preserve the memory of that touch did not wash their hands before going to eat and doing other things their fancy dictated? Now prepare yourself, and bear in mind that perhaps it will be necessary for you to do other work. I am letting you know that I no longer want good-for-nothings at my heels."

If anyone had seen the change of countenance of that poor boy or adolescent, I don't know whether compassion or laughter, or a struggle between these two, would have moved him more.

SAUL. This time I believe that "Risit Apollo."[17]

SOPHIA. Pay attention, because what you have heard up to now is only the embellishment.

SAUL. Go on.

SOPHIA. Yesterday, which was the day on which is commemorated the victory of the gods over the giants, immediately after dinner [18] she who alone governs the nature of things, and by virtue of whom everything prospers under heaven,

> The beautiful mother of twin love,
> The divine power among gods and men,
> She, through whom every being to-be-born in the world
> Is conceived, and once born, beholds the sun,
> Before whom winds and storms take flight,
> When out of the luminous East she bursts forth,
> The calm sea smiles upon her
> And the earth bedecks herself anew, with a beautiful mantle
> And presents to her through the beautiful hands
> Of the gentle Naiades, Achilles' enameled horn,
> Filled to the brim with copious branches of flowers and fruits,[19]

having proclaimed that there should be dancing, approached Jove, with that grace which would console and entice stormy Charon, and, as prescribed by protocol, was first to shake the hands of Jove.

He, instead of doing what he was accustomed to, which was to embrace her with his left arm and press her to his bosom, squeeze her lower lip with the first two fingers of his right hand, place his mouth to hers, teeth to teeth, tongue to tongue (the most lascivious caresses that can be resorted to by a father toward his daughter), and then rise to dance, said, yesterday, pointing his right hand to her breast, and holding her back (as if he were saying "Noli me tangere") [20] with a compassionate air and a face full of devotion: "Ah, Venus, Venus! Is it possible that you will ever consider our condition even once, and yours in particular? Do you think that what humans imagine about us is true, that he among us who is old is always old, that he who is young is always young, that he who is a boy is always a boy, and thus we eternally continue as we were when first taken into heaven; and that just as paintings and portraits of ourselves on earth are always seen unchanged, so likewise here our vital complexion does not change again and again?

"Today's feast renews in me the memory of the mood I was

in when I struck with lightning and overpowered those fierce
giants who dared to hurl Ossa on Pelion and Olympus on Ossa; [21]
when I was strong enough to hurl into the dark caverns of abysmal
hell terrible Briareus, whose mother Terra endowed him with one
hundred arms and one hundred hands so that he might with the
force of a hundred rocks, which he hurled against the gods, overthrow heaven; when I chained presumptuous Typhoeus [Ty-
phon], there where the Tyrrhenian Sea joins with the Ionian,
thrusting the Trinacrian Isle upon him so that to the living body
it should be a perpetual sepulcher. Whereupon a poet says:

Where dauntless and audacious Typhoeus lies,
Laden with the weight of Trinacria,
There Mt. Pelorus presses upon the right side of his ponderous corpse,
And famous Pachynus on the left.
Upon his immense shoulders, which the weight has calloused,
Rocky and vast Lilybaeum presses,
And there Mount Aetna, under which scabrous Vulcan
Tempers the thunderbolts with his mighty hammer,
Surcharges its frightening crest.[22]

"I, who upon that other giant thrust the island of Prochyta
[Procida], I, who repressed Lycaon's audacity, and at the time of
Deucalion liquefied the earth, rebellious toward heaven, and with
so many other manifest signs demonstrated myself most worthy of
my authority, now do not have the courage to oppose certain half
men, and am compelled, in spite of myself, to let the world run according to the wish of Chance and of Fortune; and may he who
best pursues Fortune attain her, and may he who conquers her
enjoy her.

"I have now become like the old Aesopian lion, whom *impune*
the ass kicks, and whom the monkey mocks, and against whom,
as if he were an insensitive stump, the pig comes to rub his dusty
belly. There, where I had most noble oracles, shrines, and altars,
now, those having been torn down and most unworthily profaned,
they have in their places erected altars and statues to certain people
whom I am ashamed to name, because they are worse than our
satyrs, fauns, and other semi-beasts, even more vile than the crocodiles of Egypt; for even these crocodiles, magically guided, showed

some signs of divinity; but those people are quite the dung of the earth.

"All of this has been brought about by the outrage of our enemy, Fortune, who has elected and elevated them, not so much to honor them, as for our greater contempt, scorn, and shame. The laws, statutes, cults, sacrifices, and ceremonies that I have already, through my Mercuries, given, ordained, commanded, and instituted, are broken and nullified; and in their stead is found the most filthy and most unworthy indolence that this blind dame could conceive, so that just as through us men used to become heroes, now they are becoming worse than beasts. To our nostrils no longer comes the smoke of the roast, made in our service, at the altars; but if, indeed, sometimes the appetite for it should come to us, it will be necessary for us to satisfy our yearning in kitchens, like pantry-pan gods. And although some altars still smoke with incense (*quod dat avara manus*), little by little, I fear, the incense will turn into smoke, so that nothing will any longer remain as a vestige of our sacred institutions.

"Indeed, we know from experience that the world is exactly like a spirited horse, who knows very well when he is mounted by one who cannot firmly manage him, and spurns the rider and attempts to remove him from his back; and once he has succeeded in throwing him on the ground, comes to pay him in kicks. Behold! My body is drying up, and my brain is moistening; I am scabbing, and my teeth are falling out; my flesh is becoming gilded, and my hair, silver; my eyelids are distending, my sight, contracting; my breathing is becoming short, my cough, stronger; when I am seated, I feel steady, but shaky when I walk; my pulse is irregular; my ribs are tightening; my limbs are becoming thin; my joints are swelling. In conclusion, I am tormented most because my heels are hardening, and their counterweight is softening; the bag of my bag-pipe is becoming elongated; and my staff is growing short.

> My Juno is no longer jealous of me,
> My Juno no longer cares for me.

"I want you, yourself, to consider your Vulcan (leaving all other gods aside). It was he who with such vigor used to strike the heavy anvil, to whose resounding noises, issuing forth into the horizon, from ignivomous Aetna, Echo used to answer from the concavities of Campanian Vesuvius and rocky Taburnus.[23] Now where is the strength of my blacksmith and your consort? Is it not spent? Is it not spent? Or perhaps does he have some strength left with which to pump the bellows for kindling his fire? Does he perhaps still have some vigor left necessary to lift his heavy hammer and strike the heated metal?

"Now, you, my sister, if you do not believe others, ask your mirror; and you will see that because of the wrinkles you have developed, and the furrows dug into your face by the plow of time, day by day, you make it more and more difficult for the painter, who, if he does not wish to lie, must paint you as you are.[24]

"Whereas once you formed, while smiling, those two very lovely dimples on your cheeks, two depressions, and two points in the center of those lovable dents, giving you that smile that used to entice the entire world, to add seven times greater grace to its countenance, when, jesting (as he still does from his eyes), Love was darting his sharp and ardent arrows; now, starting from the corners of your mouth, up to the already commemorated area, from one corner to the other there begins to appear the form of four parentheses, which, geminated, seem to want to prevent your smile, by tightening your mouth, with those circumferential arcs, which appear between your teeth and ears, so as to make you seem like a crocodile. I say that, regardless of whether or not you do smile, the internal geometer [25] within your forehead, who is drying up your vital humor, and by making your flesh come closer and closer to the bone, by thinning your skin, deepens the inscription of the parallels, four by four, pointing out to you by those, the direct path which leads you, as it were, to the offices of the Dead.

"Why do you cry, Venus? Why do you laugh, Momus?" he said, as he sees the latter showing his teeth, and the former shedding tears. Momus still knows that once one of these buffoons (each one of whom is wont to impart more truths to the ears of a prince about his affairs than all of the rest of the court put together, and because of whom, most often, those who do not dare to talk, do speak in a kind of jest, and cause to be moved and do move proposals) said that Asclepius had given you a provision of powder made from deer's horn and a paste from corals, after having removed two of your bad molars so secretly that now there is no pebble in the heaven that does not know about it.

"You see then, dear sister, how treacherous time subdues us, how we are all subject to mutation. And that which most afflicts us among so many things is that we have neither certainty nor any hope of at all reassuming that same being in which we once found ourselves. We depart, and do not return the same; and since we have no recollection of what we were before we were in this being, so we cannot have a sample of that which we shall be afterward.

"Thus fear, piety, and our religion, honor, respect, and love leave, after which depart strength, providence, virtue, dignity, majesty, and beauty, which fly from us not otherwise than the shadow together with the body. Only Truth, with Absolute Virtue, is immutable and immortal. And if she sometimes falls and is submerged, she, necessarily, in her time rises again, the same, her servant Sophia extending her arm to her.

"Let us beware, then, of offending the divinity of Fate by wronging this twin god, so greatly entrusted to it and so favored by it. Let us think of our future state, and not, as if we were little concerned with the universal deity, fail to raise our hearts and affects to that lavisher of all good and distributor of all other fates. Let us beseech it that during our transfusion, or passage, or metempsychosis, it grant us happy spirits; since, although it is inexorable, we must indeed await it with prayers, in order either to be preserved in our present state or to enter another, better, or similar, or little worse.

"I say that to be well affected toward the highest deity is like a sign of future favorable effects from it. Just as for him who is prescribed to be a man, it is necessary and ordinary that destiny guide him as he passes through his mother's womb, so, for the spirit predestined to incorporate itself into a fish, it is necessary that it first plunge into the waters; likewise for him who is about to be favored by the gods, it is necessary that he submit himself to prayers and good works."

SECOND PART
OF THE *First Dialogue*

The great father of the celestial realm, sighing from time to time as he spoke, now having terminated his discussion with Venus, decided to change the proposal calling for dancing into one convening the grand council of the gods of the round table, consisting, that is to say, of all those gods who are not false, but are genuine, and who have a head for counseling; but excluding the ram-headed, the oxen-horned, the goat-bearded, the donkey-eared, the dog-toothed, the pig-eyed, the monkey-nosed, the goat-browed, the chicken-stomached, the horse-bellied, the mule-footed, and the scorpion-tailed. However, when the call was issued through the mouth of Misenus, son of Aeolus (for Mercury now disdains his former status as trumpeter and pronouncer of edicts), all of those gods who were scattered throughout the palace soon were assembled.

Following this, all having become silenced, as Jove was walking before ascending his throne to face the tribunal, with an air no less sad and gloomy than his presence and pre-eminence were lofty and majestic, Momus presented himself to him, and with his usual frank speech, and in a voice so deep that it was heard by all, said: "This council meeting, oh father, must be postponed for another day, and for another occasion, since it seems that your being disposed to having a conclave now, immediately after dinner, was prompted by the generous hand of your affectionate cupbearer. For nectar which cannot be thoroughly digested by the stomach neither satisfies nor refreshes it, but distorts and saddens our nature, and perturbs our imagination, making some gay and without purpose, others unrestrainedly happy, some superstitiously devout, others vainly heroic, others choleric, others builders of great castles in the air, until the time when, with the vanishing of the same pipe dreams, passing through brains of different complexion, everything falls to the ground and vanishes into smoke.

"It seems, oh Jove, that somewhat daring and fluctuating thoughts have disturbed you, and that they have caused you to become sad. As regards the reason why all unjustifiably judge you to be overpowered and oppressed by gloomy biliousness, although I alone dare to say it, they do so because, from what I seem to understand and scent from discourse, you want to treat of such serious matters on this day on which we have convened not disposed to go into consultation, on this occasion on which we have gathered for a feast, at this time after dinner and under these circumstances of having eaten well and drunk better."

Now, although it is neither customary nor too lawful for other gods to argue with Momus, Jove, giving him an abortive, almost spiteful smile, without answering him, ascended to his high seat, sat down, and gazed about him and at the great Senate which stood before him in a circle. It must be said that because of his glance everyone's heart began to pound, be it from the shock of amazement, from the extreme fear, or because of the greatness of the reverence and respect which the presence of majesty inspires in mortal and immortal hearts. After having partially lowered his eyelids, and soon afterward raising his eyes upward, and heaving an ardent sigh from his breast, he burst out with these words:

Jove's speech

"Do not expect, oh gods, that I shall, as is my custom, intone into your ears an artful introduction, a polished thread of narration, and a delightful epilogical agglomeration. Do not expect an ornate contexture of words, a polished weaving of my sentences, a rich apparatus of elegant arguments, a sumptuous pomp of

elaborate discourses, and, according to the institute of orators, conceits sooner placed three times to the file than once on the tongue:
'Non hoc ista sibi tempus spectacula poscit.' [1] ('At this juncture,
time does not call for these spectacles.')

"Believe me, oh gods, because you believe the truth; already
twelve times has chaste Lucina [2] filled in her silver horns since I
became determined to order this assembly today, at this hour, and
under such terms as you see. And in the meanwhile I have been
concerned more with the consideration of those matters about
which, despite our desire to hear them, I must keep silent, than
with what has been permitted me to premeditate and to say.

"I hear that you are astounded, because at this time, calling you
away from your amusement, I have had you summoned to an
assembly, and after dinner, to sudden counsel. I hear you murmuring that on a festive day your hearts are touched by such serious
matters; and there is no one among you who is not disturbed by
the sound of the trumpet, and by the purpose of the decree. But I,
although the reasons for these actions and circumstances depend
upon my volition, which was able to institute them, and although
my will and decree are the very reason of Justice, nevertheless do
not want to fail, before I proceed to another matter, to free you
from this confusion and astonishment. Slow, I say, grave, and
pondered must be the resolutions; mature, secret, and cautious
must be the counsel; but it is necessary that the execution be
winged, swift, and ready.

"Do not believe, however, that I have been so violently assailed
by some strange humor while dining, that, after dinner, it still holds
me bound and chained, because of which I proceed to action, guided
not by reason but rather by the power of nectarean fumes. On the
other hand, from this very day last year I began to deliberate within
my own mind what I was to carry out on this very day at this very
hour after dinner. Because it is not customary to bring sad news
on an empty stomach, and I well know that you would come more
willingly to a celebration than to a council meeting, which is
studiously avoided by many of you. For some fear it, lest they
make enemies, some because of uncertainty about which side will
win and which will lose, some because of fear that their counsel
will be scorned, some because of spite, their opinion sometimes

not having been approved, some because they want to be neutral in causes that might be prejudicial to one side or the other, some because they do not wish to burden their consciences—some for one reason, others for another.

"Now I remind you, oh brothers, sisters, and children, that those whom Fate has permitted to taste ambrosia, to drink nectar, and to enjoy the dignity of majesty are also enjoined to bear the heavy responsibilities that accompany privilege. The diadem, the miter, the crown, which do not weigh heavily upon the head do not honor it; and the royal garment and the scepter do not adorn the body without some inconvenience to it.

"Do you wish to know why I have, to this end, employed the festival day, and specially one such as the present? Does it seem to you then, does it seem to you that this be a day worthy of a feast? And do you think that this should not be the most tragic day of the entire year? Which of you, after he has well reflected, will not judge it a most vituperable thing to celebrate the commemoration of the victory over the giants at a time when we are despised and contemned by the rats of the earth? Oh that it might have pleased omnipotent and irrefragable Fate that we had been expelled from the heaven at that time, when our rout, owing to the dignity and valor of our enemies, would not have been so vituperable! For today we are worse in heaven than if we were not there, worse than we would have been had we been driven out of it, considering that that fear of us, which used to render us so glorious, is extinguished.

"The great reputation of our majesty, providence, and justice has been destroyed. What is worse, we do not have the faculty and strength to remedy our evil, to redress our shames; because Justice, by which Fate governs the rulers of the world, has completely deprived us of that authority and power which we so badly employed, our ignominies being revealed and laid bare before the eyes of mortals, and made manifest to them; and it causes heaven itself, with such clear evidence, as the stars are clear and evident, to render us testimony of our misdeeds. For there are clearly seen the fruits, the relics, the reports, the rumors, the writings, the histories of our adulteries, incests, fornications, wraths, disdains, rapines, and other iniquities and crimes; and to reward ourselves for our transgressions, we have committed more transgressions, elevating to heaven the triumphs of vice and the seats of wickedness, leaving virtues and Justice banished, buried, and neglected in hell.

"And to begin, let us take minor matters, such as venial sins. Why, I ask, has that Triangle, Deltoton, alone obtained four stars, near the head of Medusa, under the buttocks of Andromeda, and above the horns of the Ram? It is to show the partiality that is found among the gods. What is the Dolphin [Delphinus] doing joined to Capricorn from the north side, and with fifteen stars in his possession? The Dolphin is there so that we may contemplate the assumption into heaven of him, who was a good middleman, not to say a pander, between Neptune and Amphitrite. Why do the seven daughters of Atlas sit near the neck of the white Bull? It is because their father, his majesty being slighted by us gods, wanted to boast that he sustained us and the disintegrating heaven; or simply to show the divinities, who conducted the seven daughters to that spot, their frivolities.

"Why has Juno bedecked the Crab with nine stars, besides the four surrounding stars, which form no pattern? It is only out of caprice, because Alcides' heel was nipped by the Crab at the time he was fighting the huge giant. Who could give me any reason, other than the simple and irrational decree of the gods, why Serpentarius, called Ophiuchus by us Greeks, receives, with his mate, an area occupied by thirty-six stars? What grave and opportune reason causes Sagittarius to usurp thirty-one stars? It is because he was the son of Euschemo, who was nurse or wet nurse to the Muses.[3] Why was not rather his mother put there? It is because he also knew how to dance and to perform sleight of hand.

"Why does Aquarius, situated next to Capricorn, contain forty-five stars? Is it because he rescued Phacete, the daughter of Venus, from the marsh? Why has this space not been granted to others to whom we gods are so obligated, to them who are buried in the earth, rather than to this one who has rendered a service not worthy of such reward? It is because it has pleased Venus to do so.

"Although the Fishes [Pisces] deserve some favor for having expelled from the river Euphrates that egg, which, when hatched by the dove, aroused the compassion of the goddess of Paphos, yet do they seem to you subjects worthy of obtaining thirty-four stars, besides the four surrounding stars, and worthy of living out of water, in the most noble region of the heaven? [4]

"What is Orion doing, with his outstretched arms, ready to fence, all by himself, daubed with thirty-eight stars in the Southern latitude in the direction of the Bull? He is there, simply because of the caprice of Neptune, who was not sufficiently satisfied to give him privileges in matters pertaining to the sea, where he [Neptune] has his legitimate dominion, but, moreover, because of so slight a reason, desires to hold sway beyond his realm.

"Do you know that the Hare, Canis Major, and Canis Minor have forty-three stars in the Southern part of the heaven, and are so rewarded for only two or three trivial reasons not less unimportant than the reason that causes the Hydra, the Saucer, and the Raven to be next to Orion and to receive forty-one stars to commemorate the occasion when the gods sent the Raven to obtain some drinking water?

"While he was on his way, the Raven saw a tree which bore figs, 'fiche' [5] or 'fichi' (you may use the form you wish, because both genders are accepted by grammarians). Because of his gluttony, that bird waited until the figs were ripe, and, finally, having eaten of them, reminded himself of the water. He went to fill the pitcher, there saw the dragon, was frightened, and returned to the gods with the empty pitcher. The gods, in order to make evident how well they have employed their intelligence and their thinking, have described in the sky the story of so kind and adept a servant. You can see how well we have employed our time, ink, and paper.

"Who has predestined the Southern Crown, which is seen under Sagittarius' bow and feet, adorned with thirteen sparkling topazes, to be eternally headless? What fine appearance do you expect that fish of Notium to present, placed under Aquarius' and Capricorn's feet, and made visible by twelve lights besides six others that surround him?

"I shall not speak of the Altar, or the Incense Bowl, or the Shrine, or the Sacristy, or whatever we want to call it. For never was it more fitting that it be in the sky than now, when it has almost no place on earth in which to stay. Now, it stands there appropriately, as a relic, or even as a plank of the submerged ship of our religion and cult.

"I say nothing of Capricorn, for he seems to me most worthy of attaining heaven, because of his having benefited us so much by teaching us the formula through which we were able to conquer the Python; for it was necessary that the gods transform themselves into beasts if they wanted to make an honorable showing in that war. He has also given us the doctrine that teaches us that he who does not know how to become a beast cannot maintain his superiority.

"I do not speak of Virgo, because if she wishes to preserve her virginity she cannot live safely in any place but in the heaven, having as guardians a Leo on this side of her and a Scorpio on the other. The poor maiden has fled from earth, where women, because of their excessive lust, the more often they are pregnant, the more they crave coitus, where it is impossible for her to be secure from contamination, even if she be in her mother's womb; however, let her enjoy twenty-six carbuncles and the other six that surround her.

"Concerning the upright majesty of those two Asses,[6] who sparkle in the space of Cancer, I do not dare to speak, because to these, especially belongs the Kingdom of Heaven, by right and by reason, as on other occasions, with many most efficacious arguments, I propose to show you. For of so great a matter I do not dare to talk, as it were, in passing.[7] But for this alone I grieve and greatly lament: that these divine animals have been given such niggardly treatment. They are not made to feel that they are in their own home, but, in the asylum of that retrograde aquatic animal. They have been rewarded with the pittance of no more than two stars, one star being given to the one, and one to the other, the two stars together being no larger than one of the fourth magnitude.

"I do not, now, want to say anything definitive about the Altar, Capricorn, Virgo, and the Asses, although I grieve that some of them, since they were not treated according to their dignity, rather than being honored, were perhaps slighted; but I return to the other arguments that are weighed on the same scales as those mentioned above.

"Do you not expect the other rivers on earth to grumble because of the wrong that is being done to them, admitting, as reason dictates, that Eridanus should rather have its thirty-four lights, which are seen on this side and beyond the Tropic of Capricorn, than so many others no less worthy and large, and others even worthier and larger? Do you think that it is sufficient to say that Phaëthon's sisters should occupy this space? Or, perhaps, you wish to commemorate it, because it was there that the son of Apollo fell, struck by lightning from my own hand, for having abused his father's office, rank, and authority?

"Why has Bellerophon's horse ascended to heaven to take possession of twenty stars, although his master is buried on earth?

"For what reason does that Arrow illuminate the area of the Eagle and the Dolphin with the radiance of its five firmly held stars? Certainly it is greatly wronged by not being allowed to be near Sagittarius so that he might make use of its services after he has shot that arrow which he is now aiming; or at least it should not be prevented from appearing where it could give some justification for its presence.

"Then I yearn to understand what that Lyre, made of ox horns in the form of a tortoise, is doing between the remains of Leo and the head of that sweet white Swan. I should like to know whether that region is inhabited in honor of the tortoise, the horns, or the lyre. Or is it that everyone should be aware of the skill of Mercury, who made it, as a testimony of his dissolute and vain boasting?

"Here, oh gods, are our works, here our remarkable handiworks, by which we honored ourselves in the eyes of heaven! What beautiful creations, not too unlike those that children are wont to create when they work with clay, paste, small branches, and straw as they attempt to imitate the works of their elders! Do you think that we shall not have to justify these things and account for them? Can you be convinced that we will be summoned, interrogated, judged, and condemned less frequently for our idle works than for our idle words? The goddess Justice, the goddess Temperance, the goddess Constance, the goddess Liberality, the goddess Patience, the goddess Truth, the goddess Mnemosyne, the goddess Sophia, and many other goddesses and gods, are being banned not only from heaven but also from the earth; and in their stead in the lofty palaces constructed for them as their residences, by exalted Providence, are seen dolphins, goats, ravens, serpents, and other filth, levities, caprices, and frivolities.

"If what I tell you seems distasteful, and we have an uneasy conscience for the good we have failed to do, how much more you should consider, as I do, that we should be pricked and pierced by sorrow for our most grievous acts of wickedness and crime;[8] which acts having been committed, not only did we not repent and mend our ways but, what is more, we commemorated them in triumphant celebration, and also erected trophies, not in a fragile and destructible shrine, not in an earthly temple, but in eternal heaven, among the everlasting stars. We may suffer and easily condone, oh gods, errors committed because of our frailty or not too judicious levity. However, what compassion and what pity can be shown toward sins committed by those who, although they were made to be the guardians of justice, as a recompense for the most criminal errors, add greater errors by honoring, rewarding, and exalting to heaven the crimes together with the criminals?

"For what great and virtuous deed has Perseus obtained twenty stars? It is because he, in the service of infuriated Minerva, with the aid of his talaria and his shining shield, which rendered him invisible, killed the sleeping Gorgons, and then presented her with the head of Medusa.[9] And it was not enough that he alone be there; in order that she might acquire a long-lived and celebrated reputation, it was necessary that his wife Andromeda should appear, with her twenty-three stars, his son-in-law Cepheus,[10] with his thirteen, he who exposed his innocent daughter to the jaws of Cetus because of the caprice of Neptune, who was angered only because her mother Cassiopea thought she was more beautiful than the Nereids. Her mother now also is seen residing in her seat, honored by thirteen other stars, at the borders of the Arctic Circle.

"Why does that guardian of sheep with golden wool bleat on the point of the Equinox, with his eighteen stars, not counting the seven surrounding stars?[11] He is probably there so that he may sermonize on the folly and on the madness and foolishness of the king of Colchis, the lewdness of Medea, the unrestrained temerity of Jason, and on our own iniquitous providence.

"What do those two boys [Gemini] who follow Taurus in the sign-bearer, who comprise eighteen stars, not counting the seven other stars that surround them, which do not form a pattern, show that is good or beautiful in that sacred seat, except the reciprocal love of two effeminates?

"For what reason does Scorpio receive the reward of twenty-one stars, without the eight that are in the claws of Cancer, the nine that are around him, and three others that do not form a pattern? As a reward for a murder ordered by the frivolity and envy of Diana, who made him kill the emulous hunter, Orion.

"You know that Chiron and his beast obtain sixty-six stars in the Southern latitude of the sky for having been the tutor of that son born out of the stuprum of Peleus and Thetis.

"You know that Ariadne's crown, in which eight stars sparkle, and which is honored yonder in front of Boötes' breasts and the coils of the eel, is there only for the perpetual commemoration of the debauched love of father Liber, who embraced the daughter of the king of Crete after she had been rejected by her ravisher, Theseus.

"What is that Leo, who wears the basilisk on his heart, and who obtains thirty-five stars, doing next to Cancer? He is there perhaps in order to be in the company of his fellow warrior and his fellow servant in the service of irate Juno, who armed the lion that he might be the devastator of the land of Cleonae and await the coming of Alcides so that he might get the better of him.

"Indeed, to tell the truth, it does not seem fitting to me that unconquered Hercules, my hard-working son, who with the remains of his lion and with his stick seems to be protecting his twenty-eight stars, which he has earned by performing more heroic deeds than anyone else, should hold that seat whence his spirit reveals before the eyes of Justice the wrong done to my Juno's marriage bond by me and by my mistress Megara, his mother.[12]

"The ship of Argo, in which are firmly fixed forty-five resplendent stars in the wide space near the Antarctic Circle, is it there for a reason other than that of eternizing the memory of the great error committed by wise Minerva, because of whom I established the first pirates, so that the sea, no less than the earth, should have its diligent plunderers?[13]

"And in order to return to the spot where the belt of the heaven turns, why does Taurus, situated near the point where the zodiac begins, obtain thirty-two bright stars, without counting that one at the apex of the horn facing North, and eleven others, which are called formless? Because, alas, he is that Jove who robbed Agenor of his daughter, Cadmus of his sister.[14]

"Who is that Eagle who usurps for himself a corridor of fifteen stars, in the firmament, there beyond Sagittarius, toward the pole? Woe is me! It is that Jove, who there is celebrating the triumph identified with the abduction of Ganymede and those victorious conquests of burning passion and love.

"Why, oh gods, is that Ursa placed in the most beautiful and eminent part of the world, as if she were reflected in a high mirror set, as it were, in a most luminous square presenting the most celebrated spectacle that the universe could offer before our eyes? She is there, perhaps, so that no eye will fail to see the fire by which the father of the gods was seized after the conflagration caused by Phaëthon's chariot had broken out on earth, while I was protecting the ruins of that conflagration and restoring them by calling back the rivers which, frightened and fleeing, had withdrawn into caverns. And while effectuating this, in my beloved land of Arcadia, lo and behold, another fire seized my heart which, proceeding from the splendor of the face of the Nonacrian virgin, struck my eyes, ran through my heart, heated my bones, and penetrated to my marrow; so that there was no water, no remedy, which could give succor and cool the fire within me. In this fire was the arrow, which pierced my heart, the love knot, which bound my soul, the claw, which seized me and made me a prey to her beauty.

"I committed the sacrilegious act of stuprum, violated Diana's companion, and hurt my most faithful consort, for which deed, the ugliness of my foul debauchery was presented before me in the form of a Bear.[15] But I was far from conceiving horror at that abominable sight, and that monster seemed to me so beautiful and pleased me so greatly that I willed that her lifelike image should be exalted in the highest and most magnificent site in the architecture of the heaven. This is that error, that ugliness, that horrible blot, which the waters of the ocean disdain and loathe to cleanse, for which Thetis, fearing to contaminate her waves, does not even wish to approach her abode, and for which Dictynna [16] has forbidden her ingress to her forests for fear that she might profane her sacred college, and for the same reason the Nereids and Nymphs deny her the rivers.

"I, a wretched sinner, admit my guilt, my most grievous guilt, in the presence of upright and absolute Justice, and before you, that up to now I have most grievously sinned; and because of my bad example, I have extended even to you the permission and privilege to do likewise. And with this I confess that I, together with yourselves, have deservedly incurred the wrath of Fate, which no longer allows us to be recognized as gods; and since we have yielded heaven to the scum of the earth, it has ordained that the temples, pictures, and statues that we possessed on earth should be smashed, so that there be deservedly lowered from on high those who have unworthily raised to the heights vile and base things.

"Woe is me, oh gods! What are we doing? What are we thinking? Why are we delaying? We have prevaricated; we have been perseverant in errors; and we see suffering joined to, and continued with, error. Let us prepare ourselves then, let us prepare ourselves for our destinies; because just as Fate has not denied us the possibility of falling, so it has conceded us the possibility of rising again; therefore, just as we were ready to fall, so are we prepared to get back on our feet. We shall be able to depart without difficulty from that suffering into which through our error we have fallen, and from worse than that which could befall us, by means of reparation which lies in our hands. By the chain of errors we are bound; by the hand of Justice we free ourselves. Where our frivolity has abased us, there it is necessary that our seriousness exalt us. Let us be converted to Justice, because since we have departed from her, we have departed from ourselves; so that we are no longer gods, are no longer ourselves. Let us then return to her, if we wish to return to ourselves.

"The order and manner of making this reparation is that, first, we lift from our shoulders the heavy load of errors that impedes us; that we remove from our eyes the veil of little consideration that hinders us; that we remove from our hearts the self-love that retards us; that we expel from ourselves all those vain thoughts that weigh upon us; that we adapt ourselves to demolishing the machines of errors and the edifices of perversity that impede our passage and encumber our path; that we revoke and annul, as much as possible, the triumphs and trophies of our criminal deeds; so that there may appear in the tribunal of Justice true repentance for committed errors.

"Come now, come now, oh gods! Let there be expelled from the heaven these ghosts, statues, figures, images, portraits, recitations, and histories of our avarice, lusts, thefts, disdains, spites, and shames. May there pass, may there pass this black and gloomy night of our errors; for the enticing dawn of the new day of Justice invites us. And let us prepare ourselves, in such a manner, for the sun that is about to rise, so that it will not disclose how impure we are. We must cleanse and make ourselves beautiful; it will be necessary that not only we but also our rooms and our roofs be spotless and clean. We must purify ourselves internally and externally.

"Let us prepare ourselves, I say, first in the heaven which intellectually is within us, and then in this sensible one which corporeally presents itself before our eyes. Let us drive away from the heaven of our mind the Bear of Deformity, the Arrow of Detraction, the Foal of Levity, the Canis Major of Murmuring, the Canis Minor of Adulation. Let there be banned from us the Hercules of Violence, the Lyre of Conspiracy, the Triangle of Impiousness, the Boötes of Inconstancy, and the Cepheus of Harshness. Let there stay far away from us the Dragon of Envy, the Swan of Imprudence, the Cassiopea of Vanity, the Andromeda of Indolence, and the Perseus of Vain Concern. Let us crush the Ophiuchus of Slander, the Eagle of Arrogance, the Dolphin of Lust, the Horse of Impatience, the Hydra of Concupiscence. Let us dispel from within us the Cetus of Gluttony, the Orion of Pride, the River of Superfluity, the Gorgon of Ignorance, the Hare of Vain Fear. May there no longer be in our hearts any part of the Argo-Navis of Avarice, the Bowl of Insobriety, the Scale of Iniquity, the Cancer of Ill Regress, the Capricorn of Deception. May it not come about that the Scorpio of Fraud, the Centaur of Animal Affection, the Altar of Superstition, the Crown of Pride, the Fish of Unworthy Silence, approach us. With these let there fall the Gemini of Unwholesome Familiarity, the Taurus of Concern for Lowly Things, the Ram of Inconsideration, the Leo of Tyranny, the Aquarius of

Dissolution, the Virgo of Infructuous Association, the Sagittarius of Detraction.

"If thus, oh gods, we shall have purged our dwelling place, if thus we shall have renewed our heaven, new will be the constellations and influences, new the impressions, new the fortunes; for upon this higher world everything depends; and contrary effects are dependent upon contrary causes. Oh happy, oh truly fortunate we, if we shall have made a good colony of our mind and thought! To those of you who do not like the present state, may the present council be pleasing! If we wish to change our state, let us change our customs. If we desire that that state be good and better, these [customs] must not be what they are now, or worse.

"Let us cleanse our interior affect, since after the formation of this internal world, it will not be difficult for us to make progress toward the reformation of this sensible and external one. The first purgation, oh gods, I see you are accomplishing; I see that you have accomplished it. Your determination, I see; I have seen that it was arrived at; and it was arrived at swiftly, because it is not subject to the counterweights of time. Come now, let us proceed to the second phase of our purgation. This phase concerns the external, corporeal, sensible, and inhabited world. However, before we make up our minds we must wait, compare one problem with the other, this reason with that one. Although the disposition of corporeal things depends on time, its execution cannot be realized in a moment.

"You have before you a period of three days, in which you do not have to decide or determine among yourselves whether or not this reform is to be carried out; because as soon as I proposed it to you, carrying out Fate's command, all of you judged it to be most desirable, necessary, and excellent. It is not as an external sign, figure, and shadow that I perceive your affect, but as reality and truth, just as you in turn see mine. And no less quickly than I moved your ears to listen to me by my proposal, you have moved my eyes to tears by the splendor of your immediate consent.

"What remains to be done then is that you consider and confer among yourselves and give some thought concerning the manner in which we shall deal with those things which we remove from the heaven, for which it will be necessary to procure and set aside other lands and dwellings; and also you must consider how to fill these seats so that the heaven shall remain, not deserted, but rather better cultivated and inhabited than before. When the three days have passed, you will come into my presence, after having meditated upon one place and another and one thing and another, so that only after you have had every possible discussion, shall we convene on the fourth day to determine and make a pronouncement upon the form of this colony. I have spoken."

Thus, oh Saulino, Father Jove himself, who attracted the ears, kindled the spirits, and moved the hearts of the celestial Senate and people, while he prayed, clearly recognized in their faces and gestures that in their minds was concluded and determined that which was being proposed to them by him.

The great Patriarch of the gods having then made his last conclusion and imposed silence upon his speech, all with one voice and with one thunder said: "Most willingly, oh Jove, do we consent to effectuate all that you have proposed and Fate has truly predestined." There then followed the roar of the multitude, here rising as a sign of happy resolution, there as that of willing homage, here as that of a doubt, there as that of a reflection, here as an applause, there as the shaking of the heads of some interested parties, here as one thing and there as another; until finally, suppertime having arrived, some withdrew in one direction, others in another.

SAUL. Things of no small moment, oh Sophia!

THIRD PART
OF THE *First Dialogue*

SOPHIA. The fourth day having arrived, and it being exactly midday, they convened once again in the general council chamber, wherein were permitted to be present not only the most important aforesaid divinities but also those others to whom heaven is conceded by right of natural law. Then the Senate and the Nation of the Gods being seated, and Jove, in his usual manner having ascended his throne of sapphire and gold, bedecked with that form of diadem and robe in which he is wont to appear during the most solemn councils, all being ready, the multitude set at attention, and a profound silence having been established, so that the assembled gods seemed like so many statues or so many pictures, there appeared in their midst, with his orders, insignia, and circumstances, my handsome divinity Mercury. And arriving in the presence of the Great Father, he briefly announced, interpreted, and exposed what was not occult to all of the council, but which, in order to preserve the form and decorum of the statutes, must be pronounced: that is to say that the gods were ready and disposed, without simulation and guile, but with free and spontaneous will, to accept and put into execution that which would be concluded, established, and ordained by the present synod. He, after having spoken, turned to the surrounding gods and requested that they, by raising their hands, make manifest and ratify all that he, in their names, had revealed in the presence of the High-Thunderer. And so it was done.

Then the great protoparent opened his mouth, and made himself heard in such a tenor: "If glorious, oh gods, was our victory over the giants, who in a brief space of time again rose against us, they who were strangers and declared enemies, who were only fighting us from Olympus, and who could not nor attempted other than to precipitate us from the heaven, how much more glorious and worthy will be that victory over ourselves, who were victorious over them? How much more worthy and glorious, I say, is that victory over our affects, which have for so long a time triumphed over us, which are domestic and internal enemies that have tyrannized us from every side, and have shaken and removed us from ourselves?

"If, then, worthy of a feast that day has seemed to us, which for us gave birth to such a victory, whose fruit disappeared in a moment, how much more festive must this day be whose fructuous glory will be eternal in future centuries? Let, then, the day of our victory continue to be festive; but let what used to be said about the victory of the giants, be said about the victory of the gods, because on this day we have conquered ourselves. Besides, let there be instituted as a festival day the present day on which heaven is being purged; and may it be more solemn for us than could ever have been the emigration of the leprous people for the Egyptians, and for the Hebrews, the passage from the Babylonian captivity. Today, disease, plague, and leprosy are exiled from heaven into the deserts; today, broken is that chain of crimes and smashed are the shackles of errors that were binding us to eternal punishment.

"Now, then, all of you being most desirous of proceeding to this reform, and all of you having, as I understand, premeditated upon the manner by which we ought to and could come to the matter, so that these seats may not remain uninhabited and that to transmigrating beings convenient places may be ordained, I shall begin to give my opinions concerning them one by one. And when that has been accomplished, if it seems to you worthy of being approved, say so; if it seems inconvenient to you, explain yourselves; if you think it can be done better, declare it; if we must take away from it, express your opinion; if you think that something is to be added to it, make yourselves understood. For each of you has plenary liberty to proffer his vote; and whoever is silent is understood to give his assent." Now almost all of the gods arose, and with this sign ratified the proposal.

"In order, then, to give commencement and to start from the beginning," said Jove, "let us first see the things that are found on the boreal side, and make provisions concerning them; then, little by little, in an orderly manner, we shall proceed to the end. Tell me what are your opinion and judgment regarding that Ursa?"

The gods, who were touched by these opening words, delegated Momus to answer in their behalf, and he spoke thus: "It is a great ignominy, oh Jove, and a greater one than you yourself are aware of, that you have placed that Ursa in the most celebrated position of heaven, an area which Pythagoras, who conceived the world as having a head, arms, legs, bust, and a head, considers to be its highest part, to which is contrasted its opposite extreme, which he considers to be the lowest region. Compare in juxtaposition the words sung by a poet of the Pythagorean sect:

Hic vertex nobis semper sublimis, at illum
Sub pedibus Styx atra videt manesque profundi: [1]

(This pole of ours is ever lofty, but the other,
Black Styx and the shades of the underworld see beneath their feet.)

"You have placed that ugly, huge animal in that very part of the sky which sailors consult during the course of their devious and uncertain sea voyages, toward which all those who are distressed by a storm at sea, lift up their hands; there in the site coveted by the giants, where the cruel generation of Bel raised the Tower of Babel, there where the magicians look into the Chalybean mirror to consult with the oracles of Floron, one of the great princes of the Northern spirits, in that region where the Cabalists say Samael [sic] wished to raise his throne, so that he might resemble the first high-thunderer. You have placed this ugly and terrible beast, whom, not by a glance, not by a turned-out mustache, not by some image of the hand, not by a foot, not by some other less ignoble part of the body, but with a tail (which Juno, counter to the nature of the ursine species, decided should remain tied behind her), you cause to come to show to all terrestrial, maritime, and celestial contemplators the magnificent pole and axis of the world, as if she were a sign worthy of so great a place. To the same extent, then, that you did wrong in fixing her there, you will do good in removing her; and see to it that you make us understand where you want to send her, and what you want to succeed to her place."

"Let her go," said Jove, "where it seems to you and pleases you that she should go, either to the Bears of England or to the Orsini or Cesarini of Rome,[2] if you want her to live in the city in comfort." "I should like to see her imprisoned in the cloister of Bern," said Juno. "Not so much contempt, my wife," replied Jove. "Let her go where we want her to, providing she is free, and that she leave that place in which I, because it is the most eminent seat, want Truth to make her residence; for there the claws of Detraction do not reach, the lividness of Envy does not poison, the shadows of Error do not sink. There she [Truth] will dwell stable and firm; there she will not be shaken violently by waves and storms; there she will be the safe guide of those who go wandering through this tempestuous Sea of Errors; and thence she will show herself as a clear and polished mirror of contemplation."

Asked Father Saturn,[3] "What shall we do with that Great Bear? Let Momus propose." And he [Momus] said, "Let her go, because she is old, as a lady companion of that smaller and younger one; and see to it that she does not become her procuress; if this happens, may she be sentenced to serve some beggar, who, by exhibiting her and allowing her to be mounted by children and others similar, in order to cure quartan-ague and other minor diseases, might earn a living for himself and her."

"How are we to deal with this terrible Dragon, oh Jove?" asked Mars. "Let Momus speak," answered the Father. "He is a useless beast and is better dead than alive," responded Momus. "However, if it seems to you that we should do so, let us send him to graze in Hibernia or on one of the Orkneys. But be most careful;

because there is the danger that with his tail he may wreak havoc among some stars and cause them to fall headlong into the sea." "Have no doubt, oh Momus," answered Apollo, "for I shall command some Circe or Medea to use the same verses with which we put him to sleep when he was custodian of the golden apples, and soon, when he is again asleep, that he be transported very gently to the earth. And I do not think that he should die; rather, he should be exhibited wherever barbarous beauty is present. Because the golden apples will represent beauty, the dragon, ferocity, Jason, the lover, and the enchantment that put the dragon to sleep,

> There is no heart so cruel
> That it will not be moved
> By good intention, by time,
> By weeping and loving
> And sometimes paying;
> Nor is there desire so cold
> That it cannot be warmed.[4]

"Whom do you want to take his place, oh father?" "Prudence," answered Jove, "who should be in the proximity of Truth, for the latter should not govern herself, move and operate without the former, because it is not possible that the one could ever profit or be honored without the company of the other."

"Well decided," replied the gods.

Mars added: "When that Cephus was king, he knew how to wield his arms with cruelty to enlarge that realm which Fortune had granted him. Now, it is not good that he, here, in that manner in which he is acting, by extending his arms and lengthening his stride, should thus make for himself a wide expanse in the heaven." "It is well then," said Jove, "that he be given to drink of the water of Lethe in order that he may forget and become oblivious of earthly and heavenly possessions, and that he be reborn as an animal which has neither legs nor arms."

"So should it be," answered the gods; "but let Sophia succeed to his place, for the unfortunate one must also partake of the fruits and fortunes of Truth, her inseparable companion, with whom she has always communicated in sorrows, afflictions, insults, and labors; besides which, if that one is not there to coadminister them, we do not know how she could be acknowledged and honored." "Most willingly, oh gods," said Jove, "I agree with it and grant you my consent, because all order and reason demand it; especially since I would consider that I had unjustly assigned the former to her place without the latter, and there, far from her so greatly beloved sister and cherished companion, she could not be happy."

"Momus," asked Diana, "what action do you think we should take in regard to Boötes, who, so well covered with stars, guides his wagon?" Answered Momus: "Because he is that Arcas, the fruit of that sacrilegious womb, and that noble parturition, which still renders testimony to the horrible thefts of our great father, he must depart from here. Now, make provision for his habitation." Apollo replied: "Because he was Callisto's son, may he follow his mother." "And because he was a bear hunter," added Diana, "let him follow his mother, providing he does not pierce her back with the point of a partisan." Mercury added: "And because you see that he does not know how to follow any other route, may he, indeed, always go watching his mother, who should be returning to the Erymanthian forests."

"Thus it will be better," said Jove; "and because the wretched creature was forcibly violated, I wish to make amends for her injury by sending her back to that place, if it still so pleases Juno, in her pristine beautiful form." "I shall be satisfied," said Juno, "after you have first restored her to her state of virginity, and, consequently, to Diana's favor."

"Let us talk no longer of this matter for now," said Jove; "but let us see what thing we want should succeed to that one's place." After many, many discussions had been held, Jove sentenced: "There, let Law succeed, for it is now necessary that she be in heaven, owing to the fact that she is the daughter of the celestial and divine Sophia, just as that other one [5] is the daughter of the inferior Sophia, through whom this goddess sends her influence and radiates the splendor of her own light at that time when she wanders through the deserted and solitary places of the earth."

"Well disposed, oh Jove," said Pallas; "for there is no true or good law which does not have as its mother, Sophia, and as its father, Rational Intellect; being in that place, therefore, this daughter will not have to be far from her mother. And in order that down on earth men may contemplate how things must be ordered among themselves, let us now dispose in this manner, if it so pleases Jove.

"Then follows the seat of Corona Borealis, made of sapphire, enriched by so many sparkling diamonds, and forming that most beautiful perspective with four and four, which are eight ardent carbuncles. Because this [crown] is a thing made below, transported from below, it seems to me most worthy of being presented to some heroic prince, who is not unworthy of it; however, let our father see who should least unworthily be remunerated by us."

"Let it remain in the sky," replied Jove, "awaiting the time when it must be given as a prize to that future unconquered arm, which, with its club and fire, will bring back the so-longed-for peace to wretched and unhappy Europe, making impotent the many heads of this monster, worse than the monster of Lerna, which with multiform heresy spreads its fatal poison, and which at too great a pace slithers to all parts through her veins." [6]

Momus added: "It will be sufficient if that hero puts an end to that idle sect of pedants, who, without doing good, according to divine and natural law, consider themselves and want to be considered religious men pleasing to the gods, and say that to do good is good, and to do ill is wicked. But they say it is not by the good that is done, or by the evil that is not done, that one becomes worthy and pleasing to the gods, but rather it is by hoping and believing, according to their catechism.[7] Behold, oh gods, if there ever existed ribaldry more open than this, which by those alone is not seen, who do not see anything."

"Indeed," said Mercury, "he who is not acquainted with that knavery does not recognize this one, which is the mother of all. If Jove, himself, and all of us together, should propose such terms to men, we should be said to be more abominated than death, we, who like those, to the greatest prejudice of human society, are concerned only with our own vainglory."

"The worst of it is," said Momus, "that they defame us, saying that this [religion of theirs] is an institution of the gods; and it is with this that they criticize effects and fruits, even referring to them with the title of defects and vices. Whereas nobody works for them and they work for nobody (because their only labor is to speak ill of works), they, at the same time, live on the works of those who have labored for others rather than for them,[8] and who for others have instituted temples, chapels, lodgings, hospitals, schools, and universities. Wherefore they are outright thieves and occupiers of the hereditary wealth of others who, if they are not perfect, nor so good as they should be, will not be, however (as are the first), perverse and pernicious to the world, but rather will be necessary to the republic, will be experts in the speculative sciences, scholars of morality, solicitous of augmenting their zeal and concern for helping one another and of upholding society (for which all laws are ordained) by proposing certain rewards to benefactors and threatening certain punishments to delinquents.

"Besides, whereas the first say that all their concern is for invisible things, which neither they nor others ever understood, they tell us that for the attainment of those things, destiny alone is sufficient (which is immutable), with the aid of certain inner affects and fantasies upon which the gods especially nourish themselves."

"However," said Mercury, "it should neither disturb them nor arouse their concern that some believe that works are necessary; for their destiny, as well as the destiny of those who believe the contrary, is pre-established,[9] and does not alter because their belief or disbelief changes, because their belief is of one or the other kind. And for the same reason they [the Calvinists] should not be troublesome toward those who do not believe in them and who consider them most wicked; for even though they [the Catholics] come to believe and esteem those others as good men, their own destiny will not change. Besides, according to the doctrine of the Calvinists, it does not lie within the freedom of choice of these others to change to this faith. But those who have the contrary belief [the Calvinists] may legally, according to their consciences, not only be harmful to the others but also consider it as a great act of homage to the gods and of benefit to the world if they persecute, kill, and exterminate them from the face of the earth. For they are worse than maggots, sterile locusts, and those harpies who did no good but only abused and sullied with their feet the good things they could not devour, and impeded those who worked."

"All those who have natural judgment," said Apollo, "judge laws to be good, because they have experience as their end; and the best laws are those that, in comparison, offer better opportunity to better experience.[10] For of all the laws that exist, some were given by us, others were especially fashioned by men for the convenience of human life; and because some do not see the reward of their virtues in this life, there is therefore promised and presented before their eyes the good and evil of their next life, its rewards and punishments, in accordance with their deeds.

"Of all those, then, who believe and teach differently from us," said Apollo, "these alone deserve to be persecuted by heaven and earth, and exterminated as pests of the world;[11] and they are no more deserving of pity than wolves, bears, and serpents, whose extermination will be a meritorious and worthy thing. However, he who will drive them [the Calvinists] away, will deserve incomparably more; for how much greater is the pestilence and ruin brought by these than that brought by the others. But Momus correctly pointed out that the Southern Crown especially awaits him who is destined by Fate to wipe out this stinking filth of the world."

"It is well," said Jove. "Thus I want and thus I determine, that this Crown be disposed of in the manner reasonably proposed by Mercury, Momus, and Apollo, to which you consent. This plague cannot last too long, because it is violent and against human and natural law; as you can perceive, these Calvinists have a most hostile destiny or fate, for their numbers never increased except for the purpose of bringing about a more widespread ruin." "The Crown," said Saturn, "is a worthy reward for him who will drive them away; but that these wicked people should be excluded only from intercourse with men is, however, a small and disproportionate penalty. It rather seems to me more just that once they have left their present bodies, they transmigrate from body to body, through various changes and modifications, and that they go to dwell in the bodies of pigs, which are the idlest animals in the world; perhaps, indeed, they might become oysters of the sea, which are attached to rocks."

"Justice," said Mercury, "demands the contrary. It seems fitting to me that labor should be given as a penalty for idleness. Thus it is better that they become asses, in which existence they will retain their ignorance and divest themselves of their idleness; and in that supposition, as wages for their continuous labor, they should have little hay and straw for food, and many blows as a reward."

All the gods together approved this opinion. Then Jove decreed that the Crown shall forever belong to him who will have given them the last blow; and that they for three thousand years shall continue migrating from asses into asses. He further decreed that in the place of that particular Crown there should succeed the ideal and eternally communicable one, so that out of it might be created infinite crowns, just as from a lighted lamp, without its dimunition and without its at all lessening in virtue and efficacy, there are illuminated infinite others.

To this Crown he proposed that the ideal Sword should be added, which likewise has more real being than any other particular one subsistent within the limits of natural operations. By this Sword and Crown, Jove wishes to signify Universal Judgment, by which everyone in the world may be rewarded and punished according to the measure of merits and crimes. All the gods strongly approved this provision in view of the fact that it is fitting that Law should have her seat next to Judgment; for the latter must govern herself by the former, and the former must exercise herself by means of the latter; the latter must execute, and the former will dictate; in the former must consist all theory, in the latter, all experience.

After many discourses and digressions were made concerning the disposition of this seat, Momus pointed out Hercules to Jove and asked, "Now, what shall we do with this bastard of yours?" "You have heard, oh gods," answered Jove, "the reason why my Hercules must go elsewhere with the others. But I do not want his departure to be the same as that of all the rest; since the cause, manner, and reason for his assumption have been very dissimilar. Inasmuch as he has merited the heaven solely and singularly because of the virtues and the merits of his heroic exploits, he has proved himself, although spurious, nevertheless worthy of being a legitimate son of Jove. And you see clearly that he is denied the heaven owing to the fact that he is adventitious, and not naturally a god; and the error for which I am noted, because of him, as it has been said, is mine and not his. I believe, furthermore, that your conscience would prick you if any one man were excepted from that rule and determination, and that man were not Hercules.

"If, however, we remove him from here and send him down to earth, let us see to it that he be not without his honor and reputation, which should be no less than it would have been had he continued to be in the heaven." Many gods arose, I say the majority of them did, and said: "Father, with more, if that is possible." "I declare then that upon this occasion he, as is due a laborious and strong person, be given such a charge and responsibility by reason of which he will become a terrestrial god, so great that he will be honored by all as being greater than when he was made a genuine celestial demigod." And the same gods answered: "Be it so." And because some of them were neither then absorbed in thought nor now speaking, Jove turned to them and said that even they should let their thoughts be known. So, some of them answered: "Probamus"; others, "Admittimus." "Non refragamur," added Juno.

Then Jove proceeded to proclaim his decree as follows: "Because, during these times, in certain places of the world, are found monsters, which if they are not the same as they were in the days of its ancient inhabitants, are probably worse, I, Jove, father and general provider, do decree that Hercules go down to earth as my lieutenant and minister of my potent arm, if not endowed with similar or greater bodily dimension, at least endowed and enriched with a greater vigilance, more concern, and greater strength of intellect and spiritual efficacy. And just as he first proved himself great after he was conceived and born upon that earth, by having overcome and conquered so many cruel monsters, and a second time, victorious upon his return from hell, by having made an appearance as an unhoped-for consoler of his friends and unexpected destroyer of outrageous tyrants, so may he now descend to be seen for the third time by his mother in the role of a new, most necessary, and greatly longed-for provider.

"As Hercules passes over the earth, let him see whether some Nemean lion is once again destroying the Arcadian cities, and whether the Cleonaean lion is again appearing in Thessaly. May he be on the lookout to see whether that Hydra, that pest of Lerna, has again come to life to assume her newly growing heads. Let him see whether Diomedes, who used to feed his mares at the Hebrus on the blood of wanderers, has been resurrected in Thrace. Let him turn his gaze toward Libya to see whether perhaps Antaeus, who used to regain his spirit so often, has even once reassumed his body. Let Hercules see whether there is some three-bodied Geryon in the land of Iberia. Let him raise his head to see whether at this time those most pernicious Stymphalian Birds are flying in the sky. I say that he should see whether those Harpies are flying, which sometimes used to becloud the sky and impede our view of the luminous stars. Let him beware lest a bristly boar be roaming idly in the Erymanthian deserts; lest he should encounter a bull not unlike the one who used to instill horrible terror among so many peoples. Let him see whether he should allow some three-headed Cerberus, who yelps, to sally forth into the open air so that he may vomit the deadly aconite; whether some flesh-bearing Busiris is still spilling blood before cruel altars; whether a certain hind, her head adorned with golden horns, makes her appearance in those deserts, just like the one who with her brazen feet used to run as swiftly as the wind; whether a new Amazon queen has assembled her rebellious forces; whether some faithless and fickle Achelous, with his inconstant, multiform, and changeable aspect, still tyrannizes anywhere; whether any Hesperides have committed the golden apples to the guardianship of the dragon;[12] whether the unmarried, audacious queen [Penthesileia] of the Thermodonians again makes her appearance; whether a certain thief, Lancinius, is still fattening himself in the land of Italy, or some predatory Cacus defends his plunder by means of smoke and flames.

"If these or similar or other new and unheard-of monsters should encounter and attack him as he goes exploring on the spacious back of the earth, may he turn them away, reform, expel, persecute, imprison, subdue, despoil, scatter, break, tear, shatter, abase, submerge, burn, destroy, kill, and annihilate them. In reward for these deeds, and for his numerous and most singular labors, I ordain, if Fate does not contradict me, that in the places where he will effectuate his heroic undertakings, there be erected trophies, statues, colossi, and other shrines and temples."

"Truly, oh Jove," said Momus, "now you do seem to me to be quite a just god; because I perceive that your paternal affection does not transport you to the point of ignoring the terms of retribution owed to your Alcides, according to his merits. Not only is he deserving of so much, but he is perhaps worthy of something more, even in the judgment of Juno, who, I see by her laughing, also approves of what I say."

But here is my long-awaited Mercury, oh Saulino, for whose sake it is fitting that this discussion of ours be deferred to another occasion. However, be good enough to leave us so that we can talk in private.

SAUL. Well, then, good-by until tomorrow.

SOPHIA. Here is he to whom I addressed my prayers yesterday. He finally comes to me, after having delayed a little too long. My prayers should have reached him last evening, should have been listened to during the night, and answered by him this morning. If he did not quickly respond to my call, a matter of great concern must have detained him; for indeed I consider myself no less loved by him than by myself.

Here he is. I see him coming out of that bright cloud, which, moved by the southern spirit, speeds toward the center of our horizon, and yielding to the flashing rays of the sun, opens up into a circle, as if it were crowning my noble planet. Oh sacred father, thou high majesty, I thank thee, because I behold my winged divinity appearing from the center of the circle, with his wings extended, striking the air, happy, with the caduceus in his hand, cleaving the heaven in my direction with greater speed than Jove's bird, more gentle than the breath of Juno, more excellent than the Arabian Phoenix. Having dashed toward me at great speed, he now politely stands before me and reveals himself to me uniquely affectionate.

MERCURY. Because you sent for me, here I am, oh Sophia, obedient and favorably disposed toward your prayers. And as for your entreaty, it did not reach me, according to its custom, in the form of aromatic vapor, but as the piercing and well-feathered arrow of resplendent light.

SOPHIA. But you, my divinity, what is the reason why you did not immediately, as according to your custom, present yourself to me?

MERC. I shall tell you the truth, oh Sophia. Your prayer came to me at the time when I had already returned to hell, to commit into the hands of Minos, Aeacus, and Rhadamanthus 246,522 souls, who, through divers battles, tortures, and necessities, have completed the course of animation of present bodies.[13] There, with me, was the heavenly Sophia, vulgarly known as Minerva and Pallas, who, from its appearance and movement, immediately knew that that message was yours.

SOPHIA. She could well recognize it; because it frequently was wont to negotiate with her, no less than with you.[14]

MERC. And she said to me: "Turn your eyes, oh Mercury, because this message comes for you from our terrestrial sister and daughter. I want that one who lives by my spirit and at a greater distance, close to the shadows, and proceeds from my father's light, to be recommended to your care."

"It is a superfluous thing," I answered her, "oh thou born of Jove's brain, to recommend to me our so greatly beloved common sister and daughter." Then, I approached your message, embraced it, kissed it. I summarized it, unbuttoned my cloak, and stuffed it between my shirt and my breast, under which the pulse of my heart was beating repeatedly.

Jove (who was present, somewhat removed, conversing secretly with Aeolus and Oceanus, who were booted, about to return quickly to their affairs down here on earth) saw what I had done, and interrupting the conversation in which he was engaged, became so curious as to ask me forthwith what memorandum it was that I had placed in my bosom. And after I had answered him that it was a matter concerning you, he said: "Oh, my poor Sophia! How is she faring? What is she doing? Alas, the poor thing! Judging from that cornet of paper, which is not too elegantly rolled, I understood that the news could not be other than what you say. It is indeed a long time since we have received any news concerning her. Now, what is she asking of you? What does she need? What is she proposing to you?" "Nothing else," I said, "but that I be in her presence to listen to her for an hour."

"It is well," he said; and he returned to finish his conversation with those two gods; and then, hurriedly he summoned me to his presence, saying, "Come, come, quickly let us put our affairs in order before you go to see what that poor creature wants; and I shall return to see this most troublesome wife of mine, who certainly weighs upon me more heavily than all the weight of the universe." He immediately demanded that I make a note in my own hand of all that today must be provided for on earth (for thus it has recently been decreed in heaven).

SOPHIA. Let me hear of some of these matters, if it pleases you, since you have aroused this concern in my heart.

MERC. I shall tell you.[15] Jove has ordained that today, at noon, two melons, among the others found in Franzino's [16] melon patch, be fully ripened, but that they not be picked until three days later, at which time they will not be considered fit for eating. He wishes that, at the same time, thirty jujubes, perfectly ripe, be picked from the jujube tree which stands at the foot of Mount Cicala on the property of Gioan Bruno; [17] thirty of them should be picked perfectly ripe, seventeen should fall to the ground unripe, and fifteen should be worm-eaten.

He decreed that Vasta,[18] the wife of Albenzio, while she tries to curl the hair on her temples, shall burn fifty-seven of them because she overheated her iron, but that she will not burn her head, that she will not swear this time upon smelling the stench, but rather bear it with patience.

He decreed that two hundred fifty-two maggots be born out of the dung of Albenzio's ox; that of these, fourteen be trampled upon and killed by Albenzio's foot; that twenty-six of them die from being turned upside down; that twenty-two live in a cavern; that eighty wander about the courtyard; that forty-two go to live under the tree stump near the door; that sixteen turn their feelers wherever they see fit; and that the rest go in search of their fortune.

He decreed that Laurenza [19] lose seventeen hairs when she combs herself; that thirteen be pulled out; and that of the former number, ten grow back within three days, and seven return no more.

He decreed that Antonio Savolino's[20] bitch conceive five puppies, of which three will live out their time, and two will be thrown away; and that of those three, the first should resemble the mother, the second be different, the third resemble partly his father and partly Polydorus'[21] father.

He ordained that at that time the cuckoo should be heard singing from Starza,[22] and that he must "cuckoo" neither more nor less than twelve times; and that he then must depart to make his way to the ruins of the Cicala Castle,[23] for eleven minutes out of every hour, and thence fly away to Scarvaita.[24] And as to what is to be done afterwards, we shall provide later on.

He decreed that the gown that Master Danese[25] is cutting on his bench should be spoiled.

He decreed that twelve bedbugs come out of the boards of Costantino's[26] bed and make their way to the pillow, seven being of the largest, four of the smallest, and one of average size; and for what is to become of them at candlelight, we shall provide.

He decreed that at fifteen minutes of the same hour, the old woman of Fiurulo,[27] by the motion of her tongue moving about in her palate, will succeed with the fourth movement in causing the third molar in her right lower jaw to fall out. Its loss will be bloodless and painless, because the said molar has come to the end of its state of trepidation that has lasted exactly seventeen annual revolutions of the moon.

Jove ordained that Ambruoggio,[28] after the one hundred twelfth thrust, will interrupt and postpone his affair with his wife, and that he will not impregnate her this time, but will do so on another occasion with that semen into which is converted that hot leek which he is eating now with juice and millet bread.

He ordained that pubic hair begin to appear on the mons pubis of Martinello's son;[29] and that at the very same time his voice begin gradually to crack. Furthermore, the red lace of Paolino's[30] breeches will break off because of the violent movement he will make while trying to pick up a broken needle from the ground; "for which reason, if he should swear, because of it [said Jove], I want him to be punished in the following manner: tonight, his soup should be too salty and have a smoky taste; his flask, filled with wine, should fall and break; if he should swear because of it, we shall attend to it later on."

He ordained that of seven moles, which left the bowels of the earth four days ago, taking various routes toward the open air, two shall come to the surface at the same hour, the one at the stroke of noon, the other fifteen minutes and nineteen seconds after, removed from one another by three paces, one foot and one half finger's length, in Antonio Faivano's garden. Concerning the time and place of the others, provision will be made later on.

SOPHIA. You have much to do, oh Mercury, if you wish to tell me about all of these acts of Providence performed by Father Jove; and in wanting me to listen to these specific decrees, one by one, you seem to me like one who would want to take a count of all the grains of sand on earth. You have taken so long to report a few insignificant occurrences out of an infinite number that took place simultaneously in a small area of the countryside, where there are four or five not-too-significant beings; now what would happen if you had to relate in detail the things that were ordained for this city situated at the foot of this Mount Cicala? Certainly, a year would not suffice for you to explain them one by one in the manner in which you have begun to do so.

What do you believe would happen if, besides, I wanted to report about the things that happened in the city of Nola, in the kingdom of Naples, in Italy, in Europe, and on all of the terrestrial globe, and every other globe in the infinite,[31] as indeed the worlds placed under Jove's Providence are infinite? In truth, in order to report only that which happened and was decreed to be contained in one moment, in the orbit of only one of these globes or worlds, it would not be enough for you to ask for one hundred iron tongues and mouths, as the poets do,[32] but a thousand thousand million of them for the period of one year, and then you would not have reported the one thousandth part of it.

And to tell you the truth, oh Mercury, I do not know what this report of yours signifies, with which some of my worshipers, called philosophers, believe that this poor, great Father Jove is much concerned, occupied, and disturbed; and they believe that his fortune is such that there is not even one mortal who should envy his state. I say that during that time he spent in proposing and decreeing these effects, there occurred on an infinite number of occasions an infinite number of opportunities for him to decree, and to have decreed, other effects; and if you should want to discharge your office while relating them to me, you will have had to go through and will have to go through, other infinities an infinite number of times.

MERC. You know, Sophia, if you are Sophia, that Jove does all things without effort, solicitude, and trouble; because he provides for innumerable species and infinite individuals by giving them order and by having given them order, not by a certain successive process, but instantaneously and all at once. He does not create things according to particular efficient causes, one by one, by means of many actions, arriving at infinite acts by means of infinite actions; but with one simple and singular act, he creates all of the past, present, and future.

SOPHIA. I know this very well, oh Mercury: that you gods do not relate and execute these things all at once, and that they are not of one simple and singular subject; therefore, the efficient cause must be proportionate to those things, or at least become proportionate to them through the act.

MERC. What you say is true. It must be so, and not otherwise, in the particular, immediate, and natural efficient; because the measure and reason of the particular act, regarding the particular subject, follow according to the reason and measure of the effective particular virtue. However, that is not so in the universal efficient, for it is proportioned, if we can express it thus, to the total infinite effect, which depends on it, according to the reason of all places, times, modes, and subjects, and definitely not to specific places, subjects, times, and modes.

SOPHIA. I know, oh Mercury, that universal knowledge is different from the particular, just as the finite differs from the infinite.

MERC. Or better say: as unity differs from infinite number. And you must also know, oh Sophia, that unity is in infinite number, and that infinite number is in unity; that besides, unity is an implicit infinite, and that the infinite is explicit unity. Therefore, where there is no unity, there is no number, either finite or infinite; and wherever there is number, either finite or infinite, there, necessarily, is unity. The latter, therefore, is the substance of the former, so that he who sees unity, not as accident (as some particular intellects do), but as essence (as universal intelligence does), understands unity, the one and the number, the finite and the infinite, the end and goal of intelligence, and the abundance of all things; and he is able to perform all things, not only in the universal but also in the particular. So since there is no particular that is not contained in the universal, there is no number in which unity is more truly contained than number itself. Thus then, Jove, without difficulty or annoyance, provides for all things, in all places and times, just as being and unity are necessarily found in all numbers, in all places, in all times and atoms of time, places, and numbers; and the only principle of being is in infinite individuals who were, are, and will be. But this disputation is not the reason for which I have come here and for which, I believe, I was summoned by you.

SOPHIA. It is true that I know well that these are matters which are worthy of being decided upon by my philosophers, and are not fully understood by me, who can only understand them with difficulty, in comparisons and similes, but are understood by the heavenly Sophia and by you. By your narration, however, I have been moved to consider such a matter before I discuss that which regards my particular interests and designs. Indeed, oh judicious divinity, you seem to me to have entered into that discussion of such insignificant and lowly matters without purpose.

MERC. I have done it, not with vanity, but with great providence, Sophia, because I have judged necessary this animadversion of you, who, from what I understand, by your many afflictions are in such manner disturbed that easily your affect might be transported toward wanting not too piously to opine concerning the rule of the gods; it is just and sacrosanct, *ad finem finalem,* although things appear, in the manner in which you see them, most confused. I have wanted, therefore, before dealing with other things, to provoke you to such contemplation so as to render you free from the doubt you might entertain and, perhaps, many times demonstrate; because you, being earthly and discursive, cannot clearly understand the importance of Jove's providence and the concern of us, his collaterals.

SOPHIA. But yet, oh Mercury, how do you explain the fact that this zeal has moved you rather more at present than at other times?

MERC. I shall tell you (that which I have deferred telling you up to the present) why your entreaty, your prayer, your message, although it arrived in heaven and came to us swiftly and readily, was, however, frozen in midsummer, was irresolute, was trembling, as if it were thrown into the lap of Fortune rather than sent and committed to Providence; as if it were dubious that it could have the effect of reaching ears such as ours, attentive to things esteemed more important. But you deceive yourself, Sophia, if you believe that minimum matters are not of so much concern to us as important ones, inasmuch as very great and important things do not have worth without insignificant and most abject things. Everything, then, no matter how minimal, is under infinitely great Providence; all minutiae, no matter how very lowly, in the order of the whole and of the universe, are most important; for great things are composed of little ones, and little things of the smallest, and the latter, of individuals and of minima. I am of the same opinion concerning great substances as concerning great efficacies and great effects.

SOPHIA. It is true; for there is no architecture so great, so magnificent, and so beautiful that it does not consist of things which appear and are judged to be small, most lowly, and formless.

MERC. The act of divine cognition is the substance of the being of all things; and, therefore, just as all things have either finite or infinite being, so are all known and ordained and provided for. Divine cognition is not like ours, which follows after things, but is before things and is found in all things, so that if it were not there, there would be no proximate and secondary causes.

SOPHIA. And therefore, oh Mercury, you want me not to be dismayed by anything minimal or great that befalls me, not only by anything principal and direct but also by anything indirect and accessory; and [to know] that Jove is in all and fills all and listens to all.

MERC. It is so; however, in the future remember to make your message warmer, and not to send it so carelessly clad and cold in the presence of Jove; and both he and your Pallas have enjoined me that before I speak of anything else to you, I should, aided by sagacity, make you aware of this.

SOPHIA. I thank you all.

MERC. Now explain the reason why you summoned me to you.

SOPHIA. Because of the mutation and change of customs, which I apprehend in Jove, and because of what I, through other discussions, have learned from you, I have attained the confidence with which to ask and entreat him about that which, at other times, I did not dare to, when I used to fear that some Venus or Cupid or Ganymede might reject and send back my message when it presented itself before the door of Jove's chamber. Now that everything has been changed, and that other doormen, guides, and assistants have been ordained, and that he is well disposed toward Justice, I desire that my request, which deals with the great wrongs being perpetrated against me by several kinds of men on earth, be presented to him through you, and that you beseech him to be favorable and propitious toward me, according to what his conscience shall dictate.

MERC. Since this request of yours is lengthy and of no small importance, and also since it was recently proclaimed in heaven that all messages, whether of a civil or criminal nature, be recorded in the chamber, not without their due ceremony, pomp, and circumstances, it is therefore necessary that you place it in my hands in writing, and that I present it so to Jove and the heavenly Senate.

SOPHIA. What is the reason for this new decree?

MERC. In order that, in this manner, each one of the gods will be compelled to dispense justice; because through recording, which eternizes the memory of acts, they may fear to incur eternal shame and eternal blame with the condemnation which must be expected from Absolute Justice, which reigns over all rulers and presides over all the gods.

SOPHIA. I shall do so, then. But one needs time to think and to write; therefore, I beseech you to come back to me tomorrow, or indeed the day after tomorrow.

MERC. I shall not fail. Ponder upon what you are doing.

End of First Dialogue

Second Dialogue

FIRST PART
OF THE *Second Dialogue*

SAUL. If you please, Sophia, before we proceed to other matters, give me the reason for this order and disposition of divinities which Jove has made among the stars. And first let me hear why he has decided that in the most eminent seat (for so it is commonly believed to be by the vulgar) Truth should be placed.

SOPHIA. Easily. Above all things, oh Saulino, is situated Truth; because she is the unity that presides over all, is the goodness that is pre-eminent among all things; because the entity, the good, and the true are one, as are likewise the true, the entity, and the good. Truth is that entity which is not inferior to anything; for if you wish to imagine something which is before Truth, you must consider that thing to be other than Truth. And if you imagine it to be other than Truth, you will necessarily understand it as not having truth within itself and, being without truth, as not being true; whence, consequently, it is false, it is worthless, it is nothing, it is not entity. I say that nothing can be before Truth, if it is not true that it is first and above Truth; and there can be no true being except by virtue of Truth. So it cannot be another thing together with Truth, and be that same thing without Truth; so that if by virtue of Truth, it is not true, it is not entity, it is false, it is nothing. Likewise, there can be nothing after Truth, because if it is after her, it is without her; if it is without her, it is not true, because it does not contain truth within itself; it must then be false, it must then be nothing.

Thus Truth is before all things, is with all things, is after all things, is above all, with all, after all; she contains the reason for the beginning, middle, and end. She is before things, as cause and principle, inasmuch as through her, things have their dependence; she is in things and is herself their substance, inasmuch as through her they have their subsistence. She is after all things inasmuch as through her they are understood without falsity. She is ideal, natural, and notional; she is metaphysics, physics, and logic. Above all things, then, is Truth; and that which is above all things, although it is conceived differently according to another reason and otherwise named, nevertheless, in substance must be Truth herself.

Because of this, then, Jove reasonably has desired that in the most eminent place of the heaven Truth should be seen. But certainly this [truth] which you sensibly see and which you, by the loftiness of your intellect, can understand, is not the highest and first, but a certain figure, a certain image, a certain splendor of her, who is superior to this Jove about whom we often speak, and who is the subject of our metaphors.

SAUL. Deservedly, oh Sophia, for Truth is the most sincere, the most divine of all things. Rather, Truth is the divinity and sincerity, the goodness and beauty of things, who is neither driven away by violence, nor corrupted by antiquity, nor diminished by occultation, nor dispersed by communication. For sense does not confound her, time does not wrinkle her, place does not hide her, night does not interrupt her, shadow does not envelop her. Rather, the more and more she is impugned, the more and more she is resuscitated and grows. Without a defender and protector, she defends herself; and yet she loves the company of a few wise men. She hates the multitude, does not show herself before those who do not seek her for her own sake, and does not wish to be declared to those who do not humbly expose themselves to her, or to all those who fraudulently seek her; and therefore she dwells most high, whither all gaze, and few see. But why, oh Sophia, does Prudence follow her? Perhaps because those who wish to contemplate Truth and who want to preach her must be governed by Prudence?

SOPHIA. This is not the reason. That goddess who is joined to and close to Truth has two names: Providence and Prudence. She is called Providence inasmuch as she influences and is found in superior principles, and she is called Prudence inasmuch as she is effectuated in us; just as the sun is wont to be referred to as that body which both warms the earth and diffuses light and as that light and diffused splendor which is found in the mirror and in other subjects besides.

Providence, then, is said to be in the highest things, is the companion of Truth, and is not found without her; and she is both liberty itself and necessity itself; so that truth, providence, liberty, and necessity, unity, truth,[1] essence, and entity are all absolutely one, as I shall better demonstrate to you on other occasions. But for the convenience of present contemplation, know that she instills Prudence in us, which Prudence is placed and is consistent in certain temporal discourse; and she [Prudence] is the principal law that flows toward the universal and the particular. She has as her handmaiden, Dialectic, and as her guide, Acquired Wisdom, commonly known as Metaphysics, who considers the universals of all things that fall into human cognition; and these two refer all their considerations to the use of Prudence. She has two[2] insidious enemies who are vicious: To her right are found Cunning, Craftiness, and Malice; to her left, Stupidity, Inertia, and Imprudence. And she flows toward consultative virtue, as does strength toward impetuosity of wrath, moderation toward assent to concupiscence, justice toward all operations, external as well as internal.

SAUL. Through Providence, then, you want Prudence to influence us, in the archetype world the former to correspond to the latter, who is in the physical world. It is the latter who gives to mortals the shield through which, by means of reason, they fortify themselves against adverse things; through which they are taught to take more speedy and perfect caution where very great losses threaten and are feared; through which inferior agents adapt themselves to things, to times, and to occasions, and minds and wills do not change but adapt themselves. Because of this, to those who are well affected nothing comes as if it were sudden and unexpected; they doubt nothing, but expect all; they suspect nothing, but guard themselves against everything by remembering their past, planning their present, and foreseeing their future. Now tell me why Sophia follows and is close to Prudence and Truth?

SOPHIA. Sophia, like Truth and Providence, is of two species. The one is that superior, supracelestial, and ultramundane one, if one can express it thus, and she is Providence herself, both light and the eye; the eye which is light itself, light which is the eye itself. The other is the consecutive, mundane, and inferior; and she is not Truth, herself, but is truthful and partakes of Truth; she is not the sun, but the moon, the earth, and the star which shine because of another. So she is Sophia, not in essence, but by participation; and she is an eye which receives light and is illuminated by an external, wandering light; she is not an eye in herself, but is so because of another. She has no being in herself, but through another. For she is not the one, not the entity, not the true; but she is of the one, of the entity, of the true; out of the one, out of the entity, out of the true; because of the one, because of the entity, because of the true; within the one, within the entity, within the true; from the one, from the entity, from the true.

The first is invisible, both infigurable and incomprehensible, above all, in all, and among all. The second is figured in the heaven, illustrated in minds, communicated through words, digested through art, refined through conversation, delineated through writings. For her, he who says that he knows what he does not know, is a rash sophist; he who denies knowing what he does know, is ungrateful to the active intellect, injurious toward Truth, and outrageous toward me. And all those become likewise who do not seek me for my own sake, or for the sake of the supreme virtue and love of the Divinity which is above all Joves and all heavens, but would rather sell me for money or honors, or for other kinds of gain, or desire me, not so much for knowing, but rather to be known, or to detract, and to be able to impugn and stand against the happiness of certain troublesome censors and rigid observers. And of these, the first are wretched, the second vain, the third wicked and of base mind. Those, however, who seek me so that they may edify themselves are prudent; those who observe me so that they may edify others are humane; those who seek me absolutely are curious; those who inquire after me for love of the supreme and first Truth are wise, and consequently happy.

SAUL. Whence does it happen, oh Sophia, that not all who similarly possess you are similarly affected; rather sometimes, he who best possesses you is least edified?

SOPHIA. Whence does it come about, oh Saulino, that the sun does not warm all those upon whom it shines, and sometimes warms least such persons upon whom it shines most?

SAUL. I do understand you, Sophia; and I apprehend that you are she who in various ways contemplates, comprehends, and explains this truth and the effects of that supreme influence of your being, toward which, through various steps and diverse ladders, all aspire, strive, study, and, by rising, force themselves to reach. And the same end and scope appear and present themselves in different studies, and succeed in actuating diverse subjects of intellectual virtues, according to diverse measures, as they direct it toward that one and simple Truth. Just as there is no one who can touch her at all, so there is not found here below anyone who can perfectly understand her; because she is understood and equaled only by that [being] in whom she dwells as essence, and this is none other than she herself.

And therefore, outwardly she is seen only as shadow, similitude, a mirror, both in surface and in manner of appearance, whom no one in this world approaches more closely through the act of Providence and the effect of Prudence than you, Sophia, while you lead diverse sects to her. Of these some aspire toward Truth by wondering, others by parabling, others by inquiring, others by opining, others by judging and determining; others by a sufficiency of natural magic, others by superstitious divination; others by means of negation, others by means of affirmation; others by way of composition, others by way of division; others by way of definition, others by way of demonstration; others by means of acquired principles, others by means of divine principles. Meanwhile she cries out to them, nowhere present, nowhere absent, proposing to them before the eyes of sentiment, by means of writing, all natural things and effects, and intones in the ear of their inner mind, by means of conceived species of visible and invisible things.

SOPHIA. Sophia is followed by her daughter, Law; and through Law, Sophia wishes to operate, wishes to be employed; through Law princes reign, and kingdoms and republics are maintained. Law, adapting herself to the complexion and customs of peoples and nations, suppresses audacity through fear, and sees to it that goodness is secure among the wicked. And she is the reason for which, among the wicked, there is always remorse of conscience, with the fear of justice and the expectation of that punishment which crushes proud boldness and introduces humble consent, with its eight servants, which are talion, prison, blows, exile, ignominy, servitude, poverty, and death.

Jove has placed her in heaven and exalted her with this condition: that she allow that the powerful be not secure because of their pre-eminence and power; but that by referring all to greater providence and superior law (through which civil law is regulated, as is the divine and natural), she make it understood that for those who come out of spiders' webs there are ordained nets, cords, chains, and fetters, since by decree of Eternal Law it is sanctioned that the most powerful be most powerfully compressed and bound, if not under one mantle and inside of one cell, then under another mantle and within another cell, which will be worse.[3]

Then he ordained and enjoined her that she deal with and be especially rigorous regarding things for which, from the beginning and first and principal cause, she has been ordained (concerning, that is to say, whatever appertains to the communion of men, to civilized behavior), in order that the potent be sustained by the impotent, the weak be not oppressed by the stronger; that tyrants be deposed, just rulers and realms be constituted and strengthened, republics be favored; that violence not tread upon reason, ignorance not despise knowledge; that the poor be aided by the rich; that virtues and studies, useful and necessary to the commonwealth, be promoted, advanced, and maintained, and that those be exalted and remunerated who profited from them; and that the indolent, the avaricious, and the owners of property be scorned and held in contempt.[4]

Let there be preserved the fear and the cult of invisible powers, and honor, reverence, and respect toward our proximate living rulers. Let no one be placed in power who himself is not superior in merits through the virtue and the intelligence in which he may prevail, either by himself, which is rare and almost impossible, or even through the communication and counsel of others, which is proper, ordinary, and necessary.

Jove has given Law the power to bind, which will consist chiefly in this: that she will not become such as to incur contempt and indignity, which she might encounter by directing her steps along two paths, of which one is that of iniquity, by commanding and proposing unjust things, the other, that of difficulty, by proposing and commanding things, which are both impossible and unjust. So that, therefore, two are the hands by which she has the power to bind every law; one is that of justice, the other is that of possibility. And of these the one is moderated by the other, since, although many things are possible which are not just, nothing is just which cannot be possible.

SAUL. You say well, oh Sophia, that no law that is not adjusted to the experience of human society must be accepted. Jove has well disposed of and ordered her; because whether it descends from heaven or arises from the earth, that institution or law which does not bring the utility and convenience that lead us to an excellent end must be neither approved nor accepted. We cannot conceive a greater end than that which so directs minds and reforms inclinations that from them are produced fruits useful and necessary to human behavior. For certainly that must be a divine thing, art of arts and discipline of disciplines, through which men must be governed and repressed, men, who among all animals are most distinct in complexion, most varied in customs, and in inclination most divided, in wills most diverse, in impulses most inconstant.

But alas! oh Sophia, that we should have come to such a pass (who would ever have thought it possible?) that the religion considered most highly should be that which maintains that actions and good works are insignificant and lowly, and considers them errors, some saying that the gods are not concerned with good works, and that through these works, however great they may be, men do not become just.[5]

SOPHIA. Certainly, oh Saulino, I must be dreaming. I believe that what you are saying is a phantasm, a figment of a troubled brain and not a real thing; and yet, it is certain that there are such persons who propose this to the wretched people and make them believe it. But have no doubts; for the world will easily realize that this cannot be readily digested, as it will also easily understand that it cannot subsist without law and religion.

Now we have seen in some way how well Law has been ordained and placed. You must now hear on what conditions Judgment has been joined next to her. Jove has placed into the hand of Judgment the Sword and the Crown; with the latter she rewards those who do good works and abstain from evil; with the former she punishes those who are inclined toward crimes, and are useless and infrugiferous plants. He has charged Judgment with the defense of and concern with true law, and the destruction of wicked and fraudulent law dictated by geniuses who are perverse and inimical to a tranquil and happy human society; he has commanded that Judgment, together with Law, should not extinguish, but as much as possible should kindle, the appetite for glory in human hearts; for this appetite is the only, the most efficacious, spur that is wont to incite men and fire their enthusiasm for those heroic deeds which enlarge, maintain, and fortify republics.

SAUL. Our professors of false religion call all of these glories vain; they say, however, that we must glory in I know not what cabalistic tragedy.[6]

SOPHIA. Besides, he has commanded that she [Judgment] should not be concerned with what each one imagines or thinks, providing that words and deeds do not corrupt the tranquil state of affairs. She should especially turn toward improving and maintaining all that which is contained in works and judge the tree not by its beautiful leaves, but by its good fruit; and those who do not produce fruit should be driven away, and cede their place to those who yield them. She should not believe that the gods are in any way interested in those things in which no man feels himself interested, because the gods are concerned only with those things with which men can be concerned. And not by anything done or said or thought in behalf of them are they moved or angered, unless, because of that thing, the respect by which republics are maintained might be lost; since the gods would not be gods if they felt pleasure or displeasure, sadness or joy, in what men do or think; on the contrary, the former would be more wanting than the latter, or, at least, the former would receive benefit and profit from the latter, as the latter from the former.

Since the gods are removed from all passion, they, consequently, can have only active and not passive anger and pleasure; and therefore, they threaten punishment and promise reward, not for any evil or good which arises in them [men], but for that which is committed among peoples and civilized societies, which they have succored with their divine laws, human laws not being sufficient for them. Yet, it is unworthy, foolish, profane, and reprehensible to believe that the gods seek the reverence, fear, love, worship, and respect of men for any other good end and benefit than that of men themselves. Since they are glorious in themselves, and since no glory outside of themselves can add to theirs, they have instituted laws, not so much in order to receive glory, as to spread it among men. Thus the farther human laws and opinions are removed from the goodness and truth of Law and Judgment, the farther they remove themselves from regulating and approving that which is especially contained in the moral actions of men in relation to other men.

SAUL. By this ordinance of Jove's, oh Sophia, it is efficaciously demonstrated that the trees that are in the gardens of laws are ordained by the gods to bear fruits, and especially those fruits upon which men feed and nourish themselves and by which they are preserved. And it is demonstrated that the gods delight themselves with the fragrance of no other fruits than these.

SOPHIA. Listen! From this, Jove wants Judgment to infer that the gods especially want to be loved and feared for the purpose of benefiting mankind, and want to warn men especially against those vices which bring them annoyance. Internal sins, however, must be considered sins only to the extent that they produce, or could produce, an external effect; and internal justice is never justice without external practice, just as plants are plants in vain without producing fruits either in the present or in expectation. And he wants us to know that, in comparison with others, those errors are the greatest which have a prejudicial effect upon the republic; that those prejudicial to a particular and interested party are lesser errors; that that which occurs between two individuals in agreement with one another is the least error; and that those sins are nought which arise in the complexion of the individual from his accidental impulses, and do not proceed to set a bad example or have a bad effect. And these are the same sins which cause the eminent gods to be offended most, less, least, and not at all; and by works which are contrary to these sins, they esteem themselves served most greatly, least, or not at all.

Furthermore, Jove has commanded Judgment that in the future she approve of Repentance, but that she not place her on an equal footing with Innocence; that she approve of Belief and Respect, but never on an equal footing with Execution and Work. He proposes that she do the same regarding Confession and Discourse, with deference to Correction and Abstinence; and that she commend thoughts to the extent that they are resplendent in expressed signs and possible effects.

She should not permit that he who in vain tries to subdue his body should sit next to him who tries to discipline his mind; and she should not make a comparison between this lonely and useless man and that other who engages in profitable conversation. Let her distinguish between customs and religions, not so much because of differences in togas and garments, as because of their good and better garments of virtues and disciplines. Let her smile, not so much upon him who has restrained the fervor of his lust and who is probably impotent and cold, as upon another, who has mitigated the violence of his wrath, and who certainly is not timid, but patient. Let her applaud, not so much the man who probably has unnecessarily obligated himself not to show himself lustful, as the other man who resolves no longer to be a slanderer and malefactor. Let her not consider a proud appetite for glory, out of which there results some good for the republic, to be a greater sin than the sordid lust for money. Let her give great acclaim, not so much to one because he has healed a humble and useless lame man who, cured, is worth little, or no more than when he is infirm, as to another one who has liberated his country and reformed a perturbed spirit. She should not esteem as a heroic jest one's having been able, in some mode and some manner, to extinguish the fire of an ardent furnace, without water, as much as or more than his having extinguished the seditions of an inflamed people, without bloodshed.

May she not allow that statues be erected to good-for-nothings who are hostile to the state of republics and who, with prejudice to customs and human life, offer us words and dreams, rather than to those who raise temples to the gods, increase the cult and zeal for such a law and religion, through which are kindled magnanimity and ardor for that glory which is derived from the service to the fatherland and is to the advantage of mankind; whence there seem to have been instituted universities for the disciplines of customs, letters, and arms. And let her guard against promising love, honor, and the reward of eternal life and immortality to those who approve of pedants and prattlers, rather than to those who, by their striving toward the perfectioning of their own intellect and that of others, by their service to the community, and by their express observance of acts of magnanimity, justice, and mercy, are pleasing to the gods.

For this reason they [the gods] exalted the Roman people above others; because with their magnificent deeds they, more than the other nations, knew how to conform with and resemble them, by pardoning the subdued, overthrowing the proud,[7] righting wrongs, not forgetting kindness, helping the needy, defending the afflicted, relieving the oppressed, restraining the violent, promoting the meritorious, abasing criminals and spreading terror and the utmost destruction among them by means of scourges and axes, and honoring the gods with statues and colossi. Whence, consequently, that people appeared more bridled and restrained from vices of an uncivilized and barbarous nature, more excellent and ready to perform generous enterprises than any other people that has ever been seen. And as long as such were their law and religion, their customs and deeds, such were their honor and their happiness.

SAUL. I should like to have seen Jove ordain that Judgment take specific action against the temerity of these grammarians who in our times are fattening themselves throughout Europe.[8]

SOPHIA. Very well, oh Saulino, has Jove commanded, ordered, and enjoined that Judgment see whether it seems true to her that those men [the Calvinists] induce peoples to the contempt of, or at least to little concern for, legislators and laws, by making it clear to them that they propose impossible things, and rule as if in jest, that is to say, by letting men know that the gods well know how to command that which they cannot put into execution. Let her see whether, while they say that they want to reform the deformed laws and religions, they do not succeed in spoiling all that which is good in them, and approve and raise to the stars all that can be, or seems to be, perverse and vain in them. Let her see whether these men bring any fruits other than those used to suppress discussions, to dissipate harmony, to dissolve unity, and to cause children to rebel against their fathers, servants against their masters, subjects against their superiors; to cause schisms between peoples and peoples, nations and nations, comrades and comrades, brothers and brothers; to create division among families, cities, republics, and kingdoms.

And in conclusion, let her see whether, while they utter greetings of peace, they do not carry, wherever they enter, the Knife of Division and the Fire of Dispersion, taking away the son from his father, neighbor from neighbor, the inhabitant from his country, and causing other divorces, horrendous and against every nature and law. Let her see whether, while they call themselves ministers of one who resurrects the dead and heals the infirm, it is they who, worse than all the others whom the earth feeds, cripple the healthy and kill the living, not so much with fire and with the sword as with their pernicious tongues. Let her see what sort of peace and harmony they propose to the wretched peoples, and whether they perhaps want and eagerly desire that all the world agree with and consent to their malicious and most presumptuous ignorance, and approve their wicked conscience, while they want neither to agree with, nor consent to, any law, justice, and doctrine; and let her see whether in all the rest of the world and of the centuries there appear so much discord and dissonance as is evidenced among them.

So among ten thousand such pedants there is not one who has not compiled his own catechism, and who, if he has not published it, at least is about to publish that one which approves of no other institution but his own, finding in all the others something to condemn, reprove, and doubt; besides, the majority of them are found in disagreement among themselves, rescinding today what they wrote the day before.

Let her see what success these have, and what customs they inspire and provoke in others in that which appertains to acts of justice and compassion and the conservation and increase of public wealth. And let her see whether, through their doctrine and teaching, academies, universities, temples, hospitals, colleges, schools, and institutions of disciplines and art are erected; or whether, even where those things are found, they are not the same things established by the same faculties that were in existence before these people came and made their appearance among nations. Afterward, let her see whether, because of their concern, these things have increased or, rather, because of their negligence, have decreased, fallen into decay, dissolution, and dispersion. Furthermore, let her see whether they are the appropriators of the goods of others or, rather, the bestowers of their own goods; and, finally, let her see whether those who side with them increase and stabilize public wealth, as their opponents and predecessors used to do, or, rather, together with these, dissipate, dismember, and devour it; and whether, while they belittle good works, they extinguish in people all enthusiasm for the construction of new works and the preservation of the old.

Jove commands that if what they [the Calvinists] say is true (and they are so persuaded and convinced of it), and if after they are warned, revealing themselves incorrigible, they stand firm on their feet of Obstinacy, Judgment should, under penalty of disgrace and losing of that rank and pre-eminence she holds in heaven, dissipate, scatter, and annihilate them; and that she, by the use of any kind of force, power, and industry, should extinguish the very memory of the name of such a pestiferous germ. And to this he adds that she should make known to all the generations of the world that they, under penalty of their destruction, must arm themselves in favor of that Judgment until such time as there shall be fully put into execution Jove's decree against this blot upon humanity.

SAUL. I believe, oh Sophia, that Jove will not ultimately want so rigidly to dissolve this wretched kind of men, and will not begin to affect them in such a manner, meting out final ruin to them, until he has tried to correct them and, by making them aware of their curse and error, provoke them to repentance.

SOPHIA. Yes, it is well. Jove, however, has ordered Judgment to proceed in that manner which I prescribe. He wants them to be deprived of all those properties[9] that those who used to preach, praise, and teach good works had acquired, which were left and set in order by those who used to labor and had confidence in good works, and were established by those who believed that by those works, benefits, and legacies they would become pleasing to the gods.

And so let them still execrate the fruits of those trees which issue forth from that seed so hateful to them; and let them maintain, preserve, defend, and nourish themselves solely on those fruits, on those incomes and aids which those who believe, approve, and defend this opinion bring and have brought to them. And, furthermore, let it not be lawful for them to occupy by rapine and violent usurpation, by expedients contrary to a contrary end, that which, to common utility, the others, with a free and grateful mind, have generated and sown. And so let them depart from those profaned dwellings and not eat of that accursed bread; but let them go and inhabit those pure and uncontaminated houses and feed upon those victuals that have been destined to them by means of their reformed law,[10] and recently brought forth by these pious individuals—they who hold completed works in such low esteem, and only because of an importune, vile, and foolish imagination consider themselves rulers of heaven and children of the gods, and believe more in, and attribute more to, a vain, bovine, and asinine faith than to a useful, real, and magnanimous effect.

SAUL. Soon, oh Sophia, it will be seen how capable of earning an inch of land for themselves these [Calvinists] are, who are so effusive and prodigal in giving away kingdoms of heavens, and it will be known of these rulers of the empyrean heaven how liberally they, who perhaps because of the little faith they have in works of charity, will reduce their Mercuries, their celestial messengers, made of their own substance, to the necessity of going to work the fields or of pursuing another trade. These [the Calvinists], without otherwise puzzling their brains, reassure the others concerning I do not know what justice of another [Christ] that has become their own. They tell them that because of the purity and justice of this man alone they [the Calvinists] will be forgiven, they who are dismayed because of the assassinations, rapine, violence, and homicides that they may have committed, and who do not at all confide, rely, and have hope in acts of charity, liberality, compassion, and justice.

SOPHIA. How is it possible, oh Saulino, that consciences so affected can ever have a true love of doing good, and a true repentance and fear of committing any kind of ribaldry, if for committed errors they are so reassured, and regarding acts of justice are thrown into such doubt?

SAUL. You see the effects, Sophia; for it is a true and certain thing, as they are true and certain, that when a man changes from any other belief and faith to this one, he, from one who was once liberal, becomes avaricious; he, from one who was once gentle, becomes insolent. You see him change from humble to proud; from a donor he becomes a robber and usurper of other peoples' wealth; from a good man he becomes a hypocrite; from a sincere man he becomes wicked; from a simple man he becomes cunning; from a grateful man he becomes most arrogant; from one who is capable of some goodness and learning, he becomes prone to every kind of ignorance and ribaldry; and in conclusion, from one who was capable of being bad, he has become so very bad that he could not be worse.

SECOND PART
OF THE *Second Dialogue*

SOPHIA. Now let us continue the discussion that was interrupted yesterday by the arrival of Mercury.

SAUL. It is high time that after the reason has been given for the collocation and the placement of the good divinities in the places where those beasts used to be, we examine those who were ordained to succeed to the places of the others, and, if it pleases you, let it not be burdensome to you always to let me know the reason and cause. We had yesterday reached the point in our narration where we saw how Father Jove had dispatched Hercules; and, consequently, we must first see who it is Jove has allowed to be his successor.

SOPHIA. I, oh Saulino, have in reality understood that there occurred in heaven as regards the debate among Wealth, Pleasure, Sanity, and Strength more than that which Crantor [1] sees in phantasy, in dreams, in shadows, and in the spirit of prophecy. For when Jove had excluded Hercules from heaven, Wealth quickly came forward and said: "This is a fitting place for me, oh Father." To which Jove answered, "For what reason?" And she replied: "I am rather amazed that you have so long deferred placing me, and that before remembering me you not only gave seats to other goddesses and divinities, who should yield to me, but besides have maintained that it was necessary that I myself come to oppose and stand against the harm and wrong you do me."

And Jove replied: "Do you plead your case, Wealth, although I do not think that I have wronged you by not giving you one of the seats already provided for. Nor do I believe that I am doing you an injustice by denying you this seat, which is to be decided upon; and perhaps, indeed, you may become aware of something worse than you expect."

"And what worse could and must befall me, in your judgment, than that which has befallen me," retorted Wealth. "Tell me, for what reason have you preferred Truth, Prudence, Sophia, Law, and Judgment, if I am she by virtue of whom Truth is esteemed, Prudence is dispensed, Sophia is valued, Law reigns, Judgment disposes, and without whom Truth is worthless, Prudence is wretched, Sophia is neglected, Law is mute, Judgment is lame? Why do I give space to the first, give fiber to the second, light to the third, authority to the fourth, strength to the fifth, jocundity, beauty, and ornament to all of them together, and liberate them from trouble and misery?"

Replied Momus: "Oh Wealth, you speak the truth no more than falsehood; for you are also she because of whom Judgment limps, Law maintains silence, Sophia is trampled upon, Prudence is incarcerated, and Truth is humiliated, when you become the companion of liars and ignoramuses, when you, with the arm of chance, favor madness, when you kindle and make minds captives to pleasures, when you minister to violence, when you resist justice.

"And, afterward, you bring him who possesses you no less trouble than jocundity, no less deformity than beauty, no less ugliness than ornament; and you are not that one who puts an end to troubles and misery, but that one who modifies and changes them into other species. Indeed, according to opinion you are good, but in truth you are, rather, wicked; in appearance you are dear, but in existence, worthless. According to the imagination you are useful, but in effect you are most pernicious; since, according to your teaching, when you invest a certain perverse person with yourself (for ordinarily I always see you in the house of wicked people, rarely in the vicinity of good men), you have, down there on earth, caused Truth to be banished out of the cities into the deserts, have broken the legs of Prudence, have embarrassed Sophia, have shut the mouth of Law, have deprived Judgment of courage, and have made all most cowardly."

"And in this, oh Momus," answered Wealth, "you are able to recognize my power and excellence: that I, by opening and closing my fist and by imparting myself here or there, make it possible for these five divinities to prevail, to have power, and to act, or, indeed, on the other hand, for them to be scorned, banished, and rejected; and, frankly speaking, I can chase them into heaven or hell."

Here Jove answered: "We want only good divinities in heaven and in these seats. Let those divinities who are wicked be driven away from here, both those who are more evil than good and those who are indifferently good and evil, among whom I believe you belong, you who are good with good people and very bad with the wicked."

"You know, oh Jove," answered Wealth, "that in myself I am good and am not in myself indifferent or neutral, or of the one and the other kind, as you say, except inasmuch as others want to use me well or badly."

Here Momus made answer: "You then, oh Wealth, are a manageable goddess, serviceable, tractable, and do not govern by yourself, and are not really that one who governs and disposes of others. But you are she of whom others dispose, and who is governed by others; whereupon you are good when others manage you well, bad when you are badly guided. You are, I say, good in the hands of Justice, Sophia, Prudence, Religion, Law, Liberality, and other divinities; you are wicked if their opposites manage you, such as Violence, Avarice, Ignorance, and others. Since, then, you are in yourself neither good nor bad, so I believe, if Jove consents, that you in yourself have neither shame nor honor; and that, consequently, you do not deserve to have your own seat either on high, among the heavenly gods and divinities, or below, among the infernal deities, but deserve to wander eternally from place to place and from region to region."

All the gods laughed upon hearing the words of Momus, and Jove pronounced the following sentence: "Indeed, Wealth, when you belong to Justice, you shall reside in the seat of Justice; when you belong to Truth, you shall reside in the seat of that goddess' excellence; when you belong to Wisdom or Sophia, you shall sit on her throne; when you belong to voluptuary pleasures, you shall be found where they are; when you belong to gold and silver, then hide yourself in money bags and coffers; when you belong to wine, oil, and grain, then bury yourself in cellars and storehouses; when you belong to sheep, goats, and oxen, then go graze with them and lie with the flocks and herds."

So Jove ordained what she must do when she is with madmen, how she must behave when in the homes of the wise, and how she should in the future, as she has done in the past (perhaps because it cannot be helped), allow herself to be found easily in a certain guise and with difficulty in another guise. But he did not make his motive and manner of reasoning understandable to many. Momus, however, raised his voice and gave them another reason, which, if it was not that very same reason, was as follows: "May no one be able to find you, unless he has repented for having had a good mind and a sound brain." I believe that he meant by this that one must lose his reflection and prudent judgment, must never think of the uncertainty and treachery of the times, must have no fear of the dubious and unstable promise of the sea, must not believe in Heaven, must have no interest in justice or injustice, honor or shame, calm or tempest, but entrust all to Fortune.

"And may you beware [continued Momus] of ever becoming friendly with those men of too much judgment, who seek you; and may those men see you less who pursue you with more snares, traps, and nets of providence. But may you ordinarily go there where are found the most senseless, mad, negligent, and foolish men. And, in conclusion, when you are on earth may you beware of the wisest, as you would of fire; and thus may you always approach and become familiar with semi-bestial people, and always follow the same rule as Fortune."

SAUL. It is customary, oh Sophia, that the wisest persons are not the richest, either because they are satisfied with little, and consider that little a great deal, if it is sufficient for preserving life. Or, perhaps, it is for other reasons, such as this: that while they are intent upon more worthy enterprises, they do not go wandering too much to and fro in order to meet one of these divinities, Wealth or Fortune. But, pursue your discussion.

SOPHIA. As soon as Poverty saw Wealth, her enemy, excluded, she came forward with a more than poor grace and said that for the very reason which made Wealth unworthy of that seat she should, because she was her antagonist, be esteemed most deserving of it.

To this, Momus replied: "Poverty, Poverty, you would not be completely Poverty, if you were not still so poor in arguments, syllogisms, and good consequences. Not because you are her opposite, wretched one, does it follow that you must be invested with that of which she is despoiled or deprived, and that you should be that very thing which she is not. As for instance (since it is necessary that you be given to understand by means of example), you must be Jove and Momus, because she is neither Jove nor Momus. And in conclusion, that which we deny about her should be affirmed about you, because those who are richer than you in dialectic know that contraries are not the same as positives and privatives, contradictories, variants, differentials, otherness, separateness, distinctness, and diversity. They know also that by reason of your being opposites, it follows that you cannot be together in the same place; but it does not follow that where she is not and cannot be, you must or can be." [2]

At this point all the gods laughed when they saw that Momus wanted to instruct Poverty in logic; and this proverb has remained in heaven: "Momus is Poverty's teacher, or rather, Momus instructs Poverty in dialectic." And this they say whenever they want to deride a fact counter to the fact.

"What then do you think should be done with me, oh Momus?" asked Poverty. "Determine immediately; for I am not so rich in words and ideas that I could dispute with Momus, nor so abundant in intelligence that I could learn much from him."

Then Momus asked Jove whether he would for that occasion give him permission to make a decree. To this Jove replied: "Are you not still mocking me, oh Momus, you who alone have so much license that you are more licentious (he meant to say licensed) than all the rest? Do indeed pronounce sentence upon that one without fear, because if it is a good one, we shall approve it."

Then Momus said: "It still seems to me congruous and fitting that Poverty should go walking through those squares on which Wealth is seen wandering, that she run back and forth, and that she come and go through the same countryside; for (as the canons of ratiocination require), by reason of such contraries, she should enter only those places whence the other takes flight, and must succeed the other only into places which she leaves; and Wealth must only succeed to and enter places whence Poverty departs and flees. And let the one always be at the other's shoulder, and let the one shove the other, never touching her face to face; but where one has her breath, let the other have her back, as if they were playing (as we sometimes do) the game *la rota del scarpone*." [3]

SAUL. What did Jove and the others say concerning this?

SOPHIA. All confirmed and ratified the sentence.

SAUL. What did Poverty say?

SOPHIA. She said: "It does not seem just to me, oh gods (if indeed my opinion is valid and I am not completely deprived of judgment), that my condition should be at all similar to that of Wealth." To which Momus answered: "Proceeding from the antecedent that the same tragedy or comedy is being directed and acted in the same theater, you must not draw the conclusion that you will be of the same condition, quia contraria versantur circa idem." "I see, oh Momus," said Poverty, "that you mock me, that even you, who profess to speak the truth and to speak ingenuously, do belittle me. And this does not seem to me to be your duty, because Poverty is sometimes, rather most of the time, more worthily defended than Wealth."

"What can I do for you," replied Momus, "if you are poor, altogether poor? Poverty is not worthy of defense, if she is poor in judgment, in reason, in merits and syllogisms, such as you are, you who have compelled me to speak again according to the analytical laws regarding the *Prior Analytics* and *Posterior Analytics* of Aristotle." [4]

SAUL. What are you telling me, Sophia? The gods then sometimes reach for Aristotle? And they, for example, study the philosophers?

SOPHIA. I shall not speak to you further about what is said of Pippa, Nanna, Antonia, Burchiello, the *Ancroia,* and about another book whose author is unknown, but which is in question as to whether it is Ovid's or Virgil's; and I do not remember its name, nor those of similar works.[5]

SAUL. And even now, they deal with such weighty and serious matters?

SOPHIA. And does it seem to you that those matters are not serious, are not weighty? Saulino, if you were more of a philosopher, I say more sagacious, you would believe that there is no lesson, no book, that is not examined by the gods, that, if it is not altogether without salt, is not used by the gods and that, if it is not altogether senseless, will not be approved and chained to the shelves of a public library. For they take delight in the multiform representation of all things and in the multiform fruit of all minds, because they are pleased with all things that exist and with all representations that are made; they are no less concerned that these should exist, and give orders and permission that they be made. And you, ponder on the fact that the judgment of the gods is otherwise than that of our common judgment; and not all that is sinful to us and according to us is sinful to them and according to them. Certainly those books as well as those theologies must not be common among ignorant men, who are, themselves, wicked; for which reason they obtain wicked instruction from them.

SAUL. Now, are there not books written, perhaps for an evil purpose, by men of bad repute who are dishonest and dissolute?

SOPHIA. It is true. But they are not without the instruction and the fruits of the cognition of that one who writes, who has the cognition of how he writes, of why and whence he writes, of what he speaks, of how he speaks of it, of how he is deceived, of how others are mistaken about him, of how he declines from, and inclines toward, a virtuous or wicked affect, of how laughter, vexation, pleasure, and nausea are aroused. And in all there is wisdom and prudence; and in everything there is everything; and especially, where the one contrary is, there is the other; and the latter is derived from the former.

SAUL. Now let us return to the discussion from which the name of Aristotle and the fame of Pippa diverted us. How was Poverty dismissed by Jove, after having been so scorned by Momus?

SOPHIA. I do not wish to refer to all the ridiculous discussion that took place between Momus and her, who knew how to "Momus" him no less than he, to "Momus" her. Jove declared that Poverty had certain privileges and prerogatives in these matters, which the other [Wealth] does not possess down here.

SAUL. Tell me what those things are.

SOPHIA. Said the father, "I want you, Poverty, first to be circumspect, to know how to return easily to that place from which you once departed, and to drive away Wealth, with your utmost strength; I want, on the other hand, that you be driven away by her, whom I wish to be perpetually blind. Then I want you, Poverty, to be winged, dexterous, and swift, with feathers fashioned like those of an eagle or vulture; but in your feet, I want you to be like an old ox who drags the heavy plough with which he digs deeply into the veins of the earth. And Wealth, on the contrary, should have slow and heavy wings, adapting to herself the wings of a goose or swan; but her feet should be those of the swiftest steed or deer, so that when she takes flight from some place, using her feet, you by beating your wings will present yourself there. And that place whence you remove yourself by the employment of your wings, I want her to be able to reach by the use of her feet, so that you, with the same swiftness by which you will be put to flight or pursued by her, will pursue and put her to flight.

SAUL. Why does he not make both strong of wing or both strong of foot? If nothing else, they could agree to pursue and put each other to flight, either slowly or rapidly.

SOPHIA. Because Wealth, always traveling with a load, will in some way impede her wings by her load; and Poverty, always walking barefoot, because of rugged paths will easily receive injuries to her feet. However, the latter would in vain have swift feet, and the former, speedy wings.

SAUL. This resolution satisfies me. Now continue.

SOPHIA. Besides, Jove especially wants Poverty to follow Wealth, and that she [Poverty] be driven away by her when she frequents earthly palaces and those seats where Fortune holds sway. "But [said Jove] [6] when she attaches herself to things that are lofty and removed from the wrath of time and of that blind lady, I do not want her to have such great daring or strength as to assault her in order to drive her away and to deprive her of her place. For I do not want her to depart with ease from that place whither one must arrive by means of difficulty and dignity.

"And so you [Poverty], on the other hand, show that firmness in regard to inferior things that she [Wealth] may have in regard to superior things. Rather," added Jove, "I want that, in some manner, there be between you some agreement, not one of a light nature, but one of the utmost importance. I say this so that you may not think that by being expelled from heaven, you will again be relegated to hell, any more than that you may think that, on the contrary, by being driven out of hell, you will be placed in heaven, so that the status of Wealth, of which I have already spoken, will be incomparably better than yours. However, I want the possibility to be very remote that the one might drive away the other from the seat of her greatest dominion; but rather I want one to maintain and interest herself in behalf of the other, so that between you there may be the closest friendship and familiarity."

SAUL. Let me know quickly how this could be.

SOPHIA. Jove said, adding to what he had already said, "You, Poverty, when you are a part of inferior beings, will not be permitted to be joined, bound, and locked to Wealth in superior things, just as your contrary, Wealth, could not be joined, bound, and locked to you in inferior things; because no one who is wise and wishes to know will ever deem it possible to associate himself with great things in the company of the latter, inasmuch as riches offer an impediment to philosophy, and Poverty gives us a sure and expeditious path. Then, since there cannot be contemplation where a throng of many servants stands about, where the multitude of debtors and creditors, the computations of merchants, the arguments of husbandmen, the feeding of so many ill-bred stomachs, the intrigues of so many thieves, the eyes of avid tyrants, and the exactions of treacherous ministers are importune (so that no one can relish that which is the spirit of tranquillity unless he be poor or similar to a poor man), I want that man to be great who in his poverty is rich because he is content; and I want that man to be a cowardly slave who in his wealth is poor because he is not satisfied.

"You shall be secure and tranquil, she, confused, solicitous, suspicious, and restless; you shall be greater and more magnificent by showing contempt for her than she can ever be by valuing and esteeming herself. In order that you be satisfied, I want opinion alone to suffice; but I do not want the possession of all things to be enough to make her satisfied. I want you to be greater by subtracting from your desires than the other can be by adding to her possessions. I want your friends to be revealed to you, that one's enemies, concealed from her. I want you to be rich according to the law of Nature, her, with all her studies and refined pursuits, to be very poor; because it is not that man who has little who is really poor, but he who desires much. For you (if you fasten tightly the sack of cupidity), the necessary will be a great deal, and a little will be sufficient; and may nothing be enough for her, although she may seize everything with outstretched hands. You, by suppressing your desire, will be able to contend with Jove in happiness; and may she, by widening the fringes of her concupiscence, sink more and more into the abyss of miseries." When Jove had completed Poverty's expulsion, she, very satisfied, asked leave to go on her way; and Wealth made a sign of again wanting to approach Jove in order to petition the council with some other new proposal; but she was not allowed to speak further.

"Away! Away!" said Momus to her. "Do you not hear all who are calling you, shouting for you, begging you, sacrificing to you, lamenting you, and appealing to you with such loud prayers and cries that they have by now deafened us all? And you go about tarrying so long and running to and fro in these parts? Depart at once and go to the devil, since you do not want to leave with our blessings!" "Do not interfere in this matter, oh Momus," said Father Jove; "let her leave and go whenever it seems to her she should and when it pleases her to do so." "Truly," said Momus, "she seems to me a creature deserving both of pity and of a kind of severity on the part of that one who can, but does not, provide against her going less frequently to whosoever calls and recalls her more, and approaching less frequently him who deserves her more." "I want what Fate wants," said Jove.

SAUL. Momus should have said, "Do otherwise."

SOPHIA. "I want her [continued Jove] to be deaf concerning things down there on earth, and never to respond or come when she is called, but, guided by Destiny or Fortune, to go about groping blindly to communicate with him who will come to meet her from among the multitude." "Then it will come to pass," said Saturn, "that she will more readily communicate with one of the wicked good-for-nothings and thieves, whose number equals that of the grains of sand, rather than with one who is a mediocre man of worth; and she would preferably communicate with one of these mediocre men, who are many, than with those more outstanding men, who are very few, and perhaps never, most certainly never, with one who is more deserving than the others, and is a unique individual."

SAUL. What did Jove say to this?

SOPHIA. [He said] "It is necessary that it be so. This condition was imposed upon Poverty by Fate: that she be summoned longingly by very rare and very few individuals, but that she communicate with and present herself to very many, and to the greatest multitude. May Wealth, on the contrary, who is called, desired, invoked, adored, and awaited by almost all, go and make herself abundantly accessible to a very rare number of people and to those who do not even cultivate and await her. May she be totally deaf so that she will not be moved, no matter how great the noise and clamor; and may she be so stubborn and strong that she, dragged by hooks and windlasses, will hardly be brought close to him who pursues her. And may the other be so attentive, so swift, and so ready that she will immediately answer and be present at the slightest whistle or signal, no matter from what distant part she is called, and even besides, when she ordinarily finds herself at the home of one and behind one who not only does not summon her but even most diligently hides himself from her."

While Wealth and Poverty were yielding, Momus said: "Say there, what shadow is that which is familiar with those two opposites, and which is both with Wealth and with Poverty? I am accustomed to seeing different shadows from one and the same body; but never until now have I noticed the same shadow from different bodies." To which Apollo answered: "Where there is no light, all is a shadow. If they [bodies] are without light (notwithstanding the fact that there are several shadows), they commingle and become one, just as when there are many lights, unless the density of an opaque body blocks them or interposes itself all concur to form one splendor." "Here," said Momus, "it does not seem to me to be so; because where Wealth is, and Poverty is completely excluded, and where Poverty is suppositively distinct from Wealth, one sees that shadow as a shadow that is with the one and with the other, not as two lights concurring in one illuminable subject."

"Look well at it, oh Momus," said Mercury, "and you will see that it is not one shadow." "I did not say it is one shadow," answered Momus, "but that it is joined to those two divinities as one and the same shadow to two bodies. Oh, I am considering it now. It seems to me that it is Avarice who is a shadow, that she is both the darkness that is in Wealth and the darkness that is in Poverty." "So it is," said Mercury. "She is Poverty's daughter and companion, most inimical to her mother, and takes flight from her as frequently as she can. She is enamored of, and attracted to, Wealth, and although joined to Wealth, always feels the severity of her mother, who torments her. And although she is close to her [Wealth], she is far from her; and although she is far from her, she is close to her; because even if she removes herself from her, she is, according to Truth, intrinsic to her and joined to her, according to opinion.

"And do you not see that since she is a companion of Wealth and close to her, she causes Wealth to be unlike Wealth, and being removed from Poverty, causes Poverty to be unlike Poverty? This darkness, this obscurity, this shadow, is that which causes Poverty to be bad and prevents Wealth from being good; and she is not found without rendering one of the two, or both, wicked. Very rarely is it that neither the one nor the other is made wicked; and this occurs when they are surrounded on all sides by the light of reason and intellect." Now Momus asked Mercury to explain to him how she prevented Wealth from being Wealth. To him he replied that the wealthy, avaricious man is most poor; because Avarice is not found where there are riches unless also present is Poverty, who is no less truly present therein by virtue of affect than she is by virtue of effect. So this shadow, in spite of herself, can remove herself no less from her mother than from herself."

While the gods discussed this matter, Momus, who is not without very good sight (although he does not always see things at first glance), after having given closer attention to the shadow, said:

"Oh Mercury, that which I told you seemed to me to be like a shadow, I now see as so many beasts herded together; for I see it as being canine, porcine, ram-like, monkey-like, ursine, aquiline, deer-like, falcon-like, leonine, asinine and as all the 'ines' and 'likes' that ever were. So many beasts, and yet there is but one body. It certainly appears to me to be the pantomorphosis of brute animals." "Better say," retorted Mercury, "that it is a multiform beast. It seems one and is one; but it is not uniform, since it is the nature of vices to have many forms, so that they are shapeless and, in contrast to virtues, have no faces of their own. Likewise you see that her enemy, Liberality, is simple and one, that Justice is one and simple; and, as you see, health is one, and diseases innumerable."

While Mercury was saying this, Momus interrupted his discussion and said to him: "I see that she, in her accursedness, has three heads. I thought, oh Mercury, that my sight was disturbed when upon this beast's single body I beheld one head, another, and still another; but when, turning my gaze in every direction I saw that there was nothing else that appeared to me to be similar to her, I concluded that she was nothing else but that one whom I see." "You see very well," replied Mercury. "Of those three heads, one is Illiberality, another is Dishonest Profit, the other is Tenacity." Momus asked whether those heads spoke. And Mercury answered that they did, and that the first says: "It is better to be richer than to be considered more liberal and more pleasing"; that the second says: "Do not die of hunger in order to be a gentleman"; and that the third says: "If it is not honorable, it is useful to me." "And yet they do not have more than two arms?" queried Momus. "Two hands suffice," answered Mercury, "of which the right is open, very wide open, so that it can grasp; the other hand is closed tight, very tight, so that it can hold and dispense things by means of distillation and alembic, without consideration of time and place, as well as without consideration of measure."

"Both you, Wealth, and you, Poverty, come closer to me," said Momus, "so that I can better see the grace of your beautiful handmaiden." This being done, Momus said: "There is one face, and yet there are many faces; there is one head, and yet there are several heads. She is a female, she is a female! She has a very small head, although her face is more than average in size; she is old, is vile, is sordid; she has a slothful countenance and is black. I see that she is wrinkled and has straight black hair, watchful eyes, an open and panting mouth, a hooked nose, and claws; and (it is amazing) that, although she is such a small animal, she has a belly so capacious, cavernous, stupid, mercenary, and servile that she bends back her head and raises it toward the stars. She digs, buries herself into the ground, and, in order to find something, bores her way into the depths of the earth; and so, turning her back to the light of day, she makes her way into subterranean passages and caves, where the difference between day and night never arrived. She is an ingrate, for whose perverse desire nothing that is given to her will be much, a great deal, or enough; and the more she fills herself, the more morose she becomes; just like the flame, which, the larger it grows, the more voracious it becomes.

"Send, send away, and drive, immediately drive away, oh Jove, both Poverty and Wealth from these regions; and do not permit them to approach the abodes of the gods, unless they come without this vile and abominable beast!" Jove answered: "They will come after you and fall upon you as soon as you are disposed to receive them. For now, let them depart according to our present resolution; and let us quickly return to our task of determining which divinity will occupy this area."

And behold, as the father of the gods turns around, Fortune, on her own and with a not uncommon arrogance, impudently comes forward and says: "It is not right, oh you gods of the Council, and you, Jove, great judge, that where Poverty and Wealth speak and can be heard for so long a time, I be looked upon as pusillanimous, observing silence because of cowardice, rather than as one who presents herself before you and, with every justification, shows her resentment. I, who am so worthy and so powerful, advance Wealth, guide and move her wheresoever it seems to me I should and it pleases me to do so; and I can expel her whence I want and lead her whither I want, by effecting her succession and vicissitude in relation to Poverty.

"And everybody knows that felicity of external Goods can be ascribed no longer to Wealth, as her principle, but to me; just as the beauty of the music and the excellence of someone's harmony should not be attributed more to the lyre and to the instrument than to the art and to the artist who produces them. I am that divine and excellent goddess so much longed for, so sought after, and so dearly treasured, for whom most of the time thanks are given to Jove, from whose open hand proceed riches, and because of whose clenched palms all the world weeps, and cities, kingdoms, and empires are overthrown. Who ever offers prayers to Wealth or Poverty? Who ever thanks them? Everyone who desires and yearns for them calls upon me and invokes me, sacrifices to me; [7] whoever is satisfied by them, renders thanks unto me, shows gratitude unto Fortune. Because of Fortune, one burns aromatic herbs; because of Fortune, the altars send forth smoke.

"And I am a cause who, the more I am obscure, the more I am to be venerated and feared; the less friendly and familiar I become, the more I am desirable and appetible; for in things which are less revealed, more occult, and most secretive, there are ordinarily found more dignity and majesty. It is I who, by my brilliance, obscure virtue, blacken truth, subdue and scorn the greatest number and the best of these goddesses and gods whom I see prepared and arranged in such a manner as to form themselves into a square in heaven; and furthermore it is I, alone, who here in the presence of such and so great a Senate instill terror in all. For (although I do not have sight which can serve me), I still have ears through which I apprehend the teeth of a great number of them, chattering and clicking from the fear they conceive in my formidable presence, they who in spite of all do not lose the daring and presumption to come forward, to have themselves designated, there where it has not first been decreed by my authority, by which I, often, nay more than often, hold sway over Reason, Truth, Sophia, Justice, and other divinities. These, if they do not want to deny that which is most evident to the entire universe, will be able to say whether they can render an account of the number of times that I have thrown them down from their chairs of learning, benches, and tribunals, and, for my own purpose, have repressed, bound, shut in, and incarcerated them. And again, thanks to me, they then and on other occasions have been able to sally forth, to free, to re-establish, and to re-strengthen themselves, never without fear of misfortunes from me."

Momus said: "Commonly, oh blind lady, all the other gods expect for themselves the reward of these seats for the good works they have done, are doing, and can do. And for such [good works] the Senate has proposed to reward those people; and you, while you plead your case, produce the list and the proceedings of those crimes of yours, for which you should be banned not only from heaven but from earth as well."

Fortune replied that she was no less good than other good ones; and if she was so, she was not wicked; for whatever Fate decrees is all good; and if her nature were the same as that of the viper, which is naturally poisonous, this would not be her fault but the fault of Nature, or of another who made her so. Furthermore, nothing is absolutely bad; for the viper is not deadly and poisonous to the viper; nor the dragon, the lion, and the bear, to the bear, to the lion, to the dragon. But each thing is bad in respect to something else. "Just as you, virtuous gods, are bad in respect to those who are corrupt," said Fortune, "so those who believe in day and light are bad in respect to those who believe in night and obscurity. And you are good among yourselves, and they are good among themselves; just as now happens among sects of the world, hostile to one another, where the opponents call themselves children of the gods and just; and these, no less than the others, call the most outstanding and honored men the worst and most reprobate of men. I, Fortune, then, although in the opinion of some am a reprobate, in the opinion of others am divinely good; and it is the judgment, approved by the greater part of the world, that the fortune of men is suspended from heaven; whence it is said that there is no star, tiny or great, that appears in the firmament of which I do not dispose." [8]

Here Mercury answered, saying that too often her name was taken equivocally; for, sometimes, by Fortune we mean only an uncertain turn of events, which uncertainty in the eyes of Providence is nothing, although it is of the greatest importance in the eyes of mortals. Fortune did not hear this, but continued talking, and to what she had said, added that the most remarkable and excellent philosophers of the world, such as Empedocles and Epicurus, attribute more to her than to Jove himself, rather, more to her than to the entire Council of the gods put together. "So," she continued, "all others consider me both a goddess and a celestial goddess, according to this verse, which I believe is not new to your ears (and there is no primer which does not relate it), and which declares as follows: "Te facimus, Fortuna, deam, caeloque locamus.' [9] ('Fortune, we make you a goddess, and place you in heaven.')

"And I want you to know, oh gods, with how much justification I am called mad, foolish, rash, by some, whereas it is they who are so mad, so foolish, so rash, that they cannot adduce an explanation for my being. And where I find those who are esteemed more learned than the others, who do in effect demonstrate and conclude to the contrary, when they are compelled to do so by truth, they say that I am irrational and am without discourse, although they do not, because of this, consider me brutal and foolish; because by such a negation they do not want to detract from me, but rather attribute more to me, just as I sometimes want to deny small things in order that I may concede greater things. I am understood by them, not as one who is reasonable and who operates by reason and with reason, but rather as one who is beyond all reason, beyond all discourse, and beyond all intelligence. I even say that, in effect, people are aware and do confess that I especially obtain and exercise rule and dominion over those who are rational, intelligent, and divine. And there is no wise man who will say that I affect with my authority things deprived of reason and intellect, such as stones, beasts, children, the insane, and others who have no apprehension of final cause, and who do not know how to work toward a goal."

"I shall tell you, oh Fortune," said Minerva, "why you are said to be without discourse and reason. He who lacks a certain sense lacks some knowledge, and especially that knowledge which is dependent upon that sense. Now, take yourself into consideration, you who are deprived of the light of eyes, which are the greatest source of knowledge." Fortune answered that Minerva either was deceiving herself or wanted to deceive Fortune, and was confident of doing so, because she saw that the other was blind. "But although I am deprived of my eyes, I am not deprived of ears and intellect," said Fortune to her.

SAUL. And do you think that this is true, oh Sophia?

SOPHIA. Listen and you will see how she is able to distinguish philosophies and how they are not occult to her, Aristotle's *Metaphysics* [10] among other things. "I know," she said, "that there are those who say that sight is most to be desired for acquiring knowledge; but never did I know a man so foolish who asserted that it is chiefly sight that enables us to understand. And when someone said that sight was most to be desired, he meant to say, however, that it was necessary only for the cognition of certain things, such as colors, figures, corporeal symmetries, beauties, charms, and other visible things, which are rather wont to disturb the imagination and alienate the intellect, but was not absolutely necessary for all or the best species of cognition. For he knew very well that many, in order to become wise, have plucked out their eyes, and that of those who have been blind, by accident or by nature, many are considered most admirable, among whom I could show you many Democrituses, many Tiresiuses, many Homers, and many like the blind man of Adria.[11]

"Then I want you to understand, if you are Minerva, that when a certain Stagirite philosopher said that sight is most to be desired for the acquisition of knowledge, he was not comparing sight with other means of acquiring knowledge, such as hearing, cogitation, and intellect, but was making a comparison between this end of sight, which is knowledge, and any other end that sight might set forth for itself. However, if it does not displease you to go to the Elysian Fields to speak to him (providing he has not made his departure for another life and drunk of the waters of Lethe), you will see that he will make this comment: 'We desire sight chiefly for the purpose of knowing,' and not the other comment: 'Of all the other senses, we desire sight chiefly for the acquisition of knowledge.' "

SAUL. It is wondrous, oh Sophia, that Fortune should be able to discuss and to understand texts better than Minerva, who is pre-eminent in this intelligence.

SOPHIA. Do not be amazed. For when you will have seriously considered them and when you will have frequented and very attentively conversed with them, you will have found that those gods who are graduates in the sciences, in eloquence and laws, are not more judicious, not wiser, and not more eloquent than the others.

Now, Fortune, to continue the discussion concerning her cause, which she was defending before the Senate, speaking to all, said: "My blindness deprives me of nothing, of nothing at all, oh gods, of nothing that is of value, of nothing that is necessary for the perfectioning of my being; for if I were not blind, I should not be Fortune. Rather than that you should be able to diminish or attenuate the glory of my merits because of this blindness, it is I, who from the very thing whence I draw the argument in favor of the greatness and excellence of the above-mentioned men shall succeed in convincing you that I, by that blindness, am less attracted by acts of self-interest and cannot be unjust in my distributions." Said Mercury to Minerva: "You will not have done little, when you have demonstrated this."

And Fortune continued: "For my justice, it is fitting to be so. For true justice the function of sight is not necessary, is not suitable, is rather repugnant and offensive. The eyes are made for distinguishing and recognizing differences (although I do not want now to demonstrate how often those who judge are deceived by their sight).

"I am a kind of justice who does not have to distinguish, who does not have to differentiate; but just like all beings I am principally, truly, and finally one entity, one and the same thing (for the entity, the one, and the true are the same). So I am compelled to put all beings on a basis of a certain equality: to esteem all alike, to consider all things one, not to be more inclined to look upon one being, not to be more inclined to call upon one being rather than another and to be more favorably disposed toward giving to one rather than to another, and to be more favorable toward one who is near rather than toward one who is far away. I do not perceive miters, togas, crowns, knowledge, and intelligence, do not discern merits and demerits. Because even if those things are found, they are not things that are of a nature that is one thing in this, and another in another, but rather, most certainly, because of circumstances, occasion, or accident that offers itself, of a nature that meets and flows in this thing or that. And therefore, when I give, I do not see the person to whom I am giving; when I take from someone, I do not see him from whom I take, so that in this manner I may succeed in treating all equally and without any distinction whatsoever. And in this way I do indeed succeed in understanding and doing all things fairly and justly, and dispense to all justly and fairly.

"I put all beings into one urn, and in its most capacious stomach, blend, mix, and stir them. Then it is the game of *zara* as to whose lot it is.[12] And it is well for him whose lot is good, and it is unfortunate for him whose lot is bad! In this manner, within the urn of Fortune the greatest being is no different from the smallest. There, rather, all beings are equally great and equally small, because difference in them is understood by another, rather than by me, before they enter the urn and after they leave the urn. While they are within, all are tossed around by the same hand, in the same vase, and by the same shake. Therefore, after the lots are drawn, it is not reasonable that he whom ill luck befalls complain either of whosoever holds the urn or of the urn itself, either of its movement or of her who puts her hand into it. But he must, with the best and greatest patience of which he is capable, bear with what Fate has decreed, with how it has decreed it or with how it is disposed to decree it, inasmuch as he was inscribed in the same way as the others, had a scroll similar to that of all the others, was likewise numbered, put into the urn, and shaken.

"I, then, who treat the entire world equally and consider all as one mass, of which I esteem no part more worthy or unworthy than the other, because it is a Vessel of Opprobrium—I who throw all into the same urn of mutation and motion am the same to all, look upon all equally, or do not look upon any particular being more than upon another—succeed in being most just, although the opposite might appear true to all of you.

"Now, when the hand that enters the urn takes and draws the lot for him whose turn it is to receive evil and for him whose turn it is to receive good, a great number of unworthy and, rarely, worthy beings present themselves. This proceeds from the inequality, iniquity, and injustice of you who do not make all equal and who have eyes for comparisons, distinctions, inequalities, and categories, through which you learn and through which you create differences. From you, I say, from you proceed every inequality and every iniquity, because the goddess Goodness does not give of herself equally to all. Wisdom does not communicate with all in equal measure; Temperance is found in few; and Truth shows herself to very few. So you, good gods, are deficient in judgment, are most biased, when you make the widest differences, enormous inequalities, and most confused disproportions in particular things. It is not I, not I who am iniquitous, I who look upon all without distinction and appear to all as of one character, as of one quality, as of one condition. When my hand draws the lots, it more frequently happens that because of you more ordinarily the wicked rather than the good, the stupid rather than the wise, the false rather than the truthful, run up against not only evil but also good, not only ill-fortunes but also good fortunes.

"Why this? Why? Prudence comes and drops only two or three names into the urn. Sophia comes and puts only four or five names into it. Truth comes and leaves only one name in it and would leave less if it were possible. And then, out of the hundreds of thousands of lots which are poured into the urn, you expect that my sorting hand should chance upon one of these eight or nine, rather than the eight or nine hundred thousand others.

"Now, you do the opposite! You, Virtue, I say, see to it that the virtuous be more numerous than the wicked. Wisdom, see to it that the number of the wise be greater than that of the fools. You, Truth, see to it that you become open and manifest to the greatest number of people. And certainly, most certainly, more of your people, rather than their opposites, will encounter the usual rewards and punishments. See to it that all are just, truthful, wise, and good; then certainly, most certainly, no rank or dignity that I may dispense could reach the mendacious, the wicked, and the insane.

"Therefore, I, who treat and affect all in the same manner, am not more unjust than you yourselves, who do not make all equal. Consequently, when it happens that a poltroon or rogue rises to the position of prince or man of wealth, it is not my fault. But it is because of the iniquity of you, who since you are deficient in light and splendor, do not 'unpoltroon' and 'unrogue' him before, or do not 'unpoltroon' and 'unrogue' him now, or at least afterward succeed in purging him of his roguish poltroonery, so that such a person shall not be in power. It is not an error that a prince be made a rogue, but it is an error that a rogue be made a prince. Now, there being two things, that is to say, principality and roguishness, the fault certainly does not lie in the principality that I grant, but in the roguishness that you allow to exist.

"Because I shake the urn and draw the lots, I do not consider one more than another. And therefore, I did not first ordain that one be a prince or a rich man (although it is necessary that determinately one man, among all the others, fall into my hands). But you, who make distinctions with your eyes by looking upon some, and communicating, more with some and less with others, too much with some, not at all with others, have succeeded in allowing that man to be determinately a rogue and a poltroon. If then iniquity consists not in the making of a prince and in enriching him, but in determining who shall be a subject of roguery and poltroonery, then, it is not I who shall be iniquitous, but you. Behold then how Fate has made me most just and could not have made me wicked. For it makes me without eyes, so that in this manner I shall be able equally to promote all."

Now Momus added: "We do not say that you are iniquitous because of your eyes, but we say that you are because of your hand." To this Fortune responded: "Not even because of my hand, oh Momus, for I, I, who take them [the lots] as they come, am no more the cause of evil than are they that do not come out as I reach for them. I mean to say that they come to me without discrimination as I, without discrimination, reach for them. I am not the cause of evil if I take the lots as they chance to come, but they that present themselves to me as they are, and the others [the gods] who do not allow them to be otherwise, are the cause. It is not I who am perverse, I who, blind, indifferently extend my hand to whatever presents itself, whether clear or obscure, but he who makes it so, leaves it so, and so directs it to me."

Momus added: "But if all [beings] should come indifferent, equal, and similar, you would, nevertheless, not fail to be iniquitous. Because even though all are equally deserving of a principality, you will not make all of them princes, but only one among them." Smiling, Fortune answered: "We are speaking, oh Momus, of one who is unjust and not speaking of one who is said to be unjust. And certainly with your manner of proposing or answering you seem to me most sufficiently convinced, since you have proceeded from that which, in fact, is, to that which is said to be. And inasmuch as you cannot say that I am iniquitous, you proceed to say that I am said to be iniquitous. It follows then, according to your concession, that I am just, but am said to be unjust, and that you gods are unjust, but are said to be just.

"Yet to what has been said I add, moreover: not only am I not less just, but would not be less just even if you offered me all equal beings. Because, as regards that which is impossible, neither justice nor injustice is expected. Now it is not possible that a principality be given to all; it is not possible that all should have one lot. But it is possible that it be offered to all without distinction. From this possibility follows the necessity that among all, only one must succeed, and it is not in this that injustice and evil consist; because it is not possible that there be more than one. But the error lies in what follows: that that one is cowardly, that that one is a rogue, that that one is not virtuous. And Fortune, who gives him the being of a prince and the being of an affluent man, is not the cause of this evil, but rather the cause is the goddess Virtue, who does not give him, nor did give him virtuous being."

"Fortune has stated her reasons most excellently," said Father Jove, "and she seems to me in every way worthy of having a seat in heaven. But that she should have a seat of her own does not seem fitting to me, since she already has no fewer seats than there are stars. For Fortune is in all of them, no less than she is on earth, since they are worlds, no less than the earth. Besides, according to the general opinion of men, Fortune is said to be suspended from all of them; and certainly, if they [men] had a more abundant intellect, they would say something useful. However (let Momus say what he pleases), since, oh goddess, your reasons seem to me to be indeed all too efficacious, I come to the conclusion that if the gods do not bring forth allegations against your defense, stronger than those hitherto adduced, I should not dare to assign you to one seat, as if indeed I wished to confine or tie you to it. But I do give you, rather I leave you with that power that you seem to have throughout heaven, since you, in your own right, have so much authority that you open for yourself those places that are closed to Jove himself as well as to all the other gods. And I do not want to say any more about that for which all of us are very, very much obligated to you. By unlocking all doors and clearing all paths for yourself and by availing yourself of all seats, you make all things yours that belong to others. And therefore it does not fail that the seats that belong to others should be yours also. For all that which is governed by the fate of mutation passes through the urn, through its revolution, and through the hand of your Excellency."

THIRD PART
OF THE *Second Dialogue*

[Continuation of Sophia's speech]

In such a manner then did Jove deny Hercules' seat to Fortune, but he left that seat and all the others that are upon the universe at her disposal. From this sentence, such as it was, none of the gods dissented. And the blind goddess, seeing the determination they had arrived at, in the face of all her insults, took leave of the Senate, saying: "I then go away, both most revealed to, and most concealed from, all the universe. I frequent exalted and humble residences, and, no less than death, know how to raise most lowly things and abase the highest things; and finally, by dint of vicissitude, I succeed in making everything equal. And with an indefinite succession and irrational reason (because I am found above and outside of particular reasons), and by indeterminate means, I turn the wheel and shake the urn, so that my intention will not be censured by any individual.

"Now, Wealth, come to my right side, and you, Poverty, to my left. Take with you your retinue, you, Wealth, your aids, who are so pleasing, and you, Poverty, yours, who are so annoying to the multitude. I say, let Trouble and Joy follow first, then Happiness and Unhappiness, Sadness and Mirth, Gladness and Melancholy, Labor and Rest, Idleness and Occupation, Sordidness and

Adornment. Then let Austerity and Delight follow, then Luxury and Sobriety, Lust and Abstinence, Inebriety and Thirst, Debauchery and Hunger, Appetite and Satiety, Cupidity, Weariness and Superabundance, Fullness and Emptiness. Besides, let Giving and Taking follow, Profusion and Parsimony, Investing and Divesting, as well as Gain and Loss, Income and Expenditure, Profit and Cost, Avarice and Liberality, Number and Measure, Excess and Deficiency, Equality and Inequality, Debit and Credit. Afterwards there should follow Security and Suspicion, Zeal and Adulation, Honor and Contempt, Reverence and Scorn, Homage and Disrespect, Favor and Disgrace, Assistance and Destitution, Discomfort and Comfort, Envy and Congratulation, Emulation and Compassion, Confidence and Diffidence, Dominion and Slavery, Liberty and Captivity, Company and Solitude.

"You, Occasion, walk ahead, precede my footsteps, open thousands and thousands of paths to me. Go irresolutely, unrecognized, and hidden, because I do not want my coming to be too easily foreseen. Slap the faces of all seers, prophets, diviners, fortune-tellers, and prognosticators. Rap the ribs of all those who come to impede our journey. Remove from the path of my feet every possible stumbling block. Clear away and uproot each and every thicket designed to be harmful to a blind divinity, so that through you, my guide, it will easily be made clear to me where I must climb or rest, turn to the right or left, move or stop, and step forward or backward. In one moment and simultaneously, I go and come, establish myself and move, rise and sit, as I extend my hands to diverse and infinite things by various means that Occasion offers. Let us, then, flow from all, through all, in all, to all, here with gods, there with heroes, here with men, there with beasts."

Now this quarrel having been terminated and Fortune having been expelled, Jove, turning toward the gods, said: "It seems to me that Courage should succeed to the seat of Hercules; for where there are Truth, Law, and Judgment, Courage must not be far off; because that will that administers judgment with prudence through law, according to truth, must be constant and strong. Since, just as truth and law form the intellect and prudence, judgment and justice regulate the will, so constancy and courage lead us to the effect. Whence it is said by a wise man: 'Do not become a judge, unless by means of your courage and virtue you are strong enough to crush the machines of iniquity.' "

All the gods answered: "You have disposed well, oh Jove, that up to now Hercules should have been the model of courage that was to be contemplated among the stars. You, Courage, succeed to that seat, with the lantern of reason before you, because otherwise you would not be courage, but rather stupidity, fury, and audacity. And you would not be considered courage, nor would you even be courage, because by your madness, error, and alienation of mind, you would not come to fear evil and death. That light will see to it that you will not be daring where one must fear, since only the fool and madman do not fear whatever one should fear, the more prudent and wise he is. It will see to it that where public honor and service, the dignity and perfection of one's own being, and the observance of divine and natural laws are concerned, you will not be frightened by terrors that threaten death. It will see to it that you will be swift and expeditious where others are torpid and slow, that you will easily endure that which others bear with difficulty, and that you will consider little or nothing that which others esteem much or a great deal.

"Temper your bad companions, both her who walks on your right side with her aids, Temerity, Audacity, Presumption, Insolence, Fury, and Familiarity, and her who walks on your left side with Poverty of Spirit, Dejection, Fear, Cowardice, Pusillanimity, and Desperation. Lead your virtuous daughters, Sedulity, Zeal, Tolerance, Magnanimity, Longanimity, Intrepidity, Alacrity, and Industry by means of the book that contains the catalogue of things governed by Caution, or by Perseverance, or by Flight, or by Sufferance, in which are jotted down things that the courageous man must not fear: that is, those things which do not make us worse, such as hunger, nudity, thirst, grief, poverty, solitude, persecution, and death; and among the others, such things as crass ignorance, injustice, infidelity, prevarication, avarice, and similar things, which, because they make us worse, are to be avoided with every diligence.

"So by tempering yourself, bowing neither right nor left, and not by removing yourself from your daughters, by reading and following your catalogue, by not extinguishing your light, you will be the only protection of virtues, unique custodian of justice, and singular tower of truth. You will be impregnable to vices, unconquered by labors, steadfast against perils, inflexible against pleasures, scornful of Wealth, a subduer of Fortune, and triumphant over all. You will not recklessly dare, not rashly fear, you will not pursue pleasures, not turn your back on sufferings. You will not be delighted by false praise and will not be awed by vituperation. You will not be exalted by prosperous times, will not give up because of adversities. The gravity of affliction will not weigh you down, the wind of frivolity will not uplift you. Wealth will not inflate you, and Poverty will not confuse you. You shall scorn excess and shall have little consciousness of want. You shall turn away from lowly matters and shall always be intent upon high undertakings."

"Now what disposition will be made regarding my Lyre?" asked Mercury. To this Momus answered: "Keep it for yourself as your pastime, for the time when you are on a boat, or even when you are at an inn. And if you choose to make a present of it by giving it to the man who comports himself most meritoriously, and do not have too strong a desire to wander off looking for him, go off to Naples to the Piazza de l'Olmo,[1] or to Venice to the Piazza San Marco,[2] toward evening. For in these two places there appear the coryphaei of those who mount the bench, and there you may come across that best man to whom *iure meriti* it must be given." Mercury asked: "Why, rather to the best of this species than to the best of another?" Momus answered that in these times the lyre has become the principal instrument for charlatans, by means of which they win over and hold their audience and more easily sell their pills and vials, just as the rebec has now become the instrument of blind mendicants.

Mercury asked: "Is it within my power to do with it that which pleases me?" "So it is," said Jove, "but not indeed to let it remain in the heaven at this time. And I want (if it still is agreeable to you of the Council) that in the place of this Lyre of his, with the nine strings, the great Mother Mnemosyne should succeed together with the nine Muses, her children." Here all the gods nodded their heads in a sign of approbation, and the goddess who had been promoted with her daughters, rendered thanks.

Arithmetic, who is her first-born, said that she was thanking them more times than she conceived of individual numbers and numerical species, and more thousands and thousands of times than the intellect, by means of additions, could conceive. Geometry said that she was thanking them more times than there are forms and figures that can be designed and points she could encounter through her fantastic solutions of continuatives. Music said that she was rendering them ever more thanks than there are harmonic forms and symphonies that phantasy could combine. Logic said that she was rendering them more thanks than there are absurdities made by her grammarians, more than there are false persuasions made by her rhetoricians, and more than there are sophisms and false demonstrations made by her dialecticians. Poetry said that she was thanking them more times than her singers have feet for the circulation of their many fables, for as many times as her singers have composed, and are about to compose verses. Astrology thanked them more times than there are stars in the immense space of the ethereal region, more, if more could be said. Physics rendered them as many thanks as there can be proximate principles, first principles, and elements in the bosom of Nature, Metaphysics, more thanks than there are genera of ideas and species of ends and efficients concerning natural effects, according to the reality that is in things, as well as according to the representative concept. Ethics thanked them as many times as there could be customs, habits, laws, just acts, and crimes in this and other worlds of the universe. Mother Mnemosyne said: "I render you as many thanks and rewards, oh gods, as there are particular beings, subject to memory and oblivion, to knowledge and ignorance."

And in the meanwhile Jove ordered his first-born, Minerva, to hand him the box he kept under the pillow on his bed, after which he drew forth nine boxes containing nine collyria, prescribed to purge the human mind in respect both to its knowledge and to its disposition. And to begin with he gave three of them to the first three [Muses], saying to them: "Here for you is the best unguent with which you will be able to purge and make clear your perceptive virtue as regards the number, the size, and the harmonious proportion of sensible things." He gave one to the fourth and said: "This will serve to regulate the inventive and judicative faculties." "Take this," he said to the fifth, "which, by bringing about a certain melancholic reaction, has the power to incite enjoyable frenzy and prophecy." He gave the sixth hers, showing her the way by means of which she could open the eyes of mortals to the contemplation of archetypal and supernal things. The seventh received that one through which the rational faculty is best remolded as regards the contemplation of nature. The eighth received the other no less excellent one, which moves the mind to the comprehension of supernatural things as regards their influence on nature, and which are in a certain manner detached from it.

The last, largest, most precious, and most excellent one he put into the hands of the last-born, who is as much worthier than the others as she is posterior to them in birth; and said to her: "Here, Ethics, you have that one with which you prudently, together with sagacity, shrewdness, and with generous philanthropy, will know how to institute religions, ordain cults, give laws, and execute judgments, and approve, strengthen, preserve, and defend all that which is well established, regulated, put forth, and executed, by adapting, as much as possible, affects and effects to the cult of the gods and to the society of men."

"What shall we do about the Swan?" asked Juno. Momus answered: "Let us send it in the name of its devil to swim with the others, either in Lake Pergus, or in the Caystros River, where it shall have many companions."[3] "I do not want it to be so," said Jove, "but ordain that its beak be branded with my seal and that it be put into the Thames. For there it will be more secure than elsewhere, since, because of fear of capital punishment, it will not so easily be stolen from me."[4] "Wisely, oh great father, have you provided," added the gods, and they waited for Jove to decide as to its successor. Whereupon, the first presiding god continued with his decree, and said: "It seems to me most fitting that Repentance, who, among the virtues, is like the swan among the birds, should be placed there. For she does not dare, nor is able, to fly high because of the weight of her modesty and her low estimation of herself; so she stays low. Nevertheless, removing herself from the odious earth and not daring to rise to the sky, she loves the rivers, plunges into the waters, which are the tears of compunction in which she tries to wash, purge, and purify herself, displeased after she has sullied herself on the muddy shore of error, and, moved by the feeling of such grief, is seized with the determination of correcting herself and of becoming, as much as it will be possible, like candid innocence. By means of this virtue, the souls that have tumbled from heaven and have been immersed in shadowy Orcus rise again, having passed through the Cocytus of sensual pleasures, and having been burned by the Pyriphlegethon of covetous love and appetite for generation; the first of which encumbers the spirit with sadness, and the second renders the soul proud.

"Returning to herself, as it were, because of the memory of her high lineage, she is displeased with herself on account of her present state; she regrets that in which she once delighted, and wishes it had not been pleasing to her. And in this manner, she succeeds little by little in divesting herself of her present state, by attenuating the weight of its carnal matter and crass substance. She bedecks herself entirely in feathers, is kindled and heated by the sun, conceives a fervent love of sublime things, becomes aërial, betakes herself to the sun, and once again is converted to its principle."

"Repentance is deservedly placed among the virtues," said Saturn, "because although she is the daughter of Father Error and of Mother Iniquity, she is nevertheless like the vermilion rose that comes forth from dark and piercing thorns. She is like a brilliant and clear flame which leaps forth from the black and hard flint, rises and reaches toward her cognate, the sun." "Well decided upon, well determined!" said the entire Council of the gods. "Let Repentance sit among the virtues; let her be one of the heavenly deities!"

Upon hearing this general sentence, furious Mars, before another could talk about Cassiopea, raised his voice and said: "Let there be no one, oh gods, who will deprive my bellicose Spain [5] of this matron, who, so arrogant, haughty, and magisterial, was not satisfied to ascend to heaven without taking her chair with its canopy. I should like you (if it so pleases the great thundering father and if you do not want to displease me, at the risk of suffering the same in good measure when you fall into my hands) to determine that she sojourn there, because she possesses the customs of that nation and seems to have been born, nourished, and raised there." And Momus answered: "Let no one take away arrogance and this woman, who is a living picture of it, from the brave squadron captain." To which Mars answered: "With this sword I shall not only teach you, you poor thing who have no other virtue and strength than that of a rotten tongue without salt, but, besides, anyone else (outside of Jove, because he is superior to all) who says that beneath that which you call my boastfulness there are not found any beauty, glory, majesty, magnanimity, and strength worthy of the protection of the Martian shield. And these insults, I say, are not unworthy of being vindicated by this terrible sword point, which has resolved to subdue both men and gods."

"Indeed, have her," added Momus, "and a curse be with you, because among us other gods you will not find another so bizarre and mad that he, in order to earn for himself one of these diabolic and raging beasts, wants to expose himself to the risk of having his head broken."

"Do not become furious, Mars, do not become angry, Momus," said the benign protoparent. "This request, oh God of War, which is not of too great importance, can be easily and freely granted to you, inasmuch as we are sometimes compelled, in spite of ourselves, to permit that you with the sole authority of your flashing sword commit so many acts of stuprum, so many adulteries, so many thefts, usurpations, and assassinations. Go, then, for I, together with the other gods, shall commit her completely to your libidinous desire, providing that you do not any longer allow her to linger among the stars near so many virtuous goddesses. Let her go down with her chair and lead Boastfulness with her. And let her yield her place to Simplicity, who turns away from the right side of her who feigns to have and boasts about more than she possesses, and from the left side of Dissimulation, who hides and pretends not to possess that which she does have and indicates that she possesses less than that which is present. This handmaiden of Truth must not wander far from her queen, although sometimes the goddess Necessity compels her to turn toward Dissimulation, so that she, Simplicity, or Truth will not be trodden upon, or to avoid other inconvenience. Since this is done by her not without plan or order, it can also easily be done without error and defect."

As she went to take her place, Simplicity seemed to have a sure and confident gait, contrary to Boastfulness and Dissimulation, who, as they demonstrated by their timid steps and frightened countenances, walked not without fear. The countenance of Simplicity pleased all the gods, because, by means of her uniformity, she in a certain manner represents, and has a resemblance to, the divine aspect. Her face is amiable, because it never changes; and therefore, because of that reason by which she once begins to please, she will always please. And not because of her fault, but because of that of another, does it happen that she ceases to be loved.

But Boastfulness, who is wont to please because she gives us to understand that she possesses more than she has, will when she is recognized easily incur not only displeasure but sometimes even contempt. Similarly, Dissimulation, because she is recognized to be otherwise than that which we allowed ourselves to be convinced of, can, not without difficulty, come to be hated by him to whom she was at first pleasing. Of these, then, the one and the other were deemed unworthy of heaven and of being united to what is used to being found in its midst. But not so, Dissimulation, of whom the gods are still wont to make use; because sometimes Prudence, in order to avoid envy, criticism, and abuse, is accustomed in the garments of that one to dissemble Truth.

SAUL. It is well and good, oh Sophia. And not without spirit of truth did the poet of Ferrara show that she is much more convenient to men, even though sometimes she is not disagreeable to the gods.[6]

Although dissimulation is most often reprehended
And gives proof of bad intention,
It is indeed found in many things,
And in many things to have produced benefits, numerous and obvious,
And to have obviated injuries, blames, and death;
For in this mortal life, much more gloomy than serene,
Filled with envy throughout,
We do not always converse with friends.[7]

But I should like to know, oh Sophia, in what way you understand Simplicity as having resemblance to the divine countenance. SOPHIA. In this manner: that she cannot add to her being with boastfulness, or subtract from it with dissemblance. And this proceeds from her not having intelligence and understanding of herself, just as that man who is most simple, since he does not want to be other than most simple, does not understand himself. For that which is discerned and contemplated becomes in a certain way much, and, to put it better, one thing and another, because it becomes object and potency, knowing and knowable; for in the act of intelligence, many things come together into one. That most simple intelligence, however, is said not to understand herself as containing a reflected act of the intelligent and the intelligible; however, because she is a most absolute and most simple light and inasmuch as she cannot be occult to herself, she is said to understand herself only negatively. Simplicity then, inasmuch as she is not aware of, and does not meditate upon, her being, is understood to have a divine aspect. Arrogant Boastfulness, a great distance removed from her, shuns her. But not so, studious Dissimulation, for whom Jove sometimes makes it lawful to show herself in heaven, although no longer as a goddess, but sometimes as the servant of Prudence, sometimes as the shield of Truth.

SAUL. Now let us proceed to consider what has been done regarding Perseus and his seat.

SOPHIA. "What will you do, oh Jove, with this bastard of yours to whom you had Danaë give birth?" asked Momus. Jove answered: "Let him go, if it so pleases the entire Senate (because it seems to me that some new Medusa is upon earth who, no less than she who lived a long time ago, has the power to convert into stone by her gaze whosoever looks upon her), let him go to her, not as one sent by a new Polydectes but as one sent by Jove and the entire celestial Senate. And let him see whether by means of the same skill he can overcome a monster, as horrible as it is recent." Here Minerva answered, saying: "And I, for my part, shall not fail to furnish him with a no less useful shining shield with which he may dazzle the sight of the hostile Phorcides, designated as custodians of the Gorgons; and, under present circumstances, I wish to assist him until that time when he has severed the head of this

Medusa from her body." "Thus, you will do much good, my daughter," said Jove, "and I impose this responsibility upon you, to which I want you to apply yourself with all diligence.

"But I should not want him again, at the expense of the poor peoples, to bring about from the drops that will flow from Medusa's incised veins, the generation of new serpents on earth, where, against the will of the wretched, they are found both in great and, indeed, in too great numbers. Let him ride, however, mounted on Pegasus, who will come forth from her fecund body (protecting himself from the flow of the poisonous drops),[8] no longer through Africa, where he may become captive of some captive Andromeda and be bound in diamond chains by her, bound in those of iron. But let him ride through my beloved Europe mounted on his winged steed. Let him there investigate to ascertain where those proud and monstrous Atlantides are, enemies of Jove's progeny, by whom they fear that the golden apples that they keep hidden in the custody and within the enclosures of Avarice and Ambition will be taken away from them. Let him linger where there are more generous and more beautiful Andromedas, who, because of the violence of false religion, are bound and exposed to sea monsters. Let him see whether some violent Phineus, hard pressed by the multitude of pernicious ministers, comes to usurp the fruits of another's industry and labors. Let him see whether a number of ingrate, obstinate, and incredulous Polydecteses are governing there. Let the mirror come very quickly before them, present itself before their eyes where they may look upon her [Medusa's] loathsome image, and, having been turned to stone by her horrible appearance, they may lose every perverse sensation, movement, and life."[9]

"All has been well ordained," said the gods. "For it is suitable that Perseus, joined to Hercules, who with the arm of Justice and the club of Judgment has been made the subduer of corporeal forces, should appear, he who, with the luminous mirror of doctrine and with his presentation of the detestable portrait of schism and heresy, may drive a nail into the pernicious conscience of nefarious and obstinate minds, depriving them of the function of their tongues, hands, and senses."

SAUL. Come now, Sophia, and enlighten me as to who is to succeed to the place whence that one made his departure.

SOPHIA. A virtue who is in the garb and with gestures not at all dissimilar to him, and is called Diligence or Solicitude. She has Labor as her companion and is considered a companion by Labor, by virtue of whom Perseus was Perseus and Hercules was Hercules, and every strong and industrious man is industrious and strong. Through her the great grandson of Abas has deprived the Phorcides of light, cut off Medusa's head, taken away the winged steed from the truncated body, the sacred apples from the son of Clymene and Iapetus, snatched the daughter of Cepheus, Andromeda, from Cetus, defended his wife against his rival, revisited Argos, his fatherland, deprived Proetus of his kingdom,[10] restored it to his brother, Acrisius, after having revenged himself against the ungrateful and discourteous king [Polydectes] of the island of Seriphus. Through her, I say, every care is conquered, every adverse circumstance is truncated, every road and access is made easy, every treasure is acquired, all violence is subdued, every captivity is put to an end, every desire is obtained, every possession is defended, every port is reached, all adversaries are beaten down, all friends are exalted, and all insults are avenged, and finally, every design is attained.

Then Jove ordained, and all the gods approved this decree, that hard-working and diligent Solicitude should come forward. And then she appeared, having assumed the talaria of divine impulse with which she tramples what is considered the highest good by the vulgar, scorns the gentle caresses of pleasures, which like insidious sirens attempt to hinder her from the course of the work that solicits and awaits her.

After having seized with her left hand the shield, radiant with the brilliance that encumbers indolent and inert eyes with stupid wonderment, and having held in her right hand the serpentine lock of pernicious thoughts, under which lies that horrible head whose unhappy face, deformed by a thousand passions of contempt, wrath, fright, terror, abomination, wonderment, melancholy, and lugubrious repentance, petrifies and stupefies whoever fixes his eyes upon it, she rides mounted on that winged horse of studious perseverance with which, the more she perseveres, the more she reaches and attains, overcoming every obstacle of a steep mountain, every hindrance of a deep valley, every impetus of a rapid river, every barrier of the densest hedges and of walls, however thick and high.

Then, having come into the presence of the sacrosanct Senate, she heard these words from the highest presiding god: "I want you, oh Diligence, to obtain this noble space in heaven, because you are she who nourishes generous minds with work. Ascend, overcome, and pass over in one breath, if it is possible, every rocky and rugged mountain. Render your affect so fervent that you will not only resist and conquer yourself but also will have no sense of your difficulty, will have no consciousness of your being Labor. For this reason Labor must not be labor to herself, just as a serious man is not serious to himself. You will not, however, be worthy labor, if you do not likewise conquer yourself, you who do not consider yourself to be what you are, that is Labor; since whenever you have sense of yourself, you cannot be superior to yourself. But if you are not depressed or suppressed, you will at least come to be oppressed by yourself.

"The highest perfection lies in not feeling labor and suffering when we undergo labor and suffering. You must conquer yourself with that sense of pleasure which does not sense pleasure, that pleasure, I say, which if it were naturally good, would not be scorned by many as the origin of diseases, poverty, and censures. But you, Labor, when outstanding works are concerned, be pleasure unto yourself and not labor. Become, I say, one and the same with her who outside of those works and acts will not be pleasure unto herself, but intolerable labor. You then, if you are a virtue, do not be concerned with lowly things, with frivolous things, with vain things. If you want to be there where the sublime pole of Truth will be vertical to you, pass over these Apennines, ascend these Alps, cross this reefy ocean, conquer these rude Riphaeans,[11] traverse this barren and frozen Caucasus, penetrate the inaccessible slopes, and enter into that happy circle where light is continuous and neither shadows nor cold is evident, but where there is a perpetual warm climate and where, for you, dawn or daytime will be eternal.

"You advance then, oh goddess Solicitude, or Labor; and I want (said Jove) Difficulty to run before you and flee from you. Crush Misfortune, seize Fortune by the hair. Hasten, when it seems best to you, the course of her wheel and, when it seems fitting to you, drive a nail into it so that it will not run. I want Sanity, Robustness, and Safety to come with you. Let Diligence be your shield-bearer and Exercise, your standard-bearer. Let Acquisition follow you with her defenses, which are Corporeal Well-Being, Spiritual Well-Being, and, if you will, Material Well-Being. And of these three, I want you to love those that you yourself have acquired more than that one that you receive from another, not unlike a mother who, being the one who knows them best, loves her children more because they are hers. I do not want you to be able to divide yourself, because if you dismember yourself, being concerned partly with works of the mind and partly with bodily activities, you will become defective in the one and the other part. And the more you devote yourself to one side, the less you will prevail upon the other; if you completely turn toward material things, you will amount to nothing in intellectual things, and vice versa. I command that when it is necessary, after having called you in a loud voice, or by a sign, or in silence, Occasion should exhort you or entice you, incite you or compel you.

"I command Advantage and Disadvantage to advise you when heavy weights must be loaded and when they must be put down, and when it is sometimes necessary that you go forward. I want Diligence to remove every obstacle before you; I want Vigilance to be your sentinel, watching about and around you, so that nothing will approach you unexpectedly. I want Indifference to warn you against concern for, and attention to, vain things; and if she is not listened to by you, Repentance should finally come to you, she who will make you realize that it is more laborious to have waved empty hands than, with hands filled, to have thrown stones. You, run and hasten as fast as you can with the feet of Diligence, before *force majeure* intervenes and takes away Liberty, or extends her might and arms to Difficulty."

So Solicitude, having thanked Jove and the others, started on her way and spoke in the following manner: "Behold, I, Labor, move my feet, gird myself, and bare my arms. Go away from me, all torpor, all laziness, all negligence, all idle sloth! Depart, all sluggishness! You, my Industry, place before the eyes of Consideration your advantage, your goal. Render salutiferous all the many calumnies of others, the many fruits of the malice and envy of others and that understandable fear of yours which drove you away from your native dwelling, which alienated you from your friends, which removed you far from your country and banished you to not-too-friendly countrysides. Industry of mine, make glorious with me my exile and travails. Above that fatherland let there reign quiet, tranquillity, comfort, and peace.

"Come, Diligence, what are you doing? Why do we idle and sleep so much alive, if we so very long must idle and sleep in death? Indeed, although we still await another world or another manner of being ourselves, that life will not be the same as that possessed by us at present; so that this life, without ever expecting to return, passes on forever.

"You, Hope, what are you doing, since you do not stimulate me, since you do not arouse me? Come now, make it possible that I may expect a salutary outcome from difficult matters, unless I flee from circumstances and do not yield to them. And do not allow me to promise myself anything, no matter how attractive, no matter how very attractive.

"You, Zeal, always be my assistant, so that I may not attempt things unworthy of a worthy deity, and so that I may stretch out my hands to those labors which may be the cause of greater labor. Show me before my eyes how ugly it is to behold love of glory and how base a thing is concern for security at the outset and beginning of labor.

"Sagacity, see to it that I do not recoil from uncertain and doubtful things, or turn my shoulders away, but that I remove myself from them little by little in safety. You, yourself, as you follow me, obliterate my footsteps, so that I will not be found again by my enemies, and their furor be vented upon me. You, make me direct my steps through paths that are far removed from the seats of Fortune, since her hands are not long and she can seize only those who are close to her, and shake only those who are inside her urn. You will see to it that I do not attempt anything except when I can aptly perform it; and in labor, make me more cautious

than brave, if you cannot make me equally cautious and brave. See
to it that my work be both concealed and open, open so that not
everyone will look for and inquire about it, concealed so that not
all but a very few will find it. For you know well that concealed
things are investigated, and that those that are locked up invite
thieves. Furthermore, that which is seen is deemed of little worth,
the open safe is not diligently searched; and that object is considered to be of little worth that is not seen to be put into safe-
keeping with great diligence.

"You, Boldness, when Difficulty presses, outrages, and resists
me, do not fail frequently to intone into my ear with the voice of
your great ardor that saying: 'Tu ne cede malis, sed contra auden-
tior ito.' [12] ('Do not yield to misfortunes, but go forth to meet them
all the bolder.')

"You, Consultation, will give me to understand when it is
fitting that I dissolve or discontinue ill-employed occupation, which
will justly take as its goal, not the gold and opulence of vulgar
and sordid minds, but those treasures that, less hidden and dispersed by time, are celebrated and cultivated in the field of eternity;
so that it will not be said of us as of those scarabs: 'Meditantur sua
stercora scarabaei.' ('Scarabs contemplate their excrement.')

"You, Patience, strengthen me, restrain me, and administer to
me that elect Leisure of yours, not that one of whom Sloth is a
sister, but that one who is a brother of Tolerance. You will make
me turn away from Inquietude and bow to non-meddlesome Solicitude. Then you will forbid me to run when it interests me to run
whither there are precipitous, infamous, and mortal obstacles.
Then you will not allow me to lift anchor and loosen the stern
from the shore when it happens that I entrust myself to the in-
superable turbulence of the stormy sea. And at this time you will
give me first, the leisure to confer with Consultation, who will
make me look at myself, second, the employment that I must
engage in; third, you will tell me to what end and why, fourth,
under what circumstances, fifth, when, sixth, where, seventh, with
whom. Administer to me that leisure with which I can do more
beautiful, better, and more excellent things than those I leave behind, because in the house of Leisure there sits Counsel, and there
one is concerned with a life of blessedness, which is better than

in any other place. There events are better contemplated. From that place one can leave for his labor with more efficacy and strength, because without being sufficiently rested at first it is not possible for one to run well later.

"You, Leisure, give me the assistance as a result of which I may be considered less idle than all the others, in order that through you it will come about that I by my speech and exhortation shall serve the republic and help the defense of the fatherland more than the soldier, the tribune, and the emperor with their sword, lance, and shield.

"Come close to me you generous, heroic, and solicitous Apprehension, and by your stimulus see to it that I am not the first to perish either from the ranks of the illustrious or from the ranks of mortals. See to it that before Torpor and Death deprive me of my hands I find myself so well provided that they cannot deprive me of the glory of my works.

"Solicitude, see to it that the roof is completed before the rain comes; see to it that the windows are protected before the North Winds and the South Winds of moist and restless winter blow.

"You, Memory of a well-employed span of life, shall see to it that old age and death take me before my mind is deranged. You, Fear of losing glory acquired in life, will make my old age and my death not bitter but dear and longed for."

SAUL. Here, oh Sophia, is the most worthy and honored prescription to remedy the sadness and pain of our mature age and the inopportune terror of death, which from the hour we have use of our senses is wont to tyrannize over the spirit of us living beings. Of this the Nolan Tansillo rightly said:

> They rejoice who are not displeasing to Heaven,
> And who were not cold to, and disrespectful of, high enterprises.
> They then, when snow and frost fall
> Upon the hills, barren of grass and flowers,
> Have no reason for which to mourn their happy seasons,
> If they, changing in hair and countenance,
> Will change life and pursuits.
> The farmer has no reason to grieve,
> If, at the proper time, he gathers his fruit.[13]

SOPHIA. Very well said, Saulino. But it is time that you retire, for here is my most friendly divinity, that most desirable grace, that most eminent countenance, who is approaching me from the direction of the east.

SAULINO. Fine then, my Sophia, tomorrow at the accustomed hour, if it so pleases you, we shall see each other again. And I in the meanwhile shall go and outline for myself all that I have heard from you today, in order that I may better renew the memory of your concepts when it is necessary, and more easily in the future make another participate in it.

SOPHIA. It is amazing that he is coming to meet me with wings, speedier than usual. I do not see him coming according to his custom, playing with his caduceus and gently striking the very clear air with his wings. I seem to see him fretfully intent on business. Here he is looking at me, and he has his eyes turned toward me in such a manner that makes it manifest that his perturbed state is not caused by me.

MERC. May Fate always be propitious toward you! May the anger of time be impotent against you, my beloved and charming daughter, sister, and friend!

SOPHIA. Although, as far as I am concerned, you are no less liberal than on other occasions with your most jocund grace, what is it, oh my handsome god, that makes you so perturbed in countenance? Why have I seen you come in haste and more ready to go on than disposed to linger awhile with me?

MERC. The reason for this is that I was hurriedly sent by Jove to make provisions for, and take protective measures against, the fire that mad and fierce Discord [14] has threatened to kindle in this Parthenopaean Realm. [15]

SOPHIA. In what manner, oh Mercury, has this pestiferous Erinys hurled herself from beyond the Alps and the sea upon this noble country?

MERC. She was summoned by the foolish ambition and insane audacity of someone; was invited with very liberal but no less indefinite promises. She was impelled by fallacious hope, and is awaited by a twofold jealousy, which creates in the nation the desire of wanting to maintain itself in the same state of liberty in which it has always found itself, and the fear of entering into a more stringent servitude; and it creates in the prince the fear of losing all because of having wanted to embrace too much.

SOPHIA. What is the prime origin and principle of this?

MERC. Great Avarice, who continues working with the pretext of wanting to preserve Religion.[16]

SOPHIA. In truth the pretext seems false to me, and, if I am not mistaken, is inexcusable. For protection or care is not required where no ruin or peril threatens, where minds are exactly the same as they were, and where the cult of that goddess does not linger.

MERC. And if it were so, it is not up to Avarice but up to Prudence and Justice to remedy it, because here we have this prince who has aroused the people into a furor; and on this occasion the time seems to be at hand for inviting rebellious spirits, not so much to defend a just liberty as to aspire to an unlawful license and to govern themselves according to pernicious and contumacious lust, for which the bestial multitude was always ready.

SOPHIA. Tell me, if it is not burdensome to you, in what manner would you say Avarice wishes to remedy matters?

MERC. By worsening the punishments of delinquents in such a manner that many innocent people, and sometimes the just, will share the punishment of a criminal, so that by this, the prince will grow fatter and fatter.

SOPHIA. It is a natural thing that sheep who have a wolf as their ruler should be punished by being devoured by him.

MERC. But it is to be feared that sometimes merely the ravenous appetite and gluttony of the wolf are sufficient to make them appear guilty in his eyes. And it is against every law that the lambs and their mother should be mulcted because of a defect in their father.

SOPHIA. It is true that I have never found such an opinion, except among savage barbarians; and I believe that it was first found among Jews, because they are such a pestilent, leprous, and generally pernicious generation, who deserve to be extinguished before they are born. So, to get back to our business, is this the reason for which you are disturbed and in suspense, and for which it is urgent that you leave me soon?

MERC. So it is. I have wanted to take this journey in order to visit you before getting to those parts whither I have directed my flight, so as not to make you wait in vain and not to break the promise I made yesterday. I have placed before Jove some matters regarding your misfortunes, and I find him more than usually inclined to please you. But for four or five days, and today among others, I do not have the leisure to deal and confer with you about the negotiation concerning the petition you must make. But in the meanwhile you will be patient, since it is better to go to see Jove and the Senate when they are free from other concerns than when they are in the state in which, as you can imagine, they are at present.

SOPHIA. I should like to await that time, since the matter, because it will be proposed later, can be more easily arranged. And to be truthful, I, being in great haste (in order not to fail in my duty regarding the promise I had made to you to commit the request into your hands today), have not been able to satisfy myself, since I believe that things should be disclosed in greater detail than they have been in this note. Here, I give it to you, so that you may see (if you chance to have leisure during your journey) the number of my complaints.

MERC. I shall look at this note. But you will do well to avail yourself of the convenience of this time to make a longer and clearer memorandum so that all can be fully provided for. Now, so that I may confound Strength, I first want to to go to arouse Astuteness,[17] so that, having attained Deception, she [Strength] may dictate a letter of betrayal against Rebellion, alleged to be ambitious, by which false letter the maritime power of the Turk[18] may be diverted and stand against Gallic fury, which in long strides is approaching by land on this side of the Alps. So because of the defect in Strength, may Daring be subdued, the people be tranquilized, the prince be assured, and may Fear quench Thirst for Ambition and useless Avarice. And with this, finally, may banished Harmony be recalled; and with the abolition of perilous and ungrateful Innovation, may Peace be placed on her throne through the strengthening of the ancient Way of Living.

SOPHIA. Go then, my divinity, and may it please Fate that your designs be felicitously fulfilled, so that my enemy, War, shall not come to disturb my state as well as that of others.

Third Dialogue

FIRST PART
OF THE Third Dialogue

SOPHIA. It will not be necessary, Saulino, to let you hear in detail all those arguments that were brought forth by Labor, or Diligence, or Solicitude, or whatsoever you want to call her (because she has more names than I could relate to you in one hour). But I do not want to pass over in silence that which occurred as soon as she with her ministers and companions went to take for herself the place in which we said busy Perseus was.

SAUL. Speak, for I am listening to you.

SOPHIA. Soon (because the spur of Ambition often knows how to encourage and incite all heroic and divine minds, even these companion gods, Leisure and Dream) it happened that hardly had

Labor, or Diligence, disappeared when they were seen coming forward, not lazily and sleepily, but solicitously and without delay. Because of this Momus said: "Deliver us, Jove, from trouble, because I clearly see that after the expulsion of Perseus we will not lack intrigues, just as we have not lacked them since Hercules' banishment."

To which Jove replied: "Leisure would not be Leisure, and Dream would not be Dream, if they had to trouble us for too long a time, because they have to apply too much diligence or labor. For the former [Diligence] is far away from here, as you see, and they [Leisure and Dream] are here only by a privative virtue, which exists in the absence of their opposite and their enemy." "All will go well," said Momus, "if they do not make us so lazy and slow that we cannot determine what we must decide concerning the principal matter of this day."

Leisure then began to make herself heard in this manner: "Thus, oh gods, Leisure is sometimes bad, just as Diligence, or Labor, is very often bad. So Leisure very often is convenient and good, just as on certain occasions Labor is good. I do not think then that if justice is found among you, you will want to deny me equal honor, unless it is right that you consider me less worthy. Rather, by means of reason I am confident that I shall make you understand (through certain arguments that I have heard alleged in praise and favor of Diligence, or Occupation) that when we are placed on the scale of reasonable comparison, I, Leisure, at times am found not to be equally good, I will [at other times] prove myself to be far better, so that you will consider me not only a virtue but on the other hand, also a vice.

"Who is it, oh gods, who has preserved the so highly praised Golden Age? Who has instituted it, who has maintained it, if not the law of Leisure, the law of Nature? Who has taken it away? Who has extinguished it almost irrevocably from the world, if not ambitious Solicitude, diligent Labor? Is it not she who has perturbed the centuries, who has created schism in the world and has led it into a ferrous, muddy, and argillaceous age, having put people on a wheel and in a kind of a whirling and tumble, after having incited them to pride, love of innovation, and lust of possessing the honor and glory of one particular individual? That one, who in substance is not dissimilar to all of them and is sometimes in dignity and merit very much beneath them, has perhaps been superior to many in malice and therefore succeeds in acquiring the power to overturn the laws of Nature, to make his lust law, which may be served by a thousand disputes, a thousand disdains, a thousand stratagems, a thousand concerns, a thousand of each of the other companions with whom Labor so haughtily has gone ahead, not to name the others who, covered and hidden under the garments of those similarly covered and hidden, have not departed outright, such as Astuteness, Vainglory, Disdain for Others, Violence, Malice, Falsehood, and their followers, Oppression, Usurpation, Grief, Torment, Fear, and Death, who have not yet appeared in your presence. These are the executioners and avengers, never those of quiet Leisure but always those of solicitous and diligent Industry, Work, Diligence, Labor, also known by as many other names by which she calls herself and by which, in order to be less known, she succeeds in hiding rather than in revealing herself.

"All praise the beautiful Golden Age during which I used to make minds quiet and tranquil, free from this virtuous goddess of yours. As the condiment for the appetite of their bodies, acorns, apples, chestnuts, peaches, and roots, which benign Nature used to administer, were sufficient to make the most delightful and commendable meal when she with such nourishment would feed them better, fondle them more, and keep them alive for a longer time.[1] This so many other artificial condiments could never do, which Industry and Diligence, ministers of that one [Solicitude], have discovered. These, by deceiving the taste and enticing it, administer poison as if it were something sweet; and since more things are produced that please the taste than those that are helpful to the stomach, they, while intent on pleasing our gluttony, succeed in disturbing our health and life.

"All magnify the Golden Age and then esteem and consider as a virtue that scoundrel who extinguished it, she who has come upon 'mine' and 'yours.' It is she who has divided and made the property of this one and that one not only the earth (which is given to all its living beings) but the sea besides, and perhaps even the air. It is she who has laid down the law concerning the pleasures of some, and has caused what was enough for all to be too much for these and too little for those others, whereupon, the first debauch in spite of themselves, and the others die of hunger.

"It is that one who has crossed the seas in order to violate those laws of Nature by intermingling those peoples whom the benign mother set apart, and in order to propagate vice from one generation to another. For virtues are not so propagative, except if we want to call those things virtues and acts of goodness that are so named because of a certain deception and custom and so believed to be, although their effects and fruits are condemned by every impulse and all natural reason. These are the obvious acts of ribaldry, of foolishness, and of malice arising from the confiscatory and proprietary laws of 'mine' and 'yours' and the laws of one considered the most just, who was the strongest possessor, and of him considered most worthy, who was most solicitous and industrious and was the first owner of those endowments and parts of the earth that Nature and, as a consequence, God give to all without distinction.

"Shall I, perhaps, be less favored than she, I who with my sweetness that comes from the mouth of the voice of Nature have taught you about quiet living, untroubled by and contented with this present and established life, and to take with grateful affection and a grateful hand the sweetness that Nature extends to us? And let us not as ingrates and unappreciative ones deny that sweetness that she gives to us and commands us to employ, because God himself, her author, to whom we shall be likewise ungrateful, gives of it to us and commands us to employ it. I say will that one be more favored who, so rebellious and deaf to advice and withdrawn from, and disdainful toward, natural gifts, adapts her thoughts and hands to artful enterprises and machinations, on account of which the world is corrupted, and perverted is the law of our mother? Do you not hear how in these times the world, belatedly becoming aware of its evils, mourns that age during which I with my rule kept the human species gay and satisfied, which age the present century (in which Solicitude, or industrious Labor, as she throws us into confusion, claims to regulate everything with the spur of ambitious Honor) abominates with loud cries and laments?

Oh, thou beautiful Golden Age!
Not because the river with milk did flow
And the woods honey did distill,
Not because the lands yielded their fruits, untouched by the plough,
And without anger and without venom the serpents did roam,
Not because the dark cloud did not then spread its veil
And the heaven did smile with light and serenity
In eternal spring, now aglow and verdant,
Not because the pine bark to another's shore
Conveyed not the wanderer, or war, or goods,
    But only because that vain name without subject,
That idol of errors, idol of deceit,
Later called honor by the insane rabble,
Which they made tyrant over our nature,
Did not intermingle its anguish with the happy sweetness of the loving
    flock.
Nor was its harsh rule known among those souls to liberty accustomed,
But a golden rule and happy,
Engraved by Nature: "If it pleaseth, it is permitted unto you." [2]

"This one [Solicitude], envious of the quiet and happiness or
even of the shadow of pleasure that in this being of ours we are
able to take for ourselves, having placed a restraint upon coitus,
food, sleep—because of which we not only can delight ourselves
less, but most often are grieved and tormented—causes that which
is a gift of Nature to be considered a theft, and wants the beautiful,
the sweet, and the good to be despised and wants us to have esteem
for cruel and guilty crime. She induces the world to leave the
certain and present good it possesses and to concern itself with,
and to get involved in, every slaughter for the sake of the shadow
of future glory. I come from all sides of that internal edifice that
Truth reveals with as many mirrors as there are stars in the sky,
and that Nature proclaims from without with as many voices and
tongues as there are beautiful objects, in order to impress it upon
you, and to declare:

Leave shadows and embrace the truth.
Do not exchange the present for the future.
You are the hound who drops his bone into the stream,
As he desires the shadow of the one he holds in his mouth.

It was never in the mind of the wise man or the shrewd
To lose one good in order to acquire another.
For what reason do you seek paradise at so great a distance,
If in yourselves you find it?
    Rather let him who loses the one good, while on earth,
After death not expect the other.
Because Heaven so disdains to give a second
To him who does not hold the first gift dear.
So believing that you elevate yourselves, you go to the bottom,
And removing yourselves from pleasures, you sentence yourselves to
    sorrows,
And with endless deceit
Striving toward heaven, you remain in hell." [3]

Here Momus answered, saying that the Council did not have
so much leisure that it could answer one by one the objections that
Leisure, because she has not had a penury of leisure, has been
able to weave and arrange. He said that she should at this time,
however, profit from her own nature by going away and waiting for three or four days. For it may be possible that the gods,
finding themselves with leisure, may be able to decide some matters in her favor, which they find impossible to do now.
    Leisure added: "Let me be allowed, oh Momus, a couple of
additional reasons in no more terms than are contained in the
form of a pair of syllogisms, more efficacious in subject matter than
in form. The first of these is the following: To the first father of
men, when he was a good man, and to the first mother of women,
when she was a good woman, Jove granted me as a companion.
But when the latter and the former became wicked, Jove ordained
that the first father should seize her so that she would be his mate
and that he might cause her belly to sweat and his forehead to
ache." [4]
SAUL. He should have said: "Cause his forehead to sweat and her
belly to ache."
SOPHIA. "Now consider, gods," Leisure said, "the conclusion that
depends on the fact that I was declared the companion of Innocence and she, the companion of Sin. Since like is accompanied by
like, the worthy by the condign, I become a virtue and she be-

comes a vice, and thus I become worthy and she becomes unworthy of such a seat.

"The second syllogism is this: The gods are gods because they are most happy; the happy are happy because they are without solicitude and labor. They who are not disturbed and angered do not have labor and solicitude. It is they especially who possess leisure. Therefore the gods are gods, because they have leisure at their disposal."

SAUL. What did Momus say to this?

SOPHIA. He said that because he had studied logic in Aristotle he had not learned to answer arguments in the fourth figure.[5]

SAUL. And what did Jove say?

SOPHIA. That from all that she [Leisure] had said and he had heard, he remembered only the last reason concerning her having been the companion of the good man and woman. Regarding that reason, it occurred to him that horses, however, are not donkeys because they find themselves in their company; nor is the sheep ever a goat among goats.

And he added that the gods had given intellect and hands to man and had made him similar to them, giving him power over the other animals. This consists in his being able not only to operate according to his nature and to what is usual, but also to operate outside the laws of that nature, in order that by forming or being able to form other natures, other paths, other categories, with his intelligence, by means of that liberty without which he would not have the above-mentioned similarity, he would succeed in preserving himself as god of the earth. That nature certainly when it becomes idle will be frustrative and vain, just as are useless the eye that does not see and the hand that does not grasp. And for this reason Providence has determined that he be occupied in action by means of his hands, and in contemplation by means of his intellect, so that he will not contemplate without action and will not act without contemplation.

In the Golden Age then, men were not because of Leisure more virtuous than beasts have hitherto been, but they were perhaps more stupid than many of the beasts. Now that difficulties have been born and needs have arisen among them, because of their emulation of divine acts and their adaptation to inspired affects, their minds have become sharpened, industries have been invented, skills have been discovered, and always, through necessity, from day to day new and marvelous inventions are summoned forth from the depths of the human intellect. Whence, always removing themselves more and more from their bestial being by means of their solicitous and urgent occupations, they more closely approach divine being. You must not be amazed at the injustices and roguery that arise from employments; because if oxen and monkeys had as much virtue and intelligence as men, they would have the same apprehensions, the same affects, and the same vices. Thus, those among men who have the quality of the pig, of the ass, or of the ox are certainly less wicked and are not infected with so many criminal vices; but they are not, however, more virtuous except in that manner by which beasts, because they are not participants in as many vices, come to be more virtuous than they.

We do not praise the virtue of continence in a sow because she allows herself to be mounted by only one pig and but once a year, but we do praise this virtue in a woman, who is urged on not only once by her nature because of its need for procreation, but many times by her own discourse because of her concern for pleasure, that concern being indeed the object of her acts. Moreover, we do not praise the continence of a female or male pig very much, but rather very little. For it rarely happens, and with little reason, that the pig because of the stupidity and harshness of its complexion is urged on by lust, any more than one man is urged on because he is cold and badly formed, and the other, because he is decrepit. That continence must be considered otherwise, which is truly continence and truly a virtue, in a complexion more gentle, more cultivated, more ingenious, most perspicacious, and more understanding. However, taking regions in general, virtue is found with great difficulty in Germany, a great deal in France; there is more virtue in Italy, still more virtue in Libya. If you ponder more profoundly upon the matter, Socrates, when he admitted the judgment of the physiognomist concerning his natural inclination toward the filthy love of boys, not only revealed a certain defect but also gained praise for his continence in spite of it.

"If then, Leisure [said Momus],[6] you consider what must be considered from this discussion, you will find, notwithstanding, that men were not so virtuous in your Golden Age, because they were not so wicked as they are at present. Since there is much difference between not being wicked and being virtuous, not so easily is the one separated from the other, considering that there are no like studies, no like minds, inclinations, and complexions where there are no like virtues. In comparison with us, however, it happens that barbarians and savages are considered better than we gods, because being of wild and equine minds, they are not notable for the same vices. Therefore beasts, which are much less noted for these vices than they, will for this reason be considered much better than they.

"It will not be very fitting that you, Leisure and Somnus,[7] and that Golden Age of yours, sometimes and in some manner be vices; but it will not be fitting that you will never and in no way be virtues. So whenever you, Somnus, will have ceased to be Somnus, and you, Leisure, will have become Activity, you will then be numbered among virtues and be exalted."

Now Somnus rubbed his eyes a bit and took a little step forward to utter a few more trivia and deliver a brief speech before the Senate, so as not to seem to have come there in vain. Momus then saw him moving leisurely, ravished by the grace and loveliness of the goddess Oscitation. Just as the dawn precedes the sun, she, about to utter her prologue, preceded him who dared not reveal his love in the presence of the gods because it was not permissible for him to caress his handmaiden. She (after having heaved a warmish sigh), enunciating every letter so as to render him more reverence and honor, caressed her master in this fashion:

Somne, quies rerum, placidissime somne deorum,
Pax animi, quem cura fugit, qui corpora duris
Fessa ministeriis mulces reparasque labori.[8]

(Oh Sleep, you rest of things, Sleep, most gentle of gods,
Peace of the mind, from whom care takes flight, you who
    soothe bodies
Wearied by difficult duties and restore them for labor.)

Hardly had Momus, the god of censures (who for the afore-
mentioned reason had forgotten about the duties of his office), re-
sumed his long talk, when Somnus, who had been attracted by the
pronouncement of so many praises and had been caressed by the
softness of the tone of Oscitation's voice, invited Drowsiness, who
was lodging within his entrails, to come for an audience. After
Drowsiness had made reference to the fumes that resided in his
stomach, all of them rose together to that god's brain and thus
made his head heavy, and with this, his senses left him. Now while
Snore was blowing his whistles and trombones before him, Somnus, trembling, bent down and put his head on Lady Juno's breast.
And while he was inclining, it happened (since this god always
wears a shirt without breeches and since it was too short) that he
showed his buttocks, his anus, and the point of his *campanile* to
Momus and to all of the other gods who were on his side.

Upon this occasion Laughter, who came to the fore presenting
to the eyes of the Senate the view of many little bones, all of which
were teeth making themselves heard with the dissonant music of
many cachinnations, interrupted Momus in his oration. Momus,
not being able to be resentful against Laughter, turned all of his
disdain against Somnus, who had provoked him at least by not
rewarding him with good attention. Moreover, he, with many
solemnities, offered Somnus and his Jacob's staff and bag, purgatory, as a sign of the greatest contempt for his adulatory and ama-
tory *dicendi genus;* whereupon it was noticeable that the gods were
laughing not so much because of the state Somnus was in, as because of the strange circumstance that had befallen him, and because he was the player and the subject of this comedy.

And when Shame had covered his face with a red veil, Momus
asked: "Upon whom does it fall to rid us of this dormouse? Who
causes this mirror of ridicule to be present before our eyes for so
long a time?" Meanwhile the goddess Laziness, moved by the
angry complaint of Momus (who is not one of the most vulgar
gods that heaven holds), took her husband into her arms. And
then she, quickly carrying him away, took him toward the cavern
of a mountain near the Cimmerii; [9] and with them departed their
three children, Morpheus, Icelus, and Phantasus.[10] They all soon
found themselves there whence perpetual fogs are exhaled from

the earth, causing the sky to have eternal twilight, where the wind does not blow and mute Quiet still has one of her palaces near Somnus' royal abode. Before its courtyard is a garden of yews, beeches, cypresses, boxtrees, and laurels. In the midst of it there is a spring that rises from a small river that comes there from the steep passage of the river Lethe, turning away from shadowy hell to the surface of the earth to disclose itself to the open sky. Here they put the sleepy god into his bed, the boards of which were of ebony, the mattresses of plumes, the canopy of white and cerulean striped silk.

In the meanwhile, after having taken his leave, Laughter departed from the conclave. And the mouths and jaws of the gods having been again set in order, for one of them came close to losing his jaw, Leisure, who alone had remained there, saw that the judgment of the gods was not too inclined in her favor and despaired of profiting further in some manner, since almost all of her most important reasons were not accepted but were, as many of them as existed, on the contrary, cast down to the ground, where because of the violence of the repulse some lay half alive, some had died, some had broken necks, others had completely broken into pieces with a crash. Every moment of waiting seemed a year to her until she could take the opportunity of removing herself from their midst, before there might perhaps befall her some disgraceful misfortune similar to that which befell her companion, out of respect for whom she doubted that Momus would worsen his censure against her.

But Momus, noticing the fright that that one had of matters not hers, said to her: "Do not doubt, you poor wretch, for I, established by Fate as the advocate of those in need, do not want to fail to plead your case." And having turned to Jove, he said to him: "From what you say, oh father, concerning the cause of Leisure, I understand that you are not fully informed regarding her being, her seat, and her ministers and court. But certainly if you come to know her, I am easily convinced that, if you do not wish to enthrone her in the stars as Leisure, you will at least permit her to dwell as Employment, together with that other one said and considered to be her enemy, with whom, without the one harming the other, she may make perpetual sojourn." Jove replied that he was seeking the opportunity of being able, with justice, to satisfy Leisure, in whose caresses there is no mortal nor god who is not often wont to delight himself. He declared, however, that he would willingly listen to him if he would present some strong case in her favor.

"Does it seem to you, Jove," he asked, "that in the house of Leisure there is leisure as regards active life, there where there are so many gentlemen in waiting with servants who arise most punctually in the morning to wash their masters' faces and hands three and four times with five or seven kinds of water, and with a hot iron and with the sap of a fern spend two hours waving and curling their hair, imitating lofty and great Providence, by whom there is not a hair of a head that is not examined in order that it be disposed of according to its law? It is there where afterward the dress coat is adjusted with such diligence, the folds of the ruff are arranged with such sagacity, the buttons are fastened with such moderation, the cuffs are adjusted with such refinement, the nails are cleaned and filed with such delicacy, the breeches are matched with the dress coat with so much justice, moderation, and equity, those knots of the laces are arranged with so much circumspection. With such great sedulity they work with the hollow of their palms again and again, to adjust their stockings; with such great symmetry of movement they go about proportioning the ends and borders of the legs of their breeches where the openings unite with the stockings around the bend of the knee; with so much patience are the tightest bindings or garters borne, so that the stockings do not slide down to form folds and confuse their proportion with the legs.

"Where does Judgment with the strength of obstinacy dispense and discern that since it is not attractive and fitting that the shoe accommodate itself to the foot, the foot should become wide, twisted, knotty, and rough, in spite of itself, so as to accommodate itself to the narrow, straight, polished, and elegant shoe? It is there where with such grace one steps, one moves about in order to be gazed upon in the city, visits and entertains the ladies, dances and performs caprioles, courantes, branles, and trescas; and when there is nothing else to do, because one has tired oneself in the abovementioned operations, to avoid the inconvenience of committing errors, one sits down to play table games, withdrawing from the more strenuous and tiring games.[11]

"And in such manner all sins are avoided, if there are not more than seven mortal and capital sins; for as a Genoese gambler said: 'What pride do you expect of a man who, having lost one hundred scudi to a count, sits down to play to win four reales from a servant?'[12] What avarice can that man have for whom a thousand scudi do not last a week? What lust and covetous love can be found in him who has placed all the attention of his spirit upon playing? How will you be able to manifest wrath against him who, for fear that his partner will leave the game, bears a thousand insults and answers with politeness and patience a proud man who is before him? In what manner can he be gluttonous who employs every kind of waste and applies every care in doing so? And what envy of what another possesses can there be in that man, if he throws away and seems to despise that which is his own? What sloth can there be in that man who, beginning from midday, and sometimes from morning until midnight, never ceases to play?

"And does it seem to you that he in the meanwhile keeps in idleness both his servants who must assist him and those who must administer to him in the temple, in the market, in the tavern, in the kitchen, in the stable, in bed, in the brothel?

"And to demonstrate to you, oh Jove, and to you other gods that in the home of Leisure there are not lacking learned and lettered persons occupied in studies, besides those occupied in employments of which we have spoken, I ask: Does it seem to you that in the house of Leisure one is at leisure as regards contemplative life, there where grammarians are not lacking who dispute about what was first, the noun or the verb? Why does it happen that the adjective is placed before and after the substantive? Why in some expressions is a certain conjunction, such as for example, 'et,' placed before and some other, such as for example, 'que,' placed after? How is it that the 'e' and 'd' with the addition of the stem and the scission of the 'd' through its middle clearly form the image representing that divinity of Lampsacus, who because of envy committed the murder of the ass?[13] Who is the author to whom legitimately must be ascribed the *Priapea,* the Mantuan Maro [Virgil], or rather the Sulmonan Naso [Ovid]?[14] I shall not talk about so many other fine matters that are similar and nicer than these.

"There, there is no lack of dialecticians who will inquire as to whether Chrysaoreus,[15] who was a disciple of Porphyry, was considered a golden-tongued man because of his nature, or because of his reputation, or only because he was so designated; whether the *Peri Hermeneias*[16] must go ahead, or come before or after, or be placed ad libitum before and after the *Categories;* whether the indefinite individual should be put in the aggregate and placed in the middle as a predictable sixth, or rather as a shield-bearer of the species and page of the genus;[17] whether after having become experts in the syllogistic form, we must first apply ourselves to the study of the *Prior Analytics,* in which the judicative art is fully dealt with, or indeed immediately examine the *Topics,* in which the perfection of the inventive art is treated; whether that one must practice captious sophistries *ad usum vel ad fugam vel in abusum;* whether the modes that form the modalities are four, or forty, or four hundred. I do not want to ask you a thousand other fine questions.

"There, there are the physicists who doubt whether there can be knowledge of natural things; whether the subject is a mobile entity or mobile body, or a natural entity or a natural body; whether matter has any other act than the entitative where the line of coincidence exists between the physical and mathematical; whether or not there is creation or production from nothing; whether matter can be without form; whether many substantial forms can be together, and other innumerable and similar inquiries concerning things which are most manifest; and whether these things are placed in doubt by useless investigations.

"It is there where the metaphysicians bother their heads concerning the principle of individuation; concerning the subject entity, in what manner it is entity; concerning the proof that arithmetical numerals and geometric magnitudes are not the substance of things; concerning whether it is true that ideas have subsistential being in themselves; about whether being is the same or different, subjectively and objectively; concerning being and essence; concerning accidents that are the same in number, in one or more subjects; concerning equivocation, 'univocation,' and analogy with entity; concerning the conjunction of intelligences with the stelliferous worlds, whether it is by means of soul or rather by means of a mover; whether infinite virtue can be in finite greatness; concerning the unity or plurality of the prime movers; concerning the gradation of finite or infinite progression in subordinate causes; and concerning so many, many similar matters that cause so many cowls to rave, cause the juice of the napes of so many 'proto-sages' to distill."

Now Jove said: "Oh Momus, it seems to me that Leisure has won over or suborned you, you who so idly waste your time and discourse. Conclude, because we have well determined what we are going to do with that one later."

"I shall discontinue," said Momus, "referring to other likewise innumerable, busy people who are employed in the house of that goddess, as for example to so many vain versifiers who against the wishes of the world want to pass themselves off as poets, to so many writers of fables, to so many new reporters of old histories, reported a thousand times by a thousand others, better told to the tune of a thousand doubloons.[18] I do not mention the algebraists, the squarers of circles, the drawers of figures, the methodizers, the reformers of dialectics, the instaurators of orthographies, the contemplators of life and death, the true postillions[19] of paradise, the new condottieri of eternal life recently corrected and reprinted with a great many most useful additions, the good nuncios who promise better bread, meat, and wine, in comparison with which the Greek wine of Somma, the malvasia of Candia, and the asprino of Nola could not be better.[20] I shall omit fine speculations concerning Fate and will, concerning the ubiquitariness of a body, concerning the excellence of the justice found in leeches."

Now Minerva said: "If you do not shut this chatterbox's mouth, oh father, we shall waste our time in vain discourses and it will not be possible for us to expedite our principal business today." Therefore, Father Jove said to Momus: "I do not have time to discuss your ironies. But to come back to your expulsion, Leisure, I tell you that that Leisure which is laudable and diligent must sit and sits on the same throne with Solicitude, because Labor must be regulated by Leisure, and Leisure must be tempered by Labor. For the benefit of Leisure, Labor will be more reasonable, more expeditious, and ready, because with difficulty does one proceed from labor to labor. And since actions without premeditation and consideration are not good, they are likewise worthless without premeditating leisure. Likewise the progress from leisure to leisure cannot be sweet and pleasing, because idleness never is sweet unless it issues forth from the bosom of Labor. Now it will never be, Leisure, that you can really ever be pleasing except when you follow worthy occupations. I want worthless and inert leisure to be the greatest labor that a generous spirit can encounter unless it appears to him after laudable exercise and work. I want you to approach Old Age as its master, and to cause her often to turn her eyes backward. And if she has not left worthy vestiges, you shall make her disturbed, unhappy, fearful of the approaching judgment of the impending season that leads her to the inexorable tribunal of Rhadamanthus, so that she thus may come to sense the horrors of death before it comes."

SAUL. Tansillo spoke well regarding this matter:

> Do believe in him who to you can swear
> That the world has no condition so sad
> To equal that of remorse,
> Since there be no one who can his past relive.
> And, although each repentance to us brings torment,
> That which most oppresses, most outrages us,
> And wounds impresses, which it alloweth not to heal,
> Is the thought of the time when man of much was
>   capable, and nothing did.[21]

SOPHIA. "I want," said Jove, "the success of useless enterprises to be not less sad, but sadder than some of those that Momus has related to us are found in the seat of Leisure; and I want the wrath of the gods to fall heavily upon those busy idlenesses that have thrown the world into greater troubles and travails than any employment could ever have done. Those people, I say, want to convert all of the nobility and perfection of human life into mere idle beliefs and fantasies while they so greatly praise the concerns and works of justice for which they say man does not become better (although he manifests himself to be so), and while they so vituperate vices and dissension for which they say that men will not become less pleasing to those gods to whom they were pleasing, although it should be so and worse. You, inert, useless, and pernicious Leisure, do not expect that your seat will be disposed of in heaven and by the heavenly gods, but rather expect that it will be disposed of in hell, and by the ministers of rigorous and implacable Pluto."

Now I have no desire to relate to you how idly Leisure comported herself as she walked away, and how she, urged on by so many shoves, could barely proceed, and only when compelled by the goddess Necessity, who kicked her, removed herself from that place, deploring the Council that had not been willing to grant her a few more days and a time limit for departing from their company.

SECOND PART
OF THE *Third Dialogue*

[Continuation of Sophia's Speech]

Then Saturn petitioned Jove to be more expeditious in the disposition of the other seats because evening was approaching; and he
also petitioned that only the principal business of removal and seat-
ing be attended to, and that that concerning whatever appertained
to the rule by which the virtues of goddesses and others must
be governed, should be decided at the advent of the next important festival, which will take place on the eve of the Feast of
the Pantheon, at which time it will be necessary that the gods
again convene in a body. To this proposal all the other gods with
a nod of their heads made a sign of assent except Haste, Discord,
Untimeliness, and others. "So it seems to me indeed," said the
loud Thunderer.

"Come now," added Ceres, "where do we want to send my
Triptolemus, that charioteer whom you see there, him for whom
I gave wheaten bread to men? Do you want me to send him to
the countryside of the one and the other Sicily [1] where he may
make his residence, since there, there are three of my temples,
which, thanks to his diligence and labor, were consecrated to me:
one in Apulia, another in Calabria, the third in Trinacria [2] herself?"

"Do what you wish with your worshiper and minister, my daughter," said Jove. "To this seat should succeed, if you still are of the same opinion, oh gods, Humanity, who in our language is called the goddess Philanthropia, of whom this wagoner especially seems to have been the type. I remind you that it was she who encouraged you, Ceres, to send him and that it was she who then guided him to execute your good deeds toward mankind."

"It is certainly so," said Momus, "because it is she for whom Bacchus puts such fine blood into men, and Ceres, such fine flesh, which could not be possible in the days of chestnuts, beans, and acorns. Then let Misanthropy together with Penury flee before her, and as is customary and fitting, of the two wheels of the chariot let the left be Counsel, the right, Aid; and of the two most gentle dragons who pull the thill, let the one on the left be Clemency, the one on the right, Favor."

Then Momus suggested to Mercury what he would like to do with Serpentarius; for he [Serpentarius] seemed to him to be well adapted to be sent to act as the Marsian charlatan because he had that grace with which to manage without fear and danger a serpent of so great a size.[3] Regarding Serpens he also asked radiant Apollo whether he wanted it as something to be used by his magicians and malefactors, that is to say by his Circes and Medeas, in order to perpetrate their poisonings, or indeed whether he wanted to offer it to his doctors, that is to say to Asclepius, to make theriaca from it. He also asked Minerva whether this one could be of service to her, so that she might send him to take vengeance against some resurrected, hostile Laocoön.

"Let anyone who wants him take him," responded the great Patriarch, "and let him do whatever he wants with Serpens as well as with Ophiuchus, providing they are removed from there; and let Sagacity succeed to their place, she who is accustomed to seeing and admiring herself in Serpens." "Then let Sagacity follow," said all, "since she is not less worthy of heaven than her sister, Prudence. In order that the former may know where and how to command and plan that which is to be done and to permit it to attain a certain design, let the latter first know and then judge, with the aid of fine intelligence, what that design is; and let her drive away Grossness, Inconsideration, and Hebetude from the squares where matters are called into question and deliberated upon. Let her drink of knowledge from the vessels of Wisdom, whence she will conceive and give birth to acts of prudence."

"As for the Arrow," said Momus, "because I was never curious to know to whom it belonged, that is to say, whether it was the one with which Apollo slew the great Python, or rather that one with which Lady Venus caused that indolent lad of hers to wound fierce Mars, who in revenge then plunged a dagger up to the hilt below the belly of that cruel woman, or whether it was a memorable dart with which Alcides did away with the queen of the Stymphalian Birds, or the other by which the Caledonian boar collapsed for the last time, or indeed whether it is some relic or trophy of a certain triumph of the most chaste Diana. Be it what it may, let its master take it back and put it wherever he pleases."

"Well," answered Jove, "let it be taken from there together with Insidiousness, Calumny, Detraction, Envious Action, and Slander; and let Close Attention, Observance, Choice, and Collimation of well-regulated intention succeed in its place." And he added: "Concerning the Eagle, a divine and heroic bird and the symbol of Empire, I determine and so wish that it go to live again in flesh and blood in bibacious Germany. There, more than in any other place, it will find itself celebrated in form, in figure, in picture, and in image, in as many paintings, in as many statues, in as many engravings as the stars that may present themselves in the heaven before the eyes of contemplative Germany. It is not necessary for it to take along Ambition, Presumption, Temerity, Oppression, Tyranny, and other companions and aids of these goddesses, for there they would have to be idle because the countryside is not wide enough for them. But let them take flight far away from that cherished and genial land where their shields are bowls, their helmets are pots and washbowls, their swords are bones sheathed in salted meat, their trumpets are drinking glasses, goblets, and mugs, their drums are barrels and casks, the field is the drinking table (I meant to say eating table), their fortresses, bulwarks, castles, and bastions are canteens, eating houses, and inns, which are found in an even greater number than dwelling places."

Now Momus said: "Forgive me, great father, if I interrupt

your talking. It seems to me that these goddesses and their companions and aids are there, without your sending them there. Because in that region alone, Ambition, who seeks to be superior over all in becoming a pig, Presumption of the Belly, which expects to receive no less from above than the throat can send below, Temerity, with which the stomach vainly tries to digest that which very soon and very quickly it finds necessary to vomit, Oppression over the senses and natural passion, and Tyranny of vegetative, sensitive, and intellectual life—there, these hold greater sway than in any other parts of this globe." "It is true, oh Momus," added Mercury, "but such tyrannies, temerities, ambitions, and other similar cacogoddesses with their cacodemonesses arise, not at all from aquiline natures, but from the natures of leeches, gluttons, starlings, and pigs.

"Now to come back to the discussion of Jove's sentence, it seems to me to be very prejudicial to the condition, life, and nature of this royal bird, which because it drinks little and eats and devours much, because it has bright and clear eyes, because it is swift in its flight, and because, due to the buoyancy of its wings, it rises into the sky and is an inhabitant of dry, rocky, lofty, and mighty places, cannot have any association and union with those rural people, the double weight of whose heavy breeches seems by their strong counterweight to pull them down toward the deep and shadowy center. And these people become so slow, sluggish, and inept, not so much in pursuing and in fleeing as in being strong enough to hold firm in wars, and are greatly subject to eye disease, and drink incomparably more than they eat." "That which I have said is said," answered Jove. "I said that it [the Eagle] should appear in flesh and blood in order to see the pictures of itself, but not indeed that it should stay there as if it were in prison, or that it should fail to find itself there wherever with other more worthy reasons it is in agreement in spirit and truth with the above-mentioned divinities. And let it leave this glorious seat to all those virtues of whom it could have been the vicar, of, let us say, the Goddess Magnanimity, Magnificence, Generosity, and other sisters and their aids."

"Now what shall we do with that Dolphin?" asked Neptune. "Does it please you that I put him into the sea off Marseilles, whence by way of the Rhone River he will return time after time to visit and revisit the 'Dolphinate'?"⁴ "So let us hurry," said Momus, "because, to tell the truth, it seems to me a matter no more to be laughed at if someone, 'Delphinum caelis appinxit, fluctibus aprum' ('Painted a dolphin of the heavens as a wild boar of the sea'), than if 'Delphinum sylvis appinxit, fluctibus aprum'⁵ ('He painted a wild boar of the sea as a dolphin of the forest').

"Let him go where it pleases Neptune," said Jove; "and allow Emblematic Love, Affability, and Service with their companions and aids to succeed in its place." Minerva asked that the horse, Pegasus, leaving his twenty brilliant spots of light, should together with Curiosity go to the equine fount, now for a long time confused, ruined, and contaminated by oxen, pigs, and donkeys. And let him see whether by means of his kicks and bites he can do enough to avenge that place against such a villainous multitude, so that the Muses may see the water of the fount settled and restored and may not disdain to return there, and there establish their schools and promotions.⁶ And in this place in heaven let there succeed Divine Fervor, Rapture, Enthusiasm, Prophecy, Study, and Ingenuity with their kin and aids, whence eternally from above the divine water will be distilled, so as to purge the minds and quench the affects of humans."

"If it so pleases you gods," said Neptune, "let this Andromeda be taken away, who has been bound by the hand of Ignorance to the reef of Obstinacy with the chain of perverse reasons and false opinions so as to be swallowed by the Cetus of perdition and final ruin that moves through the fickle and tempestuous sea; and let her be committed into the provident and friendly hands of solicitous, laborious, and sagacious Perseus, who, having then freed and removed her from her unworthy captivity, should take her into his own worthy possession. And let Jove dispose as to who must succeed her in her place among the stars."

"There," answered the father of the gods, "I want Hope to succeed, she for whom there is nothing too arduous and difficult with which she does not fail to kindle all spirits capable of having some sense of end, with an expectation of a fruit worthy of their works and labors." "Let there succeed," answered Pallas, "that most holy shield of the human breast, that divine foundation of all the edifices of Goodness, that most secure refuge of Truth, that one who never loses confidence because of any strange accident whatsoever since she senses within herself the seeds of her own sufficiency, of which she, no matter by what stroke ever so violent, cannot be defrauded. Let her succeed, by virtue of whom it is reported that Stilpo won a victory over his enemies, that Stilpo, I say, who after having escaped from the flames that were burning to ashes his country, his house, his wife, his children, and his riches, replied to Demetrius that he had all of his possessions with him, since he had with him that courage, that justice, and that prudence through which he could best hope for the consolation, safety, and support of his life and because of which he would easily disdain life's sweetness." [7]

"Let us abandon this display," said Momus, "and quickly come to the examination of what must be done with that Triangle or Delta." Shield-bearing Pallas answered: "It seems fitting to me that it be placed in the hands of the Cardinal of Cusa [Cusanus], so that he can see whether with this he can liberate the disturbed geometricians from that troublesome inquiry into the squaring of the circle, by adapting the circle and triangle to that divine principle of his of the commensuration and coincidence of the maximum and minimum figures, that is to say, of that figure that consists of the minimum, and of the other that consists of the maximum number of angles. Let this trigon then be drawn with a circle [see Fig. 1] that contains it and with another that will be contained by it; and with the relation of the two lines (of which the one goes from the center to the point of contact of the internal circle with the external triangle, the other from the same center being extended toward one of the angles of the triangle) let there come about the achievement of the squaring, for such a long time and so vainly sought after." [8]

Now Minerva rose again and said: "But I, in order not to seem less courteous to the Muses, want to send to the geometricians a gift incomparably greater and better than this and any other that up to now was ever given, for which the Nolan, to whom it will be first revealed and by whose hand it may be spread to the multitude, should owe me not only one but one hundred hecatombs. [9]

Because by virtue of contemplation upon the equality that is found between the maximum and the minimum, between the outermost and innermost, between the beginning and the end, I shall give him a method that is more fecund, richer and more secure, and will not only demonstrate how the square is made equal to the circle but besides will quickly demonstrate how every trigon, every pentagon, every hexagon and finally how every polygonal figure whatsoever, and howsoever many-sided, is made equal to the circle in which line will no less be equal to line than surface to surface, area to area, and volume to volume in solid figures."

SAUL. This will be a most excellent thing, and an inestimable treasure for "cosmometrists."

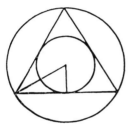

Fig. 1

Fig. 2

SOPHIA. So excellent and worthy that it seems to me that it will certainly counterweigh the invention of all the rest of the geometric faculty. Rather upon this rests another more complete, greater, richer, easier, more exquisite, shorter, and no less certain method that succeeds in commensurating any polygonal figure with the line and surface of the circle and the circle with the line and surface of any polygon.

SAUL. I should like to know the method, as soon as possible.

SOPHIA. So spoke Mercury to Minerva. She answered: "First (in the same manner that you used) within this triangle I describe the largest circle [see Fig. 2] that can be described; then outside of this triangle I shall describe another, the smallest that can be described, up to contact with the three angles. And now I do not wish to proceed to your bothersome squaring, but to an easy 'trigonism,' seeking a triangle that has its line equal to the line of the circle, and another that will have a surface equal to the surface of the circle. This will be one [triangle] described about that triangle in the middle [see Fig. 3], equidistant from the one that contains the circle, and the other triangle that is contained by the circle.[10] This one I shall let another interpret in like manner with his own mind, because it is sufficient for me to have demonstrated the locus of loci. Likewise in order to square the circle it will be necessary to take, not the triangle, but a quadrangle that is between the largest [square] inside and the smallest outside the circle [see Fig. 4]. In order to 'pentagonize' a circle one will take the middle figure between the greatest pentagon contained by a

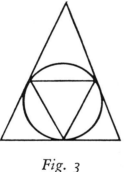

Fig. 3   Fig. 4

circle and the smallest containing a circle. One must do likewise in order to make any other figure equal to the circle in area and in line. So furthermore, because the circle of the square is found equal to the circle of the triangle, the square of this circle will be found equal to the triangle of the other circle of the same quantity as the latter."

SAUL. In this manner, oh Sophia, all the other figures can be made equal to other figures with the aid and relation of the circle, which you make the measure of measures. That is, if I want to make a triangle equal to the quadrangle, I take the middle triangle between the two contiguous to the circle with that middle [quadrangle] between the two quadrangles contiguous to the same circle, or indeed to another that is equal. If I want to draw a square equal to the hexagon, I shall delineate within and without the circle both the latter and the former, and shall draw the middle one between the two of the one and the other.

SOPHIA. You have understood it well. So then we have not only the equaling of all the figures to the circle but besides, that of each figure to all the others by means of the circle, always preserving equality according to the line and according to the surface. Therefore, with little consideration or attention we shall be able to take every equality and proportion of any chord whatsoever with any arc whatsoever while it, whole or divided, or augmented with certain ratios, will form such a polygon, so that in the said manner it will be contained by such a circle or will contain it.

"Now let us quickly determine," said Jove, "whom we want to place there." Minerva answered: "It seems to me that Faith and Sincerity will be comfortable there, without whom every contract is confused and dubious, every conversation is dissolved, every society is destroyed. See to what point the world is reduced, because it has become custom and proverb that in governing faith is not observed. Moreover, faith is not observed with infidels and heretics; so therefore [they say] let faith be broken with him who violates it. Now, what will happen if this is put into practice by all? What will the world come to if all republics, kingdoms, dominions, families, and individuals say that one must be a saint with the saint, perverse with the perverse? And will they excuse themselves for being wicked because they have a wicked man as a companion or neighbor? And will they think that we should not force ourselves to be absolutely good, as if we were gods only for the convenience and for the occasion, like toxic and poisonous serpents, wolves, and bears?"

"I want," added the father, "that Faith be most celebrated among virtues. And may it never be permissible that Faith, even if she is given with the conditions of another faith, be broken because that other faith has been broken—although it is the law of some bestial and barbarous Jew and Saracen (not of a civilized and heroic Greek and Roman), to whom it is permitted that they pledge their faith sometimes and with certain kinds of people, only for their own convenience and as a pretext for resorting to deception, making it an aid to tyranny and treachery."

SAUL. Oh Sophia, there is no offense more infamous, criminal,

and unworthy of mercy than that which is done to one man because of another, owing to the fact that the one has believed the
other. There is no offense more infamous than that through which
the one is harmed by the other, because he placed faith in him,
esteeming him a worthy man.

SOPHIA. "Then I want," said the mighty Thunderer, "this virtue
to be seen celebrated in heaven, so that she in the future will be
more esteemed on earth. Let her be seen in the place where the
Triangle used to be seen, by whom Faith has been and is appropriately signified, because the triangular body (as one that consists of a lesser number of angles and is farther from being circular) is with more difficulty mobile than a body formed in any
other manner. In this manner will be purged the northern coast,
where usually three hundred sixty stars are observed, three very
large ones, eighteen large, eighty-one medium-sized, one hundred
seventy-seven small, fifty-eight very small, thirteen exceedingly
small, with one nebulous star and nine obscure stars."

SAUL. Now let us be expeditious and briefly relate what was done
with the rest.

SOPHIA. "Decree, oh father," said Momus, "what we must do with
that protoparent of lambs, he who first allows pale plants to come
forth from the earth, who opens the year and with a new flowery
and leafy mantle recovers and beautifies this world." [11] "Because
I fear," said Jove, "to send him to be among those of Calabria, or
Apulia, or happy Campania, where they [the lambs] are often
killed by the rigors of winter, and it does not seem fitting to me
to send him among the others of the African plains and mountains, where they die because of the excessive heat, it seems to me
most suitable that he should find himself near the Thames, where
I see so many beautiful, good, fat, white, and nimble ones. And
they are not enormous like those in the region near the Nigero,
not black, as they are near the Silere and the Ofito, not emaciated,
as they are near the Sebeto and the Sarno, not bad, as they are
near the Tiber and the Arno, not ugly to see, as they are near
the Tagus, since that place [England] suits that season by which
it is dominated, because of the fact that there the sky is more temperate, more than in any other place beyond and on this side of the
Equinox. [12] This season, having abolished from the above-men-

tioned land the excessive rigor of snows and overabundant favor of the sun, makes it fortunate as a land of continuous and perpetual spring, as is testified by the perpetually green and flowery terrain.

"Add to this that there, embraced by the protecting arms of the ample ocean, he [Aries] will be secure against wolves, lions, bears, and other fierce animals and hostile forces of terra firma. And since this animal resembles the prince, the duke, and the condottiere, because he has the qualities of the shepherd, the captain, and guide, as you see in heaven where all the signs of this girdle of the firmament run after him, and as you see on earth where, when he leaps or rushes headlong, when he turns about or straightens up, when he descends or rises, the entire flock easily succeeds in imitating him, in agreeing with him, and in following him, I want that there should succeed in his place Virtuous Emulation, Exemplariness with Good Accord, and with other virtues, sisters, and aids. These have as their contraries Scandal and Bad Example, who have as ministers Prevarication, Alienation, and Bewilderment, as guides Malice or Ignorance, or the one and the other together, as a follower Foolish Credulity, who as you see is blind and attempts to walk groping with the cane of obscure inquiry and insane persuasion, and as perpetual companions Cowardice and Worthlessness. Let all of these together leave these seats and go as wanderers throughout the earth." "Wisely decreed," answered all the gods.

And Juno asked Jove what he wished to do with his Taurus, his bull, with that consort of the Holy Manger.[13] He answered her: "If he does not wish to go near the Alps or to the shores of the Po, or, I say, to the metropolis of Piedmont where is situated the delightful city of Taurino, named after him just as Bucephala was named after Bucephalus, or to the islands named after the goats, which are opposite Parthenope toward the west, or to Corveto in Basilicata, named after the ravens, or to Myrmidonia, named after the ants, or to the 'Dolphinate,' named after the dolphin, or to 'Aprutio,' named after the boars, or to Ofanto, named after the serpents, or to Oxford, named after I know not what other species, let him go as a companion to nearby Montone [Mentone], where (as testified by their flesh, which because of the advantages of the fresh grass and the delicacy of the pastures, is considered the most esteemed in the world) he will have the most beautiful companions to be seen in the remaining space of the universe." [14]

And when Saturn asked about the successor, Jove replied thus: "Because this one is an animal, patiently laborious, who endures labors, I have wanted him up to now to be the archetype of Patience, Tolerance, Sufferance, and Longanimity, virtues indeed most necessary to the world; and then with him let there depart (although I do not care whether they go with him or do not go with him) Wrath, Indignation, and Fury, who are wont to be in the company of this sometimes wrathful animal.

"Here you see leaving Wrath, the daughter borne by apprehension of Injustice and Insult; and she leaves mournful and vindictive because it seems unfitting to her that Contempt should gaze upon her and slap her cheeks. See how her flaming eyes are turned toward Jove, toward Mars, toward Momus, toward all! Observe how Hope of Revenge goes to the ear of her who, it would seem, consoles and restrains her by showing her the favor of menacing Possibility against Spite, Contumely, and Torment, her provokers! There is Impetus, her brother, who gives her strength, vigor, and fervor, there, Fury, her sister, who accompanies her with her three daughters, namely Heat of Passion, Cruelty, and Madness. Oh how difficult and troublesome it is to contemplate her and restrain her! Oh, with how much more difficulty can she be stomached and digested by other gods than by you, Saturn, this one who has open nostrils, an impetuous forehead, a hard head, mordacious teeth, venomous lips, a cutting tongue, scratching hands, a poisonous heart, a shrill voice, and a sanguine color!"

Now Mars earnestly entreated in behalf of Wrath, saying that she sometimes, rather most of the time, is a most necessary virtue, as one who favors Law, gives strength to Truth, to Judgment; and she sharpens the mind and opens a path to many eminent virtues, which tranquil souls do not understand. To this Jove said: "Then let her, and in that manner by which she is a virtue, hold steadfast and stay among those to whom she makes herself propitious. Never allow her, however, to approach heaven, unless Zeal goes before her with the lantern of Reason."

"And what shall we do with Atlas' seven daughters, oh father?" said Momus. To this Jove answered: "Let them go with their seven lamps to give light to that nocturnal and midnight holy wedding.[15] And let them see to it that they go before the door is closed and before cold, ice, and the white snow begin to descend from above, since otherwise they will raise their voices and knock in vain for the door to be opened to them as the doorman who holds the key answers: 'I do not know you.' Advise them that they will be fools if they allow the oil in the lantern to run low. If it is always moist and never dry, they will not sometimes be deprived of the light of worthy praise and glory. And to this region which they leave let Conversation, Companionship, Marriage, Confraternity, Church, Society, Agreement, Covenant, and Confederation come to establish their residences. And let them there be joined to Friendship, because where she is not, there are instead, Contamination, Confusion, and Disorder. And unless they [Conversation, Companionship, etc.] are guided, they are not themselves, because they never find themselves in truth (although most of the time they do in name) among wicked people, but possess the nature of Monopoly, Conventicle, Sect, Conspiracy, Mob, Plot, or something with another detestable name and being.

"They are found, not among the irrational and among those who are not intent upon good end, not where idle belief and understanding are one and the same, but where one agrees upon the same action regarding things similarly understood. They persevere among the good and remain a short time and are inconstant among the perverse, among such as those of whom we spoke in the discussion concerning Law and Judgment—among whom agreement is not truly found—as well as among those who do not reflect upon virtuous actions."

SAUL. Those people are not in agreement in equally understanding, but in equally ignoring and maligning and in not agreeing according to various reasons. They do not concur in equally working for a good end, but they do in equally thinking little of good works and in esteeming all heroic actions unworthy. But let us return to ourselves. What was done with the two young boys [Gemini]?

SOPHIA. Cupid requested that he [Jove] give them to the Grand

Turk. Phoebus wanted them to be the pages of some Italian prince, Mercury, cubicular attendants in the great chamber. It seemed to Saturn that they should serve as bed warmers for some old and great prelate, or even for himself, a poor, decrepit man. To this Venus remarked: "But who, oh white beard, will assure them that you will not bite them, will not eat them, if your teeth do not forgive your own children, by whom you are defamed as an anthropophagus and a parricide?" [16] "And worse," said Mercury, "for there is concern that out of some sullen fear that may seize Saturn he might thrust the point of his scythe into their bodies.

"I say that even if it may be given to these to remain in the court of the gods, there will no longer be any more reason for their affecting you, oh good father, than for their affecting many others less venerable than you, who may have laid their eyes upon them."

Here Jove decreed that he would not permit that *in posterum* there be admitted into the court of the gods pages, or other servants who do not have much sense, discretion, and beards; and that these [Gemini] be submitted to lots, whereupon it would be decided to which of the gods it would fall to relinquish them to some friend on earth. And although some entreated him to decide concerning them, he declared that, regarding these invidious matters, it was not his wish to generate suspicion of partiality in their minds by seeming to incline more to one side of the discordants than to another.

SAUL. A good decree to safeguard against the dissensions that might have arisen on account of these boys!

SOPHIA. Venus asked that to that seat should succeed Friendship, Love, and Peace with their witnesses, Intimacy, Kiss, Embracing, Caressing, Charm, and all the brothers and servants, aids, assistants, and bystanders of twin Cupid. [17] "The request is just," said all the gods. "Let it be done," said Jove.

Afterward, since they had to determine what to do about Cancer (who, because he seems scorched by the flame of the fire and reddened by the heat of the sun, finds himself in heaven not otherwise than if he were condemned to the tortures of hell), Juno asked, it being a matter which concerned her, what the Senate wished to do with him. The majority of the Senate left him to her discretion. And she said that if Neptune, the god of the sea, allowed it, she desired that he be plunged into the waves of the Adriatic Sea, where there are more companions than there are stars in the heaven. Besides, she wished that he be placed near the most honorable Venetian Republic, who, as if she too were a crab, is retrogressing little by little from the orient to the occident.[18] That god who carries the great trident consented. And Jove said that the Tropic of Conversion, Emendation, Repression, and Retraction would, in the place of Cancer, go well with virtues contrary to Bad Progress, Obstinacy, and Pertinacity.

And he immediately suggested the discussion of Leo, saying: "But let this fierce animal abstain from following Cancer and from wanting to continue to be his companion, because if he goes to Venice, he will find another, stronger than he could ever be. For that one not only can fight on land but also knows how to fight well on water and much better in the air, since he has wings, is canonized, and is a lettered person. It will therefore be more expedient for him to descend to the Libyan deserts, where he will find a wife and companions. And it seems to me that we ought to transfer to that place that Magnanimity, that so Heroic Generosity, who knows how to spare the subjugated, have compassion toward the infirm, subjugate Insolence, trample upon Temerity, reject Presumption, and overthrow Pride." "Very well," said Juno and the greater part of the consistory.

I shall refrain from mentioning with what solemn, magnificent, and fine pomp and with what a great retinue this virtue took her leave; because at present, owing to the want of time, I wish it to be sufficient for you to hear what is most important concerning the reform and disposition of seats. For when I conduct you from seat to seat as we gaze upon and examine these courts, I shall inform you concerning all the rest of them.

SAUL. It is well, oh dear Sophia. Your most courteous promise greatly satisfies me. I shall be satisfied, however, if you, with the utmost brevity with which it pleases you to do so, give me an inkling of the order, space, and changes assigned to the other seats.

SOPHIA. "Now what will become of Virgo?" asked chaste Lucina, the huntress Diana. "Ascertain," answered Jove, "whether she wants to go to be a prioress or abbess of sisters or nuns, who are in the convents or monasteries of Europe, I say in those places where they have not been put to rout and have not been dispersed by the plague.[19] Or indeed, ascertain whether she wants to go to govern the young ladies of the court so that they will not be seized with the desire to eat the fruit before or out of season, nor with the desire to become companions to their mistresses." "Oh, Dictynna said that she cannot and that she does not want to return to any place whence she was once driven away and whence she so many times has fled." The protoparent added: "Let her then remain firm in heaven and take good care that she does not fall; and see to it that she is not contaminated in this place."

Said Momus: "It seems to me that she can continue to be pure and clean, if she will continue to be far away from reasonable animals, heroes, and gods, and if she will stay among the beasts, as she has up to the present, having on her occidental side fiercest Leo and on her oriental side poisonous Scorpio. But now I do not know how she will get along, there where Magnanimity, Loving Kindness, Generosity, and Virility are close to her. They, by clinging to her in friendly intercourse, and making her draw toward her the magnanimous, the amorous, the generous, and the virile, will from a female easily cause her to become male and from a wild and Alpine goddess and a divinity ruling over satyrs, sylvan deities, and fauns, convert her into a gallant, humane, affable, and hospitable god."

"Let her be what she must be," answered Jove, "and in the meantime let there be joined in the same seat with her, Chastity, Virtue, Continence, Purity, Modesty, Reserve, and Honesty, contrary to prostituted Lust, effusive Incontinence, Immodesty, and Brazenness. It is on account of these virtues that I perceive Virginity to be a virtue, although she of herself is not a thing of worth. Because of herself she is neither a virtue nor a vice, and does not contain goodness, dignity, or merit; and when she does not serve governing Nature, she becomes crime, expressed impotence, madness, and foolishness. And if she obtempers some urgent principle, she is called Continence and has the being of a virtue to the extent that she participates in such firmness and contempt for pleasures, which contempt is not vain and frustrative, but contributes to human society and to the honest satisfaction of others."

"And what shall we do with the Scales [Libra]?" asked Mercury. "Let them go everywhere," answered the first presider. "Let them go among families in order that through them fathers will see in which direction their children best incline, whether toward letters, whether toward arms, whether toward agriculture, whether toward religion, whether toward celibacy, whether toward love.[20] For it is not good that the ass be employed in flying and pigs in ploughing. Let the Scales roam through the academies and universities where they may examine whether those who teach are of correct weight, whether they are too light or tip the scales, and whether they who presume to teach from their chair and writings need to listen and study. And by balancing their intellect, let them [the Scales] see whether that intellect gives those who teach wings or weighs them down. Let them see whether it has the nature of the sheep or rather of the shepherd, and whether it is fit for the feeding of pigs and asses, or rather of creatures capable of reason.

"Let them go through the Vestal buildings in order to make those men and those women understand what and how much the momentum of the counterweight should be to violate the Law of Nature by another supra- or extra- or contranatural one according to, or outside of, every principle and obligation.[21]

"Let them go through the courts in order that the offices, honors, seats, favors, and exemptions may be obtained according to the weight they give to the merits and dignity of each individual, because those who do not know how to rule according to order do not deserve to be presiders over order, and do preside, to Fortune's great prejudice.

"Let them frequent republics in order that the weight of administrations counterbalance the sufficiency and capacity of the subjects. And let responsibilities be distributed, not by the weighing of the grades of blood, of nobility, of titles, of wealth, but by the weighing of the virtues that give birth to the fruits of enterprises, so that the just may preside, the wealthy may contribute, the learned may teach, the prudent may guide, the strong may fight, those who have judgment, advise, those who have authority, command.

"Let them go throughout all states so that in peace treaties, confederations, and leagues one will, by attending to the measure and weight of his own faith and that of those with whom it is contracted, not prevaricate and turn away from the just, honest, and useful commune.

"And in enterprises and matters of war let one consider in what equilibrium his own forces compete with those of the enemy. Let one consider what is present and necessary with what is possible in the future, the facility of proposing with the difficulty of execution, the ease of entering with the inconvenience of leaving, the inconstancy of friends with the constancy of enemies, the pleasure of offending with the concern for defending one's self, the easy disturbing of other people's property with the uneasy preservation of one's own, the certain wasting and loss of one's own with the uncertain acquisition and gain of somebody else's. Let the Scales go among all individuals so that everyone will counterweigh what he wants with what he knows, what he wants and knows with what he is able to do, what he wants, knows, and is able to do with what he must do, what he wants, knows, is able to do, and must do with what he is, does, has, and expects."

"Now what shall we put in the place of the Scales? What will replace Libra?" asked Pallas. Many replied: "Equity, Righteousness, Retribution, Reasonable Distribution, Favor, Gratitude, Good Conscience, Self-Recognition, Respect due to elders, Equanimity due to equals, Benignness due to inferiors, Justice without rigor in respect to all, which may extinguish Ingratitude, Temerity, Insolence, Daring, Arrogance, Lack of Respect, Iniquity, Insult, and other servants of these." "Well! Well!" declared all the gods of the consistory.

After this utterance handsome, long-haired Apollo stood up and said: "The hour indeed has arrived, oh gods, in which we must give merited expedition to Scorpio, this infernal worm, who was the principal cause of the horrible accident and cruel death of my beloved Phaëthon. Because when that wretched, doubtful, and timid boy was driving the chariot of my eternal fire with the ill-reputed steeds, this pernicious, menacing monster drew close to him to give him such a blow with the tip of his death-dealing tail that it caused him to be beside himself with horrendous fright and made the reins fall from his yielding hands onto the backs of the horses. From this proceeded the so widely heralded destruction in the sky, which in the area called the Milky Way still appears to be burned, the so famed devastation of the world, which in many, many parts seemed to be reduced to ashes; and from this there seemed to have ensued so shameful an ignominy against my godliness. It is also shameful that for so long a time such foulness has occupied the space of two signs in the sky."

"See then, oh Diana," said Jove, "what you wish to do with that animal of yours, who alive is wicked, and dead serves no purpose." "Permit me (if it so pleases you)," said the virgin goddess, "to have him return to Chios on Mount Chelippos where he was born by my command, in spite of presumptuous Orion; and there let him be decomposed into that matter out of which he was produced. With him let Fraud, Deception, Betrayal, Pernicious Deceit, Cunning Hypocrisy, Lie, Perjury, and Treason depart, and to this place let the contrary virtues, Sincerity, Execution of Promises, Observance of Faith, and their sisters, followers, and ministers succeed." "Do with him what you please," said Momus, "because the facts concerning that one will not be placed before you in controversy, as were those concerning the two boys in the case of old Saturn.

"And let us quickly see what must be done with the son of Euschemo [Eupheme], who now for so many thousands of years, with the fear of sending it away without obtaining another, holds that widowed arrow fitted to the bow, aiming at that point where the tail extends from the spine of Scorpio's back. And certainly since I indeed consider him to be most experienced in sighting, in aiming at, as they say, his target, which is half of the sagittal art, I could still deem him not ignorant of the rest of it concerned with shooting at and striking the target, which comprises the other half of this exercise. I should advise that we send him to gain a little reputation for himself on the British Island, where some of those gentlemen are wont, some in jackets, others in doublets with tails, to celebrate the feast of Prince Arthur and of the Duke of Shoreditch.[22] But I fear that, lacking the principal verb relating to what appertains to hitting the target squarely, he may insult the art. In the meanwhile, you see what you want to do with him, because (to tell the truth as I understand it) he does not seem to me suitable for anything else than to be a scarecrow for birds, as for example a guardian of beans or melons." "Let him," said the Patriarch, "go where he wants to; indeed let one of you give him the address that behooves him; and in his place let there be Imaginative Speculation, Contemplation, Study, Attention, Aspiration, Drive toward an excellent goal, with their circumstances and their companies."

Here Momus added: "What, father, do you wish done concerning that saintly, pure, and venerable Capricorn, your divine and godlike co-fosterer, that vigorous and more than heroic fellow warrior of ours against the perilous attack of the gigantean stubbornness, that great war counselor who found a way of studying that enemy, that dreadful antagonist of the gods, who arrived in Egypt from the cave of Mount Taurus, that Capricorn who (because we should not have had the daring to assault him [the enemy] outright) taught us the lesson of transforming ourselves into beasts [23] so that craft and astuteness might supplement the deficiencies in our natural strength and yield us honored triumph over the adversary forces? But woe is me! This merit is not without some demerit, because this good is not without some evil adjunct, this being so, perhaps, because it is prescribed and defined by Fate, or I do not know by what other cause, that no sweetness be absolved from some trouble and bitterness."

"Now what evil," questioned Jove, "could he [that enemy] have brought us that could be said to have been conjoined to so great a good? What indignity is there that could have accompanied such a triumph?" Momus answered: "With this he brought about that the Egyptians should come to honor live images of beasts, and should adore us in the form of those, whence we came to be mocked, as I shall tell you." "And this, oh Momus," said Jove, "do not consider as bad, because you know that animals and plants are living effects of Nature; this Nature (as you must know) is none other than God in things."

SAUL. So, *natura est deus in rebus.*

SOPHIA. "However," he said, "diverse living things represent diverse divinities and diverse powers, which, besides the absolute being they possess, obtain the being communicated to all things according to their capacity and measure. Whence all of God is in all things (although not totally, but in some more abundantly and in others less). Therefore, Mars can more efficaciously be found in a natural vestige and mode of substance, not only in a viper and scorpion but also in an onion and garlic, than in any manner whatsoever of inanimate painting or statue. Think thus, of the Sun in the Crocus, in the narcissus, in the heliotrope, in the rooster, in the lion; you must think thus of each of the gods for each of the species under various genera of the entity. Because just as Divinity descends in a certain manner, to the extent that one communicates with Nature, so one ascends to Divinity through Nature, just as by means of a life resplendent in natural things one rises to the life that presides over them."

"What you say is true," answered Momus, "because indeed I see how those wise men through these means had the power to make intimate, affable, and friendly toward themselves, the gods, who, by means of cries they sent forth through statues, gave these wise men advice, doctrines, divinations, and superhuman institutions; whence with magic and divine rites they rose to the height of Divinity by means of the same ladder of Nature by which Divinity descends even to the lowest things in order to communicate herself.[24]

"But that which seems to me should be deplored is the fact that I see some senseless and foolish idolaters who no more imitate the excellence of the cult of Egypt, than the shadow approaches the nobility of the body, and who seek Divinity, for which they have no reason whatsoever, in the excrements of dead and inanimate things. These idolaters, nevertheless, mock not only those who are divine and sagacious worshipers but also those of us who are reputed to be beasts. And what is worse, with this they triumph by seeing their mad rites in so great repute and those of the others entirely vanished and broken."

"Let this not trouble you, oh Momus," said Isis, "because Fate has ordained the vicissitude of shadows and light." "But the evil," answered Momus, "is that they hold for certain that they are in the light." And Isis added that the shadows would not be shadows to them if they were known by them. Those worshipers, then, in order to procure certain benefits and gifts from the gods through the knowledge of profound magic, entered into the midst of certain natural things in which, in such manner, Divinity was latent and through which she was able to and wanted to impart herself to such effects. Therefore, those ceremonies were not vain fantasies, but live words which touched the very ears of us gods. Just as we want to be understood by these worshipers, not through utterances of language, which they may be able to contrive, but through utterances of natural effects, they wished to strive to be understood by us through these utterances, as well as through acts of ceremonies. Otherwise we should have been deaf to their prayers, just as a Tartar would be toward the Greek tongue, which he had never heard.

Those wise men knew God to be in things, and Divinity to be latent in Nature, working and glowing differently in different subjects and succeeding through diverse physical forms, in certain arrangements, in making them participants in her, I say, in her being, in her life and intellect; and they therefore, with equally diverse arrangements, used to prepare themselves to receive whatever and as many gifts as they yearned for. Then, for victory, they libated to magnanimous Jove in the eagle, where, in accordance with such an attribution, Divinity is latent. For prudence, in their sacrifices to sagacious Jove, they libated to the serpent; against betrayal, they libated to menacing Jove in the crocodile. So for other innumerable ends, they libated to other innumerable species. All of this was done not without a magic and most efficacious doctrine.

SAUL. How do you say so, oh Sophia, if Jove was not known in the days of the Egyptian cults, but existed among the Greeks a long time afterward?

SOPHIA. Do not be concerned with the Greek name, oh Saulino, because I speak according to the most universal custom and because names (even among the Greeks) are *postiches* of Divinity. Furthermore, all know well that Jove was a king of Crete, a mortal man, whose body no less than that of every other man becomes putrefied or is turned into ashes. It is not unknown that Venus also was a mortal woman, who was a most delightful, uncommonly beautiful, gracious, and liberal queen in Cyprus. Likewise, you must understand that all the other gods have been known as men.

SAUL. Why then did men adore and invoke them?

SOPHIA. I shall tell you. They did not adore Jove as if he were

Divinity, but adored Divinity as it was in Jove, because seeing in him a man in whom majesty, justice, and magnanimity were outstanding, they understood that in him there was a magnanimous, just, and benign god; and they prescribed and established as a custom that such a god or rather, Divinity, inasmuch as it imparted itself in such manner, should be called Jove, just as divine wisdom, interpretation, and manifestation were known under the name of Mercury, a most wise Egyptian. So that in the latter and in the former only the name and representation of Divinity are celebrated, that Divinity which, with the birth of these men, had come to impart itself to men, the course of whose work, with their death, was understood to have been completed and Divinity to have returned to heaven.

Thus the eternal gods (without placing any inconvenience against that which is true of divine substance) have temporal names, some in some times and nations, others in others. As you can see from revealing stories, Paul of Tarsus was named Mercury and Barnabas, the Galilean, was named Jove,[25] not because they were believed to be those gods themselves, but because men believed that that divine virtue that was found in Mercury and in Jove in other times then found itself present in these, because of the eloquence and persuasion that were in the one and because of the useful effects that proceeded from the other.

Here then is why it is that crocodiles, roosters, onions, and turnips were worshiped, but were worshiped as gods and Divinity in crocodiles, in roosters, and in other things. This Divinity in certain times and periods, places, and regions, successively and at the same time, found, finds, and will find herself in various subjects, which, although they are mortal, have a relationship with Divinity according to how close to and familiar she is with them, not according to what she is in herself, that is, most exalted, absolute, and without association with things produced. You see then that there is one simple Divinity found in all things, one fecund Nature, preserving mother of the universe insofar as she diversely communicates herself, casts her light into diverse subjects, and assumes various names. See how we must diversely ascend to her by partaking of various endowments; otherwise we, in vain, attempt to contain water in nets and catch fish with a shovel.

Then they attributed the life that gives forms to things to two most important principles, that is to say, to the two bodies that are most important in the neighborhood of our globe and maternal divinity, the sun and the moon. Afterward, they construed that life according to seven other principles, distributing it among seven lights called wandering lights, to which, as like unto an original principle and fecund cause, they reduced the differences of species of any genus whatsoever, saying of plants, of animals, of rocks, of influences, and of many other things that these were Saturn's, these Jove's, these Mars's, these and those things of this and the other.[26] So it is with parts, with members, with colors, with seals, with characters, with signs, with images, which are distributed into seven species. But they did not fail, because of this, to construe that there is found in all things, Divinity, who, since she diffuses and imparts herself in innumerable ways, has innumerable names and who, by innumerable paths with principles pertaining and appropriate to each way, is sought after as we honor and cultivate her with innumerable rites, because we seek to receive from her innumerable kinds of favors.

In this, however, we need that wisdom and judgment, that skill, industry, and use of intellectual light that are revealed to the world by the intelligible sun, sometimes more and sometimes less, sometimes most greatly and sometimes most minutely. This custom is called Magic, and she, inasmuch as she depends upon supernatural principles, is divine; and, inasmuch as she turns toward the contemplation of Nature and to the scrutiny of her secrets, she is natural. And she is said to be intermediate and mathematical, inasmuch as she depends upon the reasons and acts of the soul that is at the horizon between the corporeal and the spiritual, the spiritual and the intellectual.

Now, to return to the discussion from which we departed, Isis said to Momus that the stupid and senseless idolaters had no reason to laugh at the magic and divine cult of the Egyptians, who in all things and all effects, according to the respective principles of each, contemplated Divinity. And they knew how, by means of the species that are in the bosom of Nature, to receive those benefits they desired from her. Just as she gives fish from the sea and from rivers, wild animals from deserts, minerals from mines, apples from trees, so from certain parts, from certain animals, from certain beasts, from certain plants, emerge certain destinies, virtues, fortunes, and impressions. Therefore Divinity in the sea was named Neptune, in the sun, Apollo, on the earth, Ceres, in deserted regions, Diana; and she was differently named in each of the other species, which, as diverse ideas, were diverse divinities in Nature, all of which were related to the one Divinity of Divinities and source of ideas regarding Nature.

SAUL. From this it seems to me that that Cabala of the Jews (whatever wisdom may be found in its genus) has proceeded from the Egyptians, among whom Moses was instructed.[27] First, that Cabala attributes an ineffable name to the first principle from which, second, there proceed four names, which afterward are converted into twelve, in a straight line change into seventy-two, and obliquely and in a straight line into one hundred forty-four, and farther on are unfolded by fours and by twelves into names as innumerable as species. And likewise, according to each name (inasmuch as it befits their own language), they name one god, one angel, one intelligence, one power, who presides over one species. From this we see that all Deity finally reduces itself to one source, just as all light is reduced to the first and self-illuminated source and images that are in mirrors as diverse and numerous as there are particular subjects are reduced to their source, the one formal and ideal principle.

SOPHIA. So it is. So, then, that God, as absolute, has nothing to do with us except insofar as he communicates with the effects of Nature and is more intimate with them than Nature herself. Therefore, if he is not Nature herself, he is certainly the nature of Nature, and is the soul of the Soul of the world, if he is not the Soul herself. However, according to the special reasons that they wanted to accommodate to themselves in order to receive his assistance, they had to present themselves before him in the manner of ordered species, just as he who wants bread goes to the baker, he who wants wine goes to the cellarer, he who longs for fruit goes to the gardener, he who wants instruction goes to the master, and the same applies to all other things. Likewise, one Goodness, one Happiness, one Absolute Principle of all riches and fortunes, contracted into various laws, pours forth gifts according to the exigencies of particular beings.

From this you can infer how the wisdom of the Egyptians, which is lost, worshiped not only the earth, the moon, the sun, and other stars of the heaven but also crocodiles, lizards, serpents, onions. This magic and divine rite (through which Divinity so easily imparted herself to men) is mourned by Trismegistus, who said when reasoning with Asclepius: "Do you see, oh Asclepius, these animated statues full of feeling and spirit that are the cause of such and so many worthy works, these statues, I say, prognosticators of future things that bring infirmities, cures, joys, and sadnesses, according to the merits of human affects and bodies? Do you not know, oh Asclepius, that Egypt is the image of heaven or, better said, the colony of all things that are governed and practiced in heaven? To speak the truth, our land is the temple of the world. But woe is me! The time will come when Egypt will appear to have been in vain the religious cultivator of divinity, because divinity, remigrating to heaven, will leave Egypt deserted. And this seat of divinity will remain widowed of every religion, having been deprived of the presence of the gods, for which reason there will succeed in that land strange and barbarous people without any religion, piety, law, and cult.

"Oh Egypt, oh Egypt! Of your religions there will remain only the fables, still incredible to future generations, to whom there will be nothing else that may narrate your pious deeds save the letters sculptured on stones, which will narrate, not to gods and men (because the latter will be dead and deity will have transmigrated into heaven), but to Scythians and Indians, or other people of a similarly savage nature. Shadows will be placed before light, death will be judged to be more useful than life, no one will raise his eyes toward heaven. The religious man will be considered insane, the impious man will be considered prudent, the furious man, strong, the most wicked man, good. And believe me, capital punishment will still be prescribed for him who will apply himself to the religion of the mind, because new justices will be found, new laws. Nothing holy will be found, nothing religious; nothing worthy of heaven or of celestials will be heard. Only pernicious angels will remain, who, mingling with men, will force upon the wretched ones every audacious evil as if it were justice, giving material for wars, rapines, frauds, and all other things contrary to the soul and to natural justice. And this will be the old age and the disorder and irreligion of the world. But do not doubt, Asclepius, for after these things have occurred, the lord and father God, governor of the world, the omnipotent provider, by a deluge of water or of fire, of diseases or of pestilences or of other ministers of his compassionate justice, will doubtlessly then put an end to such a blot, recalling the world to its ancient countenance."

SAUL. Now return to the discussion that Isis had with Momus.

SOPHIA. Now, apropos of the calumniators of the Egyptian cult, she recited to him this verse of the poet: "Loripedem rectus derideat, Aethiopem albus." [28] ("Let the straight-legged man laugh at the bandy-legged, the white man at the Ethiopian.") "Senseless fools and true brutes [Isis continued] laugh at us gods for being worshiped in beasts and plants and stones and at my Egyptians, who in this manner used to recognize us. And they do not consider the fact that Divinity reveals herself in all things, although by virtue of a universal and most excellent end, in great things and general principles, and by proximate ends, convenient and necessary to diverse acts of human life, she is found and is seen in things said to be most abject, although everything, from what is said, has Divinity latent within itself. For she enfolds and imparts herself even unto the smallest beings, and from the smallest beings, according to their capacity. Without her presence nothing would have being, because she is the essence of the existence of the first unto the last being. To what is said, I add and ask, why do they reprehend in the Egyptians that for which they are still understood? And to come to those who either fled from us or were driven like lepers into the deserts,[29] did they not in their necessity resort to the Egyptian cult, when in a time of need they worshiped me in the form of the idol of a golden calf, and at the time of another necessity bowed, bent their knees, and raised their hands to Thoth [30] in the form of the brass serpent, although because of their innate ingratitude, after having been granted the favor of the one and the other deity, they broke the one and the other idol?[31]

"Afterward, when they wanted to honor themselves by calling themselves saints, divine and blessed ones, in what manner were they able to do so, except by naming themselves beasts, as is seen when the father of the twelve tribes,[32] in giving his children a blessing as a testament, magnified them with the names of twelve beasts? How often they call their old god an aroused lion, a flying eagle, an ardent flame, a resounding wave, a vehement tempest, and the god,[33] recently recognized by those other successors of theirs, a bloody pelican, a solitary sparrow, a slain lamb.[34] And thus they call him, thus they paint him, and thus they understand him wherever I see him in statue and painting, in his hand a book, which, I do not know whether I should say it, none other than he can open and read.

"Furthermore, all of those who are about to believe in him, are they not called deified by him and, taking glory in it, do they not still call themselves his sheep, his pasture, his flock, his fold, and his herd? I say that I see the same people signified by asses [35] and by the servant mother, that is to say, the Jewish people and the other generations that were to be joined unto them, by placing their faith in them because of the wild ass of a son.[36] You see how these gods then, these elected people, are signified by these poor and lowly beasts. And then they laugh at us, who are represented by other stronger, worthier, and more imperious beasts?

"I say that since all illustrious and remarkable generations want to show themselves and to be made known by means of their signs and emblems, behold, you see them as eagles, falcons, kites, cuckoos, screech owls, night owls, horned owls, bears, wolves, serpents, horses, oxen, and he-goats and sometimes, because they do not even deem themselves worthy of becoming entire beasts, behold, they present you with a piece of those beasts: a leg, or a head, or a pair of horns, or a tail, or a sinew. And do you not think that if they could transform themselves into the substances of such animals, they would not do it willingly? With what end in mind do you think they picture beasts on their shields, even imitate them in their pictures and in their statues? Do you think that perhaps they mean to signify anything else but, 'This man, this man, oh spectator, whose picture you see, is that beast that stands completed near him,' or else, 'If you want to know who this beast is, know that it is he whose picture you see here and whose name is written here?'

"How many are there who, in order better to appear as beasts, cover themselves with the skin of a wolf, of a fox, of a badger, of a ram, or of a he-goat, whereupon, in order to be one of such animals, it seems that all they need is a tail? How many are there who, in order to show how much they have in them of the bird and of the winged creature and to let it be known with what lightness they could soar to the clouds, plume their hats and caps?"

SAUL. What will you say of noble women, of those who are great as well as of those who want to play the role of greatness? Do they not pay greater attention to beasts than to their own children? There they are, as if they were saying: "Oh my son, made in my image, as you show yourself to be a man, would that you also showed yourself to be a rabbit, a she-puppy, a marten, a cat, and a sable. Just as surely as I have committed you into the arms of this servant, of this domestic, of this ignoble nursemaid, of this filthy, dirty, drunken woman, so infecting you with her fetidness (because it is also necessary that you sleep with her), she will easily cause you to die. I, I myself should be she who should carry you in her arms, should nourish you, suckle you, comb you, sing to you, caress you, kiss you, as I do with this gentle animal whom I do not want to become friendly with anyone but me. I should not let you be touched by anyone but me, and I should not let you stay in any other room and sleep in any other bed than mine.

"If that cruel Atropos should take this animal away from me, I shall not suffer him to be buried like you, but shall embalm him, shall perfume his flesh; and upon that flesh, as upon a divine relic where such members as the fragile head and feet are missing, I shall mold his figure in enameled gold, besprinkled with diamonds, with pearls, and with rubies. And so when it behooves me to make a distinguished appearance, I shall take him with me, now hanging him around my neck, now drawing him to my face, to my mouth, to my nose. Now I shall rest him on my arm and now, allowing my arms to fall perpendicularly, I shall permit him to hang down over my skirts, so that there will not be a part of that animal that is not placed in perspective."

Therefore you clearly see how these most generous women

are affected with more sedulous concern for an animal than for one of their own children, in order to show how much greater is the nobility of those beasts than that of the latter, how much more honorable are the former than the latter.

SOPHIA. And to return to more serious matters, those who are or who consider themselves greater princes, in order to make evident their power and divine pre-eminence over the others by express signs, fix a crown upon their heads, which is only the figure of many horns that wreathe them in a circlet, id est, "horn" their heads.[37] And the loftier and more eminent those horns are, the more magisterial a representation they make, being a sign of more greatness.

Therefore a duke is envious, because a count or marquis shows a crown as large as he does. A larger crown is more fitting for a king, the largest, for the emperor; a triplicate one falls to the pope, as that highest patriarch who must share it between himself and his companions. Yet pontiffs have always worn their miters pointed with two horns. The doge of Venice appears with a horn on the middle of his head; the Grand Turk allows it to issue forth high and straight from out of his turban in a round pyramidal form. All this is done to give testimony of one's greatness, to show, I mean to say, that by adjusting upon one's head, with the greatest skill, this beautiful member that nature has conceded to beasts, he has the nature of the beast.

No one before, nor anyone since, has been able to express this more efficaciously than the leader and lawgiver of the Jewish people. I ask in what manner did that Moses, who departed from the court of Pharaoh learned in all the sciences of the Egyptians, who in the multitude of his manifestations surpassed all of those who were experts in magic, demonstrate his excellence so as to be a divine emissary to that people and a representative of the authority of the god of the Jews? Do you think that he, coming down from Mount Sinai with the great tablets, came in the form of a mere man, in view of the fact that he appeared venerable, with a great pair of horns that branched out from his forehead?[38] Since the courage of that wandering people who gazed upon him failed before that magisterial presence, it was necessary that he cover his face with a veil, which he also did for the sake of dignity and in order not to render too familiar that divine and more than human aspect of his.

SAUL. Likewise I hear that when the Grand Turk does not grant an intimate audience, he wears a veil before his face. In a similar manner, I have seen the Monks of Castello[39] in Genoa showing the veiled tail for a short time and allowing it to be kissed, saying: "Touch it not, kiss it. This is the holy relic of that blessed she-ass, which was made worthy of carrying our Lord from the mount of Olives to Jerusalem. Adore it, kiss it, offer alms. 'Centuplum accipietis, et vitam aeternam possidebitis.'[40] ('You will receive a hundredfold, and will possess eternal life.')"

SOPHIA. Let us leave this and return to our discussion. According to the law and decree of that chosen people, no one becomes king unless oil is placed upon his head with a horn. And from that sacred horn it is ordained that that royal liquid issue in order that there should come forth whatever dignity is possessed by the horns that preserve, spread, and give birth to regal majesty. Now if a piece, a relic, of a dead beast, is in so much repute, what must you think of a live and whole beast that has horns planted upon it only because of the eternal kindness of Nature?

I pursue the argument according to Mosaic authority, which in law and scripture never uses any other threat than this, or others similar to this:[41] "Here, my people, is what our Jehovah says: 'I shall cut off the points of your horns, oh ye transgressors of my precepts.[42] Oh ye false advocates of my law, I shall weaken and dissolve your horns.[43] Ribalds and criminals, I shall duly dehorn you.'"[44] Likewise he does not ordinarily use any other promises than this or similar to this: "I shall surely give you horns; I swear by my faith, by myself, that I shall place horns upon you, my chosen people.[45] My faithful people, be certain that your horns will not receive injury, and that none of the horns will drop off. Holy generation, my blessed children, I shall elevate, magnify, and make your horns sublime, because the horns of the righteous must be exalted."[46] Whence it clearly appears that in horns there exist splendor, excellence, and power, because these are possessions for heroes, beasts, and gods.

SAUL. Whence does it come about that it has become a custom to call one "a horned man" in order to describe him as a man without reputation, or as a man who has lost some reputed kind of honor?[47]

SOPHIA. Whence does it happen that some piggish ignoramuses sometimes call you a philosopher (which, if it is true, is the most honored title a man could have), and say it to you as if to insult or vituperate you?

SAUL. From a kind of envy.

SOPHIA. Whence does it come about that some madman and fool is sometimes called a philosopher by you?

SAUL. From a kind of irony.

SOPHIA. Thus you can understand that either because of a kind of envy or because of a kind of irony, it happens that those who are, or who are not, honored and magnificent, are called "horned ones." In regard to Capricorn, Isis then concluded that because of his having horns and because of his being a beast and, besides, because of his having caused the gods to become "horned" and beasts (he who contains within himself a great doctrine and judgment of natural and magic things, concerning the various reasons through which form and divine substance either immerse, or enfold, or distribute themselves through all, with all, and from all subjects), he is not only a celestial god but also one worthy of a greater and better place than this.[48]

And regarding that for which the most vile idolaters, indeed the most vile in Greece and in other parts of the world, abuse the Egyptians, she answers, according to what is said, that even if there is indignity committed in the cult, which is in some way necessary, and if those sin who, because of many conveniences and necessities, worship the Deity, one and simple and absolute in itself, multiform and omniform in all things, in the forms of live beasts, live plants, live stars and in inspired statues of stone and metal (in which we cannot say that there is anything more intimate with all things than their very form), how incomparably much worse is that cult, and how much more vilely do they sin who, without any convenience and necessity, rather outside of every reason and dignity, under divine garbs, titles, and insignia, adore beasts and worse than beasts?

The Egyptians, as wise men know, from these external natural forms of beasts and live plants used to ascend and (as their successes demonstrate) used to penetrate Divinity. But those then descend, because of the magnificent external robes of their idols [49] (adjusting on the heads of some the golden rays of Apollo, upon others the grace of Ceres, upon others the purity of Diana, upon others the eagle, into the hands of others the scepter and splendor of Jove), to adore in substance as gods those who hardly have as much spirit as our beasts, because their worship terminates in a belief in mortal, useless, infamous, foolish, vituperous, fanatical, dishonorable, and unfortunate men, inspired by perverse geniuses without intelligence, without eloquence, and without any virtue, who alive, were not worth anything to themselves, and dead, cannot possibly be of any worth to themselves or to others. And, although through them so manured and sullied is the dignity of the human race that instead of being imbued with sciences it is imbued with more than bestial ignorance, whence it is reduced to being governed without truly civilized justice, all has occurred, not because of their prudence, but because Fate gives its time and vicissitude to darkness.

And, turning toward Jove, she added these words: "And I am disturbed by you, oh father, because it seems to me that you make many beasts unworthy of heaven because they are beasts, although, as I have demonstrated, their dignity is so great." The mighty Thunderer answered her: "You are deceived, daughter, in thinking that it is so because they are beasts. If the other gods had disdained to be beasts, there would not have occurred so many and such metamorphoses. However, not being able nor being bound to keep you in hypostatic substance, I want them to remain for you as an image, which may be significant as an index and representation of the virtues that are established in those places. And, although some beasts have an express signification of vice because they are animals capable of vengeance against the human species, they, however, are not in another manner without divine virtue, and are most favorable to the same and other species, because nothing is absolutely bad, but is bad in a certain respect, as are the Bear, the Scorpion, and others. I do not want you to reject this point in the argument, but I want you to support it in the manner that you may have seen and will see. It does not disturb me, however, that Truth should be under the guise and with the name of the Bear, that Magnanimity should be under the guise of the Eagle, Philanthropy, under that of the Dolphin, and the same with the others.

"And to come back to the proposal concerning your Capricorn, you know what I said from the beginning when I made the enumeration of those who were to leave heaven, and I believe that you remember that he is one of those retained. Then let his seat rejoice, as much for the reasons brought forth by you as for many others, not less important, which could be advanced. And with him, because of the respects due him, let there sojourn Liberty of Spirit, to whom Monachism (I do not say that of the eaters of spoon meats),[50] Hermitage, and Solitude sometimes administer, they who are wont to give rise to that divine image that is Good Contemplation."

Then Thetis asked what he wanted to do with Aquarius. Answered Jove: "Let him go to visit men and unravel that question of the deluge and declare how it was possible that it was universal, and why it was that all of heaven's cataracts burst loose. And let it no longer be believed to have been a particular deluge, since it is thought impossible that the sea and the rivers could have covered both hemispheres, or even one on this side of, and beyond, the Tropics or the Equinox. Then he should make them understand how this remnant of the human race, swallowed by the waves, went to our Olympus of Greece, and not to the mountains of Armenia, or to Mongibello[51] of Sicily, or to any other place. Furthermore, he should give them to understand that the generations of men are found on various continents, not in the manner in which are found so many other species of animals that have come forth from the maternal bosom of Nature, but by dint of transfretation and by virtue of navigation. And he should tell them, for example, that they were transported by those ships which existed before our first one was invented (I leave other accursed reasonings aside regarding the Greeks, the Druids, and the tablets of Mercury, which reckon more than twenty thousand years—I speak not of lunar years, as some puny glossarists say, but of those round ones similar to the ring, which are computed from one winter to another, from one spring to another, from one autumn to another, from one season to the same next season).

"He should give them to understand that a new part of the earth, called the New World, has been recently discovered, that there they have memorials of ten thousand years and more, which years are, as I tell you, whole and round, because their four months are the four seasons and because when the years were divided into fewer months, they were at the same time divided into longer months.[52] But let him, in order to avoid the inconveniences that you yourself might contemplate, go and skillfully preserve this belief, finding a suitable manner in which to adjust those years; and that upon which he cannot comment and for which he cannot find an excuse, let him boldly reject, saying that more faith must be placed in the gods (whose letters patent and seals he will carry) than in men, who are all liars." Here Momus continued, saying: "And it seems better to me to make an excuse for that belief by putting it in this manner, that for example, those of the new land are not of the human generation, because they are not men, although they are very similar to them in members, shape, and brain and, in many circumstances, show themselves wiser, and not even ignorant in dealing with their gods."

Mercury answered that this was too hard to digest. "It seems to me," he said, "that we can easily deal with whatever pertains to the records of time by making these years greater or, on the contrary, those years smaller; but I think that it is advantageous to find some nice explanation for a few gusts of wind or for some abductions by whales which have swallowed persons of one country and have gone to vomit them alive upon other parts and other continents.[53] Otherwise we Greek gods will be confused, because it will be said that you, Jove, through Deucalion are the restorer, not of all men, but only of a certain part of them." "Of this and of the manner in which we shall provide for it we shall speak when we have more leisure," said Jove.

He added to that one's [Aquarius'] mission the responsibility of deciding whether he [Jove] had up to now been in heaven as a father of the Greeks, or of the Jews, or of the Egyptians, or of others, and whether he has the name of Deucalion, or Noah, or Otreus, or Osiris. "Let him finally determine [said Jove] whether he [Jove] is that patriarch, Noah, who, drunk because of his love of wine, demonstrated to his children the organic principle of their generation,[54] in order to make every single one of them understand wherein existed the 'returnative' principle of that generation swallowed and engulfed by the waves of the great cataclysm, whereupon stepping backward, two vigorous men threw their clothing upon the uncovered breast of their father. Let him determine whether he is that Thessalian Deucalion, to whom, together with his consort, Pyrrha, was shown among the rocks the principle of human restoration, at which time a male and female of the two human beings, stepping backward, threw the rocks over their shoulders at the uncovered breast of Mother Earth.[55]

"And let him teach us [said Jove] which of these two modes of speaking is the fable and which is history (because both the one and the other cannot be history); and if both are fables, which is the mother and which is the daughter. And let him see if he can reduce them to a metaphor of some truth worthy of being concealed. But let him not infer that the sufficiency of Chaldaean magic has come out of, and is derived from, the Jewish Cabala; because the Jews have been proved to be the excrement of Egypt, and there is no one who could have imagined with any verisimilitude that the Egyptians have taken some worthy or unworthy principle from them. Therefore, we Greeks recognize Egypt, the great monarchy of letters and nobility, as parent of our fables, metaphors, and doctrines, and we do not so recognize that generation that never had a span of land which naturally or by virtue of civilized justice was theirs. Whence we can with sufficiency conclude that they have neither naturally nor because of the long enduring violence of fortune ever been part of the world."

SAUL. Then, oh Sophia, consider this, said by Jove in envy, because they are deservedly called and call themselves holy, on account of their being a generation heavenly and divine, rather than terrestrial and human. And since they do not have a worthy part of this world, they are approved by angels as heirs of the other, which is not so worthy that there is no man either great or small, either wise or foolish, who cannot acquire it and most securely hold it as his own, by the power either of will or destiny.

SOPHIA. We are on the subject of the disposition of seats, oh Saulino.

SAUL. Now, tell me, what successor did Jove have in mind for that place?

SOPHIA. Temperance, Civilization, Urbanity, sending down to earth Intemperance, Excess, Harshness, Savagery, and Barbarity.

SAUL. How, oh Sophia, does Temperance obtain the same seat with Urbanity?

SOPHIA. As the mother, she can live together with her daughter. Whereas it is because of intemperance concerning sensuous and intellectual affects that families, republics, societies, and the world are dissolved, put into disorder, dispersed, and visited by floods, it is Temperance who reforms all, as I shall give you to understand when we go visiting these seats.

SAUL. That is well.

SOPHIA. Now to come to the Fishes [Pisces], the beautiful mother of Cupid stood up and said: "I recommend to you (in the name of the affection that you show toward me and the love you bear for me, oh gods) my godparents, who dropped at the shore of the Euphrates River that great egg, which, hatched by the dove, caused me to reveal my compassion toward them." "Let them then return there where they were," said Jove. "That they have remained here so long should suffice, and should that privilege of returning be confirmed, let not the Syrians eat them without being excommunicated.[56] And let them see to it that there come again no leader like Mercury, who, by depriving them of the eggs within them, will formulate some metaphor of a new compassion for the healing of the infirmity of the eyes of some blind man; for I do not want Cupid to open his eyes. Since if blind, he shoots so straight and wounds as many as he wishes, what would he do if he had seeing eyes? Then let them go there, and pay attention to what I have said.

"See how by himself, Silence or Taciturnity, in the form in which the image of 'Pixide' appeared in Egypt and Greece, goes to take his place with his index finger placed over his mouth.[57] Now let him pass, do not speak to him, do not ask him anything. See how from the other side Chatter, Garrulity, Loquacity, with other servants, maids, and assistants, stand out." Momus added: "Let that hair called Berenice's Hair be taken away with curses, and let it be taken by that Thessalian [Deucalion] to be sold on earth to some bald princess."

"Good!" answered Jove. "Now you see purged the space of the zodiac, which contains three hundred forty-six notable stars: five very large, nine large, sixty-four medium-sized, one hundred thirty-three small, one hundred five smaller, twenty-seven very small, three misty ones."

THIRD PART
OF THE *Third Dialogue*

[Continuation of Sophia's speech]

"Now here is how they offer to set up the third part of the heaven," said the mighty Thunderer, "the part called austral, called meridional, where first, oh Neptune, that great and terrible animal of yours presents itself to us."

"Cetus," said Momus, "if it is not that monster which served as a galley, carriage, or tabernacle for the prophet of Nineveh,[1] which served as a meal, medicine, and vomitory, if it is not the trophy of Perseus' triumph, if it is not the protoparent of Ianni de l'Orco, if it is not the terrible beast of Cola Catanzano, who descended with him to the lower regions, I do not know what bad omen it may be, although I am one of the great secretaries of the celestial republic.[2]

"Let it go, if it so pleases Jove, to Salonica; and let it see whether it can serve as some beautiful fable to the bewildered nation and people of the goddess Perdition.[3] And because when this animal is discovered upon the deep, turbulent, and tempestuous sea, it announces its [the sea's] future state of tranquillity, if not on the same day, on one of those that is to come later, it seems to me that it must have been, in its class, a good prototype of the tranquillity of the spirit."

"It is well," said Jove, "that this sovereign virtue called Tranquillity of Mind should appear in heaven if it is that virtue which strengthens men against mundane instability, the constant waves, and the insults of Fortune, keeps them removed from the responsibility of administration, keeps them little eager for novelties, makes them little troublesome to their enemies, little burdensome to their friends and in no way subject to vainglory, not perplexed because of the variety of misfortunes, not irresolute in their encounters with death."

Neptune then asked: "What will you do, oh gods, with my favorite, with my handsome darling, I say with that Orion, who (as the etymologists say) causes the heaven to 'orionate' from fright?" [4]

Here Momus answered: "Let me make a proposal, oh gods. 'A macaroni,' as the proverb in Naples says, 'has fallen into the cheese.' This is because he [Orion] knows how to perform miracles, and, as Neptune knows, can walk over the waves of the sea without sinking, without wetting his feet, and with this, consequently, will be able to perform many other fine acts of kindness. Let us send him among men, and let us see to it that he give them to understand all that I want and like them to understand: that white is black, that the human intellect, through which they seem to see best, is blindness, and that that which according to reason seems excellent, good, and very good, is vile, criminal, and extremely bad. I want them to understand that Nature is a whorish prostitute, that natural law is ribaldry, that Nature and Divinity cannot concur in one and the same good end, and that the justice of the one is not subordinate to the justice of the other, but that they [Nature and Divinity] are contraries, as are shadows and light. I want them to understand that all Divinity is the mother of Greece and is like a hostile stepmother to other generations.

"Therefore, no one can be pleasing to the gods except by Hellenizing, that is, by making himself a Greek; because the most criminal and good-for-nothing man among the Greeks, since he pertains to the generation of the gods, is incomparably greater than the most just and magnanimous man who could have issued forth from Rome during the time she was a republic, or from any other generation whatsoever, although better in its customs, sciences, strength, judgment, beauty, and authority. For these are natural endowments despised by the gods, and left to those who are not capable of greater privileges, that is to say, of those supernatural privileges which Divinity grants, such as that of being able to leap over the waters, that of making crabs dance, that of making lame men perform the caprioles, that of enabling moles to see without glasses, and other beautiful and innumerable gallantries. With this he [Orion] will persuade them that philosophy, all contemplation, and all magic that could make them similar to us, are nothing but follies, that every heroic act is only cowardice, and that ignorance is the best science in the world because it is acquired without labor and does not cause the mind to be affected by melancholy. With this, he can perhaps reclaim and restore the veneration and honor we have lost, and besides advancing these, see to it that our scoundrels should be considered gods because they are Greeks or are Hellenized.[5]

"But it is with fear, oh gods, that I give you this counsel, because some flies are buzzing in my ear that he, finally finding the prey in his hand, may possibly not keep it for himself, saying, besides, and making them believe that great Jove is not Jove, but that Orion is Jove and that all the gods are nothing but chimeras and fantasies. In the meantime, it seems to me indeed fitting that we do not permit that, *per fas et nefas,* as they say, he should want to perform so many demonstrations and acts of dexterity by which he could make himself our superior in reputation."

Here wise Minerva responded: "I do not know, oh Momus, with what sense you speak these words, give this advice, propose these precautions. I think your speech is ironical; for I do not consider you so mad that you can think that the gods beg for reputation among mortals, with such poor arguments. And as for these impostors, may their false reputation, which is founded upon the ignorance and stupidity of whosoever holds them in consideration and esteem, be their honor, rather than the confirmation of their indignity and very great shame. It is of concern to the eye of Divinity and of presiding Truth that although one is good and worthy, and no mortal may know it, dignity is attributed to another, who falsely comes to be considered a god by all mortals; because only by Fate is one made an instrument and index through whom are seen the indignity and madness of all those who esteem another to be the greater, the more he is vile, ignoble, and abject.

"Let us then, for example, take not only Orion, who is a Greek and a man of some merit, but another, belonging to one of the most unworthy and rotten generations of the world, a generation of the lowest and filthiest nature and spirit, who is adored as Jove.[6] The latter, certainly, will never be honored in Jove, nor Jove despised in him, although, masked and incognito, he will obtain that place or throne; rather, others will be despised and vituperated in him. Never then can a thief be capable of honor by virtue of this man who serves as the ape and mockery of blind mortals with his train of hostile geniuses."

"Now, do you know," said Jove, "what I am deciding to do concerning that one [Orion] in order to avoid any possible future scandal? I want him to go down to earth; and I shall command that he lose all power of performing bagatelles, impostures, acts of cunning, kind actions, and other miracles that are of no worth, because I do not want him together with the other to be in a position to destroy whatever excellence and dignity are found and exist in things necessary to the commonwealth of the world. I see how easy it is for it to be deceived, and consequently inclined toward acts of madness and prone to every corruption and indignity. I do not, however, want our reputation to depend upon the discretion of him or another similar to him. For if a king be mad who gives so much power and authority to one of his captains and generous leaders as to make him superior to himself (which can be without prejudice to the realm, which can be as well, perhaps better governed by the latter than by the former), how much more senseless and deserving of a disciplinarian and tutor will he be if he should put or leave in the same authority an abject, vile, and ignorant man, by whom everything will be depreciated, slighted, confused, and thrown into disorder, ignorance being placed by the latter where knowledge is customary, nobility where there is contempt, and villainy where there is reputation!"

"Let him go immediately," said Minerva, "and to that space let there succeed Industry, Military Training, and Military Art, through which the peace and authority of the fatherland may be maintained, barbarians be fought, beaten, and converted to civilized life and human society, and inhuman, porcine, savage, and bestial cults, religions, sacrifices, and laws be annihilated. Because in order to effectuate this for the multitude of lowly, ignorant, and criminal men that prevails over noble, wise, and truly good men, who are few, my wisdom does not suffice without the point of my lance, so deeply are such rascalities rooted, sprouted, and multiplied in the world." To this Jove answered: "Wisdom is sufficient, indeed sufficient, oh my daughter, against these last things, which in themselves grow old, fall, are devoured and digested by time, as are things built on a most fragile foundation." "But in the meanwhile," said Pallas, "we must resist and repel them in order that they do not destroy us through violent means before we reform them."

"Let us come," said Jove, "to the river Eridanus, with which I do not know how to deal and which is both on earth and in the heaven, whereas the other things that we are discussing, left the earth, making their way toward the heaven. But this Eridanus, which is here and is there, which is within and is without, and which is high and is low, and which has the nature of the celestial and has the nature of the terrestrial, which is down there in Italy and is here in the austral region, now does not seem to me to be something to which we should give a place, but rather seems to me to be something from which it is fitting that some place be taken away." "Rather, oh father," said Momus, "it seems to me to be fitting (since the river Eridanus has the property of being at the same time supposititiously and personally in various parts) that we let it be wherever it will be imagined to be, named, called upon, and revered. All of this can be done with very little expense, without any interest and, perhaps, not without good gain. But let it be in such a manner that he who will eat of its imagined, named, called upon, and revered fish will, for example, be as if he did not eat, that he who will drink similarly of its waters will be like him who has had nothing to drink, that he who will in like manner have the Eridanus on his mind will be like him whose brain is vacant and empty, that he who in the same manner will have the company of its Nereids and Nymphs will be not less alone than even he who is out of his mind."

"Well," said Jove, "in this there is no prejudice at all, since it will not happen that, because of it, the others will remain without food, without water to drink, without something remaining in their brains, and without companions; because for them, to have it in mind and to keep it in their company, in imagination, in respect, in prayers, in reverence, is to drink and eat of it. Let it be, however, as Momus proposes, and I see the others affirm. Let Eridanus be in the heaven only in belief and imagination, so that it may not prevent some other thing from being in that same place, upon which we shall determine on another of these forthcoming days; for we must think about this seat as well as about that of the Great Bear.

"Let us now provide for the Hare, whom I wanted, through Contemplation of Death, to be the prototype of Fear and also, as much as it is possible, to be the prototype of Hope and Confidence, the contraries of Fear. For if they are daughters of Consideration and serve Prudence, both the one and the other are, in a certain manner, virtues, or at least of the matter of virtues. But let Vain Fear, Cowardice, and Desperation go together with the Hare down below in order to bring about a true Hades and an Orcus of Suffering upon stupid and ignorant minds. Let there be no place so occult that this False Suspicion and this blind Fear of Death may not enter into it, the door of every remote dwelling being opened by means of the false thoughts that Foolish Faith and Blind Credulity produce, nourish, and raise. But let her no longer (unless with vain strength) approach the place surrounded by the impregnable wall of true philosophical contemplation, where the quietness of life remains fortified and raised on high, where truth is revealed, where the necessity of the eternity of all substance is clear, where one must fear to be stripped naked only by human perfection and justice, which consist in conformity with superior and unerring Nature."

At this point Momus said: "I understand, oh Jove, that he who eats hare becomes beautiful. Let us then bring it about that whosoever will eat of this celestial animal, be he male or female, shall change from one who is ugly to one who is well formed, from one who is graceless to one who is graceful, from one who is ugly and displeasing to one who is pleasing and gentle. And may the belly and stomach of him who contains, digests, and is converted to it, be blessed."

"Yes," said Diana, "but I do not want the seed of my Hare to be lost." "Oh, I shall tell you," said Momus, "a way in which the entire world will be able both to eat and to drink of her, without her being eaten and drunk, without there being a tooth that will touch her, a hand that will feel her, an eye that will see her, and perhaps, even a place that will contain her." [7]

"This," said Jove, "you will discuss with me afterwards. Now, let us come back to that ugly Canis Major who is running after her, seizing her in his mind, as he has for so many hundreds of years, and for whom, for fear that he will lose the cause for which to continue hunting, that hour never comes in which he may really catch her, and who goes barking after her for so long a time, imagining that he hears responses." "I have always lamented, oh father," said Momus, "the fact that you have provided badly, causing that mastiff dog who was sent to pursue the Theban fox to ascend to the sky, as if he were a greyhound, at the tail of a hare, causing the fox to remain down there on earth, transformed into stone." "Quod scripsi, scripsi," said Jove.

"And this," said Momus, "is the misfortune: that Jove obtains his will through Justice and his action through Fatal Decree, so as to make it known that he has absolute authority, and so as not to lend credence to the belief that he may confess his committing or his having committed error, as are wont to do other gods, who, because they have an iota of discretion, sometimes repent, retract, and correct themselves." [8] "And," said Jove, "what do you think we are doing now, you who from a particular want to infer a general meaning?" Momus excused himself for generally inferring from species, that is to say, from similar things, not from genera, that is to say, from all things.

SAUL. Jove's comment was a good one, because the comparison is not what it usually is.

SOPHIA. But he added: "Therefore, holy father, since you have so much power that you can make heaven out of earth, can make bread out of stones, can make something else out of bread, and finally, can even make that which is not and cannot be made, do bring it about that the art of hunters, that is, venation, since it is a magisterial insanity, a royal madness, and an imperial fury, should become a virtue, a religion, a sanity.[9] And let there be great honor to one who is a slaughterer because of his killing, skinning, quartering, and disemboweling a savage beast. Although it would be fitting for Diana to beg this of you, still it is I who ask you, because it is often more proper, when one seeks benefit and honor, that another should interpose himself rather than that the very one whom these await should come in person to present, introduce, and propose himself; for, to his greater shame, his prayer might probably be denied him, and what he seeks might probably be conceded him, to his lesser honor."

Jove answered: "Just as the art of the butcher must be considered an art and an exercise more vile than that of the hangman (as the practice of the butcher's art has become in certain parts of Germany), because that art is dealt with even in contracting human limbs and sometimes while justice is being administered—and is exercised on the limbs of a poor beast, always as we administer to our inordinate gluttony to which the food ordained by Nature, more fitting to the complexion and life of man, is not enough (I leave aside other, more worthy reasons)—so, the art of the hunter is an exercise and an art no less ignoble and vile than that of the butcher, since the savage brute has no less the quality of the beast than the domestic and rustic animal. Nevertheless, it seems to me and pleases me that in order not to blame my daughter Diana and in order that she be not accused with vituperation, I should ordain that being a slaughterer of men should be deemed an infamous thing, being a butcher, that is, an executioner of domestic animals, should be deemed a contemptible thing, but being an executioner of savage beasts should be deemed worthy of honor, of good reputation, and of glory." "A command," said Momus, "fitting to Jove, not when he holds fast to or follows a straight line, but when he retrogresses.

"I used to be astounded when I saw these priests of Diana, after they had killed a buck, a kid, a stag, a boar, or another such animal, kneeling on the ground, baring their heads, and raising their palms toward the sky; and then, with their own scimitars, I have seen them truncate the beast's head, then cut out its heart before touching its other parts. And then I have seen them, successively employing the small knife with divine ritual, gradually proceed to other ceremonies, whence it may be revealed with how much religion and with what pious circumstances the only one who can act as a beast is he who does not admit a companion to this affair, but leaves the others to stand around and watch with a certain reverence and expressed sense of wonderment. And while he is among the others the only executioner, he considers himself to be that very great priest for whom alone it was permissible to carry the *Shem Ha-Meforash* [10] and to put his feet inside the sanctum sanctorum.

"But what is bad about it is that it often happens that while these Actaeons are pursuing the stags of the forest, they are converted by their Diana into domestic stags by her breathing upon their faces with that magic rite and sprinkling upon them the water of the fountain, and saying three times

> Si videbas feram,
> Tu currebas cum ea;
> Me, quae iam tecum eram,
> Spectes in Galilea; [11]

> (When thou sawest the beast,
> Then thou consentedst with him;
> Await me, who was hitherto with you,
> In Galilee;)

or indeed, intoning it in the vulgar tongue in this other manner:

> You left your room
> And the beast did follow;
> With so much diligence
> Did you pursue it,
> That you your companion,
> The same in substance,
> Did make him.
> Amen.

Jove then concluded thus: "I want venation to be a virtue, considering what Isis said regarding the beasts, so that they [the Actaeons] may besides acquire, with much diligent vigilance, with religious care, the nature of the deer, of the boar, and become ferine and bestial. Let it be, I say, such a heroic virtue that when a prince pursues a doe, a hare, a stag, or another beast, let him imagine that enemy legions are running before him. When he has caught something, let him be exactly in that frame of mind he would be in if he had captive in his hands that prince or tyrant whom he fears most; whereupon, not without reason, he will perform those fine ceremonies, render those warm thanks, and offer unto heaven those beautiful and sacrosanct bagatelles."

"We have well provided for the place of the hunting dog," said Momus, "for whom it is better that he be sent to Corsica or to England. And let Preaching of Virtue, Tyrannicide, Zeal for the Fatherland and for Domestic Affairs, Vigilance, and Protection and Concern for the Republic succeed into his place.

"Now what shall we do," he asked, "with Canis Minor?" Gentle Venus then arose and asked the gods as a favor that he be occasionally allowed as a pastime for her and her maidens, to play upon their bosoms, during the time of their vacations, with that graceful movement of his person, with those big kisses, and with that gentle wagging of his tail.

"That is well," said Jove, "but you must see, daughter, that I want greatly beloved Assentation and Adulation as well as perpetually hated Fanaticism and Scorn to depart with him, for in that place I want Friendliness, Courteousness, Placability, Gratitude, Simple Respect, and Loving Service." "Do with the rest as you please," responded the beautiful goddess, "because without these little dogs one cannot live happily in court, just as in those same courts, one cannot virtuously persevere without those virtues of which you speak."

And no sooner had the goddess of Paphos closed her mouth than Minerva opened hers, saying: "Now to what end do you destine my beautiful handiwork, that wandering palace, that movable room, that storehouse and wandering beast, that whale that goes to vomit bodies, swallowed alive and intact, upon the widely separated beaches of opposite, contrary, diverse shores of the sea?" [12] "Let it go," answered many gods, "with abominable Avarice, with Contemptuous and Precipitous Commerce, with desperate Piracy, Plundering, Deceit, Usury, and other wicked servants, ministers, and followers of theirs. And may Liberty, Munificence,

Nobility of Spirit, Communication, Service, and other ministers and servants of theirs go to reside in that seat." "It is necessary," said Minerva, "that it be yielded to, and appropriated by, someone." "Do with it what you please," said Jove. "Now then," said she, "let it serve some solicitous Portuguese, or curious and avaricious Briton, so that with it he may go and discover other lands and other regions in the direction of the West Indies, in which the keen Genoese head has not made discovery, and on which the tenacious and stingy Spaniard has not set foot. And thus let it successively serve in the future the most curious, solicitous, and diligent investigator of new continents and lands."

When Minerva had finished her discourse, Saturn began to make himself heard in this sad, restive, and melancholy tone of voice: "It seems to me, oh gods, that among those chosen to remain in heaven with the Asses, Capricorn and Virgo, should be this Hydra, this ancient and great serpent who occupies the celestial fatherland with great honor, she being that one who vindicated us against the insults of the audacious and curious Prometheus, that Prometheus who was not so much favorable to our glory as he was affectionate toward men, whom he wanted by means of privilege and prerogative to be completely similar and equal to us in immortality. This animal [the Hydra] was more sagacious and crafty, prudent, cunning, fierce, astute, and shrewd than all the others, that the world produces.

"When Prometheus had suborned my son, Jove, your brother and father, to give him those skin sacks or vessels full of eternal life, it happened that after he had loaded an ass with them in order that it might transport them to the region of men, the ass (because for a certain distance of the journey it went ahead of its driver), baked by the sun, burnt by the heat, made thirsty by its labor, its lungs dried up from thirst, was invited by that one [the Hydra] to the fountain. Here (because that fountain was rather concave and deep, so that the water was two or three spans below the level of the ground) the ass had to curve and bend itself so far in order to touch the liquid surface with its lips that the skin sacks happened to drop from its back, and were ruptured, eternal life poured out, and all was wasted upon the ground and in that mire which with the grass formed a circle around the fountain. That one [the Hydra] dexterously collected some bits for herself.[13] Prometheus was confused, men remained under the sad state of mortality; and the ass, a perpetual laughingstock and an enemy of the latter, was condemned by the human generation, Jove being consentient, to eternal labors and struggles, to the worst food that could be found, and to a remuneration of frequent and terrible blows. So it happens, oh gods, that because of that one [the Hydra], men pay some attention to our affairs. For you see that now, though they are mortal, know their imbecility, and even expect to pass through our hands, they have contempt for us, scorn our deeds and give us the reputation of being monkeys and apes. What would they do if they were like us, immortal?"

"Saturn puts it very well," said Jove. "Then let the Hydra remain," answered all the gods. "But," answered Jove, "let Envy, Slander, Insidiousness, Lie, Wrangling, Contention, and Discord depart; and let the contrary virtues remain with Serpentine Sagacity and Caution.

"But I cannot suffer to see that Raven remain there. Therefore let Apollo take away that divine one, that good servant, that solicitous ambassador, diligent news-bearer, and postman, who so well executed the command of the gods when they expected to drive away their thirst through the sedulity of that one's service." "If it wants to reign," said Apollo, "let it go to England, where it will find a thousand legions of Ravens. If it wants to remain solitary, let it direct its flight toward Montecorvino, near Salerno.[14] If it wants to go where there are many figs, let it go to Figonia, that is, where the Ligurian Sea bathes the shore from Nice to Genoa. If it is attracted by a fancy for cadavers, let it go wandering through Campania and Naples, or rather on the road that lies between Rome and Naples, where so many thieves are quartered [15] that from time to time there are prepared for it more frequent and sumptuous banquets of fresh meat than it could find in any other part of the world."

Added Jove: "Let also Turpitude, Derision, Contempt, Loquacity, and Imposture descend, and into that seat, let there succeed Magic, Prophecy, and all divination and prognostication judged to be good and useful by their effects."

SAUL. I should like to hear, oh Sophia, your opinion regarding the metaphor of the Raven, which was first found and developed in Egypt and then taken by the Hebrews, through whom this knowledge was transmitted from Babylonia in the form of a story; and it was taken in the form of a fable by those who poetized in Greece. It is true that the Hebrews speak of a raven who was sent from the ark by a man called Noah in order to see whether the waters had dried up at a time when men had drunk so much that they burst, and that this animal, seized by his gluttony for cadavers, remained there and never returned from his legation and errand. This seems altogether contrary to what the Egyptians and Greeks relate, namely that at a time when the gods were almost dying from thirst, the Raven was sent from heaven by a god called Apollo by the latter, in order to see whether it could find water, and that this animal, seized by his desire for figs, tarried many days and finally returned late without bringing back water and, I believe, having lost the vessel.

SOPHIA. I do not want at the present time to go to any lengths to explain the learned metaphor to you. But I want to tell you merely this: What is said by the Egyptians and Hebrews relates to the same metaphor; for to say that the Raven departs from the ark, which is raised ten cubits above the highest mountain on earth, and that it departs from heaven, seems to me to be all one thing.[16] And that men who are found in such a place and region should be called gods does not seem too alien to me; for because they are celestial, they can become gods with little effort. And that Noah should be called the best of men by the Hebrews, and Apollo, by those others, can easily be reconciled; because the differing denomination concurs in one and the same function of regeneration, since *sol et homo generant hominem* ("the sun and man generate man"). And that it should be at a time when men had too much to drink and that it should be at a time when the gods were dying of thirst, is certainly all one and the same thing; for when the cataracts of the heaven opened up and the cisterns of the firmament burst, it necessarily followed that matters reached that point where the earth dwellers had too much to drink and the inhabitants of heaven died of thirst.

That the Raven should have been enticed by, and enamored of, figs and that the same Raven should have been attracted by his desire for dead bodies certainly add up to one thing if you consider the interpretation of that Joseph who knew how to explain dreams. For he prognosticated to Potiphar's baker[17] (who said he had seen himself in a vision carrying on his head a basket of figs, of which birds were coming to eat) that he was going to be hanged, and that ravens and vultures were going to eat of his flesh. That the Raven should have returned, but late and without any success, is the same as saying not only that he never returned but that he had never gone or been sent; for he does not go, does not do, does not return, who goes in vain, does in vain, returns in vain. And we are wont to say to one who comes late and in vain, even if he should bring back something:

> You went away, my brother, and did not return;
> In Lucca, you thought you saw me.[18]

Here then, Saulino, is how Egyptian metaphors without any contradiction can be stories to some, fables to others, and figured sentiments to others.

SAUL. This concordance of texts to which you refer, if it does not satisfy me completely, it is close to doing so. But for now follow the main story.

SOPHIA. "Now what shall we do with the Bowl?" asked Mercury. "What shall we do with the Jar?" "Let us see to it," said Momus, "that it be given, *iure successionis, vita durante,* to the greatest drinker that northern and southern Germany can produce, Germany, where Gluttony is exalted, magnified, celebrated, and glorified among the heroic virtues and where Ebriety is numbered among the divine attributes, whence with 'treink' and 'retreink,'[19] 'bibe' and 'rebibe,' 'ructa' and 'reructa,' 'cespita' and 'recespita,' 'vomi' and 'revomi,' *usque ad egurgitationem utriusque iuris,*[20] that is, of the broth, 'butargo,'[21] soup, brain, shank, and sausage, *videbitur porcus porcorum in gloria Ciacchi.*[22] With him let Ebriety depart. Do you not see her [Ebriety] there in German attire, with a pair of breeches so large that they seem like the tubs of a mendicant friar of St. Anthony's, with that large rear flap between the one and the other trouser leg, from which she reveals herself in such a manner that she seems to want to ram the heaven? See how she moves like a bear, now bumping into something with this flank, now with the other, now with her backside, now with her breast, there being no rock, pebble, thicket, or ditch toward which she does not go to pay a penalty.

"You see with her, her most faithful companions: Repletion, Indigestion, Fumosity, Drowsiness, Trepidation alias Hesitation, Stammering, Lisping, Pallor, Delirium, Eructation, Nausea, Filth, and other followers, ministers, and bystanders. And because she can no longer walk, see how she remounts her triumphal chariot, where are gathered many good, wise, and holy personages, of whom the most celebrated and famous are Noah, Lot, Chiaccone, Vitanzano, Zucavigna, and Silenus.[23] Zampaglion, the standard-bearer, carries a banner of scarlet whence appears the natural picture of two starlings with the very color of their wings, and joined by two yokes, with fine grace; four proud and glorious pigs pull the shaft, a white one, a red one, one particolored, and a black one. Of these the first is called Grungarganfestrofiel, the second, Sorbillgramfton, the third, Glutius, the fourth, Strafocazio." [24]

But I shall tell you a great deal about this on other occasions. We shall see what happened after he gave orders to Jove that Abstinence and Temperance should succeed to that seat, with their orders and ministers, all of which you will hear later. For it is now time that we begin to reason about the Centaur, Chiron. When it was his due turn to be discussed, old Saturn said to Jove: "Because, oh my son and lord, you see that the sun is about to set, let us quickly attend to these other four, if it pleases you."

And Momus said: "Now what do we wish to do with this man inserted into a beast, or this beast imprisoned in a man, in which one person is made of two natures and two substances concur in one hypostatic union? Here two things come into union to make a third entity; and of this there is no doubt whatsoever.[25] But the difficulty in this lies, namely, in deciding whether such a third entity produces something better than the one and the other, or better than one of the two parts, or truly something baser. I mean, if the human being has been joined to equine being, is there produced a divinity worthy of the celestial seat, or rather a beast worthy of being put into a flock and into a stall? Finally (no matter how many times Isis, Jove, and others may have remarked on the ex-

cellence of being a beast and said that for man to be divine it is
fitting that he have of the beast, and that when he yearns to show
himself deeply divine, he make up his mind to let himself be seen
in such measure as a beast), I can never believe that where there
is not a whole and perfect man or a perfect and whole beast, but
a piece of beast with a piece of man, there could be anything better
than where there is a piece of breeches with a piece of coat, whence
there never is derived a garment better than a coat or breeches, or
even one as good as the latter or the former."

"Momus, Momus," answered Jove, "the mystery of this matter
is occult and great, and you cannot understand it. However, since
it is a matter profound and great, it will only be necessary that
you believe it." "I know well," said Momus, "that this is a matter
that cannot be understood by me or by anyone who has a few little
grains of intellect; but in order that I who am a god, or that another who possesses as much sense as there could be in a millet
seed, may believe it, I desire first that you, in some fine manner,
make me believe it." "Momus," said Jove, "you must not want to
know more than what one must know; and believe me that this is
something one must not know." "Here then," said Momus, "is
what one needs to know and what, in spite of myself, I do want
to know. And to please you, oh Jove, I want to believe that one
sleeve and one trouser leg are worth more than a pair of sleeves
and a pair of trousers; and I want to believe much more still, that
a man is not a man, that a beast is not a beast, that a half of a man
is not a half man, and that a half of a beast is not a half beast,
that a half man and a half beast are not an imperfect man and an
imperfect beast, but rather, *pura mente colendo,* a god."

Here the gods urged Jove quickly to expedite things and to
come to a decision concerning the Centaur, according to his desire.
Jove, however, having ordered Momus to be silent, decided thus:
"No matter what remark I myself may have made against
Chiron, I now retract it; and I say that because Chiron, the centaur,
was a most just man—who once lived on Mount Pelion, where he
taught Asclepius about medicine, Hercules about astrology, and
Achilles about the cither, about healing the sick, showing how one
ascended toward the stars and how the resounding strings were
attached to the wood and were controlled—he does not seem to

me to be unworthy of heaven. Furthermore I judge him most worthy of it, because at the altar at which he presides in this celestial temple there is no other priest but him whom you see with that beast in his hand that is to be sacrificed and with a libatory flask hung around his waist. And because the altar, the shrine, the oratory, is most necessary and would be useless without the celebrant, therefore, here let him live, here let him remain and here endure eternally, if Fate does not dispose otherwise."

Here Momus added: "You have decided worthily and prudently, oh Jove, that this one should be the priest of the celestial altar and temple; because when he has well consumed that beast he holds in his hand, it is impossible that he can ever be lacking a beast, since he himself and only he can serve as the sacrifice and the sacrificer, that is, as a priest and as a beast."

"How fine," said Jove, "then let there depart from this place Bestiality, Ignorance, and the useless and pernicious Fable; and where the Centaur is, let there remain righteous Simplicity and the moral Fable. From where the Altar stands let Superstition, Faithlessness, and Impiety depart; and there let Religion, which is not vain, Faith, which is not foolish, and true and sincere Piety sojourn."

Now Apollo queried: "What will become of that Tiara? For what purpose is that Crown destined? What are we going to do with it?" "This, this," answered Jove, "is that crown which, not without the lofty disposition of Fate, not without the instinct of divine spirit, and not without very great merit, awaits the most invincible Henry III, king of magnanimous, potent, and warlike France.[26] After having obtained the crown of France and that of Poland, he promised himself, as he declared at the beginning of his reign, this other Crown, and in order to strengthen the two lowly crowns with another more eminent and beautiful one, he ordered that to that so celebrated emblem of his there should be added for encouragement this motto: *Tertia coelo manet.* This most Christian, holy, religious, and pure king can surely say: '*Tertia coelo manet,*' because he very well knows that it is written: 'Blessed are the meek, blessed are the silent, blessed are the pure of heart, for theirs is the kingdom of heaven.'[27] He loves peace and, as much as it is possible, maintains in tranquillity and devotion his beloved people. He does not like the noises, the boisterousness, and the clashing of martial instruments that administer to the blind acquisition of unstable tyrannies and principalities of the earth, but loves all acts of justice and blessedness that point out the direct path to the eternal realm.

"Let not the bold, tempestuous, and turbulent spirits of those who are subject unto him hope that while he lives he (to whom tranquillity of mind does not impart warlike enthusiasm) will want to extend aid to them, because of which they may unnecessarily go to perturb the peace of someone else's country, with the pretext of adding other scepters and other crowns; for *Tertia coelo manet*. In vain, against his desire, will the rebellious French forces go to seek out alien frontiers and shores, for there will be no proposal of unstable counsels, there will be no hope from changeable strokes of fortune, no expedient of external administrations and aids that, with the pretense of investing him with robes and adorning him with crowns, will succeed in taking from him (except by force of necessity) his blessed concern for tranquillity of mind, which is liberal with what is his, rather than avid for that of another. Let then others agitate against the vacant Lusitanian throne; let others be solicitous concerning Belgian sovereignty. Why will you puzzle your heads and rack your brains, you other and you other principalities? Why will you princes and kings suspect and fear that he will come to subdue your forces and carry off your own crowns? *Tertia coelo manet*. Then let the Crown remain [concluded Jove], awaiting that one who will be worthy of its magnificent possessions. And here also let Victory, Remuneration, Reward, Perfection, Honor, and Glory have their thrones, which, if they are not virtues, are ends of virtues."

SAUL. Now what did the gods say?

SOPHIA. There was no great or small, major or minor, male or female, god (either of one kind or of another) present at the council who did not with every word and gesture most highly approve the very wise and just Jovian decree.

Then all heaven having become joyously happy, the great Thunderer rose to his feet and extended his right hand toward the Southern Fish, the only one remaining to be decided upon, and said: "Let that Fish quickly be taken away from there, and let nothing remain there but its image. And let it be in substance taken by our cook, and right now, good and fresh, let it be set forth for the completion of our supper, partly from the gridiron, partly in stew, partly in verjuice, partly seasoned as he otherwise sees fit and likes, and prepared with Roman sauce. And let it all be done quickly, for on account of all this negotiation I am dying of hunger, and I believe you are too. Furthermore it seems fitting to me that this purgation should not be without some benefit to ourselves."

"Well, well, very well!" responded all the gods, "and let there be found there Safety, Security, Benefit, Joy, Rest, and highest Pleasure, borne by reward of virtues, and by remuneration of studies and labors."

And with this they festively left the conclave, having purged the area that besides the zodiac contains three hundred sixteen famous stars.

SAUL. And now I shall go to my supper.

SOPHIA. And I shall withdraw to my nocturnal meditations.

NOTES

Editor's Preface

1. Giordano Bruno, *Opere italiane* (ed. Giovanni Gentile and Vincenzo Spampanato), Bari, Gius. Laterza & Figli, 1925–1927, 3 vols.

Vol. I (*Dialoghi metafisici,* con note di G. Gentile) contains (1) *La cena de le ceneri* (London, 1584), (2) *De la causa, principio e uno* (Venice, 1584), (3) *De l'infinito, universo et mondi* (Venice, 1584).

Vol. II (*Dialoghi morali,* con note di G. Gentile) contains (1) *Spaccio de la bestia trionfante* (Paris, 1584), (2) *Cabala del cavallo Pegaseo,* con l'aggiunta dell' *Asino cillenico* (Paris, 1585), (3) *De gli eroici furori* (Paris, 1585).

Vol. III (*Candelaio: commedia.* Ediz. critica, con introduzione e note di V. Spampanato) contains *Candelaio* (Paris, 1582). (We shall hereafter refer to the Gentile–Spampanato edition of Bruno's *Opere italiane* as *Opere ital.*)

The Gentile text of *Lo spaccio* is the result of Gentile's painstaking collation of the original Bruno text of *Spaccio de la bestia trionfante* with that contained in Adolf Wagner's edition of *Opere di Giordano Bruno Nolano ora per la prima volta raccolte e pubblicate in due volumi,* Leipzig, Weidmann, 1830, 2 vols., and that of Paul de Lagarde's *Le opere italiane di Giordano Bruno ristampate,* Göttingen, Dieterische Universitätsbuchhandlung (Lüder Horstmann), 1888, 2 vols.

Editor's Introduction

I THE MAKING OF A HERETIC

1. Geronimo Cardano, who in his *Liber de ludo aleae* developed a systematic theory of probabilities some one hundred years before Pascal, was arrested in 1570 as a heretic, but was released after a private abjuration. He was, however, forbidden to continue teaching and to publish his books.

Bernardino Telesio's works, of which the most famous was *De natura rerum iuxta propria principia,* were placed on the *Index* after his death in 1588, because their author pointed out the superiority of the experimental method over Aristotelian authority. It would seem that in his assertions that all true knowledge is derived from the senses this nature philosopher becomes the forerunner of subsequent empirical thinkers.

Tommaso Campanella, although he supported Telesio's experimental method and shared some of his thoughts on nature, was considered orthodox in his thinking. The author of *Civitas solis,* however, in 1599 became a victim of Spanish despotism, suffering imprisonment for twenty-eight years.

The Holy Office's edict of 1616, which pronounced the Heliocentric Theory heretical, officially sanctioned an attitude that had prevailed in Italy since the publication of Copernicus' *De revolutionibus orbium coelestium* in 1543. Enforcement of this edict brought about Galileo's trial in 1632, after the publication of his *Dialogo sopra i due massimi sistemi del mondo.*

2. Bruno's baptismal name was Filippo; Giordano was his monastic name.

3. *Vide* A. Corsano, *Il pensiero di Giordano Bruno nel suo svolgimiento storico,* Florence, G. C. Sansoni, 1940, 1948, p. 39.

4. Dorothea Waley Singer, *Giordano Bruno: His Life and Thought,* New York, Henry Schuman, 1950, p. 10.

5. *Vide* J. Louis McIntyre, *Giordano Bruno,* London, Macmillan and Co., Ltd., 1903, pp. 7–11.

6. When in 1571(?) Bruno's scholarly attainments and his enthusiastic interest in the study of mnemonics came to the attention of Pope Pius V (a Dominican), to whom Bruno later dedicated his *Arca di Noè* (a lost mnemonic work), he was summoned to Rome for an interview.

Bruno was not ordained until 1572, after his return to Naples. He celebrated his first Mass in the town of Campagna at the Convent of San Bartolomeo.

7. *Istoria delle sette allegrezze* (*The Story of the Seven Joys*) is a poetical work devoted to the Seven Joys of the Virgin Mary. Although I have consulted many Catholic sources, I have not been able to discover any references to this work mentioned by Bruno at his Venetian trial. It may be an anonymous work inspired by the Franciscan interest in the Seven Joys of Mary. The Feast of the Seven Joys is celebrated by the Franciscans on August 27.

Vita de [sic] *santi Padri* (*Lives of the Holy Fathers*) is one of the medieval compilations based on the lives of the saints. Most of these *Lives* are anonymous.

8. Bruno had carelessly left these volumes behind in the monastery in Naples when he had fled to Rome.

9. According to McIntyre (*op. cit.,* p. 11), probably Bruno's first book on the art of memory. It is interesting to note that Bruno asked the Dominican Remigio Nannini for permission to publish this work, indicating that he had not yet completely severed his ties with the Church.

10. Although Bruno himself at his Venetian trial, in 1592, did not admit that he had formally embraced Calvinism during his brief stay in Geneva, we find references in the Parisian Documents which seem to bear out Berti's contentions that he had done so. Cf. Domenico Berti, *Vita di Giordano Bruno da Nola,* Turin, G. B. Paravia, 1868, p. 96. Furthermore, according to a document referred to by Mrs. Singer (*op. cit.,* p. 15, n. 26), Bruno's name was entered in a seventeenth century listing of Italian residents of Geneva who had adopted Calvinism.

11. *Vide* McIntyre, *op. cit.,* p. 14.

12. On or before August 6, 1579.

13. During this period Bruno may also have written his *Clavis magna,* an unpublished mnemonic work, to which he himself refers in his *De umbris idearum.*

14. Cf. McIntyre, *op. cit.,* p. 20.

15. We are in doubt as to where Bruno gave his extraordinary lectures during his first stay in Paris. However, we do know, from Bruno's own testimony that he was not allowed to give ordinary lectures, because this privilege was granted only to practicing Catholics. *Vide* Vincenzo Spam-

panato, *Vita di Giordano Bruno, con documenti editi e inediti,* Messina, Casa Editrice Principato, 1921, "Documenti veneti," IX, 701 (hereafter cited as *Docc. ven.*). Spampanato's *Vita di G. B.* also contains the "Documenti parigini" *(Docc. parig.),* the "Documenti romani," the "Documenti tedeschi" *(Docc. tedeschi),* the "Documenti napolitani," and the "Documenti ginevrini." The number of each document is indicated by a roman numeral.

16. *Opere ital.,* II, 225.

17. Both published in Paris in one volume in 1582.

18. *Vita di G. B.,* p. 323.

19. McIntyre, *op. cit.,* p. 18.

20. Published in Paris in 1582.

21. McIntyre, *op. cit.,* p. 18.

22. Dedicated to Giovanni Moro, the Venetian ambassador to the court of Henry III. Spampanato refers to this same work as *De architectura libri Lullii commentum. Vide Vita di G. B.,* p. 322.

23. The letter is dated March 28, 1583. Sir Francis Walsingham was the godfather and father-in-law of Sir Philip Sidney, who became a friend of Bruno's and his patron. Cf. Spampanato, *Vita di G. B.,* p. 329, n. 4.

24. Cf. *ibid.,* p. 338.

25. *Op. cit.,* p. 29. Bruno may have obtained his teaching position through the influence of the uncle of Sir Philip Sidney, Robert Dudley, Earl of Leicester and Chancellor of the university.

26. A mnemonic work, which Bruno wrote in Paris and published together with *Ars reminiscendi* and *Sigillus sigillorum* immediately upon his arrival in England in 1583.

27. *Ars reminiscendi, Triginta sigillorum explicatio, Sigillus sigillorum,* Jordani Bruni Nolani, *Opera latine conscripta, publicis sumptibus edita* [recensebant F. Fiorentino, F. Tocco, H. Vitelli, V. Imbriani, C. M. Tallarigo], Naples, Dom. Morano, Florence, Le Monnier, 1879–1891, 3 vols., II, Part II, 77–8. (Hereafter cited as *Opere latine conscripta.*)

28. *Opere ital.,* I, 164.

29. Also known as Albert a Lasco.

30. *Opere ital.,* I, 101.

31. In this work the words "heretic," "heresy," and "heretical" are used not only in their strictly religious sense but also in their broadest meaning.

32. A grateful Bruno dedicated *Triginta sigillorum explicatio, De la causa, principio et uno, La cena de le ceneri* and *De l'infinito universo et mondi* to him.

33. *Opere ital.,* I, 135.

34. John Florio was the ambassador's private secretary and tutor to his daughter.

35. *Opere ital.,* II, 3.

36. The publication of *La cena de le ceneri* may have caused the rift between Bruno and Greville. It is significant to note that Sir Fulke Greville

does not mention Bruno in his biography of Sidney; nor is there any reference to Bruno in Sidney's correspondence.

37. *Opere ital.*, II, 3–4.

38. *Ibid.*, I, 52.

39. Actually Bruno's second stay in Paris lasted only eight or nine months. *Vide* "Notizia" to *Docc. parig.*, p. 643, n. 1.

40. *Docc. ven.*, IX, 702. While returning to Paris Castelnau had been robbed of all his personal possessions, and this disaster made it impossible for him to extend further patronage to Bruno.

41. This diary was discovered by Lucien Auvray in the Bibliothèque Nationale, and was published by him in 1900. *Vide* "Notizia" to *Docc. parig.*, p. 641.

It may seem paradoxical to us that the excommunicated author of *Lo spaccio* should be attracted to a Catholic clergyman. Although intellectually in profound disagreement with the teachings of Catholicism, and indeed with Christianity itself, he still harbored a strong, emotional attachment to the Church, which he seemed to envisage as the instrument through which a universal religion could be propagated.

42. A lost work, possibly the first draft of the posthumous work which appeared in 1609 under the title of *Summa terminorum metaphysicorum.* *Vide Docc. parig.*, II, 650, n. 1.

43. *Ibid.*, pp. 650–2.

44. This fact is most interesting to us, in the light of some of the harsh remarks the philosopher has made concerning the Jews, especially in *Lo spaccio.*

45. *Ibid.*, VII, 655. Bruno's *Dialogi duo de Fabricii Mordentis Salernitani prope divina adinventione ad perfectam cosmimetriae praxim* was published in Paris in 1587.

46. In 1586 Bruno published his *Centum et viginti articuli de natura et mundo adversus peripateticos per Joh. Hennequinum propositi.*

47. Bruno had referred contemptuously in *Lo spaccio* to the enormous appetite and heavy drinking of the Germans. When Mercury asks Momus what disposition should be made of the Bowl, Momus replies: "Facciamo . . . che sia donata . . . al piú gran bevitore che produca l'alta e bassa Alemagna, dove la Gola è esaltata, magnificata, celebrata e glorificata tra le virtudi eroiche; e la Ebrietade è numerata tra gli attributi divini. . . ." *Opere ital.*, II, 221. ("Let us see to it . . . that it be given . . . to the greatest drinker that northern and southern Germany can produce, Germany, where Gluttony is exalted, magnified, celebrated, and glorified among the heroic virtues and where Ebriety is numbered among the divine attributes. . . .")

48. *Docc. tedeschi*, I, 663.

49. Spampanato, *Vita di G. B.*, p. 415. Bruno was appointed to the university through the influence of Alberigo Gentile, whom he had met in London.

50. *Opera latine conscripta*, I, Part I, 20. Among the numerous works that Bruno published in Wittenberg, besides the *Oratio valedictoria* (1588), are *De progressu et lampade venatoria logicorum* on the *Topics* of Aristotle (1587), dedicated to the chancellor of the university; *De lampade combinatoria Lulliana*, on artificial memory (1587), dedicated to the senate of the university; *Camoeracensis acrotismus, seu rationes articulorum physicorum adversus peripateticos Parisiis propositorum* (1588), an enlarged version of the *Centum et viginti articuli*.

51. Spampanato, *Vita di G. B.*, p. 447.

52. *Ibid.*, p. 442.

53. The total number of Bruno's publications exceeds sixty works, the majority written in Latin. These writings include works concerning philosophy, astronomy, mathematics, mnemonics, and the various controversies in which Bruno was engaged. For a complete bibliography of Bruno's published and unpublished manuscripts, *vide* Virgilio Salvestrini, *Bibliografia delle opere di Giordano Bruno e degli scritti ad esso attinenti*, prefazione di Giovanni Gentile, Pisa, V. Salvestrini, Libraio, 1926.

54. This iconoclastic comedy is dedicated to a mysterious signora "Morgana B.," whose identity baffles biographers and critics.

55. *Vita di G. B.*, pp. 357–8. In his *Antecedenti e imitazioni francesi del Candelaio*, Portici, Premiato stab. tip. Vesuviano, 1902, pp. 83–100, Spampanato discusses the similarities between *Il candelaio* and the following plays of Molière: *Le Malade imaginaire, Le Dépit amoureux, La Comtesse d'Escarbagnas, Le Bourgeois gentilhomme, Le Mariage forcé, Les Femmes savantes, Monsieur de Pourceaugnac, Sganarelle ou Le Cocu imaginaire, Le Médecin malgré lui*, and *Les Amants magnifiques*.

56. With the publication of these dialogues Bruno was probably the first European thinker to use the vernacular in the writing of philosophical works.

57. *Opere ital.*, I, 101.

58. At his Venetian trial, however, Bruno was to state that the dispute described in *La cena* took place at the home of Castelnau, and that one of his reasons for writing the dialogue was to mock the doctors who were present. *Vide Docc. ven.*, XIII, 733. Basing his conclusions on the internal evidence of *La cena*, Spampanato points out that the discussions occurred on February 7 and February 14, as well as on February 21 or 22 in 1584, first at the home of Greville and then at the home of Castelnau.

59. *Vide op. cit.*, p. 33.

60. *Opere ital.*, I, 156.

61. *Ibid.*, II, 241.

62. *Ibid.*, I, 269–70.

II *LO SPACCIO,* ITS FORTUNES, LITERARY ASPECTS, ALLEGORY, AND SUMMARY

1. *Vide* Vincenzo Spampanato, *Spaccio de la bestia trionfante con alcuni antecedenti,* Portici, Premiato stab. tip. Vesuviano, 1902, p. 33.

2. Bruno admitted at his Venetian trial that most of his works which bear Venetian and Parisian imprints were printed in England. Cf. Vincenzo Spampanato, *Vita di Giordano Bruno, con documenti editi e inediti,* Messina, Casa Editrice Principato, 1921, "Documenti veneti," XI, pp. 707–8.

3. *Vide* Spampanato, *Spaccio de la bestia trionfante,* p. 33.

4. No other translation of *Lo spaccio* exists in English. The title of this anonymous translation reads as follows: *Spaccio della bestia trionfante, or the Expulsion of the Triumphant Beast, translated from the Italian of Giordano Bruno,* London, 1713. The catalogue of the British Museum attributes the translation to W. Morehead, a half brother of John Toland. However, Bartholmèss ascribes it to John Toland himself, a great admirer of Bruno's works, who made a partial translation of *De l'infinito. Vide* Christian Bartholmèss, *Jordano Bruno,* Paris, Librairie philosophique De Ladrange, 1846, 1847, 2 vols., II, 70–1. This free translation of *Lo spaccio,* of which only a few copies are known to exist, omits the important "Epistola esplicatoria," and is without an introduction or footnotes. Bartholmèss also refers to an anonymous, partial translation of *Lo spaccio* in French attributed to the Abbé de Vougny, whose title reads as follows: *Le ciel réformé, essai de traduction de partie du Livre Italien, Spaccio della Bestia trionfante.* Only the date of publication, 1750, appears in the imprint. *Lo spaccio* was rendered into German with other works of Bruno by Ludwig Kuhlenbeck. The complete title of his work is Giordano Bruno, *Gesammelte Werke* (trans. Ludwig Kuhlenbeck), I–II—Leipzig, Eugen Diederichs, Berlin, H. Zossen, 1904. III–VI—Jena, Eugen Diederichs, Leipzig, O. Brandstetter, 1904–1909, 6 vols. This translation is interspersed with copious footnotes, judged by Gentile as being not always useful and sometimes inaccurate. Cf. Giordano Bruno, *Opere italiane* (ed., Giovanni Gentile and Vincenzo Spampanato), Bari, Gius. Laterza & Figli, 1925–1927, 3 vols., II, XII. (Hereafter cited as *Opere ital.*)

5. The structure of *Lo spaccio* gives it a symmetry reminiscent of that of the *Divine Comedy.*

6. The vastness of Bruno's erudition is a source of admiration to the reader of *Lo spaccio.* On this point Spampanato has said: "In closely studying one of the many writings of Giordano, the works in the vulgar tongue above all, and especially *Lo spaccio,* one is perplexed. One does not know whether to esteem more highly his mind or his erudition, so great is the number of his analogies, of his remembrances and of his quotations; to

such an extent has he mastered anterior human knowledge." *Spaccio de la bestia trionfante*, p. 71.

7. Whereas Francesco Fiorentino noted resemblances solely between *Lo spaccio* and Lucian's *Parliament of the Gods*, Spampanato, in his monograph on *Lo spaccio*, points out similarities in *Lo spaccio* with other works by Lucian.

The reader of *Lo spaccio* will also note the influences upon Bruno of other satirical writers, such as Juvenal, Horace, Aretino, and Tansillo, a friend of Bruno's family.

8. *Opere ital.*, II, 26.

9. The richly imaginative mythological background of *Lo spaccio* owes much to the *Metamorphoses*.

10. *Opere ital.*, II, 5.

11. *Ibid.*, p. 8.

12. Momus represents the ethical-religious conscience, referred to by Bruno as "synderesis." Pallas represents the intellect; Diana, discourse; Cupid, memory; Venus, love; Mars, "the covetous and irascible faculties"; and Jove, the will. All the affects symbolized by these gods are directed by what Bruno calls the "efficient light," which defines what is "just, good, and true."

The name Saulino, which is also given to an interlocutor in Bruno's *Cabala*, is derived from Savolino, the name of the philosopher's maternal ancestors. It is believed that Bruno may have had in mind Andrea Savolino, a distinguished member of that family, who in 1561 was the deputy for the town of Principato Citra. Cf. *Opere ital.*, II, 23, n. 1.

13. According to Bruno, all beings governed by Fate pass through infinite transmigrations, never returning to their former state: "Andiamo, e non torniamo medesimi; e come non avemo memoria di quel che eravamo, prima che fussemo in questo essere, cossí non possemo aver saggio di quel che saremo da poi." ("We depart, and do not return the same; and since we have no recollection of what we were before we were in this being, so we cannot have a sample of that which we shall be afterward.") Thus his Jove warns: "Guardiamoci, dunque, di offendere del fato la divinitade. . . . Pensiamo al prossimo stato futuro, e non, come quasi poco curando il nume universale, manchiamo d'alzare il nostro core ed affetto a quello elargitore d'ogni bene e distributor de tutte l'altre sorti. Supplichiamolo che ne la nostra transfusione, o transito, o metampsicosi, ne dispense felici genii: atteso che, quantunque egli sia inesorabile, bisogna pure aspettarlo con gli voti e di essere conservati nel stato presente, o di subintrar un altro megliore, o simile, o poco peggiore." *Ibid.*, pp. 40-1. ("Let us beware, then, of offending the divinity of Fate. . . . Let us think of our future state, and not, as if we were little concerned with the universal deity, fail to raise our hearts and affects to that lavisher of all good and distributor of all other fates. Let us beseech it that during our transfusion, or passage, or metempsychosis, it grant us happy spirits; since, although is is inexorable, we must indeed

await it with prayers, in order to be preserved either in our present state or to enter another, better, or similar, or little worse.")

14. *Ibid.,* p. 12.

15. According to Spampanato, the three zones, as conceived in the Aristotelian-Ptolemaic universe, contained a total of forty-six constellations: twenty in the boreal (and not twenty-one, as Bruno indicated); twelve in the zodiac (and not fourteen); and fourteen in the austral. *Vide* Spampanato, *Spaccio de la bestia trionfante,* pp. 46–8.

The firmament that Jove is to reform is the Aristotelian-Ptolemaic octave, stelliferous heaven, divided into the three zones mentioned above. According to this ancient concept, the heaven contained one thousand twenty-two stars of all sizes and descriptions: the boreal zone, three hundred sixty; the zodiac, three hundred forty-six; the austral, three hundred sixteen.

16. *Opere ital.,* II, 13. In *Lampas triginta statuarum,* referring to the will or "ethical-religious conscience," Bruno declares: "sedet in puppi et gubernator est totius compositi, ad cuius nutum omnia moventur, vibrantur nervi et musculi obtemperant. Est ergo quoddam velut libere agens et praesidet suo operi" ("it sits at the helm and is the pilot of the whole composition, at whose command all things are moved, nerves are caused to vibrate, and to which muscles submit. It is, therefore, in a certain manner, like one who is freely acting and presides over his own work"). Jordani Bruni Nolani, *Opera latine conscripta, publicis sumptibus edita* [recensebant F. Fiorentino, F. Tocco, H. Vitelli, V. Umbriani, C. M. Tallarigo], Naples, Dom. Morano, Florence, Le Monnier, 1879–1891, 3 vols., III, 342. In *Eroici furori* Bruno refers to "the ethical-religious conscience" as "la voluntade umana, che siede in poppa de l'anima, con un picciol temone de la raggione governando gli affetti d'alcune potenze interiori contra l'onde degli émpiti naturali." *Opere ital.,* II, 339. ("the human will, that sits at the helm of the soul, governing, with a small rudder of reason, the affects of certain interior forces against the waves of natural vehemence.")

17. The lion, here, refers to one of Phaedrus' fables, and not to Aesop's. *Vide* Spampanato, *Spaccio de la bestia trionfante,* p. 85, n. 3.

18. *Opere ital.,* II, 37.

19. Jove's action symbolizes "the act of ratiocination of the internal council."

According to Bruno, the Feast of the Gigantomachy, which commemorates Jove's victory over the giants, symbolizes "the continuous war, without any truce whatsoever, which the soul wages against vices and inordinate affects."

20. *Opere ital.,* II, 43.

21. The constellations of Ursa, Gemini, Perseus, and Hercules are eternal reminders of Jove's erotic life.

22. Allegorically, Jove's desire that he and the gods repent, symbolizes man's ever-present yearning for self-betterment.

III THE HERETICAL PREMISES OF *LO SPACCIO,* THEIR RELIGIOUS, SOCIAL, AND POLITICAL IMPLICATIONS

1. Giordano Bruno, *Opere italiane* (ed. Giovanni Gentile and Vincenzo Spampanato), Bari, Gius. Laterza & Figli, 1925–1927, 3 vols., II, 3. (Hereafter cited as *Opere ital.*)

2. The philosopher announces his intention of dealing more fully with moral philosophy in a future work, "according to the internal light that the divine Intellectual Sun has radiated and still radiates within me." According to Kuhlenbeck, Bruno here may be referring either to the *Eroici furori* or to another work containing a more systematic elaboration of his ethics, which may never have been completed, or, if so, may be found among his unpublished manuscripts in the Vatican archives. *Vide* Giordano Bruno, *Gesammelte Werke* (trans. Ludwig Kuhlenbeck), I–II—Leipzig, Eugen Diederichs, Berlin, H. Zossen, 1904. III–VI—Jena, Eugen Diederichs, Leipzig, O. Brandstetter, 1904–1909, 6 vols., II, 266, n. 8.

3. In his empirical attitude toward ideas, Bruno stands out as a precursor of the scientific age about to dawn over Europe.

4. *Opere ital.,* II, 84.

5. Hermann Brunnhofer, *Giordano Bruno's Weltanschauung und Verhängniss,* Leipzig, Fues's Verlag (R. Reisland), 1882, p. 140.

6. *Opere ital.,* I, 214.

7. Giordano Bruno, *Opera latine conscripta, publicis sumptibus edita* [recensebant F. Fiorentino, F. Tocco, H. Vitelli, V. Imbriani, C. M. Tallarigo], Naples, Dom. Morano, Florence, Le Monnier, 1879–1891, 3 vols., II, Part I, 299. (Hereafter cited as *Opera latine conscripta.*)

8. Domenico Berti, *Vita di Giordano Bruno da Nola,* Turin, G. B. Paravia, 1868, p. 181. Berti declares: "Bruno lumps together paganism, Judaism, Christianity, and Mohammedanism. He convokes all of these religions to the syndicate of reason, and censures all, accuses, condemns, and repudiates all." *Ibid.,* p. 182.

9. Bruno, who spoke out so boldly against positive religions, was compelled to make Aristotle a target of his attack; for it was he who had profoundly influenced the philosophical definition of God accepted by the three great religions of the West. But although the ontology and the epistemology of *Lo spaccio* are in themselves a refutation of Aristotle, the references to him contained therein are less stinging than elsewhere. Cf. *Opere ital.,* II, 118, 133, 184. However, the condemnation of the Greek philosopher, contained in the following passage from *De l'infinito,* is more typical of Bruno's attitude: "E impossibile di trovare un altro che, sotto titolo di filosofo, fengesse piú vane supposizioni e si fabricasse sí stolte posizioni . . . per

dar luogo a tanta levità quanta si vede nelle raggioni di costui." *Ibid.*, I, 315–6. ("It is impossible to find another who, under the title of philosopher, imagined more inane suppositions and fabricated such foolish stands . . . so as to give rise to as much levity as is seen in that man's reasoning.")

10. J. Lewis McIntyre, *Giordano Bruno,* London, Macmillan and Co., Ltd., 1903, p. 125.

11. *Ibid.*

12. *Ibid.*

13. Bruno was especially drawn to Iamblichus' *De mysteriis Aegyptiorum* and to a dialogue on Hermes Trismegistos attributed to Lucius Apuleius. Cf. *Opere ital.*, II, 192, n. 1.

14. Cf. McIntyre, *op. cit.*, p. 140.

15. For Bruno, as well as for Spinoza, "substance," equated with God, is the cause of itself. From his concept of "substance" Bruno derived his understanding of God as pure principle. His "eternal incorporeal substance" may be identified with Spinoza's "natura naturans"; and his "eternal corporeal substance," which is an emanation from or an extension of his "eternal incorporeal substance," may be compared with Spinoza's "natura naturata." By "eternal corporeal substance" Bruno signifies the "infinite species" of things (and not particular beings, subject to mortality), in the same manner that Spinoza's "natura naturata" is identified with "infinite modes." Cf. Benedict Spinoza, *Ethics and De Intellectus Emendatione* (trans. Andrew Boyle), London and Toronto, J. M. Dent and Sons, Ltd., New York, E. P. Dutton and Co., 1910, pp. 7, 20, 22, 24.

16. The philosopher seems to consider both merely two aspects of one and the same monistic substance; for he declares that all beings are part of "one infinite entity and substance." This concept of "substance" conflicts with the Catholic belief in the dichotomy of being.

17. Since, according to Bruno, what we are depends upon the prescribed laws of Fate working through the law of "motion and change," Sophia proclaims that man should never bemoan his state when he compares himself to a more fortunate being; nor should the latter be too exultant because of his more benign fortune.

18. *Opere ital.*, II, 23.

19. Bruno's interpretation of the doctrine of the "coincidence of contraries" seems to be an admixture of Cusanus' doctrine with that of Heraclitus and Empedocles.

20. Cf. Nicholas Cusanus, *De docta ignorantia, Opera omnia* (ed. E. Hoffmann and R. Klibansky), Leipzig, Meiner, 1932, 14 vols., I, lib. I, cap. I. The orthodox German cardinal employs geometrical symbols to demonstrate the "coincidence of contraries" in a transcendent God. Bruno, on the other hand, uses mathematical symbols to illustrate the application of the same concept to an immanent God.

21. Cf. *Opere ital.*, II, 24. On this point Bruno declares: "il superbo non può convenire col superbo, il povero col povero, l'avaro con l'avero; ma si

compiace l'uno nell'umile, l'altro nel ricco, questo col splendido." *Ibid*. ("the proud man cannot get together with the proud man, the poor man with the poor man, the greedy man with the greedy man; but the one is pleased with the humble man, the other with the rich man, the latter with the splendid man.")

22. Cf. McIntyre, *op. cit.*, p. 143.

23. "Però," declares Bruno, "se fisica-, matematica- e moralmente si considera, vedesi che non ha trovato poco quel filosofo che è dovenuto alla ragione della coincidenza de contrarii, e non è imbecille prattico quel mago che la sa cercare dove ella consiste." *Opere ital.*, II, 24–5. ("However, if the matter is considered physically, mathematically, and morally, one sees that that philosopher who has arrived at the theory of the 'coincidence of contraries' has not found out little, and that that magician who knows how to look for it where it exists is not an imbecile practitioner.")

24. Bruno's Divine Law is the source of that natural religion inherent in the earliest civilizations, and is the source of the first laws by which society was governed. Man's earliest concept of religion, according to Bruno, became distorted and corrupted as he evolved other laws and religions.

25. Perhaps no one observed the details of the sixteenth century European scene in sharper focus than did Machiavelli; but that thinker's view of his times compelled him to draw most pessimistic conclusions. Bruno, viewing reality with the same objectivity, manifested a greater faith in man's ability to emancipate himself from error, through the use of reason. He firmly believed that man, aided by law derived from a rational understanding of Nature, could evolve a society in which the governed would have complete confidence in their rulers.

26. *Opere ital.*, II, 174.

27. Bruno relates that these young men began their day by rising punctually in the morning to allow themselves sufficient time to wash their hands and faces "with five or seven kinds of water." Standing before mirrors they would spend as much as two hours in waving and curling their hair, and then consume several more hours in the act of dressing. The manner in which these idlers spent the remainder of their day is bitingly described by the philosopher: "Dove con tanta leggiadria si muoveno gli passi, si discorre, per farsi contemplare, la cittade, si visitano ed intertegnono le dame, si balla, si fa de capriole, di correnti, di branli, di tresche; e quando altro non è che fare, per essersi stancato ne le dette operazioni, ad evitar l'inconveniente di commettere errori, si siede a giocare di giuochi da tavola, ritrandosi da gli altri piú forti e faticosi: ed in tal maniera s'evitano tutti li peccati, se quelli non son piú che sette mortali e capitali. . . ." *Ibid.*, pp. 158–9. ("It is there where with such grace one steps, one moves about in order to be gazed upon in the city, visits and entertains the ladies, dances and performs caprioles, courantes, branles, and trescas; and when there is nothing else to do, because one has tired oneself in the above-mentioned operations, to avoid the inconvenience of committing errors, one sits down

to play table games, withdrawing from the more strenuous and tiring games. And in such manner all sins are avoided, if there are not more than seven mortal and capital sins. . . .") Bruno's satire of the upper classes is strongly reminiscent of Giuseppe Parini's *Il giorno.*

28. Bruno advocates the restoration of that natural law "by which it is permissible for each male to have as many wives as he can feed and impregnate."

29. *Opere ital.,* II, 196.

30. Indeed, Bruno in his wanderings through Europe had many occasions to observe that the ill use of wealth tended to corrupt both the individual and the state. On the other hand, the beneficiary of Sidney's and Castelnau's kindness had ample opportunity to observe that the wise use of wealth could be most useful to mankind.

31. Bruno here again manifests his insistence that religion should play an important role in the state, a refutation of the charges of atheism and impiety leveled against him.

32. *Opere ital.,* II, 94.

33. Although Bruno had always been critical of positive religions, he had, nevertheless, maintained that religion, in some form, was necessary as an ethical force in society. Hence, adhering to this tenet, he had considered it his moral obligation to attend Calvinist services in Geneva and, later, Lutheran services in Germany. Cf. Giovanni Gentile, *Bruno nella storia della cultura,* Palermo, Remo Sandron, Editore, 1907, p. 38.

34. Bruno does not regard the teachings of either the New or the Old Testament as revelation.

35. *Opere ital.,* II, 95.

36. *Ibid.,* p. 97.

37. However, as was mentioned earlier, in his conversations with Cotin Bruno praised the eloquence and learning of Hebrew preachers, contrasting them with Christian preachers, whom he deplored. *Vide* Vincenzo Spampanato, *Vita di Giordano Bruno, con documenti editi e inediti,* Messina, Casa Editrice G. Principato, 1921, "Documenti parigini," III, 653.

Bruno's virulent attitude toward the Jews in *Lo spaccio* may stem from the fact that he was born and grew to maturity in the Kingdom of Naples, dominated by the fanatical Spaniards, whose attitude toward the Jews need not be commented on here.

According to Lagarde, Bruno's resentment toward the Jews is explained by the fact that he regards Christianity, whose basic teachings he opposes, as a direct descendant of Jewish monotheism. *Vide* Giordano Bruno, *Le opere italiane di Giordano Bruno ristampate* (ed. Paul de Lagarde), Göttingen, Dieterichsche Universitätsbuchhandlung (Lüder Horstman), 1888, 2 vols., II, 794. McIntyre, on the other hand, asserts that Bruno's antipathy can be attributed to the views that he held concerning "the reputed avarice of the Jew: his exclusiveness, unsociability . . . his religion, which appeared to Bruno a corruption of the nobler Egyptian religion." *Op. cit.,* p. 265.

For a further discussion of Bruno's attitude toward the Jews cf. Brunn-hofer, *op. cit.,* pp. 222–3.

38. It is Plutarch in his treatise *On Isis and Osiris* in *Opera moralia* who has given us the only developed form of the myth of Osiris. Bruno seems to be attracted to the "resurrection" aspects of that myth.

39. Other Renaissance philosophers, such as Marsilio Ficino and Pico della Mirandola, noted the similarities between these biblical and non-biblical stories, but interpreted them as proof of the existence of a transcendental God, who revealed himself not only to the Hebrews but also, to a lesser extent, to other peoples. Bruno, on the other hand, interpreted them as being the revelations of the Immanent Deity, revealed through his attribute, Truth, conceived by Bruno as the "filia temporis."

40. *De mysteriis Aegyptiorum,* Venice, Aldi and Andreae Soceri, 1516, f. 130.

41. *Opere ital.,* II, 192–3.

42. F. H. Jacobi, in his preface to the second edition of *Über die Lehre des Spinoza in Briefen an Herrn Moses Mendelssohn,* Breslau, 1789, wherein he refutes the oft-repeated accusations of obscurity leveled against Bruno, indicates that he believes Bruno's exposition of the pantheistic doctrine to be one of the purest ever developed.

"Sigwart and Avenarius," declares McIntyre, "have proved that in preparing the short treatise on 'God, Man, and his Blessedness,' Spinoza must have had the *Causa* and *Infinito* of Bruno almost before his eyes . . . Pollock suggests that it may have been his free-thinking teacher Dr. Van den Ende who introduced Spinoza to Bruno's writings: there is no external evidence of the acquaintanceship, but that, it is needless to say, is of slight importance. Spinoza certainly read Italian, and he practiced in other cases the same neglect of authorities, of whose substance he was making use. . . ." *Op. cit.,* pp. 337–8.

Christoph Sigwart (1789–1844) is the discoverer of two documents referring to Bruno's stay in Germany, which he discusses in *Kleine Schriften,* Freiberg, 1889, 2 vols., Richard Heinrich Ludwig Avenarius (1843–1896), the German philosopher, was the author of *Kritik der reinen Erfahrung,* Leipzig, 1888–1900, 2 vols., in which he expounds a monistic theory of knowledge.

For a further discussion of the similarities between Bruno and Spinoza, *vide* Arthur Oncken Lovejoy, "The Dialectic of Bruno and Spinoza," *Philosophy,* Berkeley, University of California Publications, November, 1904, I, 141–71.

43. Bertrando Spaventa, *La filosofia italiana nelle sue relazioni con la filosofia europea,* a cura di Gennaro Ponzano, Padua, Casa Editrice Dott. Antonio Milani, 1941, p. 51.

44. Bruno declares in *De immenso:* "Necessitas et libertas sunt unum, unde non est formidandum quod cum agat cum necessitate naturae, non libere agat: sed potius immo omnino non libere ageret aliter agendo quam

necessitas et naturae necessitas requirit." *Opera latine conscripta,* I, 189. ("Necessity and freedom are one; whence it is not to be feared that that which is done with the necessity of nature is not done freely. But rather, I may certainly say that by acting otherwise than necessity and the necessity of nature require, would not be acting freely.")

45. *Opere ital.,* II, 186. The immanent Deity, to whom Bruno refers as "one Goodness, one Happiness, one Absolute Principle of all riches and fortunes, contracted into various laws, pours forth gifts according to the exigencies of particular beings," since he is absolute intellect and devoid of all personal attributes, "has nothing to do with us except insofar as he imparts himself to the effects of Nature." *Ibid.,* p. 192. Bruno believed that the concept of an extramundane, anthropomorphic God was accepted by theologians because they wished to appeal to the imagination of the multitude. On the other hand, he maintained that the pantheistic conception of the Deity must be accepted by philosophers and the select few.

46. For Spinoza likewise, "God is the indwelling and not the transient cause of all things." *Op. cit.,* p. 18. He declares, "God is not only the effecting cause of the existence of things, but also of their essence." *Ibid.,* p. 21.

47. *Op. cit.,* p. 51.

48. Ernst Cassirer, *Storia della filosofia moderna—Il problema della conoscenza nella filosofia e nella scienza dall'Umanesimo alla scuola cartesiana* (trans. Angelo Pasquinelli), Turin, Giulio Einaudi, Editore, 1952, 2 vols., I, 320.

49. "The act of divine cognition," declares Mercury in *Lo spaccio,* "is the substance of the being of all things."

50. *Op. cit.,* p. 320.

51. Giovanni Gentile, *Il pensiero italiano del rinascimento,* Florence, G. Sansone, 1940, p. 262.

52. Cf. Felice Tocco, *Le opere latine di Giordano Bruno esposte e confrontate con le italiane,* Florence, Le Monnier, 1889, p. 400.

53. Gentile, *Il pensiero italiano del rinascimento,* p. 266.

54. *Ibid.*

55. Lorenzo Giusso, *Scienza e filosofia in Giordano Bruno,* Naples, Conte, Editore, 1955, p. 163.

IV THE HERETIC AND HIS TRIAL

1. Bruno admitted to Giovanni Mocenigo that he had been indicted on one hundred thirty counts of heresy by the Roman Inquisition. *Vide* Vincenzo Spampanato, *Vita di Giordano Bruno, con documenti editi e inediti,* Messina, Casa Editrice Principato, 1921, "Documenti veneti," I, 680. (Hereafter cited as *Docc. ven.*)

2. Cf. Spampanato, *ibid.,* "Documenti parigini," II, 651-2.

3. *Docc. ven.*, I, 679–80.

4. *Ibid.*, II, 682.

5. *Ibid.*, I, 679–80.

6. *Ibid.*, p. 680.

7. *Ibid.*, IV, 685.

8. *Ibid.*, I, 680.

9. *Vide ibid.*, II, 682.

10. *Vide ibid.*, IV, 685.

11. Giordano Bruno, *opere italiane* (ed. Giovanni Gentile and Vincenzo Spampanato), Bari, Gius. Laterza & Figli, 1925–1927, 3 vols., II, 5. (Hereafter cited as *Opere ital.*)

12. Bruno also testified on May 30, June 2, 3, 4, and July 30, 1592. The Venetian Documents, upon which most of the discussion in this chapter is based, were discovered in 1849 and were published by Domenico Berti in 1868, in his *Vita di Giordano Bruno da Nola*. They were republished by Spampanato in *Vita di G. B.*

13. Bruno was inextricably involved in the controversy engendered by Copernicus' *De revolutionibus orbium coelestium*. But, although the philosopher in *De immenso* (Giordano Bruno, *Opera latine conscripta, publicis sumptibus edita* [recensebant F. Fiorentino, F. Tocco, H. Vitelli, V. Imbriani, C. M. Tallarigo], Naples, Dom. Morano, Florence, Le Monnier, 1879–1891, 3 vols., I, 380) (hereafter cited as *Opera latine conscripta*) indicates his warm admiration for Copernicus, in his *Cena de le ceneri,* in which he defends both the Copernican system and his own astronomical ideas, he emphasizes that he "did not see through the eyes of Copernicus . . . but through his own, as to judgment and determination." (*Opere ital.*, I, 21.)

Bruno went far beyond the thinking of Copernicus, Kepler, and Galileo, for he promulgated the hypothesis that our universe was only one of countless universes in infinite space. Thus he becomes important to us in the history of scientific ideas.

14. The publication of Pietro Pomponazzi's *De immortalitate animae,* in 1516, was vehemently attacked because of his contentions that the existence of an immortal soul cannot be proved by Aristotelian logic, but must rather be accepted as an article of faith. The author, however, defended his position in his *Apologia* (1518) and *Defensorium* (1519), by claiming the right to hold a religious-philosophical dichotomy.

15. *Docc. ven.*, XI, 708.

16. *Ibid.*, pp. 708–9.

17. Galileo Galilei, *Opera omnia,* Florence, Edizione nazionale, 1890–1909, 20 vols., X, 338, and III, 123.

18. *Docc. ven.*, XI, 709.

19. *Opere ital.*, I, 338.

20. *Ibid.*, p. 295. Regarding Bruno's concept of infinity Höffding declares: "To Bruno it seemed a contradiction that no infinite effect should correspond to the infinite cause. If the Deity, which in its original unity

embraces all that is unfolded in the universe, is infinite, then the universe which is the unfolded form of God's essence must be infinite." Harald Höffding, *A History of Modern Philosophy* (trans. from the German edition by B. E. Meyer), New York, Dover Publications, Inc., 1955, I, 128.

21. *Docc. ven.*, XI, 709–10.

22. *Ibid.*, p. 710.

23. *Ibid.*, p. 711.

24. In *Lo spaccio* Bruno, referring to the nature of Chiron, the Centaur, seizes the opportunity of satirizing Christ and the Trinity: "Or, che vogliamo far di quest'uomo insertato a bestia, o di questa bestia inceppata ad uomo, in cui una persona è fatta di due nature, e due sustanze concorreno in una ipostatica unione? Qua due cose vegnono in unione a far una terza entità; e di questo non è dubbio alcuno. Ma in questo consiste la difficultà; cioè, se cotal terza entità produce cosa megliore che l'una e l'altra, o d'una de le due parti, overamente piú vile." *Opere ital.*, II, 223. ("Now what do we wish to do with this man inserted into a beast, or this beast imprisoned in a man, in which one person is made of two natures and two substances concur in one hypostatic union? Here two things come into union to make a third entity; and of this there is no doubt whatsoever. But the difficulty lies in this, namely, in deciding whether such a third entity produces something better than the one and the other, or better than one of the two parts, or truly something baser.")

25. *Docc. ven.*, XI, 711.

26. *Opere ital.*, I, 189.

27. *Docc. ven.*, XI, 711. Since the concept of the Holy Ghost in Catholic dogma is necessarily part of the Catholic definition of God, its equation by the author of *Lo spaccio* with the aforementioned Pythagorean belief, which is the essence of the pantheistic concept of deity, would seem to be faulty logic; and inasmuch as Christian theologians have always maintained that the concept of the Holy Ghost must be accepted on faith, since it can neither be explained in rational or philosophical terms nor be divorced from the definitions of the first and second persons, Bruno's attempt to reconcile his ontology with that dogma made his position untenable.

28. *Ibid.*, p. 710.

29. *Ibid.*, XII, 716. Since, according to his pantheistic philosophy, all things are the emanation of Divinity, Bruno could readily admit that there is divinity in Christ. However, eager to safeguard himself, he declared that he would abide by the Church's definition, which interpreted the second person as being of the essence of Divinity.

The philosopher had always cautiously referred to Christ, His miracles, His Sacraments, and other Christian symbols in allegorical language, no doubt in the belief that the employment of this technique would protect him against suspicions of heresy.

30. *Opere ital.*, II, 207–8.

31. *Docc. ven.*, XI, 712.

32. *Ibid.*
33. *Ibid.*, p. 713.
34. *Ibid.*, XII, 714.
35. *Ibid.*, pp. 715–6.
36. *Ibid.*, p. 718.
37. Note contradiction between Cotin's statements concerning Bruno's attitude toward the Sacraments and those here made by the philosopher.
38. *Docc. ven.*, XII, 719. Bruno's implied admission of his acceptance of the Sacrament of Penance, and, consequently, of the Catholic concept of sin, predicated upon a belief in a personal Deity who grants rewards and punishments, stands in direct contradiction to his concept of an impersonal God; for Bruno's Deity, the source of the state, can only be impersonally concerned in what men do, and then only in those actions whose consequences will be detrimental to the state.
39. *Ibid.*, p. 720; XI, 711.
40. *Ibid.*, XII, 723–4. Bruno made similar utterances in *Lo spaccio* concerning the reformed sects, especially the Calvinist. However, his statements, which on the one hand indirectly criticize the Catholic use of force, and on the other advocate the destruction of reformers by Catholics, are seemingly contradictory.
41. *Ibid.*, p. 725.
42. *Ibid.*, p. 726.
43. *Ibid.*, p. 727.
44. *Ibid.*
45. *Ibid.*, p. 728.
46. *Ibid.*, p. 729.
47. *Ibid.*, XIII, 732.
48. *Ibid.*
49. *Ibid.*, p. 733.
50. *Opere ital.*, II, 80–1.
51. *Ibid.*, pp. 30–1.
52. *Docc. ven.*, XIII, 735–6.
53. Cf. *ibid.*, XVII, 746. Bruno's abhorrence of having to make a public confession of his heresies in Rome was to seal his fate.
54. *Vide* Spampanato, *Vita di G. B.*, p. 518.
55. The Roman Documents give us only a fragmentary account of Bruno's testimony before the Inquisition. As were the Venetian Documents, most of the Roman Documents were discovered in the Vatican Archives in 1849. They were published by Domenico Berti for the first time as an appendix to his discussion, *Copernico e le vicende del sistema copernicano in Italia nella seconda metà del sec. XVI e nella prima metà del XVII con documenti intorno a G. Bruno e a G. Galilei*, X, then in *Documenti intorno a G. Bruno* in 1868, and finally they were incorporated in *Giordano Bruno da Nola, sua Vita e sua dottrina*, Turin, G. B. Paravia, 1889. Cf. Spampanato, *Vita di G. B.*, "Notizia" to "Documenti romani," pp. 765–6.

Cardinal Angelo Mercati discovered a hitherto unknown document of the Roman trial, which he published in his *Il sommario del processo di Giordano Bruno con appendice di documenti sull'eresia e l'inquisizione a Modena nel secolo XVI (Studi e Testi)*, Vatican City, Biblioteca Apostolica Vaticana, 1942.

56. We do not possess the documents that contain the specific formulation of these propositions.

57. Vincenzo Spampanato, *Documenti della vita di Giordano Bruno*, Florence, Leo S. Olschki, Editore, 1933, "Documenti romani," XXIV, 183. In this volume Spampanato has included all of the documents found in his *Vita di Giordano Bruno*, plus other Genevan and Roman documents not contained in it.

58. Spampanato, *Documenti della vita di G. B.*, "Documenti romani," XXVI, 191.

59. The document is here inaccurately referring to *Spaccio de la bestia trionfante*.

60. Spampanato, *Documenti della vita di G. B.*, "Documenti romani," XXX, 202.

61. *Opera latine conscripta*, I, Part II, 99.

62. Albert Einstein, *The World as I See It* (new abridged edition) (trans. Alan Harris), New York, Philosophical Library, 1949, pp. 26–7.

The Expulsion of the Triumphant Beast

EXPLANATORY EPISTLE

1. Note the similarity between this passage and the following in Plato's *Symposium:* "I shall praise Socrates in a figure which shall appear to him to be a caricature, and yet I do not mean to laugh at him, but only to speak the truth. I say then, that he is exactly like the masks of Silenus, which may be seen sitting in the statuaries' shops, having pipes and flutes in their mouths; and they are made to open in the middle, and there are images of gods inside them." *The Best Known Works of Plato* (trans. B. Jowett, M.A.), Garden City, Halcyon House, pp. 288–9.

2. Gentile quotes some passages from Aretino that indicate an influence upon these words of Bruno's. *Vide* Giordano Bruno, *Opere italiane* (ed. Giovanni Gentile and Vincenzo Spampanato), Bari, Gius. Laterza & Figli, 1925–1927, 3 vols., II, 5, n. 1.

3. There is a copy of the 1584 edition of *Lo spaccio* in the Biblioteca Nazionale of Naples that contains some interesting marginal comments by an anonymous annotator, to whom Gentile refers as the "postillatore napoletano." Gentile has included these comments in his edition, and I have taken the opportunity of reproducing those that may be of particular interest to the reader. On pages 157–8, note 2, of the Neapolitan copy of *Lo spaccio* there appears the following observation by the anonymous annotator: "Non asserit. Cur igitur tam acerbe stomachatur in contradicentes?" *Opere ital.,* II, 6, n. 3. ("He does not commit himself. Why, then, does he so bitterly revile his critics?")

4. For Bruno, man in his search for Truth must possess the quality of

Prudence, with which he may discern Truth, even when time and attendant circumstances obscure his vision of her.

5. This Sophia is not to be confused with the Sophia who narrates to Saulino the results of the council's deliberations.

6. It would seem that by "mothers" Bruno signifies the Muses, their "daughters" being all the arts and sciences derived from them.

7. Bruno fails to mention, or is obscure concerning, the name of Divine Magic's second daughter. It is possible he had Augury in mind.

8. Petrarch, sonnet 193.

FIRST DIALOGUE: FIRST PART

1. The following passage from Horace, first cited by Kuhlenbeck (*vide Gesammelte Werke* [trans. Ludwig Kuhlenbeck], I–II—Leipzig, Eugen Diederichs, Berlin, H. Zossen, 1904. III–VI—Jena, Eugen Diederichs, Leipzig, O. Brandstetter, 1904–1909, 6 vols., II, 227, n. 24), is a development of the same theme:

> Agricolam laudat iuris legumque peritus
> Sub galli cantum consultor ubi ostia pulsat.
> Ille datis vadibus qui rure extractus in urbem est,
> Solos felices viventes clamat in urbe.
> > *Satires,* I. I. 9–12.
> (The jurisconsult praises the farmer
> When his client knocks at the door before cock's crow.
> He, who is removed from the country into the city, after
> > his bail has been paid,
> Declares happy only those living in the city.)

2. That is to say, the contraries that are inherent in mutation.

3. Again showing his enthusiasm for Cusanus and his theory, Bruno asserts in *De la causa:* "Profonda magia è saper trar il contrario, dopo aver trovato il punto de l'unione." Giordano Bruno, *Opere italiane* (ed. Giovanni Gentile and Vincenzo Spampanato), Bari, Gius. Laterza & Figli, 1925–1927, 3 vols., I, 264. ("It is profound magic to know how to derive the contrary, after having found the point of union.")

4. Lodovico Ariosto, *Orlando furioso* XLV. 2.

5. "Evidently," says Gentile, "the author has in mind the *Dialogues of the Dead* by Lucian." *Opere ital.,* II, 26, n. 2.

6. Allusion to Ganymede.

7. Gentile calls to our attention the slyly erotic nature of this passage. Cf. *Opere ital.,* II, 27, n. 3.

8. *Vide* Ecclesiastes I. 2.

9. The Bohemian astrologer, Cyprian Loewicz, predicted that the world would come to an end either toward the end of March or the beginning of April of the year 1584, in his book *De coniunctionibus magnis insignioribus superiorum planetarum*, published in 1564. Cf. *Opere ital.*, II, 28, n. 2.

10. Bruno's allusion to a lame Saturn, the counterpart of Cronus, may be inspired by the existence in antiquity of a cult statue of the Italian god, bound at his feet with woolen bands and untied once a year at the celebration of the Saturnalia. See also note 3, First Dialogue, Third Part.

11. Virgil, Ecologues IV. 36.

12. Seneca, *Oedipus*, chorus, vv. 1001–8, 1015–6.

13. Gentile declares: "In *De rerum principiis* Bruno says Styx or abyss designates one of the two principles of matter: the humid, agglutinating, and formative principle." *Opere ital.*, II, 31, n. 4.

14. Votaries of Bacchus, so called because they were wont to intersperse their rites to Bacchus with the cry "euoi."

15. As is well known from Petrarch's sonnet, "Voglia mi sprona," the poet fell in love with Laura on April 6, 1327.

Dante met Beatrice in the Spring of 1274 when she had just entered her ninth year, he being but a few months older.

16. Priapus, god of fertility.

17. Horace, *Odes* I. 10. v. 12.

18. Gentile notes the influence of Erasmus upon this passage. Cf. *Opere ital.*, II, 35, n. 2.

19. This is a free translation of a passage in Lucretius' *De rerum natura* I. 1–9.

20. John XX. 17.

21. Bruno, here, seems to be in error. According to the myth, Pelion was hurled on Ossa, and Ossa on Olympus.

22. This passage is a free translation of Ovid, *Metamorphoses* V. 346–54. Cf. *Opere ital.*, II, 37, n. 1.

23. A small mountain chain of Campania between the Volturno and the Calore, now known as Monte Taburno.

24. Here "sister" is used in the sense of "friend" or "companion."

25. An allegorical representation of the efficient and formative principle to which Bruno alludes in the "Explanatory Epistle."

FIRST DIALOGUE: SECOND PART

1. Virgil, *Aeneid* VI. 37.

2. Bruno is here identifying Lucina, the goddess of childbirth, with Diana, the moon goddess. Cf. Horace, *Carmen saeculare*, v. 15.

3. "Euschemia," employed by Bruno, seems to have been a variant of "Euschemo," the only form I have been able to verify. The name of the

nursemaid of the Muses and mother of Sagittarius (Crotus), however, is more commonly known to us as Eupheme.

4. This is an allusion to a Semitic myth describing the birth of Venus. The myth narrates that a great egg fell from heaven into the Euphrates. It was pushed ashore by the Fishes, where it was hatched by doves. Out of it came Venus, or Astarte, as she was known in the Near East. In gratitude for their kindness Venus asked Jove to place the Fishes, "her godparents," in heaven. Cf. Gaius Julius Hyginus, "Fabula 197—Venus," *Fabulae,* ed. H. J. Rose, Leyden, 1934.

5. The feminine form has an obscene meaning.

6. The two stars found at the head of the constellation of Cancer are called the Asses by Hyginus. Cf. Giordano Bruno, *Opere italiane* (ed. Giovanni Gentile and Vincenzo Spampanato), Bari, Gius. Laterza & Figli, 1925–1927, 3 vols., II, 48, n. 3.

7. Bruno here seems to be referring to his *Cabala del cavallo Pegaseo.*

8. Jove's words of self-criticism are not only an attack upon the religion of the Greeks but also a veiled indictment of the Judaeo-Christian religions.

9. Unless the facts of the story of Perseus and the Gorgons became garbled in a misreading of the original text or a subsequent one, Bruno erred in two details: (1) It was Perseus' cap which rendered him invisible, and not his shield, (2) Only Medusa was slain and not her sisters, who were immortal.

10. Cepheus is rather, as is well known, Perseus' father-in-law.

11. Eratosthenes and Hyginus attribute only seventeen stars to the constellation of Aries. Cf. *Opere ital.,* II, 51, n. 2.

12. Megara was Hercules' wife; Bruno meant to refer to Alcmene, Hercules' mother.

13. A possible allusion to the many incursions carried out against the coastal towns of southern Italy by the Turks during the sixteenth century.

14. Europa.

15. The constellation Ursa reminds Jove of his infidelity to Juno. Callisto, the daughter of Lycaon, king of Arcadia, was hunting with Diana on Mount Nonacris when she was seduced by Jove. Juno, in a jealous wrath, changed her into a she-bear. Jove later turned both her and her son Arcas, the legendary founder of the Arcadians, into constellations; the mother into the constellation of Ursa Major, and Arcas into Arctophylax, also known as Boötes, the Wagoner. According to another version of the myth, Arcas was turned into Arcturus, which is only one of the stars in the constellation Arctophylax.

16. Diana.

FIRST DIALOGUE: THIRD PART

1. Virgil, *Georgics* I. 242–3.

2. Here Bruno alludes to families, cities, and states whose coats of arms contain the bear. Cf. Giordano Bruno, *Opere italiane* (ed. Giovanni Gentile and Vincenzo Spampanato), Bari, Gius. Laterza & Figli, 1925–1927, 3 vols., II, 61, n. 1.

3. Bruno's use of Saturn as a participant in the heavenly deliberations is anachronistic, since Saturn (Cronus) had been banished by Zeus.

4. This is an imitation of a passage from Tasso: *Aminta*, I. 1; and V. chorus. Cf. *Opere ital.,* II, 62, n. 2.

5. Human law or the law of nations.

6. Gentile here reminds us that this passage has been erroneously compared with Dante's apostrophe to Henry VII in Canto XXV of the *Paradiso.* Cf. *Opere ital.,* II, 64, n. 3.

7. An allusion to the Calvinist and other evangelical theologians, who frequently quarreled among themselves. Bruno, who placed the greatest emphasis on works, was in violent disagreement with their reliance on faith alone.

8. A reference to the confiscation of Catholic properties by the Protestants.

9. Bruno satirizes the Calvinist dogma of predestination.

10. Bruno is saying in effect that the best laws are those predicated upon the best experiences of peoples.

11. The anonymous Neapolitan annotator inserts the following comment: "That is to say, those who deny that sanctity and justice are found in works." *Vide Opere ital.,* II, 66, n. 4.

12. Actually, it was Juno who entrusted the golden apples to the custodianship of the Hesperides, who guarded them with the assistance of the dragon Ladon.

13. Gentile notes that this passage not only is imitative of Lucian, but also alludes to contemporary events which were the cause of great bloodshed. In Spain the Inquisition against the Jews and Moors was becoming ever more fierce; Flanders was in rebellion against the tyranny of Philip II; religious wars divided Germany; civil war raged between the Catholics and Protestants in France; and in England there was persecution of Catholics and Presbyterians. Cf. *Opere ital.,* II, 71, n. 2.

14. In this strange passage Bruno is personifying the message.

15. Although this passage, with its bizarre references to providence, may seem enigmatic to us, one fact is clear: that after an absence of so many years from Nola and its environs, the exile in London found pleasure in recalling to his readers the persons and places of his happy childhood. Cf. *Opere ital.,* II, 75–7, n. 5.

16. Gentile agrees with Spampanato that Franzino is not Franzinus Alla-

manna from the town of Casamarciano, but, rather, is Don Francinus, a parish priest, known to the Savolino family. Cf. *ibid.*

17. Bruno's father. Cf. *ibid.*

18. Vasta, also known as Basta, was the wife of Albenzio Savolino, Bruno's maternal uncle. Cf. *ibid.*

19. A poor, childless, and widowed servant woman. Cf. *ibid.*

20. A relative of Bruno's. Cf. *ibid.*

21. Polydorus was the son of Giacomo and Medea Santorello, born in 1540. Cf. *ibid.*

22. Gentile has corrected the old texts which read "stanza" to "Starza," thus preserving for us a valuable autobiographical reference. "Starza," which in the Neapolitan and Apulian dialects has the meaning of "estate," here refers to the community of Starza, situated on the slopes of Mount Cicala. Cf. *ibid.*, p. 74, n. 1.

23. A castle mentioned by the sixteenth century Nolan historian, A. Leone, which dates back to the twelfth century. Cf. *ibid.*, n. 2.

24. Scarvaita, a mountain named after a section of S. Paolo Belsito, a community near Nola. Cf. *ibid.*, n. 3.

25. Bruno is referring to a certain Adanesio Biancolella. Cf. *ibid.*, pp. 75–7, n. 5.

26. A reference to a Costantino Buonaiuto, husband of Imperia and father of five children. Cf. *ibid.*

27. There is no record of the old woman of Fiurulo. Cf. *ibid.*

28. No record exists of Ambruoggio. Cf. *ibid.*

29. Martinello's son is said to be Paolo, son of a Martinello Alemanno. Cf. *ibid.*

30. A reference to a Paolino da Casoria, owner of a tavern. Cf. *ibid.*

31. Note Bruno's daring reference to an infinite universe, composed of many worlds; this, at a time when even the teachings of Copernicus, whose views on cosmology did not go as far as Bruno's, were considered heretical.

32. These words echo the following passage from Virgil: "Mihi si linguae centum sint oraque centum, Ferrea vox. . . ." *Aeneid* VI. 625–6. ("Had I a hundred tongues and a hundred mouths / A voice of iron. . . .")

SECOND DIALOGUE: FIRST PART

1. Note repetition of "truth," evidently an error.

2. Perhaps what Bruno means to say is "two groups of enemies."

3. Another reference to transmigration.

4. These words seem to indicate a socialistic tendency, which others also have observed in Bruno.

5. The anonymous Protestant Neapolitan annotator here reproves Bruno for attacking the reformers "calumniously and mendaciously, as he is wont

to do." *Vide* Giordano Bruno, *Opere italiane* (ed. Giovanni Gentile and Vincenzo Spampanato), Bari, Gius. Laterza & Figli, 1925–1927, 3 vols., II, 89, n. 3.

6. Although this passage is specifically an attack upon the teachings of the Calvinists, the reference to a "cabalistic tragedy" is, indeed, a satirical allusion to the life and passion of Christ.

7. Bruno's words bring to mind the following from Virgil: "Parcere subiectis et debellare superbos." *Aeneid* VI. 853. ("To spare the conquered and to conquer the proud.")

8. Here, the anonymous annotator points out that by "grammarians" Bruno means to refer to the Evangelical reformers "concerning whom it seems he cannot be silent." Cf. *Opere ital.,* II, 94, n. 3.

9. "That is to say," declares Gentile, "the properties of the Catholics, usurped by the Protestants, especially in England." *Ibid.,* p. 96, n. 6.

10. Our anonymous Neopolitan annotator refers to Bruno's words as "an open blasphemy against Christ." Cf. *ibid.,* p. 97, n. 3.

SECOND DIALOGUE: SECOND PART

1. A philosopher of the Old Academy in Athens.

2. On this passage Gentile comments: "Opposing contrary propositions cannot, indeed, according to Aristotelian logic, both be true; but both can be false." Giordano Bruno, *Opere italiane* (ed. Giovanni Gentile and Vincenzo Spampanato), Bari, Gius. Laterza & Figli, 1925–1927, 3 vols., II, 102, n. 4.

3. I am not sure what game Bruno is referring to. He may, however, be alluding to "scarpaccia," a game played with old shoes. *Vide ibid.,* p. 103, n. 3.

4. The reference is to the *Prior Analytics* and the *Posterior Analytics*.

5. Pippa, Nanna, and Antonia are three interlocutors in Aretino's *Ragionamenti,* published in 1535 or 1536. The barber, Domenico di Giovanni, known as Burchiello, was the celebrated Florentine satirical poet (1404–1449). Cf. *Opere ital.,* II, 104, n. 3. The work by an uncertain author is the *Priapea*. Three of the poems of this collection are now attributed to Virgil. Cf. *ibid.,* p. 184. The *Ancroia* is an anonymous Italian poem of chivalry whose complete title is *Libro de la Regina Ancroia,* Ancroia being a queen of the Saracens. This work was published in Venice in 1479. *Vide Dizionario letterario Bompiani,* Milan, 1947–1950; Johann Georg Theodor Graesse, *Trésor de livres rares et précieux,* Dresden, Kuntze, 1859–1869.

6. I have corrected what seems to be an omission of quotation marks in the text on p. 106 beginning with the words "ma allor che ella" and have interpolated "said Jove," "Poverty," and "Wealth," in order to eliminate the ambiguities of the passage.

7. Bruno's words remind Spampanato of Pliny's: "Toto mundo, locis

omnibus omnibusque horis, omnium vocibus, Fortuna sola invocatur, una nominatur, una cogitatur, sola laudatur, sola arguitur et cum conviciis colitur." *Epistles* II. 2. ("In the whole world, in all places and in all times, by the voices of all, Fortune alone is invoked, alone is named, alone is contemplated, alone is praised, alone is censured, and is worshiped with loud cries.") Cf. Vincenzo Spampanato, *Spaccio de la bestia trionfante con alcuni antecedenti*, Portici, Premiato stab. tip. Vesuviano, 1902, p. 88.

8. Bruno's Fortune is not the fickle lady conceived by the Renaissance poets, but, rather, an instrument of Fate.

9. Juvenal, *Satires* X. 366; XIV. 316.

10. Cf. *Metaphysics* I. 1.

11. Bruno is referring to Luigi Groto (1541–1585), known as the "Cieco d' Adria," an orator and poet, who is one of the few men of the sixteenth century named by him. Cf. *Opere ital.*, III, 10, n. 2.

12. A game of chance.

SECOND DIALOGUE: THIRD PART

1. The site of a crowded market place, later called Via di Porto. Cf. Giordano Bruno, *Opere italiane* (ed. Giovanni Gentile and Vincenzo Spampanato), Bari, Gius. Laterza & Figli, 1925–1927, 3 vols., II, 125, n. 2.

2. In Discourse CV of Garzoni's *Piazza Universale,* we are told that the Piazza San Marco in sixteenth century Venice was alive with a various and sundry multitude of people. In the evening it was a gathering place for charlatans, prestidigitators, puppeteers, and young gallants who related stories and anecdotes, enacted dialogues, sang, laughed, and quarreled. There were also noblemen, plebeians, beggars, peasants, and showmen who exhibited lascivious dancing girls. Cf. *ibid.,* p. 126, n. 1.

3. These lines are evidently inspired by the following passage from Ovid:

> Haud procul Hennaeis lacus est a moenibus altae,
> Nomine Pergus, aquae. Non illa plura Caystros
> Carmina cycnorum labentibus audit in undis.
> *Metamorphoses* V. 385-7.

(At a short distance from the Hennaean walls there is found a deep lake, Pergus, by name. No more songs
Of swans does Caystros hear than those heard in Pergus' gliding waves.) Lake Pergus, now known as Lago Pergusa, is located in Sicily near Enna, ancient Henna. The Caystros, now called the Kara-Su, is a river in Lydia, celebrated for its swans.

4. This, according to Gentile, is an allusion to the punishment that during the time of Elizabeth was threatened against anyone who stole one of the swans in the Thames. *Vide Opere ital.,* II, 129, n. 1. The swans of the Thames are still protected by law.

5. The proud boastfulness of the Spaniard has become proverbial among Italians and has often been alluded to in Italian literature. Cf. *ibid.*, p. 130, n. 1.

6. Lodovico Ariosto.

7. Ariosto, *Orlando furioso* XXIV. 1.

8. Bruno draws upon Ovid for the details of the Perseus myth. *Vide Metamorphoses* IV. 618–9.

9. Cf. *ibid.*, V. 248–9.

10. According to the Perseus legend, it was Acrisius, Perseus' grandfather, who was the king of Argos and not Acrisius' brother, Proetus. Perseus, as it had been decreed, accidentally killed his grandfather. Bruno seems to have confused this story with that regarding Perseus' deposition of Polydectes, king of Seriphus, on whose throne he placed Dictys, Polydectes' brother.

11. A people of Scythia.

12. Virgil, *Aeneid* VI. 95.

13. Luigi Tansillo, *Il vendemmiatore*, stanza 5 (ed. Flamini), p. 53. Bruno sometimes quotes verbatim from Tansillo, although frequently, as in this passage, he paraphrases the words of his fellow Nolan. Cf. *Opere ital.*, II, 140, n. 1, n. 3.

14. "For the color with which the working of Discord is here described," asserts Gentile, "one must recall Folengo's *Baldus* (mac. XXIV) rather than the *Aeneid* VI. 273, and the *Furioso* XIV. 83." *Ibid.*, p. 141, n. 1.

15. The Kingdom of Naples.

16. Bruno refers to the attempt of the Spaniards under Don Pedro de Toledo to introduce the Inquisition into the Kingdom of Naples in 1547, causing the uprising of May 17th of that year, which continued for two months. For this act of defiance the Neapolitans were fined 100,000 ducats by the Spaniards. Coming to the defense of the orthodoxy of Naples, the sixteenth century historian, Giovanni A. Summonte, writes: "She [Naples] has always been most religious," and free from "any blemish of heresy." Summonte asserts that the Spaniards instituted trials against alleged heretics in Naples, "not so much for the honor of God, as for deriving from them heavy confiscations of properties." *Historia della città e del Regno di Napoli*, Naples, Raimondi e Vivenzio, 1749, t. V, 280–1.

17. In 1558 the Duke of Alba, Fernando Álvarez de Toledo, working together with the astute Pope Pius IV was successful in preventing the outbreak of war between Spain and Henry II of France, who was threatening to invade the Kingdom of Naples, a war which might have jeopardized Spain's position in Southern Italy. Cf. *Opere ital.*, II, 144, nn. 1, 2.

18. According to Bruno, the Neapolitans, in rebellion against Spain, expected aid to come to them from the French and the Turks. Cf. *ibid.*, n. 3.

THIRD DIALOGUE: FIRST PART

1. Cf. Ovid, *Metamorphoses* I. 103–6.

2. Tasso, *Aminta* I. chorus.

3. The second ottava is from Tansillo, *Il vendemmiatore,* st. 20, p. 60; the first is formed by Bruno with verses taken from three different stanzas of *Il vendemmiatore* itself (st. 17–19). Cf. Giordano Bruno, *Opere italiane* (ed. Giovanni Gentile and Vincenzo Spampanato), Bari, Gius. Laterza & Figli, 1925–1927, 3 vols., II, 150, n. 2.

4. Allusion to Genesis III. 16–19.

5. "Aristotle, in fact," says Gentile, "had not spoken of syllogisms in the fourth figure." *Opere ital.,* II, 151, n. 4.

6. I have inserted quotation marks before "Se dunque, Ocio, consideri" (omitted on p. 155, Vol. II, in the Gentile text of *Opere italiane*), and have interpolated "said Momus" to indicate the resumption of direct discourse by that god.

7. God of Sleep, son of Erebus and Nyx, and father of Morpheus.

8. Ovid, *Metamorphoses* XI. 623–5.

9. Cf. *ibid.,* pp. 592–3.

10. Morpheus is the god of visions. Icelus and Phantasus are gods of dreams.

11. The "branle" is an old French dance. The "tresca" is an Italian dance, also known as the "trescone."

12. Note the philosopher's ironic employment of the concept of the seven capital sins.

13. The divinity of Lampsacus is Priapus, god of fertility. The symbol to which Bruno alludes is obviously obscene. Cf. *Opere ital.,* II, 159, n. 3.

14. Of the eighty or more erotic poems of the *Priapea,* inspired by the cult of Priapus, three are attributed to Virgil, and many more show the influence of Ovid. Four *Priapea* were included by Martial in his *Epigrams.*

15. Porphyry dedicated his *Isagoge* to Chrysaoreus. Cf. *ibid.,* p. 160, n. 2.

16. Greek title for Aristotle's logical work, *De interpretatione.*

17. Species and genus are two of the five predicates discussed by Porphyry in the *Isagoge to the Categories of Aristotle.* Cf. *Opere ital.,* II, 160, n. 4.

18. "An allusion," says Gentile, "to the literature of the century of which, it cannot be denied, Bruno shows himself to be a severe but just critic." *Ibid.,* p. 161, n. 4. Bruno was particularly vehement against the slavish imitators of Petrarch, the grammarians, theologians, pseudo-scholars, and pedants in every field of learning.

19. The "contemplators of life and death," etc., another reference to the Calvinist theologians.

20. Mount Somma is a few kilometers from Mount Cicala.

21. This passage is an adaptation of a passage in *Il vendemmiatore*, st. 7, p. 54. Cf. *Opere ital.*, II, 163, n. 2.

THIRD DIALOGUE: SECOND PART

1. Not until the Congress of Vienna, in 1815, did the Kingdom of Naples and Sicily, "the one and the other Sicily," officially become known as the Kingdom of the Two Sicilies. Cf. Giordano Bruno, *Opere italiane* (ed. Giovanni Gentile and Vincenzo Spampanato), Bari, Gius. Laterza & Figli, 1925–1927, 3 vols., II, 164, n. 3.

2. The ancient Greek name for Sicily.

3. Serpentarius is another name for Ophiuchus. The Marsians were known for their skill in magic. Cf. *Opere ital.*, II, 165, n. 2.

4. I have endeavored to convey the flavor of Bruno's pun on the Italian words for "dolphin" ("delfino") and "dolphinate" ("delfinato").

5. Horace, *Epistle to the Pisos.* v. 30.

6. Another allusion to pedants and pedantry.

7. Stilpo (or Stilpon) was a Greek philosopher of Megara (circa 380–300 B.C.). The form "Stilbone," found in the Gentile edition, seems to be an erroneous spelling of "Stilpone."

8. Both Cusanus and Bruno asserted that they had discovered a method of squaring the circle. It was definitely established, however, by the German mathematician, Ferdinand Von Lindemann, that the squaring of a circle is an impossibility, when, in 1882, he proved that π is a transcendental number. It must be pointed out, nevertheless, that for Cusanus the circle was more than a mathematical symbol: This most perfect of all figures was symbolic of God himself. It would seem, therefore, that here Bruno also uses the circle allegorically, the circle being for him the God of Nature, in whom all opposites coincide.

9. According to legend, Pythagoras offered a hecatomb upon discovering that the square on the hypotenuse of a right-angled triangle is equal to the sum of the squares on the other two sides.

10. Note that the in-between figures referred to by Bruno relating to figures 3 and 4 are not shown in the drawings.

11. The constellation Aries.

12. The Nigero is a river in Campania also known as the Tanagro. The Silere is known today as the Sele, and the Ofito, as the Ofanto. The Sele flows near the town of Campagna, at whose convent of San Bartolomeo Bruno sojourned during his youth. The Sebeto and the Sarno are rivers in Campania. *Vide Opere ital.*, II, n. 2 and n. 3.

13. The anonymous Neapolitan annotator underlines Bruno's reference to the Holy Manger, indicating his indignation. *Vide ibid.*, p. 177, n. 1.

14. Bruno's use of the old Italian spelling for Torino is a pun on Taurus.

The islands to which Bruno refers are off the Bay of Naples, the most famous being Capri, probably so named because of the goats that inhabited it. Gentile explains that there is no geographical place by the name of Corveto, and that Bruno might have confused Corveto with Montecorvino. "Aprutio" is a variant of Abruzzo. Bruno avoids going into the obvious etymology of Oxford, a town of which he did not have pleasant recollections. Cf. *ibid.,* n. 6 and n. 7.

15. The anonymous Neapolitan annotator inserts the following comment: "Irridet parabolam decem virginum: Matthew XXIV [1–13]." ("He derides the parable of the ten virgins.") *Vide ibid.,* p. 178, n. 1.

16. Saturn is, of course, known both as a parricide and a filicide, having murdered his father after castrating him, and also having swallowed his children.

17. In speaking of Cupid or Eros as a twin, Bruno may be alluding to that god's close association with his brother, Anteros, the avenger of unrequited love, the fosterer of reciprocal affection, and, sometimes, the opponent of love.

18. A reference to the declining power of the Venetian Republic after her defeat at the hands of the Turks in 1537 and 1573. Cf. *Opere ital.,* II, 180, n. 3.

19. Here Bruno is referring to the plagues that visited Italy in the years 1575–1577 and France in 1580–1583, which caused the closing of many convents. *Vide* Vincenzo Spampanato, *Vita di Giordano Bruno, con documenti editi e inediti,* Messina, Casa Editrice G. Principato, 1921, pp. 267–8.

20. Note Bruno's modern views on the rearing and the education of children.

21. An oblique reference to the religious in monasteries and convents, and an indictment of their celibacy.

22. Bruno is here referring to a feast possibly celebrated by the archery society, "the ancient order societie and Unitie laudable of Prince Arthure and his knightly armory of the round table." C. J. Longman and Col. H. Walrond, *Archery,* London, Longmans, Green & Co., 1894, p. 167.

Henry VIII is said to have promised the title of Duke of Shoreditch to a certain Barlow, one of his guards, if he should be the victor in an archery match. Cf. *Opere ital.,* II (noti aggiunte).

23. Bruno, as does Hyginus, identifies Capricorn with Pan, the god of nature. Cf. Gaius Julius Hyginus, "Fabula 196—Pan," *Fabulae,* ed. H. J. Rose, Leyden, 1934. In gratitude to goat-horned Pan for having taught the gods to become beasts, which saved them from the wrath of Typhoeus (Typhon) in Egypt, Jove changed him into the constellation Capricorn.

24. The following comments of the anonymous Neapolitan annotator show his strong disapproval of Bruno's words: "Videtur excusare, imo laudare vetus commercium daemoniorum cum hominibus in oraculis daemoniacis. Discorso detestabile." *Vide Opere ital.* II, 187, n. 1. ("He appears to be making excuses for, indeed, to be praising the ancient com-

merce of demons with men, in demoniacal oracles. A detestable speech.")

25. Bruno had in mind the following passage in the Vulgate version of the New Testament: "And they called Barnabas, Jupiter, and Paul, Mercury, because he was the chief speaker." Acts of the Apostles XIV. 11.

26. The seven wandering lights refer to the sun, moon, Venus, Jupiter, Mars, Mercury, and Saturn, which the ancients distinguished from the fixed stars.

27. Since Bruno was attracted not only by the Pythagorean belief in metempsychosis but also, to a lesser extent, by its employment of numbers as symbols, we can readily understand the philosopher's interest in the numerical symbolism of the Cabala.

28. Juvenal, *Satires* II. 23.

29. "Calumnia," says the anonymous Neapolitan annotator, "in populum Israeliticum." *Vide Opere ital.,* II, 194, n. 3. ("A calumny of the Jewish people.")

30. Egyptian god of wisdom and magic, also known as Tehuti.

31. Exodus XXXII. 184; and Numbers XXI. 9.

32. *Vide* Genesis XLIX. 14.

33. The anonymous annotator inserts the following comment: "Christum notat." Cf. *Opere ital.,* II, 195, n. 2.

34. *Vide* Apocalypse IV. 7; V. 6.

35. The anonymous annotator interprets this passage as a reference to Christ's entry into Jerusalem mounted on an ass. Cf. *Opere ital.,* II, 195, n. 5.

36. A reference to Ishmael, the son of Abraham and Hagar, Sarah's servant. Although, strictly speaking, Ishmael's descendants are the Arabs, here the allusion seems to refer to the Gentiles in general. *Vide* Genesis XVI. 12; XL. 11.

37. In the Italian text there is a witty play on the verbs "incoronare" ("to crown") and "incornare" ("to give horns to"), as well as on the nouns "corona" ("crown") and "corna" ("horns"), which cannot be easily rendered into English.

38. Bruno interprets his reference to the horns of Moses according to the Vulgate, which translates the Hebrew "keren" as "cornu" ("horn"). Thus, medieval and Renaissance statues of Moses, the most notable of which is Michelangelo's great work, depict Moses with horns protruding from his forehead. However, "keren" in Hebrew means not only "a horn" but also "a ray of light." The Soncino edition of the Bible (London, 1950) renders Exodus XXXIV. 29, as follows: "Moses knew not that the skin of his face sent forth beams while he talked with him." The King James version of the same passage reads: "Moses wist not that the skin of his face shone while he talked with him."

39. After having escaped from the Roman Inquisition in 1576, Bruno sojourned at the Monastery of Santa Maria di Castello in Genoa, which housed the holy relic to which he alludes. Cf. *Opere ital.,* II, 198, n. 3.

40. Matthew XIX. 29.

41. "Ridet propheticas comminationes" ("He scoffs at the prophetic warnings"), comments the Neapolitan annotator, as he detects a scornful note in this reference to the Scriptures. Cf. *Opere ital.,* II, 199, n. 2.

42. *Vide* Jeremiah XLVIII. 25.

43. *Vide* Psalms LXXV. 11.

44. *Vide* Amos III. 14.

45. *Vide* Luke I. 69.

46. *Vide* I Kings II. 10.

47. A cuckold, in Italian, "cornuto."

48. That the precursor of Spinoza should utilize Pan, that is, Capricorn, as the allegorical representation of pantheism clearly indicates his own strong commitments to pantheistic beliefs.

From Bruno's discussion of Capricorn and of the natural religion of the Egyptians we may infer the teaching that man is endowed with rational intelligence derived from his limited will; that he often relies too heavily on his intellect, neglecting the instinctive nature that he shares with irrational animals; and that when he refuses to be a "beast," that is to say, when he submerges his natural instinct (that instinct that makes animals incorruptible), he becomes corrupt. Therefore, only by integrating his rational nature with his intuitive nature can he arrive at the highest understanding of himself and his universe.

49. These words, a strong indictment of the religion of the Greeks, also seem to be a veiled attack upon the Catholic practice of canonization. The Neapolitan annotator observes: "Puto ista omnia dici in idolatriam papisticam et cultum divorum; nam noster iste Lucianus omnes religiones, praeter Aegyptiam et forte gentilicam omnem, inf[eriores] dig[nitate] habet." *Vide Opere ital.,* II, 201, n. 2. ("I think all these things are being said against papal idolatry and its cult of saints; for this Lucian of ours considers all religions, indeed all gentile religion, inferior in dignity to the Egyptian.")

50. A satirical reference to monks and their eating habits.

51. Mount Aetna.

52. Perhaps in order to establish his premise of the universality of the Flood and other biblical stories, and in order to refute Judaeo-Christian chronology and exegesis based on the story of creation, Bruno alludes to the mythical "tablets of Mercury that reckon more than twenty thousand years," and to the ancient civilizations and prehistoric life of Mexico.

Bruno's references to the New World were inspired by accounts of the circular Aztec Calendar Stone. Upon their conquest of Tenochtitlán, now Mexico City, in 1521, the Spaniards found and hid the Stone along with other Indian art and religious objects. The Stone came to light in 1551, but upon orders from the Spanish ecclesiastical authorities, it was reinterred in 1558. It was finally rediscovered on December 17, 1790. The Aztec Calendar consisted of eighteen months of twenty days each, which are symbolized by the eighteen smaller squares surrounding the four large squares.

53. The anonymous Neapolitan annotator observes that Bruno is ridiculing the story of Jonah and the whale. *Vide Opere ital.,* II, 203, n. 2.
54. *Vide* Genesis IX. 21.
55. *Vide* Ovid, *Metamorphoses* I. 399–402.
56. In deference to the Fishes, who brought the egg from which Venus was born to the shore of the Euphrates, and to the doves, who hatched it, the Syrians abstained from eating fish and doves.
57. The god who in Greek and Egyptian mythology is pictured with a finger on his lips is Harpocrates. Since that god is sometimes pictured seated on a box (the Greek word for "pyxis"), Bruno may have derived from it the name "Pixide." However, the name of Apollo, sometimes known as Pyxios, is often equated with that of Harpocrates, and it is possible that Bruno's "Pixide" may be an incorrect form derived from Pyxios.

THIRD DIALOGUE: THIRD PART

1. *Vide* Jonah II. 1; I. 37.
2. I have not been able to locate any references to Ianni del'Orco and Cola Catanzano.
3. Bruno is referring to the Spanish Jews who fled to Salonica in Greece. Cf. Giordano Bruno, *Opere italiane* (ed. Giovanni Gentile and Vincenzo Spampanato), Bari, Gius. Laterza & Figli, 1925–1927, 3 vols., II, 206, n. 5.
4. The anonymous Neapolitan annotator suspects that Bruno uses Orion to allegorize Christ, and that the ensuing passage is an attack upon Christ's divinity. Cf. *ibid.,* p. 207, n. 2; 208, n. 1. Bruno, however, denied a similar accusation at his Venetian trial. *Vide* Vincenzo Spampanato, *Vita di Giordano Bruno, con documenti editi e inediti,* Messina, Casa Editrice G. Principato, 1921, pp. 488–94. Bruno's use of Orion to symbolize Christ was undoubtedly suggested by the fact that Orion had been given by Neptune, his father, the power of walking on the surface of the sea.
5. Jove's paradoxical references to the Greeks reveal his deep concern with the corruption of Greek ideals as a result of the Hellenization process that helped bring about the synthesis of Greek philosophy with biblical teaching and, ultimately, the triumph of Judaeo–Christianity.
6. A reference to the Jews and to Christ.
7. Possibly an allusion to the Eucharist.
8. An implied argument against the personal God of the Judaeo–Christians.
9. Bartholmèss points out that this allusion to hunting could not help but please Queen Elizabeth. Cf. Christian Bartholmèss, *Jordano Bruno,* Paris, Librairie philosophique De Ladrange, 1846, 1847, 2 vols., II, 104.
10. *Shem Ha-Meforash* is the Hebrew for "the special name" (of God), contained in the breastplate worn by the Jewish High Priest.

11. Here Bruno deliberately replaces the Latin "furem" ("thief") with "feram" ("beast"), which Spampanato indicates has the more specific meaning of "doe," allegorical of Christ, distorting "Si videbas furem, currebas cum eo . . ." (Psalms [Vulgate] XLIX. 18), "When thou sawest a thief, then thou consentedst with him . . ." Psalms [King James] L. 18. The second part of the passage "Me, quae . . . Galilea" is inspired by the words of the angel to Mary Magdalene and to the Virgin Mary, after Christ's resurrection: "Ecce praecedit vos in Galilaeam: ibi eum videbitis" ("behold, he goeth before you into Galilee; there shall ye see him"). Matthew XXVIII. 7; Cf. V. Spampanato, "Postille storico-letterarie alle opere italiane di Giordano Bruno," *La critica*, Naples, 1911, p. 312.

12. Another allusion to the story of Jonah. Cf. *Opere ital.*, II, 216, n. 3.

13. The Hydra myth referred to by Bruno seems to be a variant of versions found in the following sources: (1) Nicander (Nicander Colophonius), *Theriaca*, ed. J. G. Schneider, 1816, vv. 343–58, (2) Aelian (Claudius Aelianus), *De natura animalium*, ed. R. Hercher, 1864–1866, vi. 51. Aelian informs us that Ibycus, Sophocles, and other early writers dealt with the same myth.

14. Montecorvino (Montecorvino Rovella) is a town less than twenty kilometers from Salerno. Cf. *Opere ital.*, II, 219, n. 1. A pun on the word "corvo," the Italian for "crow" or "raven."

15. A reference to the punishments carried out by Pope Sixtus V against the many thieves who roved the highways between Naples and Rome. Cf. Spampanato, *Vita di G. B.*, pp. 653–4.

16. Violently disagreeing with Bruno's philosophy of history, the anonymous Neapolitan annotator refers to Bruno's passage as "A lie and a myth." *Vide Opere ital.*, II, 220, n. 1.

17. In Genesis XL. 16, the passage refers not to Potiphar's baker but to Pharaoh's. Bruno's reference to the "basket of figs, of which birds were coming to eat" is also somewhat inaccurate. The biblical passage (Genesis XL. 16–17 [King James]) reads as follows: "and, behold, I had three white baskets on my head: And in the uppermost basket there was of all manner of bakemeats for Pharaoh; and the birds did eat them out of the basket upon my head." Gentile believes with Spampanato that Bruno may have been confused with Aretino's treatment, in his *Ficheide*, of the fable of the crow and the figs. *Vide Opere ital.*, II, 220, n. 2.

18. These two lines are a rewording of a popular adage of Bruno's day. Cf. *ibid.*, p. 221, n. 1.

19. Forms of the German verb "trinken," to drink.

20. Gentile calls our attention to Bruno's play on the Latin "ius," whose meaning is not only "law," but also "broth." *Vide Opere ital.*, II, 221, n. 3.

21. Egg of smoked tuna. *Vide ibid.*, n. 4.

22. Here Bruno is referring to Dante's Ciacco, known for his gluttony. Cf. *Inferno* VI. 52, 58. Gentile notes that the gluttony of the Germans is

also alluded to by Teofilo Folengo in his *Macaronea* XXVI; cf. *Opere ital.,* II, 222, n. 2.

23. For Noah see Genesis IX. 20. For Lot, who was made drunk by his two daughters so that they could lie with him, see Genesis XIX. 32; "Chiaccone," derived from a common noun in the Neapolitan dialect, means a "vine leaf." Vitanzano and Zucavigna are nicknames for drunkards. Silenus was a friend of Bacchus. *Vide Opere ital.,* II, 222, n. 6.

24. Spampanato has endeavored to trace the derivation of these bizarre names. According to him, "Grungarganfestrofiel" means "one who grubs with pride." "Sorbillgramfton" means "one who sips." "Glutius" is derived from the Latin verb "glutire," meaning "to gorge"; Bruno's "Glutius" then would seem to mean "a gorger." "Strafocazio" is derived from the Neapolitan form "strafocarsi," meaning "to swallow avidly so as to choke." *Vide* Vincenzo Spampanato, *Spaccio de la bestia trionfante con alcuni antecedenti,* Portici, Premiato stab.tip. Vesuviano, 1902, p. 89.

25. As he did in the case of Orion, Bruno makes an analogy between Christian symbols and a classical myth, this time to satirize Christ and the Trinity. When Prometheus was punished by Jove for having brought fire to mankind, he was told by Mercury that he would not be released from his agony until a god would sacrifice himself for him. It was Chiron who was willing to do so.

26. "O lying assenter!" angrily exclaims the anonymous Neapolitan annotator. *Vide Opere ital.,* II, 225, n. 2. That Bruno should heap such extravagant praise upon Henry III, who, besides having helped his mother, Catherine de Médicis, organize the St. Bartholomew Massacre, was known to have led an indolent, vicious, and corrupt life, may be surprising to the reader. This attitude, however, can only be explained in terms of Bruno's appreciation of the role played by the monarch as a patron of the arts, and of his personal interest in him.

Regarding Henry's motto, *Tertia coelo manet* (The third crown remains in heaven), Bartholmèss comments: "the Leaguers promised him this crown in the cathedral close, from the hand of a *shearer,* of an executioner, perhaps, when they predicted to him that it would escape him, as did the crown of Naples that Paul IV had intended to transfer to him with the arms of Henry II." *Op. cit.,* I, 99. Henry III was murdered in 1589 by the monk, Jacques Clément.

27. Matthew V. 3–8. Psalms (Vulgate) XXXVI. 11; (King James) XXXVII. 11.

Bibliography

EDITIONS OF *LO SPACCIO* AND GIORDANO BRUNO'S COLLECTED WORKS

Spaccio de la bestia trionfante, Paris, 1584.

Spaccio della bestia trionfante, or the Expulsion of the Triumphant Beast, translated from the Italian of Giordano Bruno, London, 1713.

Le ciel réformé, essai de traduction de partie du Livre Italien, Spaccio della Bestia trionfante (trans. anonymous), Paris?, 1750.

Spaccio de la bestia trionfante (ed. Christian Bartholmèss), Milan, Daelli, 1863.

Spaccio de la bestia trionfante (ed. G. Stiavelli), Rome, E. Perino, 1888.

Opere di Giordano Bruno Nolano ora per la prima volta raccolte e pubblicate in due volumi (ed. Adolf Wagner), Leipzig, Weidmann, 1830, 2 vols.

Opera latine conscripta, publicis sumptibus edita [recensebant F. Fiorentino, F. Tocco, H. Vitelli, V. Imbriani, C. M. Tallarigo], Naples, Dom. Morano, Florence, Le Monnier, 1879–1891, 3 vols.

Le opere italiane di Giordano Bruno ristampate (ed. Paul de Lagarde), Göttingen, Dieterichsche Universitätsbuchhandlung (Lüder Horstman), 1888, 2 vols.

Gesammelte Werke (trans. Ludwig Kuhlenbeck), I–II—Leipzig, Eugen Diederichs, Berlin, H. Zossen, 1904. III–VI—Jena, Eugen Diederichs, Leipzig, O. Brandstetter, 1904–1909, 6 vols.

Opere italiane (ed. Giovanni Gentile and Vincenzo Spampanato), Bari, Gius. Laterza & Figli, 1925–1927, 3 vols.

Vol. I (*Dialoghi metafisici,* con note di G. Gentile) contains (1) *La cena de le ceneri* (London, 1584), (2) *De la causa, principio e uno* (Venice, 1584), (3) *De l'infinito, universo et mondi* (Venice, 1584).

Vol. II (*Dialoghi morali*, con note di G. Gentile) contains (1) *Spaccio de la bestia trionfante* (Paris, 1584), (2) *Cabala del cavallo Pegaseo*, con l'aggiunta dell' *Asino cillenico* (Paris, 1585), (3) *De gli eroici furori* (Paris, 1585).

Vol. III (*Candelaio: commedia*. Ediz. critica, con introduzione e note di V. Spampanato) contains *Candelaio* (Paris, 1582).

PRIMARY AND SECONDARY SOURCES

Aretino, Pietro. *Piacevoli e capricciosi ragionamenti*, a cura di Antonio Piccone Stella, Milan, Valentino Bompiani & C., 1944.

Bartholmèss, Christian. *Jordano Bruno*, Paris, Librairie philosophique De Ladrange, 1846, 1847, 2 vols.

Berti, Domenico. *Vita di Giordano Bruno da Nola*, Turin, G. B. Paravia, 1868.

——— *Giordano Bruno da Nola, sua vita e sua dottrina*, Turin, G. B. Paravia, 1889.

Brunnhofer, Hermann. *Giordano Bruno's Weltanschauung und Verhängniss, Leipzig*, Fues's Verlag (R. Reisland), 1882.

Cassirer, Ernst. *Storia della filosofia moderna—Il problema della conoscenza nella filosofia e nella scienza dall'Umanesimo alla scuola cartesiana* (trans. Angelo Pasquinelli), Turin, Giulio Einaudi, Editore, 1952, 2 vols.

Corsano, A. *Il pensiero di Giordano Bruno nel suo svolgimento storico*, Florence, G. C. Sansoni, 1940, 1948.

Cusanus, Nicholas. *Opera omnia* (ed. E. Hoffmann and R. Klibansky), Leipzig, Meiner, 1932, 14 vols.

Einstein, Albert. *The World as I See It* (new abridged edition) (trans. Alan Harris), New York, Philosophical Library, 1949.

Fiorentino, Francesco. *Studi e ritratti della rinascenza*, a cura della figlia Luisa, Bari, Gius. Laterza & Figli, 1911.

Galilei, Galileo. *Opera omnia*, Florence, Edizione nazionale, 1890–1909, 20 vols.

Gentile, Giovanni. *Giordano Bruno nella storia della cultura*, Palermo, Remo Sandron, Editore, 1907.

——— *Il pensiero italiano del rinascimento*, Florence, G. Sansone, 1940.

Giusso, Lorenzo. *Scienza e filosofia in Giordano Bruno*, Naples, Conte, Editore, 1955.

Greenberg, Sidney. *The Infinite in Giordano Bruno*, with a translation of his dialogue *Concerning the Cause, Principle, and One*, New York, King's Crown Press, 1950.

Höffding, Harald. *A History of Modern Philosophy* (trans. from the German edition by B. E. Meyer), New York, Dover Publications, Inc., 1955, 2 vols.

Jacobi, F. H. *Über die Lehre des Spinoza in Briefen an Herrn Moses Mendelssohn* (second edition), Breslau, 1789.

Lovejoy, Arthur Oncken. "The Dialectic of Bruno and Spinoza," *Philosophy*, Berkeley, University of California Publications, November, 1904, Vol. I.

Lucian. *Dialogues* (trans. Howard Williams, M.A.), London, George Bell and Sons, 1884.

McIntyre, J. Lewis. *Giordano Bruno*, London, Macmillan and Co., Ltd., 1903.

Mercati, Angelo. *Il sommario del processo di Giordano Bruno, con appendice di documenti sull'eresia e l'inquisizione a Modena nel secolo XVI* (*Studi e Testi*), Vatican City, Biblioteca Apostolica Vaticana, 1942.

Mondolfo, Rodolfo. *Figuras e ideas de la filosofía del renacimiento*, Buenos Aires, Editorial Losada, S.A., 1954.

Salvestrini, Virgilio. *Bibliografia delle opere di Giordano Bruno e degli scritti ad esso attinenti*, prefazione di Giovanni Gentile, Pisa, V. Salvestrini, Libraio, 1926.

Singer, Dorothea Waley. *Giordano Bruno: His Life and Thought*, with annotated translation of his work *On the Infinite Universe and Worlds*, New York, Henry Schuman, 1950.

Smith, Preserved. *A History of Modern Culture*, New York, Henry Holt & Co., 1930, 2 vols.

Spampanato, Vincenzo. *Bruno e Nola*, Castrovillari, Tipi di Francesco Pattucci, 1889.

———— *Documenti della vita di Giordano Bruno*, Florence, Leo S. Olschki, Editore, 1933.

———— "Postille storico—letterarie alle opere italiane di Giordano Bruno," *La critica*, Naples, 1911.

———— *Spaccio de la bestia trionfante con alcuni antecedenti*, Portici, Premiato stab. tip. Vesuviano, 1902.

———— *Vita di Giordano Bruno, con documenti editi e inediti*, Messina, Casa Editrice G. Principato, 1921. Contains the "Documenti parigini," the "Documenti romani," the "Documenti tedeschi," the "Documenti veneti," the "Documenti napolitani," and the "Documenti ginevrini."

Spaventa, Bertrando. *La filosofia italiana nelle sue relazioni con la filosofia europea*, a cura di Gennaro Ponzano, Padua, Casa Editrice Dott. Antonio Milani, 1941.

Spinoza, Benedict. *Ethics and De Intellectus Emendatione* (trans. Andrew Boyle), London and Toronto, J. M. Dent and Sons, Ltd., New York, E. P. Dutton and Co., 1910.

Tansillo, Luigi. *Il vendemmiatore*, Rome, tipografia Capaccini, 1896.

Tocco, Felice. *Le opere latine di Giordano Bruno eposte e confrontate con le italiane*, Florence, Le Monnier, 1889.

Selected Addenda to Bibliography

Bruno, Giordano. *The Ash Wednesday Supper (La cena de le ceneri)*, Eds. and trans. Edward A. Gosselin and Lawrence S. Lerner. Hamden, Conn. Archon Books, The Shoe String Press, 1977.

———. *The Ash Wednesday Supper (La cena de le ceneri)*, Ed. and Trans. Stanley L. Jaki. The Hague, Mouton; New York, Humanities Press, 1975.

———. *Cause, Principle and Unity*. Trans. Jack Lindsay, Essex, Castle Hedingham, 1962, and New York, International Publishers, 1964; Westport, Conn., Greenwood Press, 1976.

———. *Dialoghi italiani*. Ed. Giovanni Aquilecchia, Florence, Sansoni, 1958.

———. *Des Fureurs héroïques*. Ed. and trans. Paul-Henri Michel, Paris, 1954.

———. *Due dialoghi sconosciuti e due dialoghi noti*. Ed. Giovanni Aquilecchia, Rome, 1957.

———. *The Heroic Enthusiasts*. Trans. L. Williams, London, 1887–89, 2 vols.

———. *The Heroic Frenzies*. Trans. Paul E. Memmo, Chapel Hill, University of North Carolina Press, 1964.

———. *Ombre delle idee (De umbris idearum)*. Ed. and trans. Gabriele La Porta, Rome, Atanor, 1978.

———. *On the Composition of Images, Signs and Ideas*. Trans. Charles Doria, ed. and annotated by Dick Higgins, New York, Willis, Locker & Owens, 1991.

———. *Opere di Giordano Bruno e di Tommaso Campanella*. Eds. Augusto Guzzo and Romano Amerio, Milan, R. Ricciardi, 1956.

———. *Scritti scelti di Giordano Bruno e di Tommaso Campanella*. Ed. Luigi Firpo, Turin, U.T.E.T., 1949.

———. *Spaccio della bestia trionfante*. Ed. Michele Ciliberto, Milan, 1985 (polemical introduction).

———. *Summa terminorum metaphysicorum*: ristampa anastatica dell'edizione Marburg 1609, presentazione di Tullio Gregory, Roma, Edizioni

dell'Ateneo, 1989.
———. *Über die Monas, die Zahl und die Figur.* Trans. Elizabeth von Samsonow, "Philosophische Bibliothek," Hamburg, Felix Meiner Verlag, 1991.

SECONDARY SOURCES

Aquilecchia, Giordano. *Giordano Bruno.* Roma, Istituto della enciclopedia italiana, 1971.
———. "Lezioni inedite di Giordano Bruno in un codice della Biblioteca universitaria di Jena," *Rendiconti delle classe di scienze morali, storiche e filologiche,* Accademia Nazionale dei Lincei, ser. 8, 1962, Vol. XVII, 463–85.
———. "Lo stampatori londinese di Giordano Bruno, e altre note per l'edizione della 'Cena'," *Studi di filologia italiana,* Florence, 1960, Vol. XVIII, 101–62.
Bossy, John. *Giordano Bruno and the Embassy Affair.* New Haven, Yale University Press, 1991.
Ciliberto, Michele. *Giordano Bruno,* Rome, Bari, 1990.
———. *Lessico di Giordano Bruno,* Roma, Edizioni dell' Ateneo & Bizzarri, 1979.
Kristeller, Paul Oskar. *Eight Philosophers of the Italian Renaissance,* Stanford, Calif., Stanford University Press, 1964.
Horowitz, I. L. *the Renaissance Philosophy of Giordano Bruno,* New York, Coleman-Ross, 1952.
Michel, Paul Henry. *The Cosmology of Giordano Bruno.* Trans. R. E. W. Maddison, Ithaca, Cornell University Press, 1973.
Nelson, John C. *Renaissance Theory of Love.* New York, Columbia University Press, 1958.
Yates, Frances. *The Art of Memory,* London, Routledge and Paul, 1966.
———. *Giordano Bruno and the Hermetic Tradition.* Chicago, University of Chicago Press, 1979. First published 1964.
———. "Giordano Bruno; Some New Documents," *Revue internationale de philosophie,* XVI, 1951, 174–99; reprint in *Collected Essays,* ii, 111–30.
———. *Lull and Bruno: Collected Essays,* London, Routledge and Kegan, I, 1982.

INDEX